Jerusalem Blessed, Jerusalem Cursed

And when the Lord your God brings you into the land
which you are entering to take possession of it,
you shall [know] both blessing and curse.
—Deuteronomy 11:29

On the holy mount stands the city he founded;
the Lord loves the gates of Zion
more than all the dwelling places of Jacob.
Glorious things are spoken of you, O City of God.
—Psalms 87:1–3

If I were to live a thousand years,
never would I forget [Jerusalem]
which still seems to breathe with the grandeur of Jehovah
and the terrors of death.
—Chateaubriand, 1811

Jerusalem is once again an open city
and a good place in which to live.
—Teddy Kollek, Mayor of Jerusalem, 1980

JEWS, CHRISTIANS,
AND MUSLIMS
IN THE HOLY CITY
FROM DAVID'S TIME
TO OUR OWN

Jerusalem Blessed, Jerusalem Cursed

Thomas A. Idinopulos

Chicago
Ivan R. Dee
1991

Typography by Ana M. Aguilar-Islas.

Maps by Robert A. McCamant, based upon information in *Jerusalem: Illustrated History Atlas* by Martin Gilbert; the Department of Surveys of the Municipality of Jerusalem, and other sources.

Photography and illustration credits: Photographs by Adrien Bonfils, from the collections of the Harvard Semitic Museum, pages 14, 122, 184, 191, 197, 199, 227, 229, 234; paintings and sketches by David Roberts, from the Yale Center for British Art, Paul Mellon Collection, pages 17, 187, 266; Israel Museum, Jerusalem, page 9; Art Resources, page 88; Trustees of the British Museum, page 173; Mansell Collection, London, page 188; Jewish Agency, Jerusalem, page 294; Roy Brody, pages 150, 316, 321, 325, 334.

Library of Congress Cataloging-in-Publication Data:
Idinopulos, Thomas A.
  Jerusalem blessed, Jerusalem cursed : Jews, Christians, and Muslims in the Holy City from David's time to our own / Thomas A. Idinopulos.
    p.   cm.
  Includes bibliographical references and index.
  ISBN 0-929587-66-9
  1. Jerusalem—History. 2. Jerusalem—Religion. 3. Jerusalem in Judaism. 4. Jerusalem in Christianity. 5. Jerusalem in Islam.
  I. Title.
DS109.9.I35   1991
956.94'42—dc20   91-15355

BT 30.00/16.41 - 10/91

For Lea
...my queen of Judea
and
David and Michael,
my sons
...with whom I first saw
Jerusalem

Acknowledgments

My research in Jerusalem was made easier by several good friends: Aharon Sarig, Yechiel Ilsar, Solomon S. Bernards, Bernard Resnikoff, Shemaryahu Talmon, the late Hanan Cidor, and the late Professor Uriel Tal.

For their cooperation in my study of Islamic holy sites I wish to thank officials of Jerusalem's Muslim trust (Waqf), particularly Hassan Tarboub, Adnan Husseini, Issam Awad, and the mufti and cadi of Jerusalem, Sheik Said al-Alami. I benefited from the insights of Aly Khamis; Muhammad Jarallah, official of the United Nations Work Relief Agency; and from conversations with the journalists Muhammad Abu Shilbayah and Ibrahim Douabis. I honor the memory of the late Anwar Nusseibeh, the distinguished Palestinian, with whom I talked on several occasions, and who died much too soon. I also learned much from conversations with George Hintlian of the Armenian patriarchate; Isaachar Ben-Yaacov and Naomi Teasdale of the Municipality of Jerusalem; the late Greek Orthodox patriarch Benedictos; Eminence Germanos, Archbishop of Petra; Eminence Vasileos, Archbishop of Caesarea; and former Roman Catholic apostolic delegates, Msgrs. Pio Laghi and William Carew.

The early stages of my writing were done in the agreeable atmosphere of Mishkenot Sha'ananim, an historical landmark and today the cultural center of the Jerusalem Foundation. I am especially grateful to Teddy Kollek, mayor of Jerusalem, for inviting me to Mishkenot on two occasions.

One of my joys in Jerusalem is my long association with the Ecumenical Institute for Advanced Theological Studies at Tantur, where I lectured at the kind request of rectors Dr. Jean-Jacques von Allman, Fr. David Burrel, and Fr. Thomas Stransky. This would not have been possible if the University of Notre Dame, and particularly

Fr. Theodore Hesburg, had not graciously invited me there as a resident scholar in 1973. I also treasure my association with the scholars of the Rainbow Club and the Interfaith Committee of Jerusalem.

Some day I hope to repay the kindness shown to me by HRH Crown Prince Hassan bin Talal, who invited me to Amman, Jordan, where I talked with Palestinian Jerusalemites, including the Arab mayor of east Jerusalem, Rauhi Khatib.

For invitations to lecture on Jerusalem I am grateful to the Postgraduate Hebrew Centre at Oxford University, the Leo Baeck Rabbinical College at London, the Aristotelian University of Thessaloniki, Columbia University, the Universities of Manitoba and Winnipeg, Lewis and Clark College, Milliken University, Drake University, Grinnell College, and the American Academy of Religion.

I am sincerely grateful for the generous support of my research by Miami University of Ohio and its Alumnae Association.

For valuable criticism of portions of the manuscript at different stages I am indebted to Steven Bowman, Alan Dowty, Naomi Janowitz, Austin Wright, Britton Harwood, Edward Tomarken, Annette Tomarken, and A. Weinberg. I am especially grateful for the vision and commitment of Ivan R. Dee, whose pencil was unerring. Nancy Levin labored long and well to locate the illustrations. I acknowledge my debt to John Gray's *A History of Jerusalem*, whose time line on Jerusalem I adopted, modified, and updated.

On a subject as vast and complicated, as emotional and controversial as Jerusalem, it is necessary to say that none of the people mentioned here should be held responsible for the findings of this book, or for any of my own views and opinions.

New books have old mothers who repose in libraries. Among the many institutional libraries I used, three in Jerusalem were invaluable: Ecole Biblique, Yad Ben-Zvi, and the National Library of Hebrew University.

Because of the way I have organized and presented the history of Jerusalem in this book, certain facts and events are occasionally repeated from one part of the book to another. This I have done for purposes of clarity and comprehension, and not to tax the reader.

I dedicate this book to Lea, my wife, and to my sons, David and Michael, who share my love of Jerusalem.

T. A. I.

Jerusalem
April 1991

Contents

Jerusalem in Time

B.C.E.

1000   The Judean tribal chief David seizes the Canaanite mountain stronghold of Jebus and makes it the capital of his united Israelite monarchy.

931   The united monarchy breaks up after Solomon's death; Jerusalem remains the capital of Judah, the southern kingdom.

722   The Assyrians conquer Israel, the northern kingdom.

622   The ritual reform is carried out by King Josiah in Jerusalem's Temple.

612   Nineveh falls and the Assyrian empire collapses at the hands of Babylonia.

586   The Babylonians destroy Jerusalem and the Temple; Judeans are exiled to Mesopotamia.

539   Persian King Cyrus overwhelms Babylonia, captures Judah, and invites Jews to return to the homeland.

539–333   Duration of the Persian empire in western Asia.

520–516   Jerusalem's Temple is rebuilt, inaugurating the period of the Second Temple.

445   Nehemiah arrives as the Persian-appointed governor of the restored Judean community.

397   Religious reforms are initiated by the Torah scholar Ezra.

333   Alexander the Great defeats Darius III of Persia at the Battle of Issus, commencing the spread of Greek language and culture in western Asia and the Middle East.

312   Beginning of the domination of Palestine by the Ptolemies of Egypt.

1948 Israel declares its national independence, followed by the outbreak of the first Arab-Israeli war.

1948–1967 Period of a divided Jerusalem, in which west Jerusalem serves as Israel's capital while east Jerusalem and the old city are under the control of the Hashemite kingdom of Jordan.

1967 Six Days War leads to the reunification of Jerusalem under Israeli sovereignty. A united Jerusalem is declared to be Israel's "eternal capital."

1977 Israeli-Egyptian peace treaty fails to address the question of Arab-populated Jerusalem.

1987– Outbreak of the Palestinian uprising (*intifada*) in Gaza, West Bank, and east Jerusalem.

1990 Arab Palestinians and Israelis intensify violent action against each other in Jerusalem and throughout the entire country.

Jerusalem Blessed, Jerusalem Cursed

Jerusalem Blessed,
Jerusalem Cursed

Ariel, David's city, Zion, Mountain of God—Jerusalem. Why such exalted titles for one small dusty hilltop town? Because religious people herald Jerusalem as earth's link to heaven. For centuries millions of Jews, Christians, and Muslims from every corner of the globe gathered in Jerusalem in the expectation of hearing the Word of God. They still do. This is a book about those ancient religious traditions which have made Jerusalem's name sacred and immortal.

But this is also a book about the centuries of human warfare that have permanently scarred Jerusalem, making her face both forbidding and fascinating. In this town, religion and war run side by side. Piety and blood, belief and battle have mingled here for more than three thousand years. Today Muslims, Jews, and Christians, Israelis and Palestinians, live in their isolated ghettos, each eyeing the others across town with suspicion and fear. What are these feelings that pit religion against religion, people against people in Jerusalem, whose name is synonymous with peace?

Destruction, distrust, suffering have spawned the Jerusalem Problem. It is a problem that torments diplomats who would like to bring peace and justice to the holy capital of this holy land. But the problem will not be solved unless and until some questions are answered. Who should govern Jerusalem, Jews or Arabs? Should or should not the city be divided between them? Will division bring a new peace or more war? Will the solution to the Jerusalem Problem end the wider Arab-Israeli conflict? This book will seek answers to these questions.

No one better anticipated the Jerusalem Problem than Isaiah, the eighth-century Hebrew prophet-poet. He was optimistic. After predicting the world's destruction, he located his messianic vision of future redemption in Jerusalem's hills. He prophesied that one day all the nations will end their warring and gather in final reconciliation on the highest hill, the hill called Zion. From Zion, the "mountain of the house of the Lord," the divine Law of Justice will come forth. Here are Isaiah's words:

> It shall come to pass in the latter days
> that the mountain of the house of the Lord
> Shall be established as the highest of the mountains,
> and shall be raised about the hills;
> all the nations shall flow to it. . . .
>
> For out of Zion shall go forth the law,
> and the word of the Lord from Jerusalem.
> He shall judge between the nations,
> and shall decide for many peoples;
> and they shall beat their swords into plowshares,
> and their spears into pruning hooks,
> neither shall they learn war any more.
>
> Isaiah 2:2, 4

Isaiah knew that Jerusalem is a city of daily strife embracing a vision of eternal peace. The contradiction is embedded in the landscape. Consider the hills. On the eastern face of Jerusalem are the hills of the Judean desert, an expanse of dry brown forbidding wasteland stretching down to the Dead Sea, the earth's deepest and saltiest water hole. To the west lie forested hills, a green canopy of pine trees cooling the city from the humid winds blowing up from the Mediterranean Sea but seventy kilometers away. All the prophets, priests, pilgrims, kings, and conquerors of Jerusalem climbed these hills; none entered the city's gates without first lingering on the heights to gaze on the place God chose for his dwelling place. The heights are little more than raised clumps of earth, but they bear the most cherished and the most dreaded names in the world: Mount of Olives, on whose crest the Messiah will appear; Mount Zion, from whose summit the Law will shine forth; Mount Moriah, where Abraham bound Isaac for sacrifice; the Hill of Evil Counsel, where the high priest Caiaphas condemned Jesus; the Hill of Offense, which Solomon disgraced by constructing idols on its slopes to please his pagan wives.

The valleys below leave no doubt about eternal punishment for human error. There is the Valley of Ghenna, the legendary site of hell, where infants were immolated to appease the sullen god Moloch. Across from Ghenna lies the eastern Valley of Jehosophat, where the wicked will be punished on Judgment Day. In the middle is the Kidron Valley, where Jesus warned his disciples, "If the world hates you, you know that it has hated me before it hated you."

These are the heights and depths of a city besieged, defended, conquered, damaged or destroyed, and rebuilt forty times in thirty centuries, always in the name of God. Yet Isaiah's words have not been wasted. Despite the bloody divisions of nations, creeds, and cultures, peoples of good will and abiding faith draw close to Jerusalem. The city rises taller on the wreckage of its own history. Intimations of justice, of peace, of unity rise from the hills. The people who continue to live here feel them; the hungry souls who journey here each year believe in them. Jerusalem in spite of her tormented history comforts the believers.

What drives them to this place? What is the source of energy in the hills, in the valley, behind the temples, churches, synagogues, mosques, and mausoleums that comprise the holy places in this unholy city? I asked myself these questions in seventeen years of walking the high and low places of Jerusalem. What I learned is that where modern Western cities have become functional, pragmatic, and secular, Jerusalem adheres to its ancient ways. In this town religion is not peripheral, not one of many cultural diversions. Jerusalemites would scoff at the idea that religion was a person's private affair, a personal feeling, devoid of objective content. They would denounce Marx and Freud for contending that our beliefs in sin, judgment, grace, heaven, and hell are purely psychological, a human being's weak-willed reaction to anxiety, deprivation, ignorance. To the people of Jerusalem, religious faith is not a human mirror but a response to a holy presence perceived in the stones and in the light. Here faith is an insistent, creative, fanatic, almost physical response to holiness. In Jerusalem, as in few places of the world, prayer is a form of seeing.

Seeing what? The answer points us a long way back. Jerusalem was Zion, the Mountain of God, long before Isaiah named it. Before Isaiah, before King David—whose ambitions led him to tear the veil from an obscure Jebusite stronghold and expose it to the world—were the original Canaanite inhabitants of this country.

The Canaanites knew there was something strange about Jerusalem. Standing on a small outcropping of limestone rock, on one of Jerusalem's prominent hills, the Canaanites felt the power and mystery of the sun. Here on the autumnal equinox the pagan people could witness the miracle of the sun rising directly before them and setting directly behind them. In their eyes here was the axis of the world, the meeting point of heaven and earth; here on this rock, this high stone, was the diverse source of light and warmth. Nowhere else but here was the home of the solar deities, Shahar, the god of the rising sun, and Shalim, the god of the setting sun.

Shalem gave his name to Jerusalem. *Jeru-shalem*, meaning "place of the god Shalem." Poor Shalem. When the idol makers fell prey to the Israelite idol haters, Shalem lost his place. For in the fourteenth century B.C.E., when the Israelites made their appearance in the ancient land of Canaan, they proceeded to confuse the name of Shalem with their own Hebrew word for peace, *shalom*. Thereafter Jerusalem was mistakenly called "city of peace." What a mockery history has made of their mistake!

Doubtless the Israelites were drawn to the sacred high stone of Jerusalem because the Canaanites first worshiped it. The link between the two peoples is dramatized in Hebrew scriptures by the wonderful story of Melchisedek, the legendary Canaanite priest-king of Jerusalem who anticipated monotheism, the belief in but one God. In the story, Melchisedek, standing on Jerusalem's sacred stone, consecrates an altar to El Elyon, the "god most high," whom the Israelites would name simply Elohim, "Lord." Later the patriarch Abraham, obedient to the Lord, binds his son Isaac for sacrifice on the sanctified rock now called Moriah. Eventually Moriah becomes the foundation stone of Solomon's Temple, built as the dwelling place of God. The precious rock becomes the bond between Judaism and her daughter faiths, Christianity and Islam. For it was on the Jewish Temple that Jesus prophesied Jerusalem's destruction as prelude to the arrival of God's Kingdom. And six hundred years after Jesus, with the Jewish Temple in ruins, the Muslim conquerors of Palestine show their own profound respect for the Abrahamic stone of sacrifice by building over it a magnificent octagonal shrine, naming it The Dome of the Rock.

This stone that is the source of Jerusalem's religious unity is also the symbol of the world's faith. A famous medieval map shows Jerusalem and Solomon's Temple at the center of the world, the continents of Europe, Africa, and Asia fanning out from the center like gigantic petals. It is a vision of world redemption arising from Jerusalem. Today, seeing pilgrims kneeling at Jesus' Tomb, observing Jews in prayers before the Western Wall, hearing the muezzin call the Muslim faithful to prayer, the mapmaker's vision seems confirmed. Jerusalem, whatever its problems, is still the root of redemption. The city continues to comfort the believers.

Moriah is but one stone in a stone-built city. Add stones to hills, and both to a cobalt sky and pure light, and one begins to see a city both sanctified and alluring. Jerusalem is best seen at dawn. The light of the early morning uplifts the hills and turns the stones to yellow gems. For an hour or so, before traffic noises are heard, sky, stone, hills in silence pay homage to their creator. Looking up at the hills we can readily believe that God made this city and called it Zion.

The vision of the One God unites Jerusalem's different peoples. What divides them is the daily, practical application of that vision—in a word, religion.

The vision of God is given to human beings who speak different languages and see the world differently. Religion is born of these differences. Once there were great stone idols in the Valley of Ghenna, symbols of Canaanite devotion. The idols were broken and carted away by Israelites who proclaimed the triumph of their own mighty God. But a mere thousand years after monotheism vanquished idolatrous polytheism, believers in the God of Israel quarreled in Jerusalem over who was the true messianic agent to the One God, and in that quarrel Christianity was born. Later the prophet Muhammad, rejected by both Jews and Christians, inspired an army of zealots who conquered Jerusalem. To show their pride in the triumph of Islam, they constructed the Dome of the Rock on the Temple Mount, a shrine deliberately built higher than Constantine's Golgotha basilica. The births of Christianity and Islam from Judaism were painful and bloody. The infants showed all the outward signs of their mother but hated her inwardly; the mother, Judaism, disdainful of her offsprings, disowned them. How could we not expect that Jerusalem would become the battleground of the three monotheistic faiths?

There is nothing perverse in such conflicts. If God had not wanted his creatures to fight over the holy stones of Jerusalem, he should not have chosen stones as the vehicles of his earthly presence. If today we criticize the folly of religious conflict in the Holy City, we should also lament the foolishness of God who chose a hilltop town as his earthly abode. For what pagan or Jew or Christian or Muslim could resist dominating God's dwelling place and thereby come into conflict with his brothers? Only the most attenuated believers, the abstractly "spiritualized," fail to see the fateful connection between the Jerusalem blessed by the vision of God and the Jerusalem cursed by human religions.

Not everyone sees it this way. I recall a conversation with a Mennonite theologian, a fervent believer in a spiritualized gospel. We walked together up the Mount of Olives to look down on the Temple Mount, to gaze out on all the mosques and churches and on the whole of the ancient walled city spread out before us. With a look of disgust on his face he turned to me and said, "Jerusalem is a pile of rocks. The blood shed over its shrines was wasted blood." Isaiah would have agreed with my Christian friend, for he too believed in a spiritualized gospel. But the prophet understood that spirit is never disembodied, it always assumes flesh; the ideal vision always becomes religious and sectarian. What my friend ignored is that the stones of Jerusalem's shrines are more precious to Christians, Muslims, and Jews *because* of the blood shed over them. Priests and prophets did not come to this city alone; they accompanied warriors and sanctified the ground over which war's blood first spilled. They merely imitated the gods who in this land have been obsessed with power. Were not infants sacrificed on the pagan altars of Ghenna? Did not Abraham sanctify Moriah through his willingness to shed Isaac's blood? Was not redemption purchased with Jesus' blood at Golgotha? Have not Muslims shared with Jews and Christians the belief in *herem, jihad,* holy war, that righteous

A Roman coin depicting a triumphant Roman soldier gloating over the defeat of the Jewish nation and the conquest of Jerusalem in 70 c.e.

shedding of blood pleasing to God? Nothing sacralizes stones like blood, and Jerusalem is a city founded on sanctity, sacrifice, and blood.

A lot of blood. In three thousand years most of the world's civilized peoples have exchanged places as masters and captives in a city ruined or destroyed not less than forty times. Jerusalem is a city of piled-up stones, where each layer of stone designates a different conquest. When around 1000 b.c.e. David seized Jerusalem from the Jebusites, monotheism replaced polytheism as the sovereign religion of the city. The Israelites enjoyed two generations of national and religious glory in the mountain capital. The death of Solomon led to the break up of the only truly independent Jewish monarchy. After that, Hebrew prophets denounced corrupt kings and predicted disaster for the Jewish people. The Babylonians in 586 B.C.E. destroyed Jerusalem and banished Jews from their ancestral city. The Persians allowed Jews to return to Jerusalem and rebuild their Temple, but the Greeks who followed the Persians desecrated the Temple with their pagan rites and provoked the Maccabees into the longest, most successful rebellion in Jewish history.

But the fate of Jerusalem was always decided from afar. The Romans, who had little trouble containing local rebellions, installed the Idumean half-Jew Herod as monarch of Judea, a country which held little interest for them strategically or economically. The master builder of hippodromes, roads, baths, forums, fortresses, and Jerusalem's last great temple, King Herod was a colorful and ruthless character who provided a measure of stability between Jewish rebellions. When he died there was no one to prevent Jewish zealots from arousing the Roman Beast which struck back in the year 70 when the Temple was destroyed, and struck again in 132 when Emperor Hadrian, expelling Jews from Jerusalem, leveled the city and built it anew, Roman fashion, renaming it Aelia Capitolina.

The Roman victory ushered in three hundred years of Byzantine Christian rule. The Byzantine emperors filled Jerusalem with churches and monasteries and continued to keep out the Jews, who on their high holy days would bribe their way to the ruins of the Temple to mourn with dirges, hoping with prayer to hasten the arrival of the messianic redemption. In the seventh century tribesmen from the Arabian peninsula, united in the new faith of Islam, invaded the country renamed Palestine by the Romans, after Israel's ancient enemy, the Philistines. None were more grateful that Muslims drove the Byzantines back to Constantinople than Jews who were permitted to live and worship freely in Jerusalem as long as they paid their taxes.

In 1099 the Crusader Franks, an alien, harsh, haughty people, conquered Jerusalem and held the city for a hundred years. The Crusaders purified the Holy City by slaughtering Muslims and Jews and evicting the local Greek and Arabic-speaking Christians who were thought too dark-skinned to be included in Christ's church. But in 1186 celebrations were held in synagogues, mosques, and churches throughout the Middle East after the Kurdish warrior-prince Saladin drove the Franks out of Jerusalem, Jews believing that the conquest heralded the messianic redemption.

For the next seven hundred years, while Palestine remained on the periphery of the Muslim world, native inhabitants suffered a succession of Egyptian and Turkish governors, some good, some bad, but all indifferent to the country and its holy capital. The long era of Muslim rule ended in 1917 when the British imperial army drove the Turks from the country. Local Christians cheered, but not for long. For in the thirty years of British rule the stage was set for the fierce contest between Jewish and Arab nationalists for control of the land.

Thus the bare chronicle of Jerusalem's history, recited in broad, swift strokes to make a point: none of this history is past, dead, forgotten. The story of victor and vanquished excites the imagination of people who live here. The conquests are still celebrated, the tragedies still mourned. All the great personalities—King David, Judas Maccabee, Simon Bar Kochba, Sophronios, Heraclius, Harun Rashid, Baldwin I, Saladin, Ben-Gurion, Haj Amin al-Husseini—all are remembered and honored by those for whom those memories keep the spirit alive. These are not past heroes; they are lights showing the way. Most cities look to the past, some recall ancient glory; the people of Jerusalem drag the past forward into their homes and hearts, so that the past becomes a part of them, uniting them, justifying them in their grievances, instilling hope for the future.

What helped me to understand Jerusalem's use of the past is the strikingly different appearance of monuments in this city. In Athens or Rome or Istanbul the glory is spent, and the monuments to that glory are neatly laid out and clearly separated from the busy, serious, day-to-day city which preoccupies the men and women who live there. The Parthenon, Socrates' Agora, the Coliseum, the Forum, Palatine hill, Aghia Sophia—what have they to do with the Greeks, Italians, Turks who must work, pay rent, raise their families? The monuments are for visitors, and one visits them on well-constructed footpaths, with toilets handy, leaving the modern city for a few hours to browse in antiquity.

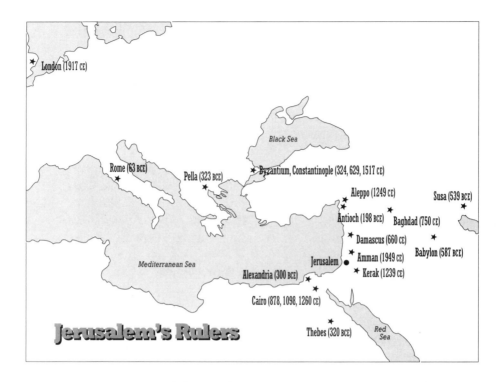

London (1917 CE)

Black Sea

Rome (63 BCE)   Pella (323 BCE)   Byzantium, Constantinople (324, 629, 1517 CE)

Aleppo (1249 CE)   Susa (539 BCE)

Antioch (198 BCE)   Baghdad (750 CE)

Damascus (660 CE)

Jerusalem ●   Amman (1949 CE)   Babylon (587 BCE)

Mediterranean Sea   Alexandria (300 BCE)   Kerak (1239 CE)

Cairo (878, 1098, 1260 CE)

Jerusalem's Rulers

Thebes (320 BCE)   Red Sea

How very different the monuments in Jerusalem. The monuments *are* the city, and the people stand close watch beside their
ancient treasures. Most conquerors have desecrated the shrines
of their vanquished enemies. Israelis remember how the Jordanians destroyed synagogues in the old city and ruined the Jewish
cemetery on the Mount of Olives. Today Muslims worry about
Jewish extremists blowing up mosques on the Temple Mount in
order to make room for the third Temple. A team of Hebrew
University archaeologists, digging for traces of David's original
capital in the Kidron Valley, are accosted by Talmudists who
charge them with desecrating Jewish graves in the area. The
Western Wall remnant of Herod's Temple is guarded day and
night by ultra-Orthodox Jews; they are afraid of the Muslims
who also revere the sacred wall as the place to which Muhammad tethered his horse Buraq before the Heavenly Ascent.
No window, pillar, or stairwell in the Church of the Holy
Sepulchre is washed or repaired without setting Greek against
Franciscan against Armenian against Copt, all of whom have
proprietary rights and mutually contradictory claims on the
church. There are no easy footpaths to these monuments. There

is nothing antique, dusty, or irrelevant about them. The history of Jerusalem is contained in these monuments. Today they are the sword's point of the ambitions and resentments of all the peoples who live here.

The mood of conquest fills the streets of this city. Once, late at night, I trailed a group of dark-bearded, black-coated young Hasidic boys from their prayers at the Western Wall up a narrow alley of the old city. They walked fast, taking long strides, moving their arms rapidly in athletic fashion. Seeing them coming, Arab boys of the same age (sons of the local merchants) quickly moved to the side of the street, and in the brief moment that we passed, they hugged the walls and cast furtive glances of fear and contempt. Always in this city one group is up and another down, and those who are down are waiting, with grudging patience, to be up again.

The spirit of conquest rules Jerusalem, and so the ancient, walled city continues to be a maze of quarters, compounds, and walls, a fortress encircling thirty thousand inhabitants, scores of churches, mosques, and synagogues, dozens of the world's most cherished holy places. And beyond the walls lie 400,000 more souls in the modern Jerusalem which extends westward into the Jewish neighborhoods of Rehaviah, Talbiah, Katamon, Rome-mah, and Talpiot, and eastward across the Arab areas of Wadi Jos, Sheikh Jarrah, Beit Hanina, and Shuafat. But there is no neat division of peoples and parties here. Memories blur the geographical lines as they deepen resentments. Forty years ago Jewish homes could be found all over east Jerusalem, and Arabs were living in Talbiah and Katamon, and on Gaza Street, a short walk from where the Hechal Shlomo now sits, the stone citadel of the rabbinate.

The walls of old Jerusalem tell the story of this city. There are walls to keep people out, walls to keep the desert from creeping close; walls to mark off sacred space from a world broken and defiled; walls to wash, to decorate, to tie one's animal to, to gaze upon in the evening light. In 1869 Mark Twain noted that it took a fast walker about an hour to walk around Jerusalem's four walls. In 1948, to celebrate the city's liberation, Israel's former prime minister David Ben-Gurion thought to tear down Jerusalem's walls—but, thank God, wiser

The Golden Gate at the eastern wall of old Jerusalem. From this gate, according to Jewish, Christian, and Muslim beliefs, the Messiah will enter. A Muslim cemetery lies at the foot of the gate. (Photographed by Adrien Bonfils ca. 1860–1890)

heads prevailed and the walls remained. In the same year Jordanian soldiers erected a concrete barrier outside the old city to keep Jews from contaminating the Muslim side of town. But in 1967, after Israel won a military victory for control of the whole city, this new wall of shame came down.

We learn from the Bible that Nehemiah repaired Jerusalem's walls. Roman emperors Titus and Hadrian, after first destroying the walls, built new ones which were repaired again by the Byzantine empress Eudocia. In the sixteenth century the Turkish conqueror Suleiman the Magnificent constructed the walls we see today.

In the last three hundred years the walls grew short from the rubble which collected at their base until Mayor Teddy Kollek, combining Nehemiah's dedication and Suleiman's industry, swept away the rubble to reveal the walls in their original height and beauty.

Walls have their gates, and Jerusalem's old city gates are wide, handsome mouths opening into a tiny universe of priests, pilgrims, peddlers, plotters, dreamers, rabbis, and Muslim holy men. But one gate is never open: the Golden Gate, through which Jesus entered the Temple Mount on Palm Sunday. The Turks sealed the Golden Gate, fearing the legend that when Christ reappears through the gate the world empires will fall.

Sealed with stones, the Golden Gate's double-doored outline seems more like an etched decoration in the eastern wall than an actual gate. But the people who live in this city know the gate is there, and they will tell you stories which speak volumes about their yearnings and fears. Legend has it that when Titus burned the Temple the Divine Presence—the *Shekinah*, as it is called in Hebrew—fled the conflagration, exiting from the earth through the Golden Gate. To this day the most pious of Jerusalem's Jews believe that on the Day of Judgment the *Shekinah* will return to earth and reenter the Temple Mount through the same gate. On that day the righteous souls will ascend to heaven through the southern (Mercy) portal and the wicked will be cast down into hell through the northern (Repentance) portal. The judgment will take place in the Valley of Jehosophat, below the Mount of Olives. Then a bridge will appear across the valley, a bridge "as thin as a hair and as sharp as a sword." Muslims believe that righteous Muslims will cross the bridge safely but that the wicked will fall to their ruin below. The Jewish version of the same legend contains a different fate. The bridges are two, one of iron, the other of paper. Muslims and Christians will cross the iron bridge which will collapse under them, while Jews will pass safely over the paper bridge.

Because of walls and gates, Jerusalem is a city of communal circles, one closed to the other, tribal ghettos, each dedicated to its tribal gods. There are ghettos of Armenians, Greeks, Melkites, Maronites, Syrians, Ethiopians, and Copts, German and Swedish Lutherans, Italians, French, Scottish Presbyterians, Evangelicals and Pentecostals; bedouins, Hebronite shopkeepers and *felaheen* (peasants), old Muslim patricians and Jewish Hasidic Talmudists. And more ghettos of young brave Zionists in the Jewish quarter, old Ashkenazi elite in Rahaviah and Talbiah, Israeli nouveaux riches in the German and Greek colonies, Jewish expatriates from America in Yemin Moishe, Arabic-speaking oriental Jews in Musrara and Katamon, and lately thousands of Russian Jews on the fringes of the city.

The psalmist, visualizing Jerusalem as a universal city of peace and unity, spoke of the city as "compact together." Actually another truth prevails, that of particularity. The drive for particularity is so great here that one cannot imagine a municipal committee composed of representatives from the different communities.

The section of town defines your religion, class, ethnic group, and political loyalty. In Jerusalem everyone has a place and adheres to it. For that reason no one really chooses his friends at large. The neighborhood determines the people one knows, makes friends with, marries. Four hundred years ago the Turkish system of *millets*, or ethno-religious "nations," defined the pattern, and the groups have adhered to it ever since. Everyone in Jerusalem is categorized, and little you say or do will alter your category. You may be atheistic or agnostic, but in Jerusalem you are defined as Jew or Christian or Muslim. And within those categories, further subcategories. No one walks about free in Jerusalem. This is what accounts for the city's burden, its perpetual seriousness. To borrow a word from theology, Jerusalem is an eschatological city, always in the end-time, awaiting any moment the cataclysm that will inaugurate the New Age. At any moment the Messiah will appear in the form of Jewish zealots or enraged Muslims or mad Christian prophets. Meanwhile everyone worries: Jews worry about the next war, Muslims worry about getting rid of the Jews, and Christians worry about whether or not they can survive the conflict between Arabs and Jews.

Jerusalem has high-rise buildings—too many of them; Jerusalem has urban renewal—too little of it. But no face-lift can alter the oldness of this city. And like every one of the world's old cities, Jerusalem has a distinctive mark, a smell, like a person's breath which sets him apart from all other persons. In *The Plague*, Albert Camus wrote of Oran, a Mediterranean seaport, completely modern, "without intimations," whose citizens live, love, and die with the same tedious indifference. Jerusalem, the antithesis of the modern, reeks of intimations. Here people love furiously and all live on the brink. As for dying, here is the only place to die and to be buried on the Mount of Olives where on Judgment Day the dead will rise, heralding the New Age. There is no colorless, odorless, gray mass in Jerusalem. Every citizen belongs somewhere, and no one gets lost.

For this reason Jerusalem is a sensuous city. Not sensuous in the ways that Rome or Paris or Venice is sensuous. No decaying beauty here. No glorious buildings, fine promenades, handsome

The Damascus Gate, so named to mark
the distance between Jerusalem and
the Syrian capital. The Mamluk
decoration above the gate shows it to
be the most beautiful entryway into old
Jerusalem. (Painted by David Roberts
in 1838)

squares here; no symbols of a proud, wealthy, lustful society.
Jerusalem's sensuousness is simple, immediate. One sees it in
the people at the Damascus Gate entry to the old city: a
procession of Arab boys in tight black pants followed by their
girl friends; green-coated Muslim women; proper Arab Christian husbands carrying market sacks; gowned priests of the
Latin and Greek churches; heavy bedouin women on their
haunches before baskets of yellow and blue grapes; sights of
working donkeys, tethered goats, lazy pigeons; fast-darting
children of ten balancing long wooden trays of warm pita bread;
smells of mint, cigarettes, and sweat from the tiny houses just
inside the gate mingling with more smells of dangling meat,
fresh fish, anise, basil, all dominated by the sweet stench of
dried donkey droppings.

Because the city is particular, ceremonies, style, form, and
civility count for much here. People not only greet each other
courteously, they go out of their way to do so. They are saying,
"Beliefs, traditions, holy wars divide us, but we are men of

the world and can greet each other as men." Jews treat Muslims with exquisite delicacy. Latin and Greek priests bow to each other when they meet in the alleys of the old city. An Armenian is the soul of courtesy and smiling good will. The Hasidim chatter endlessly to each other, rarely speaking or even smiling at the *goyim*, the gentiles; but if a person has the courage to stop a Hasid with a question about ritual or about some meaning in Talmud or Torah, the "pious one" will stop in his tracks, lower his voice to an intimate conversational level, and provide a quarter-hour's lecture on the question. Amidst the compounds in this city is an unmistakably human curiosity of one people about the other—not love exactly, but curiosity, a cultured, refined interest in one another.

The ceremonial city was on display one summer's night in 1981, at the celebration held by the Red Russian church on the anniversary of its founding in Jerusalem.

The Red Russian church is "red" because it is aligned to the patriarchate of Moscow, a virtual Soviet agency. The priests, seldom more than a dozen, all said to be Soviet spies, are shunned by the anti-Bolshevik White Russian community which has its own churches and hospices a half-mile away in the old city on the Mount of Olives. The banquet was held in the garden of what is left of the original Russian compound established in Jerusalem in 1882, north of Jaffa Gate. Most of the original buildings were sold or leased to the government of Israel, which now uses them for police headquarters and the local jail. In the center of the compound stands the cathedral Church of the Holy Trinity, during the last century a symbol of Russian Orthodox piety and power in the Holy Land.

Jerusalem's summer nights are still, cool, and smell of the young fresh pine planted all around the city. This night the air was filled with the smell of lemon, paprika, and lamb's flesh roasting over red coals. Arab Christian boys from Bethlehem tended the barbecue on the patio of the convent. Strategically placed at the open bar, priests with a diplomat's sense of tact offered Crimean wine, Russian vodka, French brandy, Greek Ouzo, German beer, Johnny Walker Scotch, and Israeli Carmel champagne. The buffet table groaned under the weight of ten salads, three different dishes of chicken, meatballs in thick cream sauce, six varieties of pickled fish, and a sizable hill of green-leafed, cigar-shaped dolmades. When a man standing next to me inquired politely about caviar, a nun reached behind her to an ice chest, extracted a sterling silver pot heaped with black fish eggs, and graciously handed the man a spoon.

Arriving in small groups, the guests were greeted with kisses on both cheeks at the gateway by a priest of about thirty-five years who seemed to know a dozen words in every language. Before sunset the garden was ringed with the local Christian powers, each occupying his small garden space. In one corner the Greek Orthodox, in another the Copts, pressed between them representatives of the Latin patriarchate. Off to one side were three black-faced Ethiopian priests. Whenever a priest from one of the tables made his way discreetly to one of the other tables, the entire group would rise, shake hands with the visitor, exchange kisses. Although they had repeated these gestures countless times at dozens of annual feast-day celebrations of all the churches, the gestures were marked by unmistakable pleasure.

Government officials, nearly all Israelis and Europeans, energetically hopped from one clump of priests to another. Stolidly, waiting at their tables like ancient princes of the realm, the priests awaited their audience. The blonde Finnish vice counsel, with enchanting cheek bones, made her way to the celibate Greek bishops, who sprang to their feet at the sight of her. She shook hands all around, and when she bent her head to kiss the ring of Patriarch Diodorus, a six-foot four-inch mountain of black robes, the patriarch half-rose from his chair, eyes aglow, to grasp her hands warmly.

There is a subtle, sensuous quality to church civility in Jerusalem: from their isolated communities people quietly, hesitantly reach out to one another.

It is not easy to say when a book was first seeded, when impressions first gave rise to words. With this book I have no doubt. It began on the last day of September 1973, my first night in Israel, on the journey from Lod Airport to Jerusalem. I had come to the country at the invitation of the Tantur Ecumenical Christian Institute to write and lecture on religious symbols of suffering in Dostoevsky, Albert Camus, and Elie Wiesel. It was Shlomo, my taxi driver, who opened my eyes to a different mode of tragedy.

It was not until we had passed the coastal plain, feeling the driver slip into low gear for the ascent into the hills, that conversation began with the burly, friendly man. He turned out to be a thirty-year-old Moroccan Jew who had immigrated to Israel with his family from Rabat, fifteen years earlier.

He began. "First time in Israel?"

"Yes. First time."

"You come to visit? Tourist?"

"I came to write a book."

"Book?"

"A book about suffering in literature."

The moonlight streaming through the windshield illuminated his face. He was smiling broadly.

"Suffering? You came to the right place. We all suffer here."

"The book is about suffering in modern literature."

"Never mind. Suffering is enough."

I tried to change the subject. "Is it difficult living in Israel?"

"Difficult? Impossible. But we don't have a choice."

"What do you mean, no choice?"

"It's no good for us in Arab countries. The people don't persecute us, but the leaders don't want us. So we go."

"Anti-Semitism?"

"Not exactly. They have their own problems. Arab problems. They hate each other. Sadat, Assad, Faisal, they all agree to hate each other. It makes them feel better. For this reason it is good to have Israel."

"If things were better, would you go back to Morocco?"

He began laughing. "Maybe. Actually, no. But it is a different life here. I don't love it. Life was quiet in Rabat, more simple. But I am an Israeli now. That's enough. I will stay here."

I pressed my question. "Is there a lot of anti-Semitism in Morocco?"

"I wouldn't call it anti-Semitism. It is politics. Look at what happened in Austria with that dirty Jew Kreisky." A few days before my arrival in Israel, Austria's Chancellor

Bruno Kreisky, in sympathy with the Palestinians, had closed Vienna's main transit camp for Soviet Jews leaving their country for Israel.

"Kreisky is a dirty Jew?" I asked.

"Yes, a dirty Jew—a Jew against Jews. Not different from Arabs."

"I suppose Israel will survive these world leaders."

"What does it matter? Israel will survive period. We survive each other. Why shouldn't we survive the politicians?"

"What do you mean, you survive each other?"

"Ah, it is your first time here. You will see. Israelis do not like each other. Everyone is pushing, yelling. We are difficult. Politicians, taxi drivers, everybody."

"Is this what you mean by everybody suffers in Israel?"

"Yes, no. Look, when we have a war, everyone changes. I believe God sends us a war every few years just to bring us together."

"You really believe God sends Israel war to unify the country?"

"I have to believe it."

"You live in Jerusalem, Shlomo?"

He shook his head, laughing.

"My question is funny?"

"It's not funny. I wouldn't live in Jerusalem...too much religion, too many rabbis, you understand? And too many stones."

"And too much suffering?"

"Yes, too much suffering."

"Shlomo, what's wrong with the stones?"

"The stones are cold. It makes Jerusalem cold, all night. I prefer to live in Petah Tikva. Warmer, no stones, not so many rabbis, better for me."

Coming out of a curve in the road at the top of the hill we had been climbing for half an hour, we reached Jerusalem. On first glimpsing the city in 1920, G. K. Chesterton wrote these words: "Suddenly, between a post of the wagon and a wrack of rainy cloud I saw it, uplifted and withdrawn under all the arching heavens of its history, alone with its benediction and its blasphemy, the city that is set upon a hill, and cannot be hid." What I saw in the night were street lights, Paz petrol stops, and a half-finished Hilton Hotel construction.

"Where are we going?"

"To the desert," Shlomo replied.

"But I thought the Tantur Institute was close to Jerusalem."

"Yes, yes, but where Jerusalem ends the desert begins."

We crossed the western side of town and made for the Bethlehem-Hebron road. Within minutes we were passing low, barren hills. An enormous stone building loomed up on our left, illuminated by moonlight. "What is that?"

"*Minzar*," the driver replied. "Mar Elias monastery. In two minutes, Tantur."

He drove by the monastery and within a couple of hundred yards slowed to negotiate a narrow gateway leading up a hill to enter another gate, a Crusader castle turret, finally stopping in front of a low glass building neatly decorated with freshly planted pine trees.

Shlomo sprang to the suitcases, jabbering in Arabic with the institute's handyman who had come out to assist us. Before he disappeared down the road he shouted to me out the car window, "Don't forget what I say for your suffering book."

After the luggage was put away, I turned to the handyman, Abu Joseph, and asked him if he would lead me to the roof so that I could see the desert in the moonlight. "My first time in the Holy Land," I said. He smiled, nodding his head with understanding. Taking me by the arm he led me up several flights of stairs.

I stood on the roof of the institute, turning my head in every direction. It was three in the morning. The full moon shone on Jerusalem to the north, sparkling with its own night lights; a smaller cluster arose from Bethlehem, two and a half miles in the opposite direction. Between the two towns in the black space was the Judean desert stretching east, all the way down to the Jordan Valley and the Dead Sea. Behind me, a stone's throw from the institute's outer wall, was the Arab Christian village of Beit Jala, sitting on its hill where the patriarch Jacob once tended his flock of sheep. I knew why I had run to this rooftop. I had to confirm the existence of these places as something more than biblical names and travel-book entries. I could smell lemon and pine and the sweet, intoxicating scent of jasmine. Below me, just outside the walls, I could hear the sound of an animal's bell. I recognized the outline of an Arab shepherd's hut. There were no other noises. No wind. Thousands of diamond stars burst forth with light, making the sky appear an immense arc, covering the whole world. I could not look up at them without feeling dizzy. I was exhausted, famished, elated. I can never forget that night. Three days later the forces of Syria and Egypt went to war against Israel. I never learned what happened to Shlomo.

PART ONE

The Meaning of Jerusalem in Jewish History

CHAPTER 1

Zion,
City of David

I am laying in Zion for a foundation a stone, a tested stone,
a precious cornerstone....
—Isaiah 28:16

I have set my king on Zion, my holy hill.
—Psalms 2:6

In June 1967 the Israeli army captured the eastern half of Jerusalem, which included the Arab-populated part of the town, the walled old city, the historic Jewish quarter, the Temple Mount, and the Western "Wailing" Wall. A few days after the capture, Israel's parliamentary Knesset decreed that east Jerusalem together with the Jewish-inhabited new city formed one undivided city, the complete and sovereign capital of Israel.

The Israelis' next step was equally practical and symbolic. Military authorities demolished the concrete wall that had prevented Arabs and Jews from mixing freely in the city during nineteen years of Jordanian control of east Jerusalem. With the wall gone, the city physically united, and with Israeli sovereignty extended over the whole of Jerusalem, Jews in Israel and throughout the world saw the healing of a wound in the body of the Jewish nation. After experiencing defeat, destruction, exile, and dispersion for eighteen hundred years, the people had now truly returned to the land, the nation could once again claim its capital. Secular-minded Jews spoke of the fulfillment of the Zionist dream; the more religious beheld the beginning of the messianic redemption.

The words of one of the young soldiers who fought in the battle for Jerusalem, a paratrooper, expressed the feelings of all Jews. After first distinguishing between Jerusalem and the Arab-populated territories of the West Bank and Gaza (also conquered in 1967), he said:

> I think you have to make a distinction between the problem of Jerusalem and the rest of the territories we're talking about. As long as security problems dictate that we stay in the territories beyond our previous borders, then we have to stay there. But the minute these problems are solved, then in my opinion we've no more right to stay there, at least as long as our only right is that of military success. And it's got nothing to do with who started the war, or the background against which it all began. But I wouldn't say the same about Jerusalem, because Jerusalem's got some far deeper meaning. It's something in our hearts, something to do with the way we feel. It was the source, the cornerstone of the whole Jewish people. Jerusalem really symbolizes our whole history, it's a thread that goes right through the story of our people. It was always the focus. Jerusalem's not just an idea; it's a whole world that embraces everything. . . . [1]

The words were timely, emotional, and largely true to the uniqueness of Jerusalem in the totality of Jewish history. They make it clear that Jerusalem has a powerful and enduring meaning for Jews, a meaning forged from all the glorious and bitter moments of the nation's historical experience. Reading back into Jerusalem's history, we cannot fail to recognize that Jewish reverence for this history shaped both Christian and Muslim estimation of Jerusalem's sanctity. In that respect there is a commonly shared sense of Jerusalem's holiness.

Perhaps more striking in reading Jerusalem's history is the diversity of beliefs, rituals, and symbols through which Jews and Christians and Muslims have expressed their love of Jerusalem. The history of the city demonstrates one thing above all: that the three peoples lived very differently in Jerusalem and experienced very different events of glory and tragedy. Thus the *meaning* of Jerusalem is very different for Jews, for Christians, and for Muslims. In this book the differences are what matter.

In this chapter, the first of three on the Jewish historical experience of Jerusalem, I aim to uncover that unique meaning which Jews gave to this city, a meaning which they have carried with them to this day. In succeeding chapters I will examine the distinct meanings of Jerusalem held by Christians and then by Muslims through their own respective historical experiences.

We can begin by recalling the words of the paratrooper: "Jerusalem really symbolizes our whole history, it's a thread that goes right through the story of our people." A thread knits together a garment, holds it in place. This is what Jerusalem has done and continues to do for Jews. The remarkable fact is that Jerusalem has acted as a strong, almost unbreakable thread despite numerous crises in which the nation fell apart politically or suffered military defeat and religious humiliation. From a purely political point of view, Jerusalem both succeeded and failed to unite the Jewish nation. Successes outweighed failures because the sources of national unity were both political *and* religious. As Jerusalem in time became grafted onto the authority of the Covenant law, so the people of ancient Israel began to believe that no defeat, no disaster would finally rob them of their homeland and capital, for no catastrophe could deprive them of God's love in the fulfillment of his promises to the nation.

The state and the politics of ancient Israel fell prey, as all small nations fell prey, to superior military powers. But the memory of Jerusalem outlived the collapse of the state because the meaning of Jerusalem, connected to the Covenant law, was inseparably political and religious. It was not a serene combination of elements. Often the prophets, as champions of Israel's Covenant law, found reason to criticize the state and denounce the capital for its idolatrous and immoral violation of the law. But the prophets were also patriots, and they too believed that Jerusalem, whatever her blasphemies, was not the enemy of the law but its setting. Isaiah said it: "Out of Zion shall come forth the law, and the word of the Lord from Jerusalem."

Out of the ashes of the Babylonian and later Roman destructions of the Judean state arose a spirit of Jewish national unity which would live on in the face of exile and dispersion throughout the world. The religious vitality of the Covenant law and the equally vital memory of Jerusalem made that spirit possible. Jerusalem was also at the heart of the messianic hope that eventually the people would return to the land to live again freely as a sovereign nation.

The great accomplishment of King David was to create a

united kingdom founded on the Covenant law and radiating from Jerusalem. David brought together in one city the newer forces for political nationalism with the older energies of religious faith and moral conduct. Thus the ancient Israelite nation-state was born. It survived by warfare and trade and foreign treaties. And like all nation-states, Israel chose to dominate rather than be dominated by her neighbors. Inevitably, military, political, and economic needs outweighed the religious and moral principles of the Covenant. The prophets criticized David and all the kings who followed him for ignoring these principles. But most of the kings knew, as David knew, that while the Covenant law showed Israel how to live in obedience to Israel's God, Yahweh, only the wise use of power ensured Israel's survival on earth. The law would come forth out of Jerusalem, but it would take an army to defend the city as Israel's capital. The connections between nation and morality, state and religion, capital and Covenant were delicate connections, easily broken, easily perverted, as we shall see.

To understand both the political and religious meaning of Jerusalem in Jewish historical experience, we must go back before King David conquered Jerusalem in 1000 B.C.E., all the way back to Mosaic times, around 1300–1200 B.C.E., when the Covenant law began to shape the consciousness of ancient Israel. If Jerusalem became the "cornerstone" of ancient Israel, it was because the Covenant law was the very earth on which Israel stood.

The Covenant law can be found on every page of the most sacred portion of Israel's bible, the Torah. The Covenant law was the mind and will of Yahweh, who chose Israel as his Covenant partner. Yahweh disclosed himself to Israel as a law-giver who demanded obedience to a set of moral principles stipulated in the Ten Commandments. The spirit of those commandments was expressed so: "You shall love God with all your heart, soul, and mind, and you shall love your neighbor as you love yourself."

In the middle of the twelfth century B.C.E., twelve Israelite tribes were living in Canaan. They formed a confederacy whose solidarity was expressed through four supreme beliefs about their God, Yahweh. First, Yahweh, not the lesser gods of the surrounding pagan nations, was the Lord of the Universe; second, Yahweh chose Israel to spread the word of his majesty to all peoples; third, Yahweh gave to Israel the land of Canaan as a dwelling place; fourth, in revealing his moral law, Yahweh showed Israel how to live in Canaan as his Covenant partner.

Annually, at the important festival times of spring planting, first fruits, and the fall harvest of the new year, the tribes would meet together to celebrate their common faith. At these times tribal rivalries were set aside as the leaders recited the Exodus story of liberation from Egyptian servitude, a story which dramatized their belief in Yahweh's love which set them apart from all other nations. The tribes would praise the majesty of Yahweh and recite the moral law which was at the heart of their Covenant faith with Yahweh.

But prayer alone could not assure survival. For more than two hundred years the Israelite tribes struggled successfully against their enemies to secure their place in Canaan. To encourage victory they carried with them into battle a talisman, the Ark of the Covenant, which symbolized Yahweh's protective love. The Ark itself was a simple wooden box containing a leather-bound copy of the Ten Commandments; the box was also fitted with arms so that it could be transported from shrine site to battle place.

Armed with swords, spears, and the Ark, the Israelites fought with bravery and secured their place in the central hill country of Canaan, from Dan in the north, near the headwaters of the Jordan River, to Beersheva southward on the edge of the Negev Desert. Concentrated in a small area, they surmounted rivalries among their tribes and effectively united against any of the Canaanite aggressors, like the Edomites or Amalekites, who would dislodge them. Then, around 1050 B.C.E., a powerful new regional enemy, the Philistines, invaded their territory.

The Philistines (or "Sea Peoples," because they came originally from the Aegean Islands) were fierce warriors. With their newly invented iron weapons they began a march of conquest inland from their own tribal cities of Gaza, Ashkelon, Ashdod, Gath, and Ekron on the Mediterranean coast of Canaan. Upon invading the tribal area of Israel they won a series of battles culminating in the capture of the shrine town of Shilo, where the Ark of the Covenant was kept.

The capture of the Ark was a humiliating event for the Israelites. Many of them felt that Yahweh, who was Israel's protector in battle, had abandoned his people as punishment for failing to obey the Covenant law. But the Philistines worried about the Ark. It seems they were intimidated by the aura of divine power surrounding the box. The biblical writer we know as the Deuteronomist, who narrated the Books of Samuel, informs us that after capturing the Ark the Philistines were so afraid that Yahweh's wrath would be exercised against them that they deliberately discarded the sacred object. Hence the Ark lay lost for years until an Israelite, David the Judean, had the luck to find it and the foresight to use it as a means of transforming a people into a nation and thence into a state.

While the Philistines dominated central Canaan for thirty years, Israelite tribal leaders feared for the survival of their confederacy. From 1020 B.C.E. on, two heroic personalities made their appearance in biblical history. The first was Saul, tribal chief of Benjamin; the second was the Judean David. The biblical story of their relationship is a commentary on the agonizing transition from Israel's tribal past, where democracy, sectional jealously, and territorial insecurity prevailed, to a new political future characterized by power, pride, and obedience to central state authority.

Saul, who became Israel's first king, effectively led the Israelites in battle against the Philistines, but his efforts paled by comparison with his protégé and rival, David. It was a rivalry mocked in the song's refrain:

> ... When David returned from slaying the Philistine, the women
> came out of all the cities of Israel, singing and dancing, to meet
> King Saul, with timbrels, with songs of joy, and with instruments
> of music. And the women sang to one another as they made merry.
> "Saul has slain his thousands, and David his ten thousands."
>
> 1 Samuel: 6–7

David's fighting skills won him leadership over the tribe of Judah and made it possible for him to best Saul for the crown of all Israel. In time he decisively defeated the Philistines, driving them back to their coastal cities where they paid tribute to Israel throughout the period of the Davidic-Solomonic empire.

David's skill was not military alone. He had a sound political understanding that the future security of the nation lay in moving beyond the tribal confederacy to a new, more unified framework of government. Where Saul had begun to unify the tribes under a single king, David completed the process. He succeeded in establishing his kingship over the various tribal leaders because they had no power to oppose him and because a sufficient number of them agreed with his perception of the nation's security.

David's genius was never more evident than in his selection of Jerusalem as the capital of the united Israelite monarchy. We cannot be certain that he had a capital in mind when one night, in a bloodless raid, he seized the hilltop town of Jerusalem (then called Jebus after its Jebusite inhabitants). But after taking the city he quickly exploited its advantages. As a natural fortress, protected on three sides by steep hills which bordered on desert wasteland, Jerusalem was an ideal site for a new royal palace. The city loomed over the Jordan Valley and afforded a unique vantage point for dominating both the northern and southern halves of the country.

The political advantages of Jerusalem were equally clear. As a Jebusite stronghold Jerusalem owed allegiance to no Israelite tribe; it was a "neutral" place which could serve as the capital of a new political union. By locating the palace in Jerusalem and not in his own tribal capital of Hebron, thirty miles southeast of Jerusalem, the king hoped to minimize sectional strife between the northern tribes and his own southern tribe of Judah. And because Jerusalem was David's personal possession by right of conquest, the king could feel free to build in the capital without worrying about offending the tribal elders who continued to exercise power from their regional cities.

Eventually all the important institutions of the monarchy were established in Jerusalem—palace, treasury, law courts, military headquarters, and the central religious shrine. In time Jerusalem became so completely shaped by the power and personality of the king that people simply refered to the capital as *ir David*, City of David, a name that the biblical writers adopted.

Early in his planning for Jerusalem, David knew that the security of his own kingship depended on ending sectional rivalries. How to get the northern Israelite tribes to join his loyal supporters in Judah in accepting Jerusalem as their own national capital? How to convince them that Jerusalem was a legitimate center of worship which could take its place alongside the regional shrine centers of Shechem, Shilo, and Bethel? And how to persuade them that his rule in Jerusalem did not violate traditional tribal ways of government and worship but rather built on them? The questions were answered through religion. The king retrieved the old tribal totem, the Ark of the Covenant, and brought it to Jerusalem as the center of a new national cult. The Ark was to link the new institutions of kingship and capital to the older ritual traditions, showing the people that David's monarchy was the legitimate successor to the tribal confederacy.

We are told by the Second Book of Samuel that David rescued the Ark from Kiriath-yearim, a few miles north of Jerusalem, where it had been discarded by the Philistines. In colorful language the Deuteronomic writer describes the festive procession of men and beasts bearing the sacred Ark to Jerusalem. It was moved to the accompaniment of "songs and lyres and harps and tambourines, castanets and cymbals." Horns announced the grand entry into the city; oxen were slaughtered every six paces in praise of Yahweh. The king led the procession. And because he wished to be accepted not only as king but as high priest of the nation's worship, David dressed (or rather undressed) for the occasion by wearing only his priestly apron, the linen ephod. The Deuteronomist tells us that the joyous king proceeded to dance nakedly "before the Lord with all his might."

Suddenly something went wrong. The oxen drawing the Ark stumbled. One of the attendants, Uzziah, stuck out his hand to steady the rig but inadvertently touched the sacred vessel of the law and was struck down by the Lord. Why did it happen? Was it magic? Divine punishment? What was the crime? No answers are given. As readers of the story we are left to wonder if Israel's God, Yahweh, really wanted his law permanently enshrined in one place, even in this one city whose promise under David was so great.

No sooner did the Ark enter Jerusalem than another dark incident occurred. David's wife, Michal, grew angry at the sight of her husband's nakedness. Was her anger a portent of the terrible events that would plague David's reign over Israel? Before the king died, his family would be torn apart by betrayal, incest, adultery, rebellion, and murder. The prophet Nathan would denounce the king for murdering Uriah in order to marry his wife, Bathsheba. And the prophets who followed Nathan would find both in the immorality of King David and in the megalomania of his son and successor, Solomon, an explanation for the dissolution of the united monarchy and for the later destruction of Jerusalem.

After the Ark arrived in Jerusalem it was housed at the king's newly built palace on the slopes of the eastern ridge overlooking the Kidron Valley. To officiate at worship services, as well as to undermine allegiance to regional shrine centers, David brought the Levite priests of Shilo to Jerusalem. But it was he, the king, who presided at the services, whose liturgy included the songs of praise that David himself wrote.

From the beginning of his reign, David also wished to be recognized as the nation's high priest. He would mediate Yahweh's blessing to the people. He would be thought of as the successor to Melchisedek, the legendary Canaanite priest-king of Jerusalem. David's priestly powers were on display annually at the autumn festival of the New Year. Where once Israelites on the New Year had gathered at the regional shrine centers of Shilo, Shechem, and Bethel to renew the Covenant bond with Yahweh, now with the king officiating at the Ark they came to Jerusalem.

In time the aura of sanctity enveloped David. His royal advisers began to speak of the king's divinity, a conception borrowed from the sacred power surrounding the kings of neighboring nations. The psalms that were written for the Ark worship and the later temple service spread the cult of the king's divinity which began in David's own time. As a good example of the cult we can take portions of the Second Psalm, where the Lord identifies David as his "anointed" (*messiah*), a divine son to whom will be given dominion over all the nations of the earth.

> Why do the nations conspire, and the peoples plot in vain?
>
> The kings of the earth set themselves, and the rulers take counsel together, against the Lord and his anointed, saying,
>
> "Let us burst their bonds asunder, and cast their cords from us."
>
> He who sits in the heavens laughs; the Lord has them in derision.
>
> Then he will speak to them in his wrath, and terrify them in fury, saying,

"I have set my king on Zion, my holy hill."

I will tell of the decree of the Lord:
He said to me, "You are my son, today I have begotten you."

The sanctification of King David and the presence of the Ark at the palace contributed to the sacralization of the city of Jerusalem. Before long the idea was heard that Yahweh had chosen Jerusalem as his eternal "dwelling place." Although worship continued at the northern shrine centers, Jerusalem increasingly became the center of the nation's religious life, a development that intensified with the building of the Temple under Solomon.

The task of transforming Jerusalem into a Hebrew national shrine center was helped by the air of holiness which had always hung over the former ancient city-state of Jebus. The Jebusites offered sacrifices to their god Shalem on the great outcropping of limestone rock on the northern hill overlooking Jebus. Biblical legend held that David acquired the hill by paying fifty shekels to its owner, Araunah, the king of Jebus, who had used the hill for threshing grain. After purchasing the site David constructed a small altar on the very stone where the Jebusites had offered their holy sacrifices; that same stone became the foundation stone of Solomon's Temple.

The Jebusite hill, looming north above David's palace, received the mystical name of Zion because the Israelites, like the Jebusites before them, believed that the divine presence dwelt there. The Jebusites had sacrificed to Shalem on this hill, and eventually Shalem gave his own name to the city below, *Urushalem*, Jeru-salem, "place of the god Shalem."[2]

The Israelites extended the sanctity of Zion by incorporating their own sacred legends into Jebusite mythology. An example of this is the tale in which Abraham passes the test of faith by his willingness to bind Isaac for sacrifice; the place of the sacrifice was set on Zion's hill. Another example is the lovely story of Melchisedek, who steps forth to bless Abraham in the name of his own Canaanite deity El Elyon, the "God Most High," whom the Israelites renamed simply Elohim, "Lord."[3]

David planned the building of a temple as a permanent home for the Ark. Although he had selected the gold and silver ingots to be used in the temple service, we do not know why he never began the actual construction. Yet the people's admiration for

David was so great that his failure to build the temple was interpreted as an expression of divine favor. According to the Deuteronomist, David approached the prophet Nathan, a royal adviser, and asked his permission to build a "house" for the Lord in Jerusalem. "I dwell in a house of cedar," David said, "but the ark of God dwells in a tent" (2 Samuel 7:1–29). The Lord, speaking through Nathan's voice, responds that he will not permit David to build him a house, but instead that he, the Lord, will build David a house, by which is meant a royal dynasty. Thus the denial of David's right to build a temple to the Lord is converted into a divine blessing or guarantee of David's royal descendants.

Perhaps the real reason for the Lord's refusal of David's offer reflected the concern of many in David's kingdom that a temple was too radical a departure from the traditions of the Ark, whose original home was a simple desert tent.[4] If this was true, then David was wise to avoid building a sacred structure, for it would only have defeated his purpose in bringing the Ark to Jerusalem. Centuries later, the rabbis provided their own explanation of the Lord's refusal. They reasoned from the rules of ritual purity that because David, a military commander, was befouled by war's blood, he was unfit to build the spotless abode required for God's earthly dwelling place. The rabbis went on to say that Solomon, on the other hand, who inherited David's kingdom and never fought, remained clean, and so built the Lord's "house."

The Lord's promise of a "house" to David was interpreted by all loyal to the king as a "commitment" by Yahweh to David and to his descendants for future generations. Yahweh would shower his loving blessing on the "house" of David, thereby assuring the nation that a Davidic king would rule over them forever. In the mind of the king and his royal advisers, Yahweh's commitment was nothing less than a new Covenant with Israel based on the Davidic royal line. It would build on but not replace the older Covenant founded on the Mosaic law. Thus David would be seen as a second Moses, and Jerusalem, David's city, would succeed Mount Sinai as the site of the law.

But in David's own time there were many Israelites, particularly among the northern tribesmen, who rejected the divine claims made for the Davidic monarchy. For them nothing could be placed on a level with the Mosaic law. No mere mortal, not even Israel's king, could be proclaimed a second Moses. And Jerusalem could never replace Sinai as the Mountain of God.

Aware of his detractors, David worked energetically to promote the sacred authority of his monarchy. Soon after he took possession of Jerusalem he set to work his royal scribes and chroniclers. The story of David's reign over Israel as we have it in the Second Book of Samuel came from the pens of those court-appointed writers. They were not historians in the modern sense of the word, striving for objectively written, factual accounts of events. Their aim was to weave a tapestry of meaning drawn from religious convictions and nationalistic confidence: that David was God's appointed king over Israel, and that because of God's unique blessing, the Davidic dynasty and the united monarchy would last forever. Yet what is remarkable about the Davidic court history is that despite its religious and political intention, the writers did not seek to hide the king's indiscretions and blunders. The court history allows us to understand both the extraordinary hope invested in the Davidic monarchy by the nation and the tragic errors that brought about its downfall.

The establishment of the monarchy, the selection of the capital Jerusalem, the relocation of the Ark—all these events were expressions of an enlarging nationalistic consciousness among the Israelites. Fueling nationalism were the territorial conquests which gradually created an empire. With the confidence that Yahweh was on its side, the army of David subjugated the Philistines and all the other native peoples of Canaan. David then sent his troops into Transjordan and made tribute-paying vassals of the Moabites, Edomites, Ammonites, and the Aramean peoples of Damascus. So greatly did the kingdom expand into foreign lands that when David died, in 960 B.C.E., his empire extended from the Euphrates to the borders of Egypt. It was an extraordinary achievement. In four decades of ceaseless fighting, tiny Israel, which for two hundred years had been an endangered confederacy of tribes in central Canaan, had united under a brilliant leader, defeated her enemies, and become a powerful regional empire. The power was based in Jerusalem, the city of the God-blessed king who had secured for the nation all the land promised to the patriarch Abraham by Yahweh.

The last years of David's life were more difficult.[5] Rebellions marred the conclusion of his reign. Although he had convinced the tribal leaders of northern Israel to follow his command in battle, he could not ultimately persuade them to yield their powers to him as absolute monarch. The forty years of David's reign saw continuing tension between the northern tribes and the king who ruled from Jerusalem. This unrest increased when David made the mistake of bypassing the tribal leaders to appoint his own bureaucracy of royal advisers, scribes, priests, chroniclers, land overseers, and tax collectors. Many of those appointed to these offices—new in the history of the nation— were not even Israelites. Often picked for their skills or loyalty, they were men who came from one of the subject nations of Canaan or Transjordan. Even David's own most trusted personal guard consisted not of Israelites but of Philistine mercenaries, Israel's former enemy. The presence of so many pagan foreigners in the court at Jerusalem widened the alienation between David and his countrymen in the north.

We are not surprised to learn that when David's son Absalom mounted a rebellion to win the throne from his father, Absalom's supporters proved to be those very northern tribal leaders who had been neglected by the king. David rallied his own Judean tribesmen against the rebels and averted the loss of his throne, but at the tragic price of losing his son in battle. In turning to Judah to battle against northern Israel, David understood that he had written a death warrant to his own long and largely successful effort to lead a united Israelite nation.

More rebellions followed. This time the leader was Sheba ben Bichri of the tribe of Benjamin, who along with many northerners still resented the rise of King David at the expense of King Saul and his descendants. They were the voices who found expression in the refrain, "We have no part in David, neither have we inheritance in the Son of Jesse; every man to his tents, O Israel" (2 Samuel 20:1).

At the root of David's problems were questions that faced the Israelites from the moment they adopted monarchy as a political framework. Was monarchy compatible with the original tribal faith which recognized only Yahweh as king? How could David pretend to rule Israel as king when Yahweh had made it clear to Moses that the moral law alone would rule Israel? Further, was kingship not the detested office of pagan despots who were gods in the eyes of their idolatrous subjects? No one thought more about these questions than the Deuteronomist. This writer, who lived in Jerusalem in the last generation before the Babylonian destruction of nation and capital, greatly admired the monarchy of David. Yet his honesty compelled him to record the bitterness as well as the joy felt toward monarchy by David's subjects in his own time.

Some of those closest to David, including his own appointed court chroniclers, believed that Yahweh had blessed Israel's kingship. At the moment when Israel faced destruction at the hands of the Philistines, Yahweh anointed David as king to lead Israel in victory. But other views of kingship were represented in the humble rejoinder of the old tribal leader Gideon when he was the first to be offered kingship: "I will not rule over you, and my son will not rule over you; the Lord will rule over you" (Judges 8:23).

The problem of kingship in ancient Israel was never solved because it defied solution. Israel's security, her survival, her developing nationalism, all seemed to require the unified leadership that monarchy provided. Yet the ancestral religion placed severe limitations on the exercise of the king, if it did not prohibit kingship altogether. King David sought to combine Israel's nationalism with her faith in the Covenant law. But the rebellions that scarred his last years as monarch show that he failed to sustain the unification initially brought about by his kingship. The main reason for that failure is clear. The people could not agree on the wisdom of being ruled by a single king, exercising his powers from one capital which was also designated as the national shrine. While the empire which David bequeathed to Solomon was powerful and wealthy, it also suffered internally from lack of unity and purpose. It was only a matter of time before its foundation cracked and the nation's leaders sought a new political framework through which to express the old faith in Yahweh and his law.

The last of the rebellions against David was a terrible omen. Shortly before his death, David faced the hostility of his oldest living son, Adonijah, who failed in his effort to seize the throne from the aging king. To counter the plot against him, the king elevated as his successor his youngest son Solomon, born of Bathsheba. In the view of the Deuteronomist, the passing of the diadem from father to son seemed to confirm Nathan's dire prediction made after David's adulterous affair with Bathsheba.

"Now therefore the sword shall never pass from your house..."
(2 Samuel 12:10). And the sword did not pass, for Solomon was
able to secure the crown only after having his older brother
Adonijah assassinated.

Solomon, who came to the throne in Jerusalem about 960
B.C.E., was not a fighter like his father but rather a builder. He
enlarged Jerusalem and rebuilt a sumptuous new palace adjacent
to the Temple. He constructed the fortified cities of Megiddo,
Gezer, and Hazor. To finance these projects he drew from a
royal treasury which at times must have seemed inexhaustible.
Money came from a variety of trading ventures. The king
controlled the lucrative caravan route along the "King's High-
way" running from Damascus to Egypt. He bought for resale
horses and camels. He exported wheat and olive oil to the
Phoenician King Hiram and bought from him cedar and cypress
woods needed for construction. He extracted copper from mines
south of the Dead Sea and on the northern edge of the Red Sea,
and equipped ships to sail the ingots to markets in distant
lands.

Surpassing all these enterprises in significance was his construction of the Temple in Jerusalem. It took workers seven
years to complete. Although a modest building, measuring
ninety feet long, thirty feet wide, and forty-five feet high, it was
an architectural achievement. As Phoenicians were employed to
design the building and perform the skilled craftwork, what
resulted was a temple in the style of earlier Syraeo-Phoenician
temples. Few would have criticized the king in his own time, but
in later centuries the complaint was heard that instead of building a house for Yahweh, Solomon's pagan architects had designed a temple in honor of their own gods.

The Temple consisted of three rooms: a vestibule or *ulam*;
the central sanctuary (*hechal*) in which the altar, candelabra, and
table of shewbread were placed; and a small, windowless, unlit
"back room" raised above the sanctuary (*debir*)—the inner
shrine or Holy of Holies, where the Ark of the Covenant was
kept. The Ark was flanked by two sphinx-like cherubim fashioned of olive wood. Copied from the temple art of the Phoenicians, the outstretched wings of these guardian angels had a
symbolic function: they protected the holy Ark below and

formed the throne seat of Yahweh invisible in the heavens above. Only the high priest was allowed to enter this inner shrine, and then only on the Day of Atonement when, facing the Ark, he petitioned the Lord's mercy on behalf of all the people of Israel.[6]

In front of the Temple was a courtyard, in the center of which was the great altar of sacrifice, a huge bronze receptacle, its brim "made like the brim of a cup; like the flower of a lily" (1 Kings 7:26). Worshipers came to the altar from throughout the kingdom on the days of the yearly festivals to petition the Lord with prayers and to pay the priests to sacrifice the ewe lambs that would bring divine blessing.

In bringing the Ark of the Covenant to his city, David had begun the process of sacralizing Jerusalem; now Solomon, by installing the Ark in the Temple, had completed the process. But it seems there were gnawing doubts in the king's mind on the day the Temple was dedicated to Yahweh. The king's prayer began confidently: "The Lord has set the sun in the heavens, but has said that he would dwell in thick darkness. I have built thee an exalted house, a place for thee to dwell in forever" (1 Kings 8:12–13). Suddenly a theological problem occurs: How can the great invisible Lord of the universe occupy earthly space? Is it not the idolatrous who make such foolish claims about their gods? Solomon understood the problem, for midway in the prayer he asks, "But will God indeed dwell on the earth?" (1 Kings 8:27). The answer was, obviously not. "Behold, heaven and the highest heaven cannot contain thee; how much less this house which I have built." How then does Yahweh occupy an earthly temple? The question was answered further on in the prayer. It seems that it is not Yahweh himself but the *name* of Yahweh which dwells in the earthly Temple.

And thus idolatry was avoided, at least for those who championed Solomon's reign over Israel.

> O Lord my God, hearkening to the cry and to the prayer which thy servant prays before thee this day; that thy eyes may be open night and day toward this house, the place of which thou hast said, "My name shall be there," that thou mayest hearken to the prayer which thy servant offers toward this place.
>
> 1 Kings 8:28–29

The reign of Solomon lasted some forty years, until 922

B.C.E., when tribal factionalism reasserted itself: northern Israel claimed its independence by seceding form the union. The breakup of the united monarchy was inevitable. King David could bequeath to his son Solomon the prestige, wealth, and sanctity of the monarchy, but he could not instill in his successor the political shrewdness necessary to maintain national unity.

The central problem of Solomon's forty-year reign was extravagance: he spent more money than he collected. In addition to the many lavish constructions of Temple, palace, fortresses, and cities, he maintained a large peacetime army and a huge state bureaucracy. Ships built to export metals to Africa returned to port with silks, perfumes, ivory, jewels, gold, baboons, and other rare animals for the royal zoo—all of it thought necessary to grace a royal court which in ostentation increasingly resembled its pagan neighbors. Late in his reign, lacking funds to pay the Phoenicians for his many purchases of wood, Solomon turned over to King Hiram some twenty productive cities on the sea coast between Acre and Tyre. In one sarcastic sentence, the Deuteronomist summed up the megalomania that finally rotted Solomon's reign over Israel: "All King Solomon's drinking vessels were of gold, none of silver, because it was not considered as anything in the days of Solomon" (1 Kings 10:22).

What alienated Solomon's Israelite subjects most were two drastic decisions affecting taxes and labor. The king reorganized the country into twelve tax districts, conducted a census, and appointed governors from his own family who saw to it that heavy revenues were extracted from the people. Then, to supplement non-Israelite slave labor (which had always been used in the empire), the king introduced forced labor drawn from the Israelite population, particularly from the northern tribal areas. It was a decision that led directly to rebellion.

The Deuteronomist informs us that in the last period of Solomon's reign the subject peoples of Aram and Edom, both sources of slave labor, broke away from the empire and established independent governments. After that, one of Solomon's trusted officials, Jeroboam ben Nabat, commander of a forced-labor battalion in northern Israel, had a change of heart (induced by the prophet Ahijah) and began a revolutionary movement when he "lifted up his hand against the king" (1 Kings 11:27).

Political and economic blunders brought down the Solomonic empire, but to the Deuteronomist the explanation was deeper. He attributed Solomon's downfall to idolatrous flirtations. To oblige his pagan wives, the king had built for them shrines to their favorite deities:

> For Solomon went after Ashtoreth the goddess of the Sidonians, and after Milcom the abomination of the Ammonites. So Solomon did what was evil in the sight of the Lord, and did not wholly follow the Lord, as David his father had done. Then Solomon built a high place for Chemosh the abomination of Moab, and for Molech the abomination of the Ammonites, on the mountain east of Jerusalem. And so he did for all his foreign wives, who burned incense and sacrificed to their gods.
>
> 1 Kings 11:5–8

Perhaps the Deuteronomist was right to charge Solomon with idolatry. But what he failed to see was that the king's tolerance of pagan practices, of a piece with his marriages to foreign princesses, was an expedient that sustained economic and political relations with such important trading partners as the Phoenicians and the Egyptians. It is difficult to know whether Solomon's "liberalism" in this regard made him less zealous for Yahweh, whether it corrupted him in a way that reduced his leadership. Perhaps idolatry was less a source of corruption than a symbol of it. What we can be sure of is that if the collapse of his kingdom was influenced by religious idolatry, it was simply additional evidence of a corruption rising out of political and economic misjudgments. Yet because idolatry was the foremost sin against the Covenant law, the Deuteronomist and the prophets saw in Solomon's idolatry a kind of poison released into the body of the nation, a poison that infected many of Israel's later kings and eventually brought destruction to Jerusalem.

The national unity which David established and Solomon sought to sustain came to an end upon Solomon's death in 921 B.C.E. Finally, the northern Israelites would not submit to Jerusalem's monarchy.

The fifty-year civil war between northern Israel and Judah that followed the breakup of the monarchy showed that neither kingship nor holy Jerusalem and its Temple could ultimately unify within one state a people divided by political and economic grievances. The ultimate source of the people's national unity was not state institutions and Temple cult but rather common loyalty to Yahweh and his Covenant law. Monarchy, capital, and Temple would work to unify the nation only if they could be cemented to the older "foundation stone" of God and law. The attachment worked more or less well when David exercised his magnetism and skill; it failed when Solomon squandered national wealth. The lesson was clear to any of the nation's kings who had eyes to see: Jerusalem as Israel's capital and seat of all its institutions provided no more national unity than Israel's leaders could provide through their loyalty to the Covenant law, their military skills, their political and economic judgments.

Having said this, we can speak of the authentic accomplishments of Israel's first monarchy. If longevity is a measure of success, then unquestionably David succeeded as a king. His military, political, and religious accomplishments convinced the people of Judah after his death that he was indeed God's "anointed." Where in northern Israel various royal dynasties replaced each other regularly by intrigue and assassination, Judah by contrast enjoyed a continuously stable existence under a succession of David's royal ancestors.

A second measure of David's success was the immortalization of his legacy in the myth of the messianic redemption. We can appreciate the power of the myth in recalling the contrasting fates of northern Israel and Judah in the centuries following the dissolution of the united monarchy. Northern Israel had the misfortune to lie directly in the path of Assyria, which destroyed her independence in 721 B.C.E. The people were banished to the distant land of Mesopotamia and never heard from again. No legend arose among the northern Israelites that spoke of a divine deliverance of people and king to the homeland and to its capital Samaria.

Judah was more fortunate than her sister kingdom. The Assyrians, who saw little material gain in invading Jerusalem, agreed to grant Judah her independence in exchange for tribute. For four hundred years the people were free to live, work, and worship until the late sixth century B.C.E. when a new conqueror, Babylon, made its appearance in the land. In the period 596–586 B.C.E. the Babylonians invaded Judah, destroyed Jerusalem, set fire to the Temple, and banished the people to Mesopotamia, where their cousins in northern Israel had preceded them. Yet what might have been seen as an experience of defeat was rather interpreted as providential. The Deuteronomist and the prophets who lived through the experience and looked back upon it interpreted it as God's will—punishment for disobedience of the moral law.

Those religious visionaries were also committed to the Davidic Covenant. For in Judah, in the centuries following the dissolution of the united monarchy, the belief in Yahweh's promises to the Davidic dynasty had acquired the proportions of a national theological myth. No military defeat of Israel counted against the myth. Just the opposite: each disaster occurred by divine design. As Yahweh had used Assyria to chastise northern Israel for her sins, so now Babylon was a divine scourge to punish the people of Judah for their disobedience of the Covenant law. But the punishment would end. Repentance would follow punishment, and after repentance would come redemption. Yahweh would remain faithful in his promises to the nation, to the Davidic dynasty, and to Jerusalem. All the dispersed peoples, northern and southern Israelites alike, would be restored to the land; Jerusalem and the Temple would be rebuilt, and a Davidic prince, God's "anointed" *(the messiah)*, would be sent to lead the nation through a new era of peace and righteousness. This vision was partly nostalgia for the "good old days" of David's kingship, partly an earnest hope that the failures of men would be corrected by God. Most of all it was the expression of a national belief that David, Jerusalem, and the Temple were at the very heart of Yahweh's Covenant with Israel. In originally fostering that belief, David indeed succeeded in cementing his kingship to the "foundation stone" of Yahweh's Covenant law.

During the long period of conquest and turmoil at the hands of Assyrians and Babylonians, the kings of Judah and of northern Israel were confronted by one supreme question: Would they submit to a humiliating foreign domination, or would they resist at the risk of annihilation? Kings Ahaz and Manasseh chose submission and gained survival; Hezekiah first decided on submission, then resisted and survived by pure good fortune; Josiah, in a burst of nationalistic and religious pride, chose resistance with disastrous results.

Much of our knowledge of Jerusalem's kings is based on the writings of the Deuteronomist and the prophets Isaiah and

Jeremiah. They favored kings like Hezekiah and Josiah because they abolished pagan sacrificial sites. Ahaz and Manasseh, on the other hand, were viewed as wicked kings who, like Solomon before them, profaned the Covenant law of Israel by tolerating pagan cultic practices in the land, even to the extent of permitting idol worship in Jerusalem's Temple. The prophets were convinced that the disasters which befell northern Israel under the Assyrians and Jerusalem under the Babylonians were directly due to the apostasy of wicked kings. But the historical record points to an ironic fact. Often Israel's so-called wicked kings, by their willingness to pay tribute and tolerate pagan worship, preserved the peace and gained survival; the pious kings, in refusing tribute and purging foreign temples, actually plunged the nation into a destructive maelstrom.

To illustrate, the Deuteronomist gave Hezekiah high praise for abolishing, in a frenzy of nationalistic pride, the pagan sanctuaries that his father Ahaz had allowed. We are also informed that he removed from Jerusalem's Temple the hated Mesopotamian snake symbol, the Nechustan. Afterward Hezekiah made the dreadful mistake of withholding tribute from Assyria, an action which signaled rebellion. The death in 705 B.C.E. of the brilliant and aggressive Assyrian ruler Sargon II had deceived Hezekiah into believing that he might win independence for Judah. Hezekiah had also gained support from the ruler of Egypt, Shabako, who had begun to rally forces for a military campaign to unseat Assyria as the dominant power in Canaan.

Planning rebellion and anticipating the Assyrian military response, Hezekiah strengthened Jerusalem's defenses by improving the city's water supply. Jerusalem was a nearly impregnable fortress, but its only ground source of fresh water was outside the city gates at the Gihon Spring in the Kidron Valley. Hezekiah ordered his engineers to build a water tunnel to bring water from the spring to a pool located inside the city walls. Diggers worked at both ends of the tunnel which when completed measured 1,749 feet, a remarkable achievement which can be seen and admired to this day.

The prophet Isaiah, who seems to have held a high position in Hezekiah's court, counseled the king not to rebel against Assyria. The fate of Judah and Jerusalem were in Yahweh's hands, Isaiah said. He told Hezekiah that just as Yahweh had sent Assyria to punish northern Israel for her moral transgressions, so now Assyria was being used as a punishing rod against Judah for her own violations of the Covenant law. When Yahweh finished with Judah, Assyria would cease to be his instrument, and this idolatrous nation would herself become a target of Yahweh's wrath. Isaiah expressed his certainty that Hezekiah must submit to the divine will, even if it meant continued submission to Assyrian power.

Hezekiah, who had already expelled Assyrian cultic idols and had whipped his nation into a nationalistic fever, resisted the prophet's advice. Tribute was withheld, the rebellion commenced. In 701 B.C.E. the Assyrian king sent a mighty military force through Judah, capturing the outpost of Lachish, only thirty miles from Jerusalem. The siege of Jerusalem was imminent. The Book of Isaiah informs us that suddenly, without explanation, the prophet counseled the king to resist the advances of the Assyrian enemy. Isaiah assured the king that no harm would come to Jerusalem. Yahweh would not permit the pagan intruder to seize the divine dwelling place.

What followed not only confirmed Isaiah's prophecy, it bolstered the authority of the prophet in the eyes of all Israelites. As the Assyrian forces were ascending the hills toward Jerusalem, an order was given to suspend the march and prepare for a long journey back to Mesopotamia. We do not know why the Assyrians broke off the offensive. Perhaps the army was needed to quell a revolt that had developed among the Chaldeans in southern Mesopotamia, a revolt that threatened to overthrow King Sennacherib. Perhaps a disease (bubonic plague?) broke out in the army camp. Whatever the reason, the withdrawal of the Assyrian aggressor was greeted by Judeans as divine miracle.[7]

As Isaiah had correctly predicted the survival of Judah and Jerusalem, no one, least of all King Hezekiah, doubted that Isaiah was truly the voice of Yahweh. Isaiah's prediction also intensified the popular belief in Jerusalem's sanctity as the earthly abode of the heavenly God. In everyone's mind, the sparing of Jerusalem was seen as a vindication of Yahweh's promise that the Davidic dynasty would rule forever from the national capital.

No one more believed in the Davidic national theology than Isaiah. He was born in Jerusalem and served four kings in the city. He attributed his prophetic career to a vision he experienced in Jerusalem's Temple, where he served as a priest. But he was no idle dreamer about Jerusalem. He knew the city well and spared it no criticism. In his judgment, Hezekiah's reforms had not halted the moral decline of the people. The Covenant law was daily violated in Jerusalem. The "faithful city has become a harlot," he charged. No one is willing to "defend the fatherless," and the "widow's cause" goes unhelped.

Because of her sins, Yahweh would not continue to spare Jerusalem. Isaiah's younger prophetic colleague, Micah, graphically portrayed the coming disaster. ". . . Zion shall be plowed as a field. . . . Jerusalem shall become a heap of ruins" (Micah 3:12). Yet Isaiah was convinced that after this punishment the Lord would remain faithful to Zion whom he chose, and that a child of the House of David would be born whom the Lord would set on the throne. It would be the beginning of the messianic redemption, an event that would herald an era of universal peace and justice. It was Isaiah's prophecy of the heavenly-sent Davidic child that the Christian religion would find fulfilled in the person of Jesus.

> For to us a child is born, to us a son is given; And the government will be upon his shoulder, and his name will be called "Wonderful Counselor, Mighty God, Everlasting Father, Prince of Peace."
>
> Isaiah 9:6

Where Hezekiah heeded Isaiah's words, his son and successor as king, Manasseh, ignored virtually every prophetic counsel to resist foreign domination. And not without reason. Manasseh had learned the lesson of survival. He paid his tribute faithfully to the Assyrian king Esharhadden and to his successor, Ashurbanipal. He made no alliances with Assyria's enemies that might provoke the Mesopotamian giant. The king's reward was a long rule of sixty-five years (696–631 B.C.E.) during which time Judah enjoyed a rare period of peace. For this one expects that Manasseh would have been remembered by the biblical authors as the wisest and best of kings. But to the Deuteronomist and the prophets Manasseh was the greatest sinner in the history of Judah because he permitted child sacrifice to be resumed in the Valley of Ghenna. Apart from child sacrifice, it is difficult for anyone to assess Manasseh's violation of Covenant faith. Undoubtedly he allowed pagan religious practices to mix with Israelite ritual, producing at worst a syncretistic Temple worship. His actions could not have differed much from those of his grandfather King Ahaz, whose liberal policy toward foreign cults was intended to maintain good relations with the leaders of the Assyrian empire.

The death of King Ashurbanipal in 630 B.C.E. marked the beginning of the end of the Assyrian empire. Assyria's hold on the western provinces of the empire loosened, and in just eight short years the empire fell under the combined impact of Media and Babylonia. The capital Nineveh was captured in 612 B.C.E.

Manasseh's successor as King of Judah was Josiah, whose royal ascendancy in 639 B.C.E. marked a fateful turning point in the life of the nation. Josiah correctly read the signs of Assyrian weakness and seized the opportunity to withhold tribute and reassert Judah's independence. Then he launched a religious reform to cleanse what he believed to be the ritual pollution brought on by King Manasseh's toleration of foreign cults. He emptied Jerusalem's Temple of idols depicting the male god Baal and the Assyrian mother goddess Asherah. Temple prostitution, magic, necromancy, astral worship, and child sacrifice were abolished. The Deuteronomist's account of this reform is so vivid that one sympathizes with idol worshipers subjected to fanaticism and butchery. We read that Josiah destroyed pagan sanctuaries in every village and town, and slaughtered priests at Bethel, north of Jerusalem, a sacred site hated by Judah's kings ever since the northern King Jeroboam had built a sanctuary there to rival Jerusalem's Temple.

It was in the midst of the king's efforts to repair the Temple that a great discovery was made in the building. Repairmen found the Book of the Law, a copy of the moral and ritual code derived from the earliest years of Israel's practice of faith. Josiah was overjoyed at what he took to be a sign of Yahweh's pleasure with his religious reform. When renovations were complete, the Temple was rededicated in a ceremony of Covenant renewal. At the heart of the ceremony was a public reading of the Book of the Law.

Josiah was driven by nationalistic as well as religious zeal. He seized every opportunity to expand the borders of Judah into the area formerly occupied by northern Israel. Ambitious to unite the two parts of the Davidic kingdom, he fought and won back from Assyria the city of Samaria. These actions led many of his countrymen to believe that their pious and courageous king was the true inheritor of the mantle of David.

But the Davidic empire was not reborn under Josiah. The king was able to carry out both religious reform and territorial expansion at a time of waning Assyrian strength. The formidable powers of Egypt and Babylonia still confronted him. Ignoring prophets like Isaiah and Jeremiah who had warned against involvement in international politics, Josiah entered into an alliance with Babylonia against Assyria. He did so in the mistaken assumption that Assyria represented the greatest threat to his kingdom. To counter Babylonian strength, Assyria had taken her old foe Egypt as a new ally. In 609 B.C.E. Babylonia attacked Assyria, and King Josiah led a force to the town of Megiddo in northern Israel to prevent Egypt from rushing troops to assist Assyria. The strategy failed miserably. The Egyptians decimated the Judean force, and Josiah lost his own life.

Josiah's death signaled the downfall of the nation. For just four years later, at the battle of Carchemish, the forces of Assyria and Egypt were vanquished by Babylonia which then became the undisputed power in the ancient Near East. The Babylonian victory threw Judah into a panic. Earlier she had sided with Babylonia against Assyria and Egypt, but as Babylonian power grew, Judah began turning to Egypt for help. After the resounding Babylonian victory at Carchemish, she did not know upon whom to rely.

The dominant figure in the last two decades of Judah's independence was not a king but a prophet, Jeremiah, who began his career with a sermon preached at Jerusalem's Temple in 609 B.C.E., the year of Josiah's death. Jeremiah lived more than fifty years and witnessed the destruction of Jerusalem in 586 B.C.E. He was adamant in his view that Judah must avoid any alliance with Egypt and submit totally to Babylonia. He advised Josiah's successor, King Jehoiakim, that only by submission could Judah survive as a nation. "Bring your necks under the yoke of the king of Babylon," he said, "and serve him and his people, and live" (Jeremiah 27:12). Jeremiah's words were not heeded. Judah continued to rely on Egypt; Babylon became angry and ultimately sent a force to punish the rebel.

If Josiah in his piety and military prowess resembled King

David, then Johoiakim in his megalomania was like King Solomon. Where Josiah had introduced moral, religious, and political reforms, Jehoiakim imposed harsh taxes to pay for the construction of lavish palaces and fortresses. Like Solomon he also relied on forced labor drawn from his own people. These abuses of power were the subject of Jeremiah's condemnation when the prophet delivered his oracles at Jerusalem's Temple. His words brought the king and the nation's influential leaders down on his head.

While Jeremiah, like Isaiah, came from a priestly family and was closely associated with Jerusalem's Temple, he seems not to have shared Isaiah's esteem for the institutions of the monarchy. In his sermon he challenged the belief that the Temple built by Solomon was a guarantee of divine favor for the nation. "Do not trust in these deceptive words: 'This is the temple of the Lord, the temple of the Lord, the temple of the Lord' " (7:4). Jeremiah called for moral repentance and renewal, not trust in the Temple. "Will you steal, murder... and then come and stand before me in this house, which is called by my name, and say, 'We are delivered'—only to go on doing all these abominations?" (7:9–10). The prophet called the Temple a "den of robbers" and reminded his listeners that the Lord punished the people by abandoning the sanctuary at Shilo, allowing it to be destroyed by the Philistines. He predicted a similar fate for Jerusalem's Temple. "...When I spoke to you persistently you did not listen, and when I called you, you did not answer, therefore I will do to the house which is called by my name, and in which you trust, and to the place which I gave to you and to your fathers, as I did to Shiloh" (7:13–14).

Jehoiakim died in 598 B.C.E. and was followed by two weak kings, Jehoiachin (598–597 B.C.E.), who served only three months, and Zedekiah (597–587 B.C.E.), the last Davidic king to sit on the throne of an independent Judah. In a badly calculated effort to improve relations with Egypt, Jehoiachin withheld tribute from Babylonia, which led to a series of invasions of Judah in 598, 591, and 586, and the capture and deportation of several thousand Judeans to Mesopotamia and other far reaches of King Nebuchadnezzar's empire. Imitating Assyrian practice, the Babylonians destroyed the potential for future rebellion by eliminating the Judean infrastructure of administrative, military, educational, religious, and commercial leadership. Only peasants remained to work the land.

The last Babylonian invasion in 586 B.C.E. led to the destruction of Jerusalem. Our most accurate account of this event is also our most poignant: the eyewitness report of the unknown author of the Book of Lamentations (wrongly attributed to Jeremiah). The book consists of a series of elegiac poems, composed shortly after the event they depict; the poems were meant to be recited in public to mourn the loss of Jerusalem and the Temple. The author leaves no doubt that as punishment for sins the Lord had withdrawn his protective grace from Judah, with the result that the Babylonians are given free rein to destroy everything in sight. The result is desolation, inconsolable grief: "The elders of the daughter of Zion sit on the ground in silence; they have cast dust on their heads and put on sackcloth; the maidens of Jerusalem have bowed their heads to the ground" (2:10).

In the final days of the siege, havoc reigns. Priests and prophets are murdered within the precincts of the Temple. Jerusalem is starved into submission. There are reports of cannibalism. Everyone suffers, but small children the worst:

> My eyes are spent with weeping; my soul is in turmoil; my heart is poured out in grief because of the destruction of the daughter of my people, because infants and babes faint in the streets of the city.
>
> They cry to their mothers, "Where is bread and wine?" as they faint like wounded men in the streets of the city, as their life is poured out on their mothers' bosom.
>
> 2:11–12

In the Book of Jeremiah we read that one of the final acts of the Babylonians before destroying the Temple was to loot the Temple treasury: "... They took away the pots, and the shovels, and snuffers, and the basins, and the dishes for incense, and all the vessels of bronze used in the temple service; ... What was of gold the captain of the guard took away as gold, and what was of silver, as silver" (53:18–19).

Looking back on the history of Israel from the time of the Babylonian destruction of Jerusalem, we recognize a great tragedy. The task of the ancient Israelite people was the unification of nationalistic and religious impulses. Briefly, for eighty years, under the leadership of David and Solomon, a unity of nation, faith, capital, and Temple were achieved. But that unity failed to outlive Solomon. The history of Israel for six hundred years following the death of Solomon is a history of political division, military defeat, and religious conflict. The two small states that resulted from the division—northern Israel and Judah—were unable to defend themselves against the superior power of Assyria, Egypt, and Babylonia.

Had the original monarchy founded by David remained intact, had there been one Israelite army instead of two frequently locked in civil war, Israel as a nation might have been able to protect itself against the encroachments of the stronger powers. We could also say, following the insight of the prophets, that had Israel minded its own business and not meddled in international politics, the superior powers might not have been provoked into invasion. For weighed in treasure, neither northern Israel nor Judah were viewed as prizes worth the cost of invasion. Almost always, foreign invasions were provoked by pretentious, shortsighted, nationalistic ambitions on the part of Israel's kings. Freedom from foreign rule is a precious thing. But even as a vassal state, Judah had the most precious freedom of religious worship, a freedom she was not always willing to grant to her pagan Canaanite neighbors. The key to Israel's survival lay in placating the foreign powers by tribute, treaty, and respect for their gods. Some of Israel's kings turned this key; others, out of religious obsession, threw it away.

But if the Davidic monarchy and its successor state in Judah expired, the Davidic principle of national unity survived both the capture of Judah and the destruction of Jerusalem. The Davidic principle meant that the Judeans—the *Jews*, as we may now call them—might be exiled to Mesopotamia and other distant lands, but they would continue to recognize *Eretz Yisrael*, the Land of Israel, as the true home of the nation. And they would continue to recognize Jerusalem as the capital of that nation, the site of the destroyed Temple. The Temple would be rebuilt on that day, the Lord's Day, when the nation would be reunited in the land and led once again by a Davidic king in Jerusalem. The prayerful hope in that coming Day of Redemption was expressed daily in countless ways by the thousands exiled to Mesopotamia. They taught the hope to a second generation, from whom arose a handful of intrepid souls who returned and colonized the ancestral land and its capital. Jerusalem would not be forgotten or abandoned.

CHAPTER 2

Fallen Temples

Is this the city which was called
The perfection of beauty,
The joy of all the earth?
—*Lamentations 2:13–15*

In those days will Judah be saved,
And will dwell safely....
—*Jeremiah 33:16*

This is the city which must be punished.
—*Jeremiah 6:6*

They are rebuilding that rebellious and wicked city....
—*Ezra 4:12*

The Babylonian conquest of Jerusalem brought to an end the six-hundred-year-old Davidic state. Save for the eighty years' interlude of Hasmonean rule (120–60 B.C.E.), Jews (after the English pronunciation of the Aramaic word for the Judean people, *Yehudim*) never again exercised political independence in the ancestral homeland until modern times.

What the defeated took away with them into exile was the religious law, the durable source of national self-identity and survival. Theological beliefs about Yahweh's majesty and goodness, moral codes about fairness and honesty, ritual observances of prayer and purity—all these were rooted in the traditions of the religious law, a law which reminded the Jew daily who he was and what was expected of him by God and his fellow Jews.

Rather than weaken the national religion, the experience of

defeat seemed to strengthen it. For now the obligations of the Covenant law were seen within the wider framework of the messianic hope. The Jews who were exiled to Mesopotamia had seen disaster with their own eyes; they had read the words of Isaiah, Micah, and Jeremiah and were convinced that what had happened to their nation, land, capital, and Temple was not the result of bad luck or mightier armies. Always faithful to the belief that everything on earth happens because of God, they attributed disaster to the punishing hand of the Almighty laid against them for their sinful violation of the law. They were equally convinced that the divine hand would graciously open with forgiveness and acceptance only when the nation rededicated itself to the Covenant law. The Deuteronomist and the prophets had preached this message of repentance, but they scarcely invented it. The demand for repentance and the hope for future redemption were already in the thoughts of the people. Ezekiel, who was among the deportees in 589 B.C.E., had given voice to them. He understood that the nation must take responsibility for its sins and not blame them on the wicked King Manasseh.

Repentance and redemption had begun to shape the national religion long before Isaiah and Jeremiah came before the people to explain the ultimate meaning of foreign invasion. In the eighth century B.C.E., Amos and Hosea in the northern kingdom had prophesied national destruction, the need for repentance, and the coming redemption. And before them were the fiery words of Elijah and Elisha, and even before that was Nathan's judgment against King David. What all these prophets agreed on was that no matter how severely Yahweh punished his erring nation, he would not abandon it—and that Jerusalem and its Temple would rise from their rubble. No one better expressed the popular confidence in the future than Ezekiel. Adopting the metaphor of death and rebirth, he spoke of the nation's resurrection.

> Son of man, these bones are the whole house of Israel.
>> Behold, they say, "Our bones are dried up, and our hope is lost; we are clean cut off." Therefore prophesy, and say to them, Thus say the Lord God: Behold, I will open your graves, O my people; and I will bring you home into the land of Israel.
>
> 37:11–12

Of course the messianic hope flew in the face of historical facts. It was meant to do so. If in exile the community's morale was to be sustained, then community leaders and people alike could not afford to dwell on past disaster. How could they when their own King Jehoiachin was among the exiled—this pathetic man who was released from a Babylonian prison with a pension to wander about the city, a visible reminder of national humiliation.

The new leaders of the exiled community were prepared to make the necessary adjustments in political, legal, and economic conduct in order to take advantage of that precious freedom of religious affairs which the Persians generously granted. The nation had lost its political independence, but it would retain its integrity through religion alone. It would be sustained by the messianic hope, but that hope would be taught quietly, in a nonpolitical manner. Why anger the ruler? Most of all, the people would not forget Zion, Jerusalem, the symbol of a national glory that was and would be again.

The Babylonian empire ruled over Judah but forty-seven years (586–539 B.C.E.), exceeding by only a few years the reign of its most famous king, Nebuchadnezzar (604–562 B.C.E.). What ended Babylonian power was the extraordinary military success of the Persian monarch Cyrus, who in 539 B.C.E. defeated Babylonian forces at the battle of Opis on the Tigris River, and a few weeks later captured the imperial capital at Babylon.

It was on the eve of Cyrus's conquest, when it was clear that Babylonian hegemony had ended, that a new voice of Hebraic prophesy was heard. The voice belonged to an unknown writer who was called the Second Isaiah because his poetic oracles were attached as later chapters to the original Book of Isaiah. To the Second Isaiah the appearance on the world scene of Cyrus was a divinely wrought event—indeed, this Persian was no less than Yahweh's intended messianic agent of Israel's redemption. It was an astounding revelation when one considers that Cyrus was not a Jew but a Persian, a gentile, and a pagan idolator to boot. This was Second Isaiah's prophesy:

> Thus says the Lord to his anointed, to Cyrus,
>
> whose right hand I have grasped, to subdue nations before him

and ungird the loins of kings, to open doors before him
that gates may not be closed: I will go before you
and level the mountains, I will break in pieces
the doors of bronze and cut asunder the bars of iron....

For the sake of my servant Jacob, and Israel my chosen
I call you by your name....

Isaiah 45:1-2, 4

The meaning of Second Isaiah's prophesy was clear: Yahweh
had commissioned Cyrus to bring down Babylonia, to restore
Israel to the Covenant land, and thus to inaugurate the era of
world redemption wherein Yahweh could be seen by all the
gentile nations to be Lord of the Universe.

We do not know what Cyrus thought of the exalted vision of
Second Isaiah or even that he was aware of it. Centuries later the
Roman-Jewish historian Josephus speculated that Cyrus's be-
nevolence in allowing Jews to return to the ancestral homeland
was inspired by the wish to live up to the prophet's expectation
of him.[1] Be that as it may, in 538 B.C.E., one year after his
victory at Opis, Cyrus ordered all Jews in Mesopotamia to
return to their homeland. He further urged the rebuilding of
Jerusalem's Temple, promising to provide funds for the reconstruction. And he agreed to return to the Temple the sacred
ritual objects of gold and silver looted by Nebuchadnezzar's
officers. But he drew the line at reconstituting the Judean state.
Accordingly, the new Jewish leader of the restored community
would not be called king but rather governor. And, lest the new
Judean people revert to old militaristic habits, the massive but
broken walls of Jerusalem would not be rebuilt.

The reconstruction of Jerusalem's Temple was but one of a
host of foreign sanctuaries rebuilt by Cyrus throughout the
empire. What explains the generosity of this ancient ruler, who
reversed the policy of deporting subject peoples practiced earlier
by Assyrians and Babylonians? We know that Cyrus was a
devout adherent of Zoroastrianism, a religion which stressed
the values of universal toleration. He was also a master of public
relations. For he so convinced the Babylonians that he had
defeated their king in the name of the Babylonian deity Marduk
that they took Cyrus as their own legitimate king and not as an
alien conqueror.[2] He seems also to have worked his mysterious

charm on Jews when he let it be known that he was a faithful champion of Yahweh. Prophets like Second Isaiah would
celebrate Cyrus's name even when it was obvious to them that
his syncretistic religion was anathema to the principles of
Judaism.

Whatever Cyrus's religious motivation in resettling Jews in
Judea, he had little fear of Judean nationalism or messianic
prophesies about the reconstitution of the Davidic state. His
actions were consistent with a sound policy to stabilize a far-
flung empire with loyal subjects.

Why did so few Jews accept Cyrus's invitation to return to
the ancestral land? The question has plagued historians for
generations, and there is no satisfactory answer. Had the decree
of restoration come to the first generation living in Babylonian
exile, one imagines that the overwhelming majority of Jews
would have gathered up their belongings and started toward
home. But the decree came to the second generation, fifty years
after the expulsion. None of them had memories of the homeland; whatever they knew of Judea they learned from their
parents. It made eminent sense to them to heed Jeremiah's
advice to "seek the welfare of the city where I have sent you into
exile" (29:4-7). They married, had children, built homes, planted gardens, and lived with security and prosperity under a set of
fairly benign Persian rulers. Undoubtedly they thought of Jerusalem
as the national capital, the site of the destroyed Temple. But
everyone knew this city as an earthly place that had fallen on
evil times. No one was willing to make of the city an idolatrous
altar of self-sacrifice. Jerusalem was not the Covenant law.
And everyone understood that the nation could lead its life
through the Covenant law outside the capital and without the
Temple.

Still, Jerusalem would not be forgotten. The messianic prayer
of deliverance was recited daily in the hope that by Yahweh's
grace, more than by Cyrus's generosity, the whole nation of
Israel would be restored to Jerusalem and the land. Remembering Jerusalem would become a sacred obligation expressed
through prayer. The psalmist articulated the feeling:

> By the waters of Babylon,
> where we sat and wept,
> when we remembered Zion. . . .

How shall we sing the Lord's song
in a foreign land?
If I forget you, O Jerusalem,
let my right hand wither!
Let my tongue cleave to the roof of my mouth,
if I do not remember you,
if I do not set Jerusalem above my highest joy!

Psalms 137:1a, 4–6

When we consider the hardships involved, the remarkable fact is not the refusal of the exiled community to pack its belongings and set off as one man for the ancestral land, but that a few small groups actually did so. There were a sufficient number of "Zionists" who were willing to leave comfortable homes and secure jobs to make a dangerous journey of six hundred miles, and then to undertake the arduous life of the pioneer. We cannot be certain how many Jews made the caravan journey back to Judah and Jerusalem. The figure of 40,360 is given in the Book of Ezra (2:64), which is probably an exaggeration reflecting the size of the entire community a century after the first return. In the eyes of Ezra and Nehemiah, the return had all the significance of the national redemption foretold by Second Isaiah in an oracle delivered shortly before Babylon's fall in 539. The prophet began by announcing that the long night of Israel's punishment had ended: "Comfort, comfort my people, says your God, speak tenderly to Jerusalem, and cry to her that warfare is ended, that her iniquity is pardoned, that she has received from the Lord's hand double for all her sins" (Isaiah 40:1–2). Second Isaiah sees night yield to day. He exults in announcing the dawn of the new age:

Get you up to a high mountain,
O Zion, herald of good tidings,
lift up your voice with strength,
O Jerusalem, herald of good tidings,
lift it up, fear not; say to the cities of Judah
"Behold your God!"

Isaiah 40:9

The immigrants who arrived in Judea around 520 B.C.E. were led by Zerubbabel, a grandson of the captive King Jehoiachin, and the designated high priest, named Joshua. Together they completed the reconstruction of Jerusalem's Temple in 515 B.C.E. Their efforts were urged on by two local prophets, Haggai and Zechariah. The latter was so convinced that Zerubbabel was the long-awaited Davidic prince of the messianic redemption that he preached his faith openly. It was a terrible blunder that may have cost Zerubbabel his office as governor, for shortly after Zechariah's prophecy Persian officials, detecting a resurgence of Judean nationalism, removed Zerubbabel from office.[3] To the great disappointment of the many who believed in Zechariah's prophecy, Zerubbabel proved to be the very last descendant of the Davidic royal family to exercise political leadership.

But there were other disappointments. The sight of the new Temple was not unanimously greeted with joy. In size and design the building resembled its forerunner from Solominic times; but the financially pressed Judean community could not afford the rich adornments that had bestowed splendor on Solomon's original structure. It is said that when the few who remembered Solomon's Temple gazed on the new building, they broke down in tears.

And more disappointments. The immigrants returned to a land still devastated by the Babylonian invasion, economically depressed from drought and famine, a diseased and dangerous land continually plundered by Edomites, Moabites, Philistines, and bedouins from the Arabian peninsula.

Equally disheartening was the degeneration of religious life among the Judean peasants and priests who had been allowed to remain during the Babylonian years. They had intermarried with the Samaritans, the descendants of the northern Israelites who had stayed in the land after the Assyrian conquest. The Samaritans, because they had also intermarried with the native Syrians of the north, were looked upon by the Jewish immigrants as carriers of ritual and ethnic impurity. The fact that the Samaritans had instituted conversion ceremonies for any of their people who entered the Hebraic faith through marriage mattered not at all to the Jews of Judah.

If the snobbery or elitism of the Jewish immigrants bothered the Samaritans, we do not know. We do know that for generations the Samaritans had made a practice of pilgrimage to Jerusalem's Temple. The Temple held a great meaning for them. They mourned its destruction and erected an altar in its ruins for the sacrifice of animals. So when they offered help to the Jews in rebuilding the Temple, no one could question their sincerity. Yet their help was refused, and relations between the two ancient houses of Israel worsened.[4]

From the Samaritan point of view, the Jews had returned to Judah for the express purpose of reasserting their dominion over the whole country. Their fears were confirmed in the middle of the fifth century when Persian officials, for reasons of security, altered their policy to permit the rebuilding of Jerusalem's walls—which in the Samaritan mind were a symbol of Judean nationalism. Relations between Samaritans and Jews remained hostile until the Samaritans in the fourth century B.C.E. finally withdrew from any association with Jerusalem's Temple and, in 332 B.C.E., built their own temple on Mount Gerizim overlooking the old northern shrine town of Shechem.

The major migration of Jews from Mesopotamia in the middle of the fifth century was led by two powerful personalities, Nehemiah and Ezra, who were selected by Persian authorities for their ability to reorganize the Judean community politically and religiously. We do not know with certainty which of the two arrived first in the Holy Land, but their collective activities not only led to a major reorganization of the community but shaped the character of normative Orthodox Judaism for later centuries.

Nehemiah, who may have arrived in Judea about 440 B.C.E., is identified in the Bible as a royal "cup bearer," in other words, a highly placed official in the Persian court. Undoubtedly it was due to his position that Nehemiah gained his commission to go to Jerusalem as its royally appointed governor. He was responsible for securing the city against marauders by rebuilding the outer fortification walls, a task which he seems to have completed in the remarkably short time of four years. He also set about healing many of the social wounds that had remained in Judah during the Babylonian captivity. He broke up the great feudal agricultural estates and divided the land among the peasants. He introduced legislation to prevent bankers and rich merchants from exploiting the poor who had mortgaged their homes or borrowed money. And he decreed that at least 10 percent of the population of Judah must live in Jerusalem. His next decree, however, that non-Jews could not live in Jerusalem, showed that he had as much concern for restoring the ritual purity of the community as he did in providing for the security and welfare of the city.

In the twenty years that he stayed in Jerusalem, Nehemiah carried out a number of reforms which laid a basis of religious renewal completed in later years by his successor, Ezra. Appalled by his discovery of how many foreign elements had infiltrated the traditions of the Jewish people, Nehemiah began by prohibiting the widespread practice of intermarriage between Jew and gentile, save through the ritually correct procedures of conversion. (Ezra later demanded that community leaders, particularly the old Temple priests, abandon their gentile wives and children.) Because the children of these "mixed" marriages had lost the ability to speak Hebrew, Nehemiah made the study and use of Hebrew a requirement in the community. The ritual of circumcision was strictly enforced, as was the Sabbath observance. Jerusalem's gates were ordered closed at night before the Sabbath so that merchants would not violate the sanctity of the day of rest as they had been accustomed to doing. The governor also insisted on a Temple tithing of one-third shekel annually. And to the anguish of farmers he further insisted on observance of the Sabbath fallow year in which the ground is allowed "to rest."[5]

These reforms were not original; they were the application in Judah of a rigidly demanding pattern of religious and social life instituted in Mesopotamia by community leaders who sought to minimize contact between Jews and the surrounding gentile world. As the Mesopotamian Jewish community had retained its social and spiritual self-identity by assiduously practicing separatism, so Nehemiah ordered the Judean community to do the same. Behind the policy of separatism in both places lay a profound theological conviction. Like every national leader before him, Nehemiah believed in the strictures of the prophets. The prophets had said that Yahweh destroyed Jerusalem for its sins, principally idolatrous association with pagan gentile peoples. The restored Judean community would not repeat that mistake.

Nehemiah did not see separatism as violating the theme of universal salvation present in the Book of Isaiah. To him, if Israel was to be a "light to the nations," the leaders and people of Israel had to see to it that their light was bright and clear.

Nehemiah's reforms were continued by the priest and Torah

scholar Ezra, who arrived in Judah in 397 B.C.E. leading a battalion of new priests eager to begin a new, purer Temple service. He brought with him a copy of the Book of the Law of Moses, and, duplicating the annual Covenant renewal ceremonies instituted in Mesopotamia, he mounted a wooden pulpit and read from the Torah law.[6] Along with this public reading of the law was a public confession of sins and petitions for divine forgiveness.

Before too many years it became clear to everyone that the character of national leadership had changed. Those who now spoke for the nation were not kings and their ministers but rather preachers, scribes, and interpreters of the law. And from them came the Torah-based synagogue, an institution of worship which developed alongside the Temple and finally survived the Temple's final destruction to become the enduring framework of Jewish life in the Diaspora, the scattered colonies of Jews outside Palestine.

The reforms of Nehemiah and Ezra, which sought to restore the purity of Israel, also inspired new feeling for the sanctity of Jerusalem. This feeling is reflected in many post-exilic psalms which extolled the Holy City. The psalms were composed for the Temple service and used during the celebration of the New Year when worshipers reconfirmed their faith in Yahweh, who dwells in Zion. In one of the most famous of these psalms, the pilgrim lavishes praise on Jerusalem, whose buildings he admires, whose peace and prosperity he prays for, a city which he views as a symbol of Israel's national unity.

> Our feet have been standing
> within your gates, O Jerusalem!
>
> Jerusalem, built as a city
> which is bound firmly together,
> to which the tribes go up,
> the tribes of the Lord,
> as was decreed for Israel,
> to give thanks to the name of the Lord.
>
> Psalms 122:2–4

In the year 333 B.C.E. the Macedonian conqueror Alexander won a crucial battle against the Persian king Darius III at Issus

in Asia Minor. The Greek victory precipitated the downfall of
the Persian empire. Within a year or so the Greeks captured
Egypt, Syria, and the land bridge between them which would be
named in Greek after Israel's ancient enemy, Philistia, and later
in Latin, *Palestina.*

Only ten years after the victory at Issus, Alexander died at
the age of thirty-three of syphilis contracted from one of the
hundreds of foreign princesses whom politics obliged him to
marry. His death provoked a major crisis of succession in which
his generals went to war against one another to gain control of
the empire. The protracted conflict between two of those generals, Ptolemy and Seleucus, and the interminable warring among
their descendants, determined the fate of Palestine and Jerusalem
for the next 150 years. Jews lived first under the Ptolemies who
ruled Egypt, and later under the Seleucids who controlled Syria.

The coming of Greek rule to the land of Israel posed two
cultural challenges to Jews: language and the *polis* (city).[7] Educated Jews readily succumbed to the power of the Greek language, learning to read, write, and speak Greek as well as any of
the newer Greek settlers to the country. For Jews, accustomed
to the belief that the whole of human wisdom was contained in
the Hebrew-language Torah, the learning of Greek was a revolutionary exposure to the dramas of Sophocles, the philosophy of
Plato, and the mathematics of Euclid.

Jewish investors and merchants were quick to learn Greek,
which became the dominant language in the commercial expansion that followed Alexander's conquests in the Middle East.
There was money to be made in the country which had recovered from the economic devastation of the Babylonian years.
The Greeks, with their wide international connections, made
possible new markets for the export of high-grade olive oil
produced on Jewish farming estates. Dead Sea asphalt could be
sold to the Egyptians for the embalming of their dead. As in
Solomonic times, the country became a transit for perfume,
silks, spices, ivory, and precious metals shipped from Arabia to
North Africa and the countries of the Mediterranean.[8]

Learning Greek to read literature and to engage in business
was the beginning of the process of Hellenization. Some Jews
went further by adopting Greek names like Jason or Menelaus,
shaving their beards, and cutting their hair short in the Greek

fashion. A few were willing to undergo the delicate surgical procedure of removing the marks of their circumcision.

It was a different matter when Jews faced the challenge of the Greek city, the *polis*.[9] Not only were many new Greek cities founded throughout Palestine and Transjordan, but such old Jewish cities as Beit Shean, Samaria, and Gaza became Hellenized by new Greek settlers. On the whole, Jews shunned the *polis* because it was founded on the Greek religion. Every Greek city had its temple, the center of the civic cult, with its devotion to Zeus, Apollo, and Aphrodite. All loyal citizens were required to support the civic cult with donations and animal sacrifices. Dedication to the Torah meant that Jews could not participate in the temple sacrifices, and this in turn prevented them from holding public office and exercising all the rights of a citizen. In addition to a temple, every *polis* had a gymnasium where studies in philosophy, mathematics, and poetry were combined with athletic games of running, discus-throwing, and other feats of strength. But here, too, because the games were sponsored through cultic worship of the gods Hercules and Hermes, most Jews shunned the gymnasium.

In no city was the challenge of Greek culture more deeply felt than in Jerusalem, where the Jewish community found itself increasingly divided between the Hellenizers, a minority of wealthy aristocrats attracted to Greek culture, and the Hasidim, the poor and pious traditionalists who, like the vast majority of peasants in the countryside, stubbornly resisted Greek culture. The tensions between these two groups did not produce a violent break in the community during the hundred years of Ptolemaic rule of Palestine only because the Greek rulers wisely forced Jews to do nothing that would violate their sense of sacred tradition.

There was little friction between Greeks and Jews in Jerusalem or in any of the Hellenized towns that contained a Jewish settlement. Jews paid their taxes to the gentile tax collector or sometimes to their fellow Jews, usually Hellenizers, who had purchased the lucrative right of tax collecting from the imperial tax office in Alexandria. Jews served in the Ptolemaic army, but they were given the right to worship on the Sabbath and to refrain from the obligatory sacrifices to the gods. Jerusalem's Jewish Temple priests were influenced by Hellenistic ways, but they too were free to conduct rites according to Hebrew tradition. They saw to it that Jerusalem did not become a *polis* like Gaza or Samaria. The city was recognizably Jewish, with thousands of Jews living within its walls. As in late Persian times, the nation's leader was an ethnarch, the Temple high priest who was assisted by a council of elders governing according to traditional ritual laws enshrined in the Deuteronomic legal code handed down from the era of King Josiah.

It was at the beginning of the second century B.C.E., after control of Palestine had passed to the Ptolemies' arch rivals, the Seleucids, that Jewish-Greek relations began to deteriorate. Only then did Jews confront the distinct threat of national dissolution in the predominant Hellenistic culture. The turning point was the appearance in 175 B.C.E. of the Seleucid king Antiochus IV, who in his characteristically arrogant manner adopted the title Epiphanios, or "God manifest." King Antiochus, an ardent champion of Greek religion, was offended that the Jews of his empire showed so little respect for the gods. But he did nothing about it until his desperate need for money drove him to tax extortion and then to a persecution of Hebrew ritual practice which changed the course of Jewish history.[10]

Antiochus's financial troubles can be traced to the continuing war with the Ptolemies of Egypt, a war that had bankrupted the Seleucid state. Antiochus had a stronger army than the Ptolemies, but the Ptolemies had a powerful ally in the Roman state which was determined not to allow the Seleucid kingdom to expand at the expense of Ptolemaic-controlled Egypt. In 188 B.C.E. Roman forces had defeated Antiochus's father upon his invasion of Egypt and then imposed a heavy debt on the Seleucid crown which the son was obliged to honor. Desperate for money, Antiochus looked covetously at the treasury of Jerusalem's Jewish Temple. The Temple was faithfully supported by gifts from a substantial number of Jewish families who had grown wealthy from decades of prosperity in agriculture and trade under the Ptolemies. There was also revenue from the annual one-third shekel tax continued from Nehemiah's time, a tax which was now levied at one-half shekel. The Temple treasury had also become a kind of bank reserve where widows and the wealthy placed their money rather than trust it with the Greek-run banks.

In a bold move to gain money, Antiochus dismissed Jerusalem's high priest Onias and replaced him with his brother

Jason who had offered the king a bribe to secure the nation's highest office. Once installed as high priest, Jason immediately raised taxes on Jews, an action which he thought would satisfy Antiochus's demands for money. An ardent Hellenizer, Jason established a gymnasium in Jerusalem and made plans for the construction of a pagan temple. He even promised that he would rename Jerusalem Antiochus after the king. Jason knew that if he offered the possibility of transforming Jerusalem into a *polis*, money would flow into the city from influential Greeks in the empire who had come to admire Jerusalem as a beautiful and historic city.

The acceleration of Hellenization in Jerusalem also affected the Jewish Temple priesthood. The writer of the First Book of Maccabees sarcastically reports that the attraction of the pagan athletic contests proved so great that the priests neglected their ritual duties in order to attend the games at the city's gymnasium. "Despising the sanctuary and neglecting the sacrifices, they hastened to take part in the unlawful proceedings in the wrestling arena after the call to the discus, disdaining the honors prized by their fathers and putting the highest value upon Greek forms of prestige" (1 Maccabees 2:14–15).

And what of Antiochus's designs on the Temple treasury? Here it seems Jason proved a stubborn moralist. He declined to allow Antiochus to desecrate the sacred fund. The king, enraged, dismissed Jason in favor of a more reliable puppet high priest, Menelaus, who wasted no time in meeting the king's demands. And with that action the king met direct mass opposition from Jews in Jerusalem and throughout the country. For it seems that Menelaus, unlike Jason, was not from the family of the high priest, and therefore by the strict ritual rules that guided the Jewish nation, Menelaus was unfit to sit as the chief administrator of Jerusalem's Temple.[11]

The popular Jewish reaction against Antiochus can be gauged by the street celebrations that broke out in the year 168 B.C.E., when it was heard (on false rumor) that the king had fallen in battle in Egypt. Many influential Jewish families, including some inclined toward Hellenism, suspended their gifts to the Temple.

When Antiochus returned home from the war in Egypt he was a bitterly disappointed man. He had successfully invaded Egypt and was on the verge of conquering the capital Alexandria, which would have fulfilled his dream of ruling both Syria and Egypt, when, as often in the past, Rome came to the rescue of the Ptolemies. Driven out of Egypt by Rome, facing new debts in a bankrupted empire, and now hearing of the Jewish riots, Antiochus took his revenge. He launched a full-scale religious persecution, the first of its kind in ancient history.

Antiochus's initial action against Jews was to order from the imperial capital of Syrian Antioch a contingent of Greek mercenaries to move to Jerusalem and settle at the Akra, the citadel in the northwestern part of the city. The presence of the Greeks would accelerate the Hellenization of Jerusalem. While Jason had begun the process of Hellenization by constructing the gymnasium, nothing had come of plans to build a Greek temple. Now, under Antiochus's order, an altar was built and animal sacrifices were offered to the Olympian gods. As more Greeks poured into the city, Jerusalem began to take on the appearance of the *polis* which the Hasidim so feared and hated; it reminded them of the wicked days of Jerusalem's shame under idolatrous King Manasseh.[12]

The Jewish reaction to the sight of Greek idols in Jerusalem was instant. Many families fled to the surrounding hills. But none could escape the physical persecution that Antiochus launched in 169 B.C.E., beginning with a ban on the reading of the Torah. A death sentence was decreed for any Jew who observed the Sabbath or circumcised his children. Jews were forced to participate in pagan temple sacrifices, including the eating of the forbidden swine. Swine were ritually slaughtered within the precincts of the Jewish Temple. A nadir of disgrace was reached when the king ordered a statue of his patron god, Zeus, erected in the Holy of Holies, where the Ark of the Covenant once reposed. It was the sight of a stone-made pagan god standing in the place reserved for Yahweh's sacred presence that caused the writer of the Book of Daniel to speak of "the abomination which makes desolation" (Daniel 9:27). The Hasidim, like Daniel, interpreted these evil events as the "end of days" which heralded the coming of the Messiah, the divine agent who would strike down the wicked and uplift the people of Israel.

Antiochus's harsh actions against the Jewish religion provided explosive material which was set afire in the year 167 B.C.E. In what at the time seemed a minor incident, an obscure Jewish priest named Mattathias Hasmon, from the village of Modein in the hills overlooking Lydda, took offense at the sight of a Jew offering sacrifice on a pagan altar. Mattathias slew him as well as the Greek officer in charge of the temple service. He then collected his five sons and, with a small group of friends, fled to the safety of the caves in the Judean desert wilderness. From there the family launched its own campaign to reverse Antiochus's decrees, beginning with a series of raids against Greek military forces. The rebels destroyed pagan sanctuaries and circumcised Jewish boys whose parents out of fear or envy had succumbed to the Greek practice of leaving their infants uncircumcised.

After striking this first blow for freedom, Mattathias lived but two years. The shield of the revolution was passed to the ablest of his sons, Judas, nicknamed Maccabee, or the "Hammerer," for his military zeal. Judas and his brothers Jonathan and Simon proved remarkably successful in rallying the people against the Seleucids, with the result that in 163 B.C.E., only six years after Antiochus began his persecution, Judah, Samaria, and the Galilee were once again in Jewish hands. After Jerusalem was won back from Greek forces, the Temple was immediately emptied of all the "abominations" of which Daniel spoke. In 164 B.C.E., on the 23rd of the Hebrew month of Kislev (December), the month in which Antiochus had committed his sacrilege against the Temple, the sacred candelabrum was lit, symbolizing the reconsecration of the Temple. It was an event of such moving religious and political significance that it entered the festival calendar to be celebrated thereafter as Hanukkah, the Feast of Dedication. Indeed, Jews had much to celebrate. After an interruption of 422 years, their state was reestablished.

The rebellion sparked by Mattathias Hasmon and led by Judas Maccabeus led to the founding of a Hasmonean family dynasty which governed the nation for almost a hundred years. Political freedom instilled among the Jews a fresh nationalistic spirit not experienced since the time of King Josiah. It was, of course, a perpetually endangered freedom which was defended against the ever-present Seleucid power both by arms and by alliances with Rome and the anti-Seleucid Greek city-states of Sparta and Athens. Fortunately for the Hasmonean rulers, the Seleucid empire from the time of Antiochus Epiphanes's death had entered an economic and military decline which enabled the Hasmoneans to win back much of the territory lost on the sea coast and in Transjordan.[13]

The Hasmonean king John Hyrcanus (134–104 B.C.E.) extended the boundaries of the state to include Idumea, Samaria, and Moab in Transjordan; and the brilliant military successes of his son Alexander Jannaeus (103–76 B.C.E.) brought Jewish control over lands in Transjordan and the coastal areas of Gaza and Dor—altogether a territory nearly equal in size to that of the united kingdom of Israel under David. During this period the city of Jerusalem expanded fivefold in the direction of the western hills and contained within its walls a population of thirty thousand.

The territorial expansion of the Hasmonean state under Hyrcanus and Jannaeus was inspired by the conviction that the whole of the country was the heritage of the Jewish nation. It was in the same spirit of religio-nationalistic pride that King Hyracanus conducted an aggressive campaign of proselytization. The peoples of Idumea (formerly Edom) on the Dead Sea were converted to Judaism, the young males undergoing forced circumcision. In a burst of vindictive rage that recalled King Josiah's destruction of the northern Israelite sanctuary at Bethel, Hyrcanus destroyed the Samaritan temple on Mount Gerizim in 128 B.C.E. He believed that in the newly purified land of Israel the Samaritans must be made to acknowledge that Yahweh's only home on earth was in Jerusalem's Temple. What irony: that the Maccabeean revolution which was originally fought to gain Jews religious freedom should result in the establishment of a zealot state which denied the very same freedom to its own kinsmen.

Territorial expansion provided a measure of military security for the state but did not end its internal troubles. The old quarrel between Hellenizers and Hasidim, which led to the Maccabeean revolution, was not overcome with the successes of the Hasmonean leaders. With the passing of years the Hasidim had given rise to a new religiously oriented party, *Perushim*, "separatists" who desired to remain ritually pure in a world of contaminating sin. We know them as the Pharisees who were often at odds with a second party, the Sadducees, who regarded themselves as the spiritual descendants of King David's chief priest, Zadok. Where the Pharisees were Torah scholars drawn from the lower classes, principally from villages and small towns, the Sadducees, coming from aristocratic circles mostly in Jerusalem, comprised the hierarchy of the Temple priesthood.

The sharpest disagreement between Pharisees and Sadducees occurred over the meaning of Torah.[14] The Sadducees believed that the Torah alone, as it was written through the inspiration of God, was the definitive guide set for the nation Israel. Further, the Sadducean priests of God's Temple could not alter the sacred words of Torah by any sort of human interpretation; rather they were commanded to adhere strictly to the literal meaning of every verbal Torah requirement. The Pharisees, by contrast, were Torah interpreters par excellence. They acknowledged that the Torah was the sole guide to Jewish life, but contended that the changing circumstances of life required the Torah scholar to search the holy words for a specific meaning and thus the right solution to any and every problem faced by a Jew in his daily life. That "searching" meant *interpreting* Torah; it further meant that the Torah scholar's interpretation was not a mere opinion, a subjective idea, but rather an actual extension of the divine Torah itself. Thus the Pharisees championed their view that the oral Torah was a valid extension of the written Torah vouchsafed by God to Moses.

Conflicts between the two parties often occurred in Jerusalem where the Sadducees formed a pro-monarchy party, with distinct Hellenizing tendencies, while the Pharisees were teachers in Torah academies, where they were idolized by students for their devotion to morals.

The conflict between Pharisees and Sadducees might have remained a family quarrel if the political situation of the Hasmonean leadership had not undergone radical change after the death of Judas Maccabeus in 161 B.C.E. Judas was succeeded by his brother Jonathan, who in turn was followed by Simon. Both brothers claimed the title of high priest, the office of national leadership after the eclipse of the Davidic monarchy. While the people knew that the Hasmoneans were not from the hereditary family of the high priest, few objected to their leadership. All the brothers were popular heroes and admired for their religious idealism. But it was a different story when in 135 B.C.E. Simon's son John Hyrcanus claimed the offices of both high priest and king. The Pharisees, idealists to the core, led the popular reaction to what was seen as Hyrcanus's usurpation of a sacred royal title which properly belonged to the Davidic family alone.[15] They reasoned that after the passing of the Davidic dynasty, Israel was meant to be ruled by Yahweh's law and the scholarly exponents of the law.

Hyrcanus himself was not confident about his claim to the Davidic crown. He had taken the title for political reasons, to put himself on the same level as the kings of foreign nations. Although as king he had the support of the Temple priests and other Hellenizers, he never held his kingship over the head of his Jewish subjects. The coins minted during his reign read in Hebrew "ethnarch" on one side, and on the other side in Greek "king."[16]

What further exacerbated relations between the Pharisees and Hyrcanus were the steps which the king took to achieve one-man rule over the country. The Pharisees opposed Hyrcanus's despotic hold over the military, civil, and religious functions of government. They reacted to the king's manipulation of the council of elders which had always assisted the high priest in governing the country. They were particularly incensed that the Israelite army was increasingly staffed with Greek mercenaries whose allegiance was less to Israel then to their patron Hyrcanus.

Nor were the Pharisees the only religious party to oppose Hyrcanus. The puritanical Essenes, in reaction to Hyrcanus's tyrannical rule, fled Jerusalem for the Dead Sea caves of Qumran and there for the next two hundred years prayed and fasted in anticipation of the messianic deliverance—until the Romans destroyed the last community in 68 C.E.

Relations with the Pharisees continued to deteriorate when Alexander Jannaeus succeeded his father as head of state. When the Pharisees engaged in a six-year rebellion against Jannaeus's despotic rule, the king reacted brutally. The historian Josephus, himself formerly a Pharisee, described the gruesome punishment. "... As [Jannaeus] was feasting with his concubines, in sight of all the city he ordered about eight hundred of [the Pharisees] to be crucified, and while they were living, he ordered the throats of their children and wives to be cut out before their eyes."[17]

The Hasmonean state outlived King Jannaeus by merely thirteen years. Jannaeus was succeeded as head of state by his wife Alexandra, who ruled for nine years (76–67 B.C.E.), during which time she strengthened the country's defenses and sought to heal the breach with the Pharisees. Unfortunately she was cursed with two incompetent sons, Hyrcanus II and Aristobulus II, who upon her death waged a bitter civil war of succession. That struggle opened wide the gates of Jerusalem to Roman forces who entered the city in 63 B.C.E., and after three months of fierce fighting in the Temple area, brought an end to Jewish national independence.

The Roman conquest of Judah was a repetition of the tragic story of the David-Solomonic monarchy which fell prey to internal disorder long before a foreign enemy made its appearance. Some would say that when the Roman forces swept into Syria after their conquest of Armenia, it was inevitable that they would annex Palestine. But there was no certainty of that. More likely, if the Jews had stood together in a solid military-political front, the Romans, like the Assyrians long before them, might have declined to engage in a long and bloody conquest of Judah and Jerusalem—particularly when the spoils of conquest were so meager.

Upon defeating the Jewish forces in Jerusalem, the conquering Roman general Pompey (soon to become Caesar) acted swiftly to consolidate his victory. First he dismembered the enlarged Judean state by reducing it to the city of Jerusalem itself and a narrow perimeter of a few kilometers beyond the city walls. This shrunken Judea was not officially added to the empire but allowed to retain its administrative autonomy as the western part of the province of Syria. Significantly, the Romans continued to use the name Judah, recognizing it as the Jewish ancestral land. John Hyrcanus II was confirmed in the office of high priest as the national leader, but he was stripped of the title of king. The Romans, like the Persians, would recognize ethnarchs but no royal pretenders to power.

No persecution of Jews followed the capture of Jerusalem because the Roman leaders had no wish to incur the eternal hatred of their taxpaying subjects. There was also a happy memory of the useful alliances with the Hasmoneans which had helped Rome weaken the Seleucid state. And so the worst that Jews suffered at the hands of the Roman conquerors was the imposition of taxes, the symbol of subjection to a foreign power.

For the Samaritans in the northern part of the country, the payment of taxes was a small price for the religious freedom accorded them by their new overlords. Now safe within Roman civil law, the Samaritans ceased coming to Jerusalem's Temple and drew apart into their own Torah-devout communities.

While Hyrcanus II was the ethnarch of Judah, real power was exercised by a half-Jewish, Roman-appointed governor named Antipater. He and his son Herod (who would rule Judah for forty years) began a new dynasty which would shape the life of the Jewish nation for more than a hundred years, until a succession of Jewish rebellions against Rome brought catastrophe to the nation, capital, and Temple.

The story of Jewish life in Jerusalem in Roman times begins with the fascinating personality whom history knows as Herod the Great. Like his father, Herod came to power as a loyal and brutally effective Roman administrator. He was charged by Rome to bring peace and order to Jerusalem after the Parthians in the year 40 B.C.E. had seized the city, deposed Hyrcanus II, and installed as ethnarch their own Hasmonean puppet, the son of Aristobulus II. Herod carried out his charge successfully. In 37 B.C.E. he led an army of Roman soldiers that reconquered Jerusalem, whereupon he took control of the country as its king, ruling for thirty-three years, without major opposition but always as an object of contempt in the eyes of Jerusalem's religious leaders.[18]

In reading about Herod we often become so preoccupied with his murderous rages (he killed his wives and children who threatened his kingship) that we tend to ignore the shrewdly successful manner in which he governed Judea during his long reign. Recognizing that his sole source of power lay with his patrons in Rome, first Marc Antony, then Augustus Caesar, he saw to it that his loyalty to the empire was never questioned. His gifts to influential Roman leaders were lavish, and he built new cities in the Greco-Roman style, complete with gymnasia, pagan temples, amphitheaters, hippodromes, and baths. Augustus Caesar was the recipient of much of his generosity. Herod built a new city near the ancient town of Samaria and named it Sebaste in honor of Augustus. The new deep-water harbor constructed at the old part of Straton's Tower was also renamed Caesarea for

Augustus. In Jerusalem Herod built a massive fortress whose towers he named after his brothers Hippicus and Phasael and his wife Mariamne. He built a fortress to protect the weak northwestern approach to the Temple Mount and named it Antonia after his original patron Marc Antony. With all these works Herod served Rome well, and Roman leaders trusted him.[19]

To pay for his many gifts and constructions, Herod maintained a strict system of tax collection which provoked numerous plots of rebellion—but none successful. Not surprisingly, the king maintained an army of spies in Jerusalem and other towns to report on every expression of discontent. To provide total security for Jerusalem, Herod built fortress-palaces at Herodion, near Bethlehem, and at Massada overlooking the Dead Sea.

Herod could occasionally be compassionate. When the country was afflicted by famine, he sold gold and jewels from his own treasury in order to pay for corn imported from Egypt.

If we discount the numerous sycophants appointed to his court, we can say that many ordinary Jews despised this man who was crowned king of Judah in Rome and set over them as their nation's leader. He began by murdering or exiling all the surviving members of the Hasmonean royal family and thus removing any potential rival to his kingship. In the eyes of Jerusalem's priests, the Hasmoneans were not wholly legitimate claimants to Israel's kingship, but Herod had even less family connection to the royal line of David than the Hasmonean usurper, John Hyrcanus. Herod, his father Antipater, and his grandfather Antipas were from the Dead Sea area of Idumea, the people whom Hyrcanus had forcibly converted to Judaism. In the eyes of Jerusalem's ritual purists, they were at best half-Jews and therefore as a family not fit legitimately to claim the exalted title of king.

Herod was also seen as a tyrant, a murderer, a Hellenizer, and an instrument of Roman imperial aggression against the Jewish nation. Much of this was true, and no one knew it better than Herod himself. He seems to have taken it to heart in that his pro-Jewish policies were formulated to gain precisely that acceptance which his pro-Roman policies otherwise denied him. He was careful never to offend Jewish ritual practice. In an effort to legitimize his kingship, he married Mariamne, the granddaughter of the high priest Hyrcanus II, and though he eventually ordered her killed he insisted that any prince marrying a daughter of the Herodian family must be circumcised. He paid for the relocation in Jerusalem of many important Jewish religious leaders and their families living in Mesopotamia and Egypt, including the family of Hillel from which would come important Torah scholars. Despite their opposition to him, he provided funds for the scriptural study centers of the Pharisees. And he won the enthusiastic support of the Sadducees when he ordered the beginning of reconstruction of Jerusalem's Temple, insisting again with ritual correctness that the actual work of building could be carried out only by the priests themselves. The work was begun in 20 B.C.E. and completed in 64 C.E., sixty-eight years after Herod's death and only six years before its destruction in war. The building was supported by Corinthian columns of white marble which, when viewed from afar, looked "like a mountain covered with snow," in Josephus's words. Herod placed his imprint so firmly on Jerusalem that his monuments are with us today in the remnants of the Temple Mount, the Western Wall, the Antonia Fortress, and the Citadel that guards the western approach to the city.

Herod also gained much support from the nationalistically minded who saw the borders of Judah expand across the Jordan River and westward to the sea coast, incorporating an area nearly equal to the size of the Jewish state under John Hyrcanus.

The death of Herod in 4 B.C.E., after a reign of thirty-three years, was followed by fifty years of direct Roman rule of Judea by governors or, later, procurators. The procurators varied in ability and character. The good ones sought to preserve the peace between Rome and the subject people of Judea. Those who were incompetent, beginning with Pontius Pilate (66–70 C.E.), worsened relations to the point of bloody clashes between Romans and Jews, a continuing confrontation which eventuated in the Great Revolt of 66–70 and the Bar Kochba Rebellion of 132–135.

While Roman blunders helped produce these conflicts, they also came about because of Jewish political and religious fanaticism.[20] Before describing these conflicts we should recall that a hundred years of independence under Hasmonean leaders had accustomed the Jewish nation to freedom. The idea of national independence was too deeply ingrained to die during the years of Roman domination of Judea. Therefore it was inevitable that Jews would find occasion in Roman governance or misgovernance to reassert their desire for independence. Despite numerous mistakes by Roman governors of Judea, Roman rule was largely wise and fair. The pity is that Jews reacted only to the blunders and fomented a continuing revolution which ultimately brought down the nation and fatefully changed the course of Jewish history.

Jewish anti-Roman agitation had begun in Herod's time. Throughout the years of Herod's rule, small bands of revolutionaries roamed the countryside. They hated Roman authority, detested the taxes extracted from the peasantry, and looked on Herod and his family as imposter Jews. The revolutionaries were also messianic in outlook. During the Hasmonean years the messianic idea had ebbed. As long as the Jewish nation was in control of its own destiny, the people generally felt that the messianic hope of national redemption was being fulfilled. Indeed, some Jews looked upon the Hasmonean leaders, from Judas Maccabeus to Jannaeus, as embodiments of the prophesied Messiah. But when Judea lost its independence under the Romans, many Jews were prepared to believe that the nation suffered the last days of the wicked Roman empire. Soon Yahweh would bring his judgment on that empire, and Israel would be free from pagan rule. An early indication of this sort of thinking was expressed in the second century B.C.E. by the prophet Daniel, who saw in the idolatries of the Greek king Antiochus Epiphanes a sure sign of God's coming wrath against paganism and its fall to Israel. Revolutionaries in Herod's time also believed that they were called upon by Yahweh to straighten the road of the redemption by refusing to pay taxes, by attacking foreign soldiers, by smashing pagan altars, and by punishing Jews who submitted to pagan rituals. In the minds of the Jewish revolutionaries, their violence expressed the original spirit of rebellion against pagan rule practiced by Mattathias Hasmon and his revered son Judas Maccabeus.

In the last years of Herod's reign and especially after his death, the revolutionaries increased in number and became a party of anti-Roman, messianically minded nationalists intent on freeing Israel from pagan rule. A portent of coming troubles occurred toward the end of Herod's life when, consistent with his policy of currying favor with the emperor in Rome, he caused the insignia of the Roman eagle to be placed over the main gate of the Temple in Jerusalem. Predictably the action outraged the local citizenry, two of whom (Pharisees we are told) led a group to the Temple with the intention of tearing down the idolatrous symbol. Herod, who was on his deathbed, ordered the execution of the men, who were received by the people as martyred heroes.[21]

Seventy years of continuing turmoil between Jews and gentiles in Judea separate the death of Herod in 4 B.C.E. from the outbreak of the Roman-Jewish wars in 66 C.E. The Roman leaders chose not to appoint a new Jewish king in Herod's place but to rely on their own bureaucrats or procurators to administer the province of Judea. While a sound decision in theory, it proved to have disastrous consequences for both Rome and the Jewish nation.

At first the procurators, exercising government from the seacoast town of Caesarea, were effective in maintaining order; they placated the Greek population of the country without offending the Jews of Judea.

Trouble did not occur until the arrival in the year 26 C.E. of Pontius Pilate as procurator. There is nothing to suggest that Pilate had a special contempt for Jews; most of his blunders can be traced to ineptness or incompetence. He offended Jewish feelings and contravened Roman policy by allowing army standards bearing the insignia of the boar to appear in Jerusalem. The depth of Jewish resentment against this action can be measured by Josephus's observation that Jews were prepared to die under the Roman sword rather than violate their religious law by ignoring the standards.[22] Fearing a major riot, Pontius Pilate removed the standards from Jerusalem. A second offense occurred when the procurator confiscated money from the Temple treasury to pay for an aqueduct to carry water from Bethlehem to Jerusalem. At a peaceful demonstration which followed, Roman soldiers chose to attack the demonstrators, with the result that several Jews were killed. In 36 C.E., ten years after his appointment, Pilate was recalled to Rome as punishment for a particularly brutal treatment of the Samaritans. Jews rejoiced, but what followed proved worse for the nation.

For it was in 37 that Gaius Caligula came to power as emperor. Caligula, who in egomania matched Antiochus Epiphanes, thought himself a deity and ordered his subjects to pay appropriate homage. For Jews it was a challenge they had not known since the time of the Greeks. A Jew who resisted paying homage to the emperor risked being branded a traitor. Since the time of Persian rule, Jewish officials in Jerusalem had always been mindful of the need publicly to express loyalty to the emperor. In Jerusalem's Temple the daily sacrifice of a bull and two lambs was an expression of loyalty—not to the emperor, significantly enough, but to the God of Israel in behalf of the emperor. Now Caligula's decree meant that Jews must desecrate their own Temple by an unequivocal act of emperor worship.

Direct confrontation between the Jewish people and Caligula's self-proclaimed divinity occurred in the year 40, when in the Jewish town of Jamnia a few Greek families erected an altar to honor Caligula and were immediately confronted by Jews who sought to destroy it.[23] When Caligula heard of the Jewish opposition, he ordered that a statue of himself by placed in Jerusalem's Temple, an action that certainly would have turned the Jewish nation against the emperor with fatal consequences.

Fortunately not everyone in the Roman hierarchy was infected with Caligula's madness. Petronius, the legate in Syria who was responsible for carrying out the emperor's decrees, delayed and even wrote to Caligula advising against the statue. Peace was saved by the unforeseen assassination of Caligula, the result of a court intrigue. For Jews the emperor's death was seen as an act of divine deliverance.

A fascinating aspect of Caligula's reign of terror (37–41) is that it overlapped with the years (37–44) when Judah was governed by the Jewish king Agrippa, Herod's grandson. As Caligula's personal friend and a trusted servant of Rome, Agrippa gained the high office of Judea's ethnarch. Yet by all accounts he was esteemed by the Jewish community. He sought to discourage Caligula against desecrating Jerusalem's Temple, he won the support of the Pharisees denied to his grandfather, and he made many converts to Judaism. With the support of the emperor, he expanded the borders of Judah to incorporate most of the lands ruled by Herod. And he gained the admiration of many Jews who were proclaiming as Messiah an obscure Galilean preacher executed under Roman authority. Despite the fact that Agrippa also maintained good relations with the Greek gentile population of the country by fostering the building of temples, gymnasia, and theaters, his name is treasured in the

Jewish history of Jerusalem. Today, where there is no monument to Herod in Jerusalem, Agrippa's name appears prominently on one of the city's main streets.

Yet the reign of Agrippa proved to be an interlude in the seventy-year succession of Roman-appointed procurators of Judea. In the twenty years following the death of Agrippa, anti-Roman feeling spread throughout the Jewish population of the country. Law and order declined. The historian Josephus points to the increase of brigandage throughout the countryside.[24] Small revolutionary groups formed. Gradually the country was slipping into a chaos that neither Roman nor Jewish authorities were able to prevent.

Matters were worsened by a succession of procurators whose insensitivity and incompetence matched those of Pontius Pilate. Incidents occurred in which Roman soldiers burned Torah scrolls or entered the Temple Mount area. In a bloody confrontation, Roman soldiers armed Samaritans who attacked Jews on pilgrimage to Jerusalem. In the 50s and 60s robbery, assassination, and rioting spread to Jerusalem. The Jewish *Sicarii* assassins made their appearance. Hatred of Roman authority and of the Jewish officials who collaborated with it was openly expressed on the streets of Jerusalem. Many Jews throughout the country turned to messianic ideas to explain disorders, and the belief spread that Rome was reaching the end of its days. Soon Israel would be reunited and restored to the land to live under the Davidic prince. Some, like the Essenes, were prepared to leave the messianic fulfillment in God's hands.

The messianic idea had a different effect on the revolutionaries who stepped forward to clear the way for God's own Judgment Day. They remembered the bold courage of Judas Maccabeus and believed that until the Jewish people took arms against the idolatrous nation, God would go on using Rome to punish Israel for her sins.

War broke out during the procuratorship of Florus (64–66), after disorders in the countryside had reached their height. What fed the general unrest were the harsh actions of Emperor Nero in Rome. One particular decision convinced the Jews that they had no standing in the empire: a local conflict between Syrian and Jewish inhabitants of Caesarea over political control of the city was decided by Nero in favor of the Syrians in the year 66, thus putting Jews in an inferior position legally and socially in the city.[25] What happened in Caesarea, Jews understood, could also happen in Jerusalem. The protection and privileges which the community had historically enjoyed in Palestine seemed to evaporate. Not only Jewish rebels were convinced that Rome had changed its policy toward Israel; the high priests of the Temple and wealthy aristocrats also began to turn against government authority. Among them was Josephus, then a Pharisee and a member of one of the most influential Jewish families, linked to the Hasmonean princes; Josephus would join the revolution as a general until his defection to the Roman side.

Social and economic conditions contributed to the outbreak of war. High taxes crippled the lower classes. Large landowners exploited the peasants to pay their own heavy taxes to the government. Small landowners who could not pay their taxes risked losing their land to the government. Many desperate souls relied on brigands or turned to brigandage themselves in order to solve their problems Robin Hood fashion. Josephus mentions the famine of 48 which devastated the country. Thus Jews were divided socially and economically long before the war turned Jews against one another. Upper-class Jews became wealthy as tax collectors, positions purchased with bribes to Romans. The high priests who took Temple fees exploited the lower classes of priests who labored for subsistence wages. It is not surprising that the war with Rome was strongly supported by the poor who saw in it the means to strike back against their oppressors in both the Roman and Jewish upper classes.

By the mid-60s Jerusalem and the countryside were in chaos. Contributing to the economic unrest was the completion of the Temple, which put eighteen thousand men out of work. The Temple high priests acted wisely when they decided to use Temple funds to reemploy many of the workers to repave the streets of Jerusalem in white stone. One can well imagine the priests' anger when it was discovered that the procurator, with the connivance of some priests, had tried to rob the Temple. Thus, as in Greek times, it was a threat to Temple funds that sparked the rebellion of Jews against their gentile masters.[26]

Josephus leaves no doubt that the Jewish revolutionaries were doomed from the outset because of their internal quarrels. The internecine conflict among the Jewish factions began during the provisional government at the end of the first year of the war in early 67, and continued even as Titus's troops were besieging

Jerusalem. Yet Rome would likely have crushed the rebellion no matter how well organized or united the rebels were. Josephus was aware of this; his own decision to switch to the Roman side sometime after the Zealot party had taken control of Jerusalem in 67–68 was influenced by a realistic assessment of Roman power.

Some Jews, like Johanan ben Zakkai, preferred to suffer indignities rather than take up arms. But they were a minority. The vast majority of Jews believed that their fight was just, that God would assure them a victory over the pagan Romans, and that the nation of Israel would once again know freedom in its own land. They mistakenly believed that Nero was too busy with his own troubles to bother with a revolt in a distant land. They underestimated the willingness of Rome to fight for Palestine as a land bridge between the rich provinces of Syria and Egypt. Instead they expected that the Parthian nation to the east, a perpetual thorn in Rome's side, would capitalize on the Jewish revolt by launching an offensive of its own—which the Parthians eventually did, but too late to the help the Jewish cause.

There were many calculations and miscalculations, but we cannot conclude, as Josephus did, that Jewish revolutionaries in fighting Rome acted basely, blinded by ambition.[27] The opposite seems true. Roman government had become hateful in Jewish eyes, and Jews, trusting in God's providence as they always had, and having the successful Maccabean revolt as precedent, took up arms against a vastly superior foe and lost a war. In hindsight we can say, as Josephus himself said while sitting in Rome years after he quit his command as general, that it would have been better for the Jewish nation had this war never happened. But to say this was to fail to appreciate what political and religious freedom meant to the Jewish nation.

The revolutionary groups were five: the *Sicarii,* a force commanded by John of Gischala, a third army led by Simon bar Giora, a fourth contingent identified as the Idumeans, and finally a group of fighters who called themselves Zealots. In the four years before the Roman conquest of Jerusalem, each group made an alliance with one or more of the others in order to defeat their rivals and win control of the revolution. It is difficult to explain this internal conflict, except to say that it was a reflection of the variegated character of Jewish society in the first

Jerusalem in 70 CE
(Before Its Destruction by Rome)

0   300 yards

Tomb of Simon the Just

Mount Scopus Tombs

Mount Scopus

Second Wall

First Wall

The Temple Mount

Herod's Family Tomb

Gihon Valley

Western or Wailing Wall

Tomb of Hulda the Prophetess

Mount of Olives

Jason's Tomb

David's Tomb

Mount of Olives Cemetery

Tomb of Zacharias

Tomb of Absalom

Kidron Valley

Silwan Tombs

Wilderness of Judea

Hinnom Valley

Ophel Hill, on which David built his fortified city

Jewish tombs and holy places

Probable layout of the ancient walls

century. As there was no one Judaism practiced in these times, so there was no one society of Jews. Jews could agree only on their hatred of Roman government and on the freedom of Israel. Beyond that they were a people deeply divided and quick to take revenge. We know this to be true because soon after the Temple was seized by the revolutionary band led by Eleazar, the Temple services were resumed, but the high priests were excluded from them. Thus from the beginning the rebellion against Rome contained elements of a Jewish civil war.

But the war against Rome proved a stronger force than the war among the Jews. At a crucial point in the revolt, when a provisional government was formed under the leadership of Ananus the high priest, it seemed that Ananus, with the support of other high priests and moderate elements, would arrange a cease-fire and achieve a political compromise with Roman authorities. Anticipating such a compromise, the Zealot party was formed in the winter of 67–78 to combat the moderates in behalf of the revolution. The assassination of Ananus spelled the end of compromise and sealed the fate of the Jewish nation, as Josephus noted with lament.[28] After destroying the provisional government, the Zealots took control of Jerusalem in 68 C.E., established their own government, and conducted a reign of terror against the wealthy and prominent. For the next two years, while Jews fought one another in the city, first Vespasian, then his son Titus were leading a Roman legion in subduing Jewish strongholds before the siege of Jerusalem.

The fierce battle for Jerusalem lasted five months; the last hand-to-hand fighting took place at the Temple. During the battle a Roman soldier, evidently without orders, set fire to the Temple which burned until the entire structure was reduced to char. Later Jewish tradition states that the Temple was destroyed on the ninth day of the Hebrew month of Av (August), the same day the Temple of Solomon fell to the Babylonians in 586 B.C.E. Famine, fire, and human savagery had once again desolated the city.

What happened in 70 C.E. represented an unprecedented humiliation of the Jewish nation. The Temple, the national symbol of freedom and faith, was gone. The Jews who survived the carnage lived to envy the dead. Able-bodied men were sent to work in the mines of Egypt and Sardinia; many were sent to Rome to work on the construction of the Coliseum, or to Corinth where Nero had ordered excavation of a great canal. Some who showed special strength were sent to cruel deaths in gladiator shows. Women and children were sold into slavery. We do not know how many perished, but the magnitude of the disaster for Jews is suggested by Josephus's report that one million died.

Many Jews, like Josephus and the religious leader Johanan ben Zakkai, escaped the carnage because they had a realistic perception of Roman power. Josephus, who first joined the revolution as a general assigned to the defense of the Galilee, switched to the Roman side and lived to write a history of the war; Rabbi ben Zakkai, who thought the Jewish rebellion was futile and foolish, arranged for his disciples to smuggle him out of Jerusalem in a coffin.

As always in the event of an important military victory, the conquering general was honored with a ceremonial procession in

Rome. Titus displayed as trophies the golden shewbread table and the candelabrum taken from the burned Temple. As a souvenir for himself he kept a scroll of the Torah rescued from the flames. Jewish humiliation was compounded when Emperor Vespasian decreed that the Temple donation which Jews sent annually to Jerusalem would now be sent to Rome to maintain the temple of Jupiter Capitolina. This was in addition to the *fiscus judaicus*, the special tax levied on Jews throughout the empire. To commemorate the Roman victory, coins were struck bearing the image of a woman weeping above the inscription *Judaea Capta.*

The destruction of Jerusalem's Temple ended the careers of the Sadducean priests, who had had no other purpose than the performance of ritual animal sacrifice. The Pharisees were left as the sole guardians of Israel's faith and freedom. In time they gave rise to the Torah scholars, the rabbis, who assumed leadership of all the Jewish communities in the land of Israel as well as in the Diaspora. After the defeat of 70 C.E. the Pharisees came together under the leadership of Johanan ben Zakkai at the coastal town of Yavneh, formally to determine that the Torah, the Deuteronomic history, the books of the prophets, the psalms, and other writings together would constitute Israel's Bible, her guide to living under God's law in a land dominated by a gentile power. From the meetings at Yavneh came a reorientation of the worship life of Israel. Scripture would replace Temple as the symbolic center of national self-expression; prayer would serve in place of animal sacrifice as the means of atoning for sin.

The war had the added effect of provoking anti-Jewish actions in the Diaspora communities, particularly in Alexandria, where Greeks, long resentful of Jews, rioted against them.[29] In the eyes of their gentile antagonists, the defeat of the Jews, the destruction of the Temple, and the banishment from Jerusalem which followed—all these were seen as just punishment of a troublesome people and a convincing discrediting of their arrogant religion of a national divinity. From 70 on, particularly in Diaspora, the Jews began to be seen as "homeless," alien beings who belonged nowhere. In this attitude the seeds of hostility were sewn and watered for the next three hundred years until the Christianization of the Roman empire under Constantine, after whom we see the first outgrowth of organized anti-Judaism.

A relief in the Arch of Titus in Rome,
built to honor the Roman victory
over the Jews in Jerusalem, 70 c.e.,
showing Roman soldiers carrying off
the Temple candelabra and other "spoils"
of war.

The war of 66–70 did not end Jewish rebelliousness. The
deterioration of Jewish-gentile relations provoked a revolt of
Jews in Lybia, Egypt, and Cyprus which lasted two years,
115–117. After that, in the third decade of the second century,
when Jews heard of Emperor Hadrian's decision to rebuild
Jerusalem as a pagan city, they began secretly to store arms.
Hadrian, who it seems had taken a scholarly interest in Jewish
religion, found himself offended by what he considered the
strange and unsavory practice of circumcision and likened it to
the criminal act of castration. When he issued an edict against
ritual circumcision, it provoked Jewish anger.

In the year 132 a rebellion began of such ferocity and
duration that additional Roman forces had to be summoned
from as far away as Britain to crush the rebels.[30] The rebellion

was initially successful because it caught Roman authorities unprepared. Led by a skillful commander named Barkoziba, Jewish forces drove the Romans out of the countryside and occupied Jerusalem for at least a year. As Barkoziba's fame spread, many Jews were prepared to believe that he was in fact the "anointed one" sent by God to initiate the redemption. No less a figure than the revered octogenarian Pharisee Akiba acknowledged the Jewish general as the messianic redeemer and renamed him Bar Kochba, "son of the star," after the biblical promise, "a star shall come forth out of Jacob, and a scepter shall rise out of Israel" (Numbers 24:17). With the confidence that the day of messianic glory had dawned for the Jewish people, the rebels minted their own coins bearing the inscription, "For the Freedom of Jerusalem."

But the era of messianic glory for Jerusalem lasted just three years. In 135 the Emperor Hadrian amassed a great force, including troops sent from Britain and Africa. Rebel strongholds were systematically attacked and destroyed. Jews took a stand north of Bethlehem at Betar, a town that would enter Jewish history as a symbol of Jewish defiance. The carnage was horrible. Altogether some one thousand Jewish villages and towns were destroyed and more than half a million people lost their lives. Roman losses were equally terrible. So many legionnaires were killed in battle that the emperor declined to communicate to Rome the usual salutation, "I am well and my army is well."

After the hostilities, Hadrian carried out his decision to rebuild Jerusalem. The city was replanned as a typical Roman garrison town, with two main transversal streets creating four quarters within the surrounding walls, quarters that are with us today. Then Hadrian, like Titus before him, banished Jews from Jerusalem, allowing them to visit the city once a year on the ninth day of Av to mourn the destruction of the Temple. More humiliations followed. A statue of Jupiter was erected in the Temple together with two statues of the emperor, one on horseback. The city was renamed Aelia Capitolina, Aelia after the emperor's family name, and Capitolina in honor of the patron god of Rome, Jupiter Capitolina. It is also during Hadrian's reign that we hear a new name for the land of Israel, *Palestina*. It was an ironic designation, honoring the very foe upon whose defeat the ancient nation of Israel had laid claim to the entire land.

Were there positive, creative, and lasting consequences of the two major rebellions which Jews waged against Roman political and military authority? Today there are those, such as Professor Yehoshafat Harkabi of Hebrew University, who believe that the Jewish rebels should have remembered Jeremiah's advice to King Zedekiah at the time of the Babylonian conquest—"Serve Babylon and live."[31]

Did Jeremiah give sound advice? The answer is certainly yes if we consider only Israel's physical survival in the ancestral land. Had resentment of Rome not developed into a fanatic, virtually suicidal campaign to rid the land of the Roman infidel, Jerusalem would not have been lost and the Temple would have been spared. Nor would Judea have been devastated if the Bar Kochba rebels had correctly calculated the military costs of their insurgency.

But if we can set aside purely political and military considerations, we may consider a different response to Jeremiah's advice. The dangers that faced Israel under Babylonian captivity were not nearly as great as those experienced under centuries of Greek and Roman rule. Jeremiah's Israel was not confronted by the real danger of national extinction through cultural dissolution. When we consider, too, that all other minority peoples living under Greek and Roman rule eventually made an accommodation with the culture of their rulers, it is astonishing to realize that only the Jews continued to resist these rulers, to fight against them repeatedly, to assert their own national rights, and to await—with pious foolishness perhaps—divine intervention.[32]

Why did the Jews resist? The answer is that they believed Israel must retain its integrity and freedom to be Israel, that is, Yahweh's Covenant partner. The Maccabeean struggle against the Greeks, the Great Revolt against Rome, the Bar Kochba Rebellion—all these conflicts preserved a sense of Jewish national uniqueness. However much we may deplore the extremism and destructiveness that marked these events, we should recognize that the revolutionaries kept alive a sense of Jewish national identity. In so doing they built a bridge spanning some eighteen hundred years of Diaspora existence—a bridge over which Zionists were to walk in pursuit of a new political framework through which the ancient sense of national identity could be realized in the modern world.

CHAPTER 3

Return to Zion

*[The Jews] hold the Holy City where stands the second Temple
of the most high God to be their mother city.*
—Philo

*How much longer shall there be weeping in Zion
and mourning in Jerusalem.*
—Abraham ibn Ezra

*The city of Zion is unlike other European towns and cities,
where everyone pays attention
to what others do, say and wear.
The inhabitants of Zion are not concerned with such things.*
—M. N. Cahanyu

*All possible winds blow in Jerusalem.
It is said that every wind before going where it lists
comes to Jerusalem to prostrate itself
before the Lord.*
—Rabbi Obadiah of Bertinoro

The rabbis who led the people after the disastrous Bar Kochba
Rebellion had one thought in mind: to make certain that the
land of Israel remained in Jewish hands. A half-million Judeans
lost their lives in the war; another half-million fled the country
or were exiled. Judea was a wasteland, resettled by Syrians and
Arabs.

The Jews of the Galilee, numbering more than 300,000, did
not join the Bar Kochba rebels. Recognizing the foolishness of
trying to free the Jewish nation from the Roman empire, they

preserved their hold on the completely Jewish cities of Sephoris and Tiberias and of much of the northern part of the country. In the next five hundred years, until the Arab invasion of Palestine in 638, the Jewish population of Palestine declined to 200,000, a radical reduction from the population of 1.3 million before Bar Kochba.

Eventually a handful of Jews crept back into Jerusalem. With their rabbinical leaders they learned to cooperate with Roman authority. Taxes were paid and laws obeyed. Daily prayers stressed the messianic hope in the reunion of the nation in Eretz Israel, in the restoration of Jerusalem, and in the rebuilding of the Temple. But the hope was not preached loudly lest the gentile ruler find another excuse to punish the nation.[1]

The theology of the rabbis was clear: No one knows the day on which God will act to redeem his nation. Until that chosen day arrives, the people are not permitted to force the hand of the Lord. They should pray for the speedy arrival of that day, and they should hope that a life of repentance will hasten it; but they must never assume, as the Bar Kochba rebels assumed, that violent revolutionary action can clear the way for messianic deliverance. Through the powerful institutions of the patriarchate and the religious court (Sanhedrin), the rabbis saw to it that no new fanatic arose to lead the nation in a suicidal drive against Rome.

Emperor Hadrian (who had studied Jewish ritual) may well have sought to punish the rebellious Jewish nation when he reinstituted his persecution after putting down the Bar Kochba insurgency. But the more likely reason for his harsh action was a shrewd appreciation of the strength of Jewish religion. He understood that the way to end unpredictable surges of Jewish nationalism was to stop the rituals and ceremonies that nourished nationalism. He prohibited circumcision as a "barbaric" practice, and banned observance of holy days, proselytization, the teaching of Torah, and the ordination of rabbis. The emperor also decreed a ban on any "circumcised" person living in Jerusalem. The ban was so sweeping that even the Jewish-born Christian bishop of Jerusalem had to be replaced by one who was an uncircumcised gentile.

Fortunately for the future of the nation, the persecution did not much outlive the emperor. Hadrian died in 137, only two years after crushing the Bar Kochba Rebellion. His successor

Antonius Pius, who enjoyed a long reign (137–161), made a halfhearted effort to continue his predecessor's anti-Jewish policy, then discontinued it with the decision that as long as Jews lived peacefully under Roman law, they could practice their religion under the leadership of their own chosen officials. They could administer their own villages and towns and use tax moneys to pay for public works. Within a few years of Pius's reign, Jews began visiting Jerusalem; pilgrims came from abroad and with bribes to Roman authorities succeeded in taking up residence in the city despite the official ban.[2]

On the whole, the situation of Jews in the empire from the time of Emperor Pius was not entirely unsatisfactory. They were not citizens, but they did not especially wish to be because citizenship imposed obligations of Roman oaths. They retained certain privileges. They did not serve in the army, their Sabbath was respected, and their synagogues were protected against vandalism.[3]

As the rabbis regrouped at Yavneh following the Great Revolt of 66–70, so now in the wake of the Bar Kochba debacle they met in the small Galilean town of Uscha to chart directions for the future life of the nation. They declared that despite the military defeats, despite the continuation of foreign occupation, Judea, Jerusalem, the whole of the land of Israel was to be recognized by all Jews everywhere as the center of the nation's existence. The Jewish communities of Mesopotamia and Egypt would defer to the homeland. The patriarch of the land of Israel would exercise his traditional right to fix the dates of the feasts and proclaim the leap years. And rabbis would be ordained only in Israel.

To ensure that the Jewish population did not continue to erode, the rabbis also introduced specific legislation prohibiting emigration as a sin and bestowing blessings on immigration.[4] One ruling held that it was more righteous to live in a mixed Jewish-gentile city in Eretz Israel than to live in a completely Jewish city in the Diaspora. Another stipulated that if one spouse decided to emigrate to the land of Israel, the other spouse was obliged to follow. These restrictions were necessary because many Jews were attracted to join their brethren in Mesopotamia where the detested Romans did not rule and where the economy flourished. Further, the land of Israel was literally to stay in Jewish hands. The rabbis were prepared to fine anyone who sold or leased a house or agricultural land to a gentile.

The rabbis were particularly concerned that scholars and students of Torah be kept in the land. Residence was officially considered a symbolic continuation of the Temple service that could no longer be held, and thus a righteous act meriting divine grace.

Consistent with the effort to retain Jews on the land, rabbinical leaders waxed eloquently on the Holy Land and the Holy City.[5] One memorable saying held that "Ten portions of beauty descended to the world; Jerusalem acquired nine and the rest of the world one." Living in the land was equivalent to obeying the whole Torah. One who lived in the land of Israel was forgiven all sins; one who lived in the land of Israel worshiped the true God while one who lived abroad worshiped false gods. There was a special merit too in being buried in the land, so the practice began for Jews to have their remains shipped to Israel for burial in its sacred soil. Mourning the loss of the land, lamenting the exile from Jerusalem, bemoaning the destruction of the Temple—all became incorporated into the daily prayers of every Jew. Further symbolic reminders of these tragedies developed into household traditions.[6] When a man painted his house he left a portion unpainted to remind him of the incompleteness of his life without the land, Jerusalem, and the Temple. To convey the same meaning, a woman would omit a piece of her jewelry, or one course of a meal would be left out. The meaning of loss qualified the happiness of the marriage ceremony. The bridegroom would crush with his foot a wine goblet to remind the wedding party of the destruction of the Temple. And since prayer substituted for animal sacrifice after the Temple's destruction, the memory of Jerusalem became central to prayer. Wherever a Jew found himself he would recite his three daily prayers facing eastward, toward Jerusalem. Included in his prayers was this benediction expressing his deepest hope: "And to Jerusalem, thy city, return in mercy and dwell therein as thou hast spoken; rebuild it soon in our days as an everlasting building, and speedily set up therein the throne of David." Thus in many ways ordinary Jews in their daily lives kept faith with the psalmist's words, "If I forget thee, O Jerusalem, let my right hand whither, let my tongue cleave to the roof of my mouth...."

The exaltation of the Holy Land in the second and third centuries induced reverence for specific holy sites. Designated holy places became special places of reverence for Jewish pilgrims.[7] Among hundreds of such places were the Oaks of Mamre, Jacob's Well, the burial place of Solomon, David's Tomb in Jerusalem, the tombs of the patriarchs in Hebron, and the foundation stone on the Temple Mount, the Western Wall remnant of the Temple. In time this veneration would spread to Christian and Muslim pilgrims, who would add their own special meanings to the sacred sites.

Within the Roman empire the Jews, led by their patriarch, formed a state within a state, even to the extent of maintaining their own foreign relations. There were numerous contacts between the Jewish communities of Mesopotamia, Egypt, and the land of Israel. The people, despite political boundaries separating them, looked upon themselves as one nation, practicing one ritual expressing a common hope of returning through God's agency to the ancestral land and its cherished capital.

Peaceful relations between the Jewish community of Palestine and the Roman state continued for two hundred years following the reign of Antonius Pius. For Jews it was a period of great literary creativity in which the legal and moral code of communal life, the Mishnah, was produced, followed by the Talmuds of Jerusalem and Babylonia, new editions of the body of Jewish law and tradition.

The ascendancy in 324 of Constantine the Great, the first Christian emperor, marked the beginning of the church's campaign to impose its dogma on both pagans and Jews. When the emperor embarked on a major program of church construction in Jerusalem, the few Jews living there left the city. The pilgrimages to the city on the ninth of Av continued, but by and large Jews found themselves staying away from Jerusalem where Christian monks might attack them or forcibly convert them. Tensions increased when rabbis expressed their rejection of the messianic claims of the church and sought to win back to Hebraic faith those Jews who had adopted Christianity.

The Emperor Constantine, although a zealous champion of his new faith, was no bigot. He permitted religious freedom to all non-Christian minorities within the empire, and Jews enjoyed no fewer rights than they had had under previous pagan emperors. But when the emperor died in 337 he was succeeded in 350 by his son Constantius II, who decreed the first of numerous anti-Jewish laws. Heeding the advice of his ecclesiastical advisers, Constantius set forth a policy to separate Jews from the Christian society of the empire. Laws were introduced prohibiting the intermarriage of Jews and Christians, including the conversion of Christian women to Judaism. A ban on Jewish possession of Christian or pagan slaves was a direct blow to the participation of Jews in the economy of the ancient world. Nothing so much expressed the new hostility toward Jews as the wording of laws in which Jews were referred to as "savage" or an "abominable sect." The religion of Judaism was called a "disgrace and an infamy."[8]

Constantius died in 361 and was succeeded by his younger brother Julian, who to the consternation of Roman church officials turned out to be an enemy of Christianity and an ardent champion of the old pagan cults. He opposed the alliance of state and church, blaming it for the economic decline of the empire. He abolished the special right granted to the Christian clergy by Constantine and Constantius, including the right to convert Jews. Cautious before the still powerful Christian bishops, he did not close churches but rather reopened the old temples to worship of the Greco-Roman gods. The policies carried out during Julian's short reign (November 361 to June 363) made Jews believe that Julian was from the mold of the Persian king Cyrus, a gentile redeemer fashioned by God for the Jewish nation.

Julian acted decently toward Jews not because he had any particular liking for them and their religion (he found repugnant the claim that Israel was God's "chosen" nation) but rather because he counted on Jews as allies in his struggle against the church. And potentially they *were* a valuable ally. For while Jews had lost much of their wealth and population in the fourth century, they still held the political balance between Christians and pagans. The emperor also solicited the support of Jewish communities in Mesopotamia in his planned invasion of Persia.

In 362 Julian permitted Jews to return to Jerusalem with the right to rebuild the Temple. In the mind of this devoutly pagan man, allowing Jews to resume sacrifices in their Temple would assure him the favor of yet another powerful deity, the God of Israel. The emperor also sought to counter the Christian interpretation of the destruction of the Jewish Temple. Christian monks argued that the destruction of the Temple was visible proof that God had abandoned the people he had once chosen to be his own. The monks preached that the Jewish exile from the land which followed both Titus's conquest of Jerusalem and Hadrian's defeat of the Bar Kochba rebels was God's punishment of the Jewish nation for its rejection of the messiahship of Jesus. They argued that where God saw fit to restore Israel to the land after the Babylonian destruction of Jerusalem, the exile of the Jews inflicted on them by pagan Rome would last forever—for the murder of Christ was a far greater crime than the mere dishonor of God's Covenant law.

By authorizing the rebuilding of the Temple the emperor intended to disprove these arguments and thus weaken the psychological power of the church. Just as in the twentieth century the British government supported Zionist colonization of Palestine to advance its own imperial interests, so in the fourth century Julian supported the reconstruction of the Jewish Temple to bolster his support of the pagan cult against the church.

Jews everywhere in the empire greeted Julian's announcement of the Temple's reconstruction with enthusiasm. Many believed they were witnessing the beginning of the messianic redemption. With the emperor supporting them, many returned to Jerusalem. A few religious leaders had mixed feelings. For since the destruction of the Temple three hundred years earlier, rabbis had taught that it would be rebuilt by God's hands alone. Some savored the ironic humiliation of the church. Here was a pagan emperor inviting Jews to restore their Temple while Christian leaders, fervent opponents of paganism, were forced to watch the reconstruction of the most hated symbol of a discredited religion.

With the rabbis supervising, the Temple reconstruction began. Legend has it that silver tools were used because the Torah prohibited iron. Workmen came from all parts of the empire; the costs were borne by the imperial treasury. Julian himself could not witness the work because he was busy fighting a war in Persia. The first major step was the removal of the pagan temple dedicated to Jupiter which Hadrian had built on the Temple esplanade.

Then in May 363, as work proceeded, there occurred an event which brought the whole endeavor to a halt. Fire broke

out among the building materials, and the workmen were engulfed in the flames. The cause of the fire was an earthquake
which caused an explosion of gases accumulated in the closed
underground room ("Solomon's Stables") where building materials were stored. Jews viewed the disaster as a sign of God's
dissatisfaction with the whole project. Christians, seeing a miracle, felt vindicated against their old enemy. The more fervent of
Christian believers confessed they saw the fire descend from
heaven to devour Jewish unbelievers. Some claimed to see
crosses appear on the coats of all Jerusalemites—white crosses
for Christians, black for Jews and pagans. The Emperor Julian
suspected arson instigated by Christians. But he took no action
against Christian leaders, who would not have to wait long to
feel revenged against the despised monarch. In June 363 Julian
was killed battling the Persians. His successor Jovian, a devout
Christian, bent to church pressure and ceased funding the
reconstruction of the Jewish Temple.

The death of Julian was a crippling blow to Jews in the
empire. Had he lived as long as Constantine, who reigned
thirty-one years, Judaism might have recovered from its defeats
and Christianity might never have triumphed. Had Julian rebuilt
the Temple and allowed Jerusalem to become a Jewish city once
again, we cannot know how long Jews would have remained
loyal to him or how long they would have gone without
reasserting their desire for national independence. What is clear
is that the Christians' anti-Jewish animosity, which developed
after Julian's death, might have been averted had the emperor
lived to a ripe old age.

The early death of Julian led to a succession of Christian
emperors who opened wide the door of anti-Jewish hostility.
That hostility took on ominous dimensions when under the
Emperor Theodosius II (408–438), the Jewish patriarchate, the
symbol of communal autonomy, was abolished. New legislation
curtailed Jewish legal rights.[9] In cases involving both Jews and
Christians, Jews could not appeal to their own courts but had to
appear before ordinary civil courts where a fair trial was doubtful. The biblical scholar Jerome, who lived in Jerusalem from
385 to 420, tells us that Jews could not serve in the army or bear
arms.[10] They were also excluded from the teaching profession
and from city councils. The ban against Jews owning Christian
slaves was reintroduced. Monks accelerated their campaign to

win Jewish conversions to the church. The celebration of holy days was restricted and Purim festivities banned altogether. From 388 on, synagogues were often attacked by mobs. In 414 the grand synagogue of Alexandria was destroyed. Many other destroyed synagogues in Palestine and Egypt were seized and dedicated as churches. In 419 the fanatic monk Bar-Sauma instigated anti-Jewish riots in Jerusalem which led to the burning of several synagogues. When the emperor forbade the construction of new synagogues, Jews appealed to Theodosius to rescind this law and received the following reply from the emperor:

> It is our duty to diminish the power and importance of the abominable Hellenes, Jews and Heretics. Therefore we inform the Jews, that we do not agree to fulfill their offensive requests, but order only ... that in future they should not be persecuted and that their synagogues shall not be seized and burnt.[11]

The Samaritans fared worse than Jews. They were allowed no synagogues at all because the Roman state refused to recognize them as belonging to the Hebraic faith and sharing in its privileges.

The imperial ban against Jews visiting Jerusalem continued, but it was not effectively enforced. As before, bribes to sentries opened the city's gates. When bribes failed, Jews would camp on the Mount of Olives outside the city walls and recite their prayers gazing down on the site of former glory. Jerome recorded the melancholy movements of Jews who were permitted on the anniversary of the destruction of the Temple to gather before the ruins to chant their lament. "Silently they come and silently they go, weeping they come and weeping they go, in the dark night they come and in the dark night they go. ..." In a tone of derision he continues:

> Until this very day faithless inhabitants are forbidden to enter Jerusalem, and that they may weep over the ruins of their state, they pay a price, purchasing their tears ... so that not even weeping is free to them. You see on the day of the destruction of Jerusalem a sad people coming, decrepit little women and old men encumbered with rags and years, exhibiting both in their bodies and their dress the wrath of the Lord. A crowd of pitiable creatures assembles and under the gleaming gibbet of the Lord and

his sparkling resurrection, and before a brilliant banner with a
cross waving from the Mount of Olives, they weep over the ruins
of the Temple; and yet they are not worthy of pity. Thus they
lament on their knees with livid arms and disheveled hair, while
the guards demand their reward for permitting them to shed some
more tears. . . . [12]

Between the death of Julian in 363 and the theological
council which took place in 451 at Chalcedon in Asia Minor, an
important demographic change occurred in Palestine. As the
Christians increased in number to replace Jews as the majority,
so Jewish numbers sharply declined, from 800,000 after the Bar
Kochba Rebellion in 135 to 150,000 to 200,000 by the time of
the Persian invasion of the country in 614. But as the numbers
of Jews decreased, so it seems their sense of religious self-
identity intensified. Greek names like Jason and Menelaus,
which Jews had adopted from early Hellenistic times, began to
disappear in the fifth and sixth centuries and were replaced by
Hebrew biblical names.

Anti-Jewish feeling intensified with the accession to the
Byzantine throne of Justinian in 527. This great builder of
churches and monasteries in the Holy Land proved his loyalty to
the church by adopting all the old anti-Jewish laws and cancel-
ing one law which had protected all Jews in the empire. In his
new codification of imperial law, Justinian omitted the proviso
that Judaism was *religio licita*, a legitimate religion. In this way
the whole legal ground of Byzantine Jewry was removed, leaving Jews open to legal and religious attacks as never before,
including an increase of forced baptism.

The seventh century was a decisive turning-point in the
history of the ancient Near East. Persia and Rome had been
fighting for four hundred years across the Euphrates border. In
the early part of the seventh century, Persian forces gained the
upper hand, and in the year 606 invaded Syria. The Byzantine
emperor Phocas was deposed in 610 and replaced by Heraclius.
In 613 the Persian general Khoream Rhumizan, also called
Shahar-baraz ("the wild boar"), captured the city of Damascus.
The Persian army had now arrived at the hills of Galilee, where
Jews welcomed them as liberators from the oppressive Byzantines. Contemporary authors claim the Jews conspired to hand
over towns to the Persian army, which included in its ranks

Mesopotamian Jews. In the year 614, after a three-day siege, Jerusalem was conquered by the forces of King Khosroes II.

The Persian king rewarded Jews for their support in the war against the Byzantines by returning to them control of Jerusalem. Once the city was in Jewish hands, religious services were resumed at the site of the ruined Temple. Jews, of course, rejoiced in the freedom to live again in their holiest of cities, but their leaders understood the precariousness of their political situation. The Persians were overseers of a country whose population was now more than 95 percent Christian.

The Christians, meanwhile, were determined to expel Jews again from Jerusalem and restore Christian rule. They had not long to wait. Within three years of their conquest, the Persians found it expedient to evict Jews from the government of Jerusalem and allow Christians to resume rule in the city. In Jewish eyes the Persian action was a betrayal. The decision was motivated by political considerations to maintain peaceful relations with the still powerful Christian majority in the city. For Jews the loss of Jerusalem meant the final defeat of their national hopes in the Holy City. Jews would not again exercise government in Jerusalem until the twentieth century.

It took about ten years for Byzantine forces to mount an effective counterattack against Persian rule in Syria and Palestine, and in 629 Emperor Heraclius regained Jerusalem. By all accounts Heraclius was a fair-minded man with little desire for revenge against the Jews; but the local bishops hungered for revenge and spared no effort in persuading Heraclius to punish the Jews by evicting them once more from Jerusalem. The bishops argued that in aiding the Persians the Jews were ultimately responsible for the theft of Christ's cross from the Church of the Resurrection built by Constantine to house Christ's Tomb. The Jews, they said, had led the Persians to the cross, which they had seized and taken back with them to Persia.

Heraclius was moved by the bishops's pleas but hesitated to lift his hand because he had promised Jewish leaders safety in Jerusalem. For the emperor to renege was a sin punishable by God. At this point, according to a famous legend, a delegation of bishops and monks appeared before the emperor and voiced a theological argument which they felt sure would persuade Heraclius to break his promise and agree to punish the Jews.[13] They proposed to take the emperor's sin upon themselves and do penance. The emperor consented. Jews were banished from Jerusalem and ordered not to come within three miles of the city. The monks undertook their penitential fasts, a practice which was observed centuries later in the Coptic church of Egypt and called the "Fast of Heraclius."

The punishment of Jews did not end with expulsion from Jerusalem. We are told that Jews were prohibited from reciting the *Shema* prayer ("Hear O Israel...") because in Christian hearts the words of the prayer expressed a confident nation. Permission was given only for the singing of hymns on the Sabbath. From this time Jewish poets exercised their ingenuity by weaving the words of the *Shema* into newly composed hymns and thus continued the ancient ritual of prayer.

After only five years a new conquering nation made its appearance in the Middle East. Mounted warriors rode out of the deserts of Arabia to battle the Byzantines and win from them control of Syria, Palestine, and Egypt. Although the real motive of their conquest was plunder, within a relatively short time the peoples of these newly conquered territories would adopt the faith of Islam, the self-proclaimed successor to Judaism and Christianity.

When the Arabs invaded Palestine in 634, Emperor Heraclius, fearing a legend that spoke of the loss of the country to a "circumcised people," ordered the forced baptism of all Jews in his kingdom, and even asked the kings of Spain and Italy to baptize their Jews. Evidently the emperor did not know that Arabs also engaged in the ritual practice of circumcision.

Arab forces captured Jerusalem in June 637 after a ten-month siege. Although there is no evidence that Jews helped the Arabs against the Byzantines, as they had earlier helped the Persians, there is little doubt that they welcomed the Arabs as liberators from the hated Christian rulers of the city. Muslims ruled Jerusalem for 350 years, until the conquest of Jerusalem by the Latin Crusaders in 1089. During this long period Jews lived with security and peace, largely as they had under earlier Persian and Roman rulers. As long as they paid their taxes and obeyed the laws, they were free to worship and to manage their own communal affairs under their chosen leaders. They continued to come to the Western Wall Temple remnant to recite prayers, which grew sadder in tone as they watched the construction of two magnificent mosques where the Holy of Holies had once stood. Because they had demonstrated courtesy by directing the first Muslim conquerors to the Temple Mount, their reward was the privilege of keeping the sacred enclosure clean of rubbish. They were also given the right to purchase burial sites on the Mount of Olives, where the Divine Presence (*Shekinah*) was believed to have rested after departing from the fallen Temple. Rabbinical tradition forbade a Jew to enter the Temple Mount area lest he offend God by stepping on the site of the Holy of Holies. But some Jews were given special permission by their rabbis to work for Muslim authorities as dusters and sweepers of the mosques.

Under Muslim law Jews together with Christians were regarded as "People of the Book," believers in Allah but erring in their refusal to accept the apostolic authority of God's prophet Muhammad. In civil terms, Jews and Christians were categorized as *dhimmis* or "protected subjects" of the Islamic state, forbidden to bear arms but taxed to pay for their protection. More than anything else, the heavy burden of taxation impoverished the small communities of Jews that continued in the land of Israel during the centuries of Umayyad and Abbasid rule. What is extraordinary is that Jews clung to the land and to the holy capital throughout this long period when they knew that it was relatively easy to leave the country to join their more prosperous brethren in Egypt or Asia Minor or Europe.

Jerusalem was a sanctified, secure, but fairly sleepy place for Jews during the four and a half centuries of Muslim rule. All that was to change with the coming of the Latin knights at the end of the eleventh century—an event which had a devastating impact on the Holy Land. The Crusaders arrived in the Holy Land in 1096, their hands already bloodied from the massacres of Jews in the German towns of the Rhine Valley. Jerusalem was besieged in 1098 and fell after five weeks of bitter fighting. In the battle for the city, Jews fought alongside Muslims to save Jerusalem from what they knew would be a monstrous rule. When the Crusaders entered the city they slaughtered many inhabitants. Jews were burned in their synagogues; those who survived were sold into slavery. The city itself suffered as great a devastation as at the time of Titus's siege. The Latin conquerors set to rebuilding the city, erecting churches, towers, fortifications, and markets which define the city to the present day.

Slowly Jews and Muslims, despite official prohibition, filtered back into Jerusalem and resumed their lives under later, less savage, but always unpredictable Christian rulers.

Throughout the hundred years of Crusader rule of Palestine, and for all the centuries of renewed Muslim rule of the country following the reconquest of Saladin in 1186, Jews remained faithful to the memory of the ancestral land. They continued to come to it as pilgrims, to settle in it in small numbers, and to transport their dead there to be buried in its holy soil, ideally on the Mount of Olives where the Messiah was first expected. One of the most famous of the travelers was Benjamin of Tudela, Spain, who visited the country in 1174, just before the Muslim reconquest of the city. He found the "street of the Jews" in Jerusalem, but only two pitiful souls lived there, employed as dyers of garments.

In the years that followed Benjamin's visit, funds were raised to support the old and devout who were willing to immigrate to the country to spend their years studying and praying in antici-pation of the messianic redemption. During the long period of Muslim rule, when the country was ruled by a succession of Ayyubid, Mamluk, and Ottoman dynasties, the image of Jerusa-lem in the mind of Diaspora Jews was often idealized as a beautiful, peaceful, near heavenly city. The reality was quite different. The city was impoverished, corrupt, dangerous, dirty, and disease-ridden. It is all the more remarkable that there were Jews sufficiently moved by the emotional memory and idealized image of Jerusalem to make the treacherous voyage across the seas to visit the land and its capital. In contrast to the passive messianists who believed that through God's agency alone the dispersed peoples would be reunited in the ancestral land, active messianists settled in the sacred land and city believing that through their presence and prayers God would be urged to act speedily. They earned the right to add the word "Jerusalemite," *yerushalmi*, to their names.

These lovers of Zion kept the memory of Jerusalem alive by prayers and poems, and ultimately by their decisions to settle in the land. Prayers were composed to be recited by the blessed ones who made the pilgrimage to Jerusalem in order to stand before the sacred ruins of the Temple. From a multitude of prayers we cite one from the eleventh century composed on the eve of the Crusader conquest of Jerusalem.

> I thank You, my God, for having sustained me and granted me life
> and strength to arrive here and behold the site of Your holy
> Temple for whose restoration all the people of Israel pray, that
> they may rest in its shade and lie in its dust. I, a servant son of
> your maidservant, have been privileged to see what I yearned for,
> and adore the object of my prayers, namely to stand in front of
> your holy Temple. Although it lies in ruins, Your holiness pervades
> it. The nations may have defiled it, but it remains chaste by virtue
> of Your presence and Your promise; although You deny it to us
> now, You have sworn to return us to it and rebuild it.[14]

One of the most beautiful poetic exaltations of Zion, the land and the city, comes from Judah Halevi, the Spanish poet, who left family, friends, his medical practice, and his native Spain to live in the land of Israel during the early decades of Crusader rule of Jerusalem. He did not wait for the Messiah nor for a messianic pretender. He immigrated in the belief that only in Israel could the Jew finally experience freedom and fulfillment. He took to heart the words of the Deuteronomist: "And you shall take possession of the land and settle in it, for I have given the land to you to possess it" (Numbers 33:53). Here are some lines from one of his most romantic poems about Jerusalem, lines meant to be recited on the ninth of Av, the traditional anniversary of the destruction of both the first and second Temples:

> Beautiful of elevation! Joy of the world! City of the Great King!
> For you my soul is longing from limits of the west.
> The tumult of my tenderness is stirred when I remember
> The glory of old that is departed—your habitation which is desolate.

In the next set of lines the poet's heart fills with emotion in expressing his yearning to see the sacred ruin and embrace it.

> O that I might fly on eagle's wings,
> That I might water your dust with my tears until they mingle
>   together.
> I have sought you, even though your King be not in you....
>
> Shall I not be tender to your stones and kiss them
> And the taste of your soil be sweeter than honey to me?[15]

From Abraham ibn Ezra, also a Spanish Jew and a contemporary of Halevi, there comes a dirge which repeats a message—

the Temple was destroyed as God's punishment of our sins—that
retained all its power fifteen hundred years after the prophets
first proclaimed it:

> How much longer shall there be weeping in Zion and mourning
>   in Jerusalem?
> O have mercy upon Zion and rebuild the walls of Jerusalem.
> At that time, the Sanctuary was destroyed because of our sins, and
>   because of our iniquities our Temple was burnt down.[16]

We can be sure that the longing for divine deliverance and
reunification in the ancestral land was a popular feeling that
extended beyond poets, scholars, and mystics; otherwise there is
little to explain the mass followings which the messianic pretenders inspired. The exile of Jews from Spain in 1492 intensified belief in the coming redemption. Isaac Abravanel was
persuaded by his reading of the Book of Daniel that the event
would come in 1502. David Reubeni predicted it for the year
1524. Following the Chmelnicki massacres of Jews in Poland
and western Russia in 1648–1649, Shabbetai Zevi, a Jerusalem
teacher of Cabbalistic mysticism, arose to organize a mass
migration of Jews to the Holy Land to await the redemption
expected in 1666. These and other preachers of the redemption
claimed the title of Messiah or had it attributed to them. They
were able to uproot whole groups of Jews from their villages
and towns, convince them to sell their goods, and set out by
foot, wagon, and ship in the direction of Jerusalem, a journey
which almost always ended in disaster. Many died in travel; few
were fortunate to reach the Holy Land. Those who did suffered
so many deprivations that some returned to their original countries.

The messianic movements proved so disruptive of Diaspora
Jewish communities that rabbinical leaders of those communities often pronounced anathemas against anyone joining them—
even when that meant sacrificing the chance to live in the Holy
Land. Yet despite their fanaticism, these messianic movements
kept the land of Israel from being swallowed up by idealized,
romantic images. The movements were events of concrete political action which returned Jerusalem to the earth.

Thousands upon thousands of Jews, however, ignored the
messianic pretenders. Like the Torah scholars of Mesopotamia,
most Jews did not repair to the ancestral land even when they

had both the freedom and the means to do so. What of them? Here we can say that Jews were as pragmatic in the late Middle Ages as they were in those ancient times following Cyrus's conquest of Palestine. In most Jewish minds God was not served by leaving the security of one's house and land in order to set out on a dangerous journey which might end in deprivation or death. The sanctity of life was more important than the sacredness of the Holy Land. And many scholars rationalized their reluctance to immigrate by arguing that it would be a sinful distraction from their study of Torah and Talmud.

Many Jews traveled individually to Jerusalem and left accounts of their impressions. In the case of the traveler Jonah the Elder, the leader of a Diaspora community at the end of the tenth century, a report on the city was sent to him before his visit. The heads of the Jerusalem community wrote to him to solicit funds, and in their letter they described the deplorable conditions in "the city which now is widowed, orphaned, deserted, and impoverished with its few scholars...." They continued, "Life here is extremely hard, food is scarce, and opportunities for work very limited." The Muslim authorities exacted high taxes, for which the community must borrow money at exorbitant interest or risk going to prison. If they refused to pay the taxes they might lose their right to pray over the dead on the Mount of Olives.[17]

Benjamin of Tudela, upon his visit to the Holy Land in 1174, found Jerusalem a city of many nations and languages—Syrians, Greeks, Georgians, and Frenchmen. He discovered two hundred Jews in the northwest corner of the city, under the Tower of David. Expressing his admiration for the Muslim shrine, the Dome of the Rock, on the Temple Mount, he was particularly impressed that Muslims, like Jews, avoided the use of idolatrous pictures of God and confined their worship to the recitation of prayers. He noted that Christians made a practice of desecrating Jewish grave sites and seized the stones to build their houses. It is from Benjamin that we also learn of ascetic Jewish sects in Yemen and Germany—"Mourners of Zion," they were called— who avoided meat, drank no wine, dressed entirely in black, lived in caves, and spent all their days in prayer to "implore the mercy of the Holy One...on account of the exile of Israel."

No traveler gained more honor for his devotion, learning, travel, and courage than the Spanish-born philosopher and poet

Moses ben Nachman, whom we know as Nachmanides. After an acrimonious theological debate in 1263 with Christians on the subject of God's providence, Nachmanides was forced to flee to the Holy Land. It was the fulfillment of a lifelong dream. He had long taught that living in the land of Israel was a *mitzvah*, a blessing, which equaled all the other blessings of the Bible. Nachmanides settled in Jerusalem in 1267, seven years after the Tartars destroyed the city. "What shall I relate about the conditions in the land?" he wrote. "There is large-scale destruction and ruin; in sum, the holier the site the more severe the damage." Nachmanides gathered a following, completed his commentary on the Torah, and built a synagogue which would bear his name. He noted that despite the city's devastation Jews continued to visit from Damascus and from distant Mesopotamia. He concluded a letter to his son with an exhortation, "May you, my son, and your brothers and all my household be permitted to see the good of Jerusalem and Zion's comfort."[18]

Rabbi Obadiah of Bertinoro, Italy, arrived in Jerusalem in March 1488 to accept the leadership of the Jewish community when the city was languishing from generations of neglect under Mamluk rulers, the Egyptian slave-soldiers who formed a caliphal dynasty in the thirteenth century. His description of Jerusalem provides us with a valuable account of the city in the last decades of Mamluk rule. Rabbi Obadiah found the city in ruins. About four thousand families resided there, including about seventy poor Jewish families, many without fathers. "Among the Jewish population there are many aged, forsaken widows from Germany, Spain, Portugal and other countries, so that there are seven women to one man...." A Jew, he observed, could not rebuild his house without purchasing permission which was often more costly than the house itself. Meat, wine, olives, and sesame oil were all in abundance and cheap. But Jews had to pay the Muslim governor for permission to make the new wine needed for the Sabbath blessing.[19]

For Jews the Ottoman conquest of Palestine in 1517 represented another of those sudden shifts of Jerusalem's wind, bringing a change of weather. The sultan's advisers did not actively encourage Jewish immigration to Palestine, but they did not prevent it. As a result, a Jewish toehold in Jerusalem, maintained through a succession of Byzantine, Crusader, Ayubid, and Mamluk rulers, was expanded in Ottoman times into a foothold. Many years later, in the second half of the nineteenth century, that foothold would expand so greatly that the Jewish inhabitants of Jerusalem would exceed in number the combined population of Muslims and Christians.

The official expulsion of Jews from Spain in 1492 and from Portugal four years later occurred twenty-five years before the Ottoman conquest of Palestine. Only a trickle of the 300,000 exiled were willing to risk the dangers of Mamluk rule and move directly to the Holy Land. Instead, many of the exiled made their way to North Africa, Italy, Greece, and Turkey, where they were to become an industrious, prosperous, and loyal people under a succession of Ottoman sultans. After the Ottoman conquest of Palestine in 1517, however, Jews in increasing numbers began to immigrate to the ancestral land. They were drawn not to Jerusalem, which continued to languish under conditions of poverty, but to Safed, a small mountain town in upper Galilee which was safe, free, and prosperous.

By the middle of the sixteenth century Safed (with a Jewish population of fifteen hundred) had replaced Jerusalem (with three hundred Jews) as the center of the Jewish community of Palestine. While many of the immigrants were religious scholars of Talmud and Torah, there were sufficient numbers of farmers, laborers, merchants, and craftsmen to revitalize the economic life of the community. Lake Tiberias was fished; wheat fields were plowed; fruit orchards were planted; sheep were raised and wool exported; and there developed a booming textile industry. Cotton garments from Safed were prized throughout the Arab east. Some Jews of Safed even grew wealthy from the local slave trade. Business also proved irresistible to many of the scholars in Safed because they, unlike ordinary people, were exempt from taxes.

But the essential business of Safed was religion. Talmudic study and Cabbalistic mysticism filled the mountain air. In the mid-sixteenth century Safed could boast of two hundred synagogues and more than three hundred rabbinical scholars. Mystical techniques were employed to determine from the sacred scriptures the exact dates of the coming redemption. The year 1522 had been favored; when it passed uneventfully, 1530 became the new favorite; after that other years were chosen. Many expected miraculous signs to foretell the redemption. One such sign would be the collapse of the pillars of the Dome of the Rock shrine in Jerusalem. Because the shrine, commemorating Muhammad's Heavenly Ascent, was a treasured Islamic monument, Safed's rabbis were careful to whisper their predictions lest the local Muslim authorities hear them.

Not everyone shared in Safed's messianic enthusiasms. Rabbi Levi ibn Habib, head of Jerusalem's Jewish community, reacted sharply to the miraculous predictions of the messianists, calling them "the tidings of fools."[20] Habib and his rabbinical colleagues saw little good in Safed's piety or prosperity. They had reason to worry that their own traditional prerogatives—fixing the dates of the holy days, declaring the leap year, and appointing religious judges—might be threatened by the growing power and wealth of Safed's rabbis. They recalled the generations following Hadrian's persecution, when the rabbis of Tiberias and Sephoris looked with envy on the security and prosperity of Mesopotamia's Jews. But where the Mesopotamian rabbis had deferred to the religious authority of the rabbis in the land of Israel, Safed's leaders seemed determined aggressively to assert their advantages over Jerusalem. So confident were the scholars of Safed in their religious powers that the word went out from the Talmudic academies, the *yeshivot,* that when the Messiah appeared he would come first to Safed. In Jerusalem's ears the words were heard as blasphemy.

The issue between the cities came to a head when Safed, under the leadership of Rabbi Jacob Berab, who arrived in Safed in 1524, began to teach his followers that redemption would follow the return to Zion. And for him Zion was located in Safed. Armed with this declaration, Berab began to appoint judges and make plans for the reestablishment of the ancient institution of the Sanhedrin in Safed. This really meant the enthronement of Safed above Jerusalem.

Jerusalem was not about to let Safed steal its age-old rabbinical prerogative. Levi ibn Habib, exercising his authority as head rabbi of Jerusalem, denounced Berab and ordered Safed's rabbis to disobey their leader. Berab was disgraced by the condemnation and fled to Damascus. Ironically, one of Berab's "illegitimately" ordained rabbinical judges was Joseph Karo, one of Judaism's greatest luminaries. Karo led the community of Safed for thirty years, and before his death in 1575 he and his fellow scholars produced a new codification of Jewish ritual law, the *Shulhan Arukh*, or Set Table, which remains an authoritative guide to this day.

The decline of Safed in the late sixteenth and early seventeenth centuries was brought about by drought in 1599, epidemic disease in 1602, and frequent attacks on the city from Druze and Arab marauders throughout the first half of the seventeenth century. Eventually the wool and clothing industry died, and the first printing press of Palestine, opened in Safed in 1577, was closed. In 1656 Druze attacks brought destruction to Safed and Tiberias, and a mass exodus of Jews to Jerusalem.

Jerusalem was ill prepared to receive the immigrants. The city continued to suffer from bad housing, a scarcity of jobs, unpredictable outbreaks of violence, and the always exploitive Muslim tax collectors who perpetuated Jewish poverty. In 1625 a reign of terror was led by Muhammad ibn Farukh, who bought Jerusalem from the Sultan in order to mine the city for its taxes. He imposed an annual tax of fifty thousand kurush on the city which bankrupted the Jewish community, and when rabbinical leaders faulted on payment he ordered them imprisoned.

At other times in Jerusalem it seemed that only God's direct intervention averted disaster. In 1637 drought and famine were predicted, events which Muslims foresaw as God's punishment for allowing Jews to dwell with them in Jerusalem. Threats were issued that unless rain fell in three days the entire Jewish quarter would be slaughtered. The Israeli historian Itzhak Ben-Zvi describes the Jewish response: "The Jews proclaimed a fast and on the third morning gathered at the tomb of Zechariah on the Mount of Olives, where they prayed till noon. In the afternoon the sky became overcast and a heavy rain began to fall, overflowing the reservoirs."[21]

Yet throughout the seventeenth and eighteenth centuries, Jews continued to arrive in Jerusalem in small numbers; they stayed, worked, studied, prayed, and had children. The community enlarged. New immigrants arrived from abroad, and pilgrims visited. Despite hardships, people sang the city's praises. An early expression of praise comes from a letter written by one such immigrant in 1625, the very year of Farukh's persecution.

> More of our people now inhabit the city of Our God than have dwelt there since Israel was exiled from its land, for daily many

Jews come to settle there, in addition to the pilgrims who come to pray to Him Who stands beyond our wall, to behold the pleasantness of God . . . and they give generously for the strengthening of Jerusalem. And the news is abroad that we dwell in peace and security, and the streets are filled with children, and from Zion comes forth knowledge and wisdom . . . to all the world. . . . It abounds in study houses open to all who would come and do holy work, and its leaders support the scholars and needy, providing each his needs. . . . [22]

From the beginning of Jewish immigration to Ottoman-ruled Palestine there developed a tradition of sending emissaries abroad annually to request money from the wealthier Jewish communities—this apart from the moneys sent to Jerusalem in fulfillment of the ancient Temple tax obligation. The leaders of the Diaspora Jewish communities were quick to respond to virtually any request from Jerusalem. In Constantinople a committee of Jews was formed to deal with the problem of Jerusalem's chronic bankruptcy. Under the noble name "Constantinople Committee of Elders and Honorary Wardens of the Holy Land," it began by interceding with the sultan to set a realistic annual tax fee for the community, a fee which the committee itself would pay. The Constantinople committee was also active in arranging pilgrimages to the Holy Land. So successful were these tours that a custom developed among Turkish Jews to visit the Holy Land at least once in a lifetime. The wealthiest among them traveled in the grand style, with ample servants, "one to prepare his coffee, a butcher, one to take care of his tobacco, another to tend his hookah [water pipe], and a secretary to record descriptions of the holy places."[23]

The end of the eighteenth century witnessed the first large migration to Palestine of Ashkenazi Jews. Coming from Lithuania, White Russia, and the Ukraine, they were followers of the Hasidic leader, the Baal Shem Tov. They settled first in Safed and later moved to Jerusalem. The revered Hasidic master himself set out with the group but turned back because, as he later confided, the times were not yet ripe for the redemption. This migration was followed by a second, still larger one by the traditional rivals of the Hasidim, the followers of Rabbi Elijah, the Gaon of Vilna, who were called the Mitnagdim ("Opponents"). Together the groups raised the Jewish population of

Palestine to ten thousand at the close of the eighteenth century. The earthquake of 1837, which devastated Safed and Tiberias, forced most of these Jews to resettle in Jerusalem, substantially adding to the Jewish population, which in 1850 consisted of four thousand Sephardim and two thousand Ashkenazim.[24]

Napoleon's invasion of Palestine in February 1799 sprang from his desire to expand the French empire into the Middle East. To win support of Jews in his military campaign he promised the restoration in Palestine of a "Jewish kingdom," as he put it. The promise was never fulfilled. After sweeping up the coastline from Gaza to Jaffa, he met determined resistance against his effort to conquer Acre. Aided by British naval batteries, the local Muslim forces of Acre's despot, Ahmad Jazzar (nicknamed "the Butcher"), repulsed some fourteen efforts of the French to breach the walls of the ancient seaport.

Had Napoleon captured Acre, doubtless he would have ordered his army inland to seize Jerusalem and Bethlehem and thus honor the memory of the medieval French Crusaders; but the Christian holy cities were not the priority in his military strategy. Failing to take Acre, Napoleon retreated to Egypt, leaving Jews to wonder if the emperor's appearance in their country had been the work of the devil. For when rumors of a restored Jewish kingdom reached the ears of Turkish authorities, the loyalty of Ottoman Jewish subjects was immediately suspect.

Napoleon's invasion of Palestine and Syria opened the door to European imperial influence. As Ottoman military and political power declined in the eighteenth and early nineteenth centuries, a number of European nations—Britain, France, Austria, Prussia, and Russia—found it desirable to establish their presence in the Holy Land. The impact of this international attention on the Jews living in Jerusalem and on those wishing to immigrate to the Holy City was dramatic. For the first time they discovered that Christian nations would support Jewish immigration to Palestine; even better, they would use their influence to protect and provide for Jews.

What principally motivated such support on the part of Britain was a grand imperial design for the Middle East. Britain, which had begun to assume responsibility for European Jews in

Palestine under a treaty agreement with the Turks known as the "Capitulations," saw in the Jews a useful vehicle for its own territorial and economic interests in the Middle East. Other less political motives were behind British support of Palestinian Jewry. Several important British leaders were Christian millenarians, scriptural fundamentalists who believed that the Jewish return to Palestine was the necessary prelude to the Second Coming of Christ.

As a direct result of European, particularly British, support, the second half of the nineteenth century saw a dramatic increase in Jewish settlement in Jerusalem, from six thousand at mid-century to 35,000 at its close. In 1914, before World War I, Jerusalem's Jews numbered 45,000, an absolute majority over 25,000 Muslims and Christians.[25]

The turning point in the nineteenth century came with the conquest of Palestine in October 1831 by Muhammad Ali and his stepson Ibrahim Pasha, rulers of Egypt. Under the remarkably enlightened nine years of Egyptian rule (1831–1840), many discriminatory practices against Jews and Christians were ended. Jews could appear in the street in colors other than black, though green (the prophet Muhammad's color) was still prohibited. A Jew's testimony in court was now accepted as equal to that of a non-Jew. For the first time Jews were appointed to government offices. The exploitiveness of government bureaucrats was ended by giving them regular salaries. Many taxes were reduced, some abolished, including the onerous tax on pilgrims. For the first time in generations, Jews did not have to resort to bribes to repair old synagogues and build new ones. At once Jerusalem's elders set out to repair the complex of four synagogues named after Rabbi Johanan ben Zakkai. And construction began on a magnificent new synagogue, named Menahem Zion. It had been decades since Jews felt as religiously free and physically safe in the country. New Jewish immigrants and pilgrims began arriving from Europe, their passage to Jerusalem secured by the police force which Egyptian authorities deployed against the notorious bandits of the Abu Ghosh clan which had grown rich from exploiting pilgrims.

But the nine years of Egyptian dominance over Palestine proved to be merely an interlude in the four centuries of Ottoman imperial rule of the Middle East. In November 1840 a combined British and Turkish force toppled the Egyptians. Still, the progressive laws of the Egyptians had had their effect. It was a chastened, reform-minded Turkish government under Sultan Abdul Majid that resumed control of Syria and Palestine, a government far more willing than any before it to respect the rights of non-Muslim subjects.

The price paid by the Sublime Porte (as the Ottoman government was called, referring to the palace gate where justice was administered) for military aid in evicting the Egyptians from Syria and Palestine was a set of concessions (called "Capitulations") which allowed Britain and other European nations to establish consuls in Jerusalem, each with the right of protecting its Christian and Jewish nationals in the country. In effect the concessions allowed for the creation of a set of small "states-within-the state," with virtually autonomous powers of taxation, judiciary, and police.

Outside the jurisdiction of these foreign consuls were the masses of Muslim, Jewish, and Christian subjects of the Ottoman empire who continued to be ruled by the sultan's laws. But even here the political concessions to foreign nations had a beneficial effect for several thousand Sephardi Jewish subjects of the sultan. After generations of suffering the venality and violence of local Muslim governors, Jews were gratified when in 1840 Istanbul established a new diplomatic office which would represent Jewish subjects of the empire directly before the Sublime Porte. Called in Turkish the Hakham Bashi (or in Hebrew *Rishon le-Zion*, "Foremost of Zion"), the office in effect re-created the ancient patriarchate, the office which had preserved Jewish autonomy under foreign rule. The sultan's advisers could not have been more pleased with the new office, since the burden of collecting taxes from the Jewish community now fell on the Hakham Bashi and not on the usually corrupt local Muslim tax farmers.

The right of foreign consuls to protect European Jews as their nationals living in Palestine was a mixed blessing. On the positive side, Britain acted to extend her protection not only to her own Jewish citizens but to virtually any European Jew who requested it. Thus the knowledge that a Jew could live in the Holy Land subject not to Turkish but to British law was a powerful spur to the immigration of thousands of Ashkenazi Jews from the countries of central and western Europe. In time approximately 20 percent of all Jews of foreign nationality in

Palestine were under the protection of the British consul in Jerusalem. In addition, France, Austria, Prussia, and even Russia (which otherwise persecuted Jews at home) extended similar protection to their own Jewish nationals.

The negative aspect of the foreign consuls in Jerusalem was an energetic campaign to win Jewish converts to Christianity, a campaign led by the clergy of the Anglican and Scottish Presbyterian churches and by some rather pious consular officials. Their target was not the Sephardi Jewish subjects of the sultan but those poverty-stricken Ashkenazi Jews who were officially under their protection. They offered charity in the form of food, money, schooling, and medicine to a people sorely in need of all of them. The city had suffered earthquakes in 1833 and 1837. The Jewish quarter lacked clean water, was plagued by periodic outbreaks of typhoid, cholera, and smallpox, and stank from the carcasses of animals deposited in alleys from the neighboring slaughterhouse. The religious absolutism of the rabbis decreed a life of poverty and ignorance for nearly all Jews. In 1806 the French traveler Chateaubriand described the misery of the Jewish quarter which (despite its derisive tone) held true of the area throughout the first half of the nineteenth century.

> On the right hand of the Bazaar, between the Temple and the foot of Mount Sion, we entered the Jews' Quarters. Fortified by their indigence...they appeared covered with rags, seated in the dust of Sin, seeking the vermin which devoured them and keeping their eyes fixed on the Temple.[26]

Given these conditions, one is hardly surprised to learn that some Jewish converts were won, but so few (scarcely more than two hundred over a fifty-year period) that church officials complained of wasting a fortune on a handful of redeemed souls. To Jerusalem's rabbis, however, one converted soul was too many.

The reaction of Jerusalem's rabbis to the missionaries was fierce. Any Jew who converted to the church was, together with his family, banished from the rabbinically controlled community. One who accepted money or medicine from the Christians risked the loss of his job, his dwelling, and community funds; he also lost his important right to have family members buried in a Jewish cemetery. In one famous story, a Jew died in a Christian hospital before his conversion. The hospital authorities transported his body to the Jewish quarter for burial, but the rabbis refused and sent his body back to the hospital where he was also denied burial in the Christian cemetery. Muslim authorities finally intervened and buried the man in "neutral territory."[27] A Jew might also be imprisoned or whipped by the rabbis for disobeying their injunctions against communication with Christians.

Christian charity and its seduction influenced two great Jewish leaders, Moses Montefiore of London and Baron Edmond de Rothschild of Paris, who waged their own campaigns to establish a safer, cleaner, more secure place for Jews in the ancestral land. They provided money for the opening of hospitals, schools, orphanages, workshops, and soup kitchens. Following the example of these Western philanthropists, the rabbis in 1857 established their own hospital, Bikkur Holim, with funds provided by wealthy religious Jews in Russia, the United States, Germany, and Austria.

Despite the great sums of money spent by Montefiore and Rothschild in the hope of revitalizing the Jewish community of Palestine, many of their projects failed because of unrelenting opposition by Jerusalem's rabbis. The reasons for this comprise one of the saddest chapters in the history of nineteenth-century Jewish Jerusalem. At the heart of the opposition was the charitable system known as *halukah* or "division." *Halukah* referred to the practice begun in the early nineteenth century of sending emissaries to solicit funds from wealthy Jewish communities for distribution among Jews in the Holy Land. The practice was not new, for the Sephardi community had often turned to wealthy Jews abroad for support. The Sephardim needed this help but could have survived without it because many Sephardi family heads gained money from crafts, trade, and common labor. In the case of almost all of Jerusalem's Ashkenazim, however, whose sole vocation was religious study, foreign support or *halukah* was a life-or-death matter, especially after 1840 when Ashkenazi numbers rapidly increased in Jerusalem.

The control of *halukah* funds gave the Ashkenazi rabbis absolute powers over the community. One statistic shows that in Jerusalem in the mid-1850s a total of 239 Ashkenazim (4 percent) worked for money while the remainder, 5,461, were dependent on *halukah* funds.[28] Another report showed that in 1914, before World War I, 60,000 out of 85,000 Jews in Palestine depended on *halukah*.[29] A picture of the stultifying effects of *halukah* on Jerusalem's Jews in the mid-1850s is provided by the British artist and writer W. H. Bartlett:

> Every Friday the synagogue servants go to the houses of those few who are a little better off, and beg loaves of bread, which they then distribute among the most needy. The disease and suffering occasioned by bad food, close crowded dwellings, scarcity of water, are beyond description, and would surely, if known, awaken the compassion and active benevolence of happy England. And one of the medical residents could testify that death from starvation is not uncommon. A well-directed system of employment is what would more than anything raise the poor Israelites of Zion from their mental and bodily degradation.[30]

The *halukah* funds received at the beginning of the year usually ran out before Passover, in the spring, when the Muslims who owned nearly all the houses in the Jewish quarter demanded payment for the next twelve months. Often the community sold what it had in order to repay loans, pay rent, or purchase drinking water. One year when payments were not made, Muslims burned down one of the city's synagogues. As Bartlett observed, the community simply starved until new *halukah* funds were available. Some Jews were willing to save their children from starvation by selling them to the Christians.[31] And often, as in the past, rumors abounded that unscrupulous rabbis kept *halukah* for themselves and distributed to the people only what was absolutely necessary.

To Montefiore and Rothschild the *halukah* system perpetuated indolence, passivity, and poverty. While neither man set out to break the system of charity, their efforts to sponsor projects that would foster economic self-sufficiency struck directly at the crippling combination of rabbinical authority and community dependency fostered by *halukah*. Moses Montefiore and his wife Judith made seven trips to Palestine, the first in 1839, the last in 1874. The hospital and pharmacy he opened in 1849 were welcomed, but other endeavors in agriculture, crafts, and small industry were vigorously opposed. A flour mill constructed in Jerusalem was never operated. A weaving school for girls was closed after protests from the rabbis. The efforts of Montefiore, Rothschild, and others to introduce progressive schooling by adding languages and mathematics to the traditional curriculum of Talmud study were so aggressively opposed by the Ashkenazi rabbis that most schools eventually closed for lack of students. What particularly incensed the rabbis were the attempts to hold mixed classes of boys and girls. The few students who attended these new schools came from Sephardi families who, while traditionally religious, seemed less threatened by modern methods of education.

Despite rabbinical opposition to almost all his projects, Montefiore must be credited with planting the first seed of a new Jerusalem outside the old city walls when in 1875 a major construction was completed half a kilometer from Jaffa Gate. Intended by Montefiore to encourage local Jewish crafts, the long narrow building consisted of twelve one-room workshops, each with a sleeping loft. Called Mishkenot Sha'ananim ("Dwellings of Tranquility"), artisans used the workrooms but were so afraid to spend the night in what was then a bandit area that they returned to the safety of the old city walls at dusk.

Mishkenot Sha'ananim was the first of a number of new buildings that radically affected the lives of Jerusalem's Jews. Encouraged by political protection and the financial benefits of *halukah*, the fifty years between 1840 and 1890 saw a major influx of Western Ashkenazi Jews, most of whom came to Jerusalem, filling the old Jewish quarter. After 1870 Jews began to leave the overcrowded quarter to found new neighborhoods west of the city walls. These neighborhoods, eventually some seventy in all, became a new, distinctively Jewish Jerusalem, a city which in the mid-twentieth century was declared the capital of modern Israel.

Among the earliest of the seventy new city neighborhoods were Yemin Moishe in 1856, Nahlat Shivah in 1869, Mea Shearim in 1875, and Bet Yacov in 1875. Stagecoach transportation was introduced to connect the suburbs. In the new city a Jewish society developed on a basis wider than traditional religious study. It included stonecutters and masons, blacksmiths and bookmakers, and craftsmen working in wood, leather, glass, silver, and gold. Because Muslims disdained crafts, they were left to Jews and Christians. And so heavily did Jews dominate the crafts both in the old city and in the new that on the Jewish Sabbath Christians and Muslims could get nothing repaired or buy little else than food.

While the new city was being built, old Jerusalem, including the Jewish quarter, was being rapidly transformed from a medieval bastion into a modern, Western-style town. The presence of foreign consuls and churchmen attracted large numbers of Christian tourists and pilgrims. New steamships brought the visitors directly to Jaffa port, and from there carriages were waiting to transport them to Jerusalem on a straight road protected from bandits. In Jerusalem they found paved streets and new clean hospices constructed especially for them. Everyone noted the sheer numbers of Jews in the city. New *yeshivot* and synagogues were going up all over the old city. Where at the beginning of the nineteenth century there was but the Ben Zakkai complex of four synagogues, by the end of the century Jews could proudly point to seventy. Overcrowding in the Jewish quarter not only forced Jews into the new city, but many found themselves renting houses and courtyards in the Muslim quarter. There, until the first anti-Jewish riots of the 1920s, they seemed able to live in peace with their Arab neighbors. Only in the Christian quarter were Jews not wanted, especially anywhere near the Church of the Holy Sepulchre where, as in the past, they ran the risk of stonings and beatings.

It was in the late nineteenth century that the Western Wall remnant of the ancient Temple began increasingly to be seen by Jews in the country and abroad as a symbol of national unity and redemption. Whenever important Jews like Montefiore or Rothschild visited the city, they were taken to the wall for special prayers and celebration. Because the area of the Western Wall itself remained in Muslim possession, Jews had to pay a tax for the right to worship at the Temple ruin. (So, too, they paid "protection money" to the villagers of Silwan not to desecrate Jewish grave sites on the Mount of Olives.)[32] The narrow path leading to the wall was usually filthy from animals; whenever tables and chairs were brought to the wall, or awnings to protect worshipers from the sun, Muslims protested that Jews were converting the wall area into a synagogue. As the wall grew in nationalistic significance for Jews in the late nineteenth century, so the wall and the Temple Mount looming above it acquired greater political and religious importance for Muslims who had begun to feel threatened by the growing number of Jews in Jerusalem. The Western Wall–Temple Mount area was to become a source of conflict between Muslims and Jews throughout the twentieth century.

By the end of the nineteenth century the historic and abiding

Jewish men and women ritually separated
in prayer at the Western Wall
remnant of Herod's Temple.
(Photographed by Adrien Bonfils ca.
1860–1890)

religious importance of Jerusalem to Jews had resulted in a
major Jewish return to the city. In 1910 Jews of the old city and
new numbered 45,000, an absolute majority over twelve thousand Muslims and thirteen thousand Christians.[33] For the first
time the sheer weight of numbers persuaded Ottoman authorities to appoint a few Jews to the local municipal council which
continued to be dominated by Muslim leaders of the city.

It was also toward the end of the nineteenth century that a new
Jewish immigration to Palestine occurred, one that the old religious settlers in Jerusalem came to resent and fear. This new
immigration resulted directly from anti-Jewish pogroms in
Russia launched by Tsar Alexander III in 1881. Some twenty
thousand to thirty thousand Russian and later Rumanian Jews
immigrated to Palestine. Although many of them were religiously observant, few believed in the messianic deliverance of the
Jewish nation in its own land. On the contrary, they believed
that only through human labor, intelligence, and sacrifice could
Jews reclaim the land of Israel, including Jerusalem. They were
representatives of a new movement among Russian Jews, *Hov-*

evei Zion ("Lovers of Zion"), which saw in Palestine the one place on earth in which Jews could live free and full lives. They were the first *halutzim*, or pioneers, who called themselves Biluim, an abbreviation drawn from the first letters of the words in the biblical passage, "House of Jacob, come and let us go" (Isaiah 5:5). They and the pioneers who followed them in the Second Aliya (Jewish immigration) of 1903–1914 were influenced by the nationalistic ideas of such early Zionist writers as Moses Hess, Leo Pinsker, and Ahad Ha'Am. The new settlers established their colonies on the seacoast, where agricultural land was available and cheap. They avoided Jerusalem because they knew they were not welcome to the Orthodox rabbis who viewed their labor socialism as a blasphemous philosophy of forcing the hand of God. Their nationalism was also rejected by the rabbis who viewed God as the only author of the Jewish nation, and the law of God as Israel's sole guide in life. When the settlers began adapting the Hebrew language to secular use, the rabbis declared it a desecration of the holy scriptures.

The tensions between Jerusalem's Orthodox rabbis and the secular Zionist pioneers did not impede the upbuilding of the Jewish presence in the ancestral land. On the eve of World War I, as the result of both religious and Zionist immigration, there were 85,000 Jews in Palestine, 45,000 in Jerusalem alone. Jerusalem's Jews were far from a monolithic lot. Save for a common devotion to religious law and commonly shared city, differences far outnumbered similarities. Rather than one community there was actually a set of subcommunities (*kolelim*) consisting of Sephardim from Europe, Asia, and North Africa, and Ashkenazim from Russia, Rumania, Hungary, and virtually every country of the West. Each community was a small Jewish universe, with its own synagogue, slaughterhouse, yeshiva, and mikva bath. In principle the whole of Diaspora Jewry was represented in Jerusalem, contributing to that international character which Jerusalem has known since King David's time.

And there too was found the tiny community of Karaites, theological descendants of the Temple Sadducees and the Samaritans, who rejected the Talmudic law of the rabbis and clung to their belief that the Torah alone, without human interpretation, bound the people of Israel. A small number of Karaites survived time and disease and clung to Jerusalem as their Holy City. Immigrating originally from the Crimea, no more than ten families could still be found in Jerusalem in the late nineteenth century, praying in an underground synagogue, living separately from the Sephardim and Ashkenazim who shunned them as heretics.[34]

Zion had not ceased to exert its magnetic power over both religious and secular Jews. They disagreed religiously and politically over what the land and their return to it meant; but it was in the one same land that they found themselves together despite their disagreement. And in the early decades of the twentieth century secular Zionist Jews began to make their presence felt in Jerusalem, where political and religious tensions over the meaning of Zion developed into open and permanent conflict.

If returning to a city and rebuilding it is evidence of loving it, then indeed Jerusalem was well loved by Jews, Orthodox and Zionist alike. The repopulation of the old city and the building of a new city together redeemed Jewish history. In spite of so many tragedies, so many destructions, exiles, banishments, stretching over more than 2,500 years, the people had returned to Zion, the land and the city. Jerusalem was reclaimed for the nation. The twentieth century would show whether the nation could fight well enough and build well enough to preserve its place in the country and its claim to the city.

PART TWO

The History of Christian Conflict and Consecration in Jerusalem

In the Footsteps
of Jesus

*...The hour is coming when neither on this mountain
nor in Jerusalem will you worship the Father.*
—Gospel of John, 4:21

*O Jerusalem, Jerusalem, killing the prophets
and stoning those who are sent to you!
How often would I have gathered your children together
as a hen gathers her brood under her wings, and you would not!
Behold your house is forsaken and desolate!*
—Gospel of Luke, 13:34

*We shall be able to enter with you the cave of the Savior,
weep at the Sepulchre, kiss the wood of the Cross,
and ascend...the Mount of Olives.*
—Saint Jerome to a prospective pilgrim

*The Heavens are equally open over Jerusalem and over Britannia
for the Kingdom of God is within you.*
—Saint Jerome

Christians have always felt ambivalent about Jerusalem. The persecution of the prophets in Jerusalem culminated with the crucifixion of Jesus. But Jerusalem is also cherished in Christian belief as the city of the Resurrection, the place to which Christ will come again to redeem the world.

Christian ambivalence about Jerusalem produces two attitudes. The first is inspired by the New Testament Gospels which recount the ministry of Jesus in Galilee and his suffering in Jerusalem. Moved by the Gospel stories, the Christian believer undertakes a pilgrimage to the Holy Land, arriving there eager to retrace the footsteps of Jesus from Bethlehem to Nazareth to Jerusalem. It is a journey which ends on the Via Dolorosa, where every Friday the faithful reenact Jesus' walk from prison cell to the cross on Golgotha.

The second attitude acts as a brake on the pious excesses of worship in Jerusalem; it restrains the pilgrim from the romantic delusion that his journey has earned him a spiritual benefit denied to those not able to visit the Holy City. Influenced by the Letters of Paul and by the Gospel of John, this different attitude holds that what is essential to salvation is not place but faith, not pilgrimage but repentance and righteousness. In this spiritually sober attitude, the real Jerusalem is not the earthly city but the Heavenly Jerusalem, where the risen Christ dwells and from which he will return to judge all the cities of sin.

The tension between Jerusalem's sacredness and sacrilege in the Christian mind points all the way back to the earliest period of the New Testament. The Letters of Saint Paul, written twenty years after Jesus' death, show their author to be so preoccupied with the Second Coming of Christ and the Heavenly Jerusalem that the actual historical city, as well as the land of Israel, held little interest for him.[1] As a devout Jew, Paul undoubtedly esteemed Jerusalem's Temple. But he was prepared to argue that the faith which he personally experienced in Jesus Christ was not restricted to his own nation of Israel; rather, faith in Christ was open to gentile as well as Jew. Because of this new conception of faith, Paul believed that all the old Hebraic meanings of law, land, capital, and Temple must receive new meanings drawn from faith in Christ. The result, in Paul's thinking, was a certain de-spatialization of Jerusalem and its Temple.[2] We see this new meaning when Paul addressed the pagan converts of Corinth:

> Do you not know that you are God's temple and that God's Spirit dwells in you? If any one destroys God's temple, God will destroy him. For God's temple is holy, and that temple you are.
>
> 1 Corinthians 3:16–17

Here in Paul's mind, the authentic temple is not the one in Jerusalem but the spiritual one that God himself has created in the heart of every believer in Christ. Elsewhere Paul explicitly subordinates the earthly Jerusalem, the symbol of Hebraic law, to the Heavenly Jerusalem, where he believes that Christ, who has fulfilled the law, dwells: "Those who live by faith in Christ already live in the life of the new Jerusalem; they are already citizens of heaven."

The tendency to spiritualize or de-spatialize Jerusalem and the Temple continued in such later New Testament works as the Gospel of John, the Letter to the Hebrews, and the Book of Revelation. It is a practice which explains the strikingly negative attitude taken toward the Holy Land by such later influential Christian thinkers as Saints Augustine (354–430), Chrysostom (349–407), and Gregory of Nyssa (335–394). The attitude of Gregory was typical:

> When the Lord invites the blest to their inheritance in the
> Kingdom of heaven, He does not include a pilgrimage to Jerusalem
> amongst their good deeds; when He announces the Beatitudes, He
> does not name amongst them that sort of devotion. What
> advantage, moreover, is reaped by him who reaches those
> celebrated spots themselves? He cannot imagine that our Lord is
> living, in the body, there at the present day, but has gone away
> from us foreigners; or that the Holy Spirit is in abundance at
> Jerusalem, but unable to travel as far as us. . . . Change of place
> does not effect any drawing nearer unto God, but wherever thou
> mayest be, God will come to thee, if the chambers of thy soul be
> found of such a sort that He can dwell in thee and walk in thee.
> But if thou keepest thine inner man full of wicked thoughts, even
> if thou wast on Golgotha, even if thou wast on the Mount of
> Olives, even if thou stoodest on the memorial-rock of the
> Resurrection, thou wilt be as far away from receiving Christ
> into thyself, as one who has not even begun to confess Him.[3]

Granted that "change of place" may not affect the question of the soul's salvation, most Christians have felt that the places of Jesus' life and death hold a special meaning. Certainly this was true of Jesus' earliest followers, including his disciples. After Jesus' death they were driven by the need to preserve the memory of his personality and teachings. The detailed narratives of Jesus' life in the New Testament Gospels are a response to that need. When the Gospel writers portrayed the messianic career of Jesus from birth in Bethlehem to youth in Nazareth, then preaching in Galilee and finally death in Jerusalem, they provided a spiritual map for the believer, a sacred geography which kept alive the memory of the one whose glory briefly appeared on earth.

The map provided was not strictly speaking an historical one, but then the faith of the Gospel-reading pilgrim to the Holy Land is not a faith strictly tied to historical facts. When the pilgrim reverently kneels at Jesus' birthplace, at his prison cell, at the very spot on which the cross stood, the least important question in his mind is historical authenticity. To the Christian pilgrim no less than for Jewish and Muslim pilgrims, the holy sites are earthly vehicles to transport the spirit to the heavens. Pilgrim devotion at holy places has always been direct, literal, and simple—a peasant devotion which would have no appeal for an intellectual theologian like Gregory of Nyssa.

Yet the historical question lingers for every reader of the New Testament, believer or nonbeliever. Do the Gospels report with historical accuracy the life and teachings of Jesus? Are his suffering and death in Jerusalem correctly reported? These questions are not easily answered because none of the four Gospels was meant to be a factual biographical account of Jesus. The Gospels were written out of faith and for the faithful. The word "gospel" stands for the original Greek word *evangelion*, which meant "good news." The Gospels were written to urge faith in "good news" of the risen Christ; this was the theme around which the stories of Jesus' life and death were woven.

While acknowledging the confessional purpose of the Gospels, is it possible to discern features of the historical Jesus? The answer is yes if we concentrate on the Gospel of Mark, the earliest of the Synoptic Gospels and principal source of Matthew and Luke. In Mark a brief historical outline of the last year of Jesus' life emerges.

We can begin by saying that in the fifteenth year of the reign of Emperor Tiberias, Jesus, who was then about thirty years of age, emerged from an active Jewish messianic sect led by John the Baptist. Striking out on his own, Jesus undertook a career of preaching, teaching, and healing in the Galilee. Like John the Baptist, he exhorted his fellow Jews to prepare themselves for the imminent arrival of God's Kingdom by repenting of their sins and leading new lives of righteousness. He described the kingdom vividly through parables, in the style of many messianic preachers of this time. Jesus expected the kingdom to come suddenly, unexpectedly, "like a thief in the night." When the kingdom arrived, the dead would be raised from their graves, the sinful judged, and the righteous blessed and given their heavenly reward. The kingdom would make an end of this wicked world and usher in a new epoch of righteousness and justice. In his preaching, Jesus stood in the tradition of Amos and Isaiah. There were many such preachers of the kingdom in Jesus' lifetime; most of these "holy men" circulated in the Galilee, a place of intense religious, moral, and political activity.[4]

Although Jesus taught with authority, won disciples, and drew crowds, he viewed his ministry in Galilee as a failure. The people heard the message of repentance, but they refused to heed it. There were other problems. Jesus' radical preaching of the coming kingdom provoked some of the local Pharisees. They were offended by his disregard for scholarly interpretation of the Mosaic law, as when he uttered his unorthodox opinion that "the Sabbath was made for man, not man for Sabbath." The Galileans were known for their ritual laxity, and so Jesus, a Galilean, was willing to heal on the Sabbath. He allowed his disciples to pull corn on the Sabbath, and he also associated with tax collectors, prostitutes, and other "unclean" persons.

Galilee in the first century was known as a region of Jewish nationalistic revolutionary activity. Evidently Jesus encountered political difficulties there. Whether correctly understood or not, his prophecy of the kingdom was interpreted by the Roman tetrarch Herod Antipas (son of Herod the Great) in a political manner. Herod, residing in Tiberias, heard of Jesus' preaching and may have mistaken him as one of the many Galilean zealots who had been plotting revolt against Rome for the preceding thirty years.[5]

While Jesus was taken to be a revolutionary nationalist by both Roman and Jewish authorities, first in the Galilee and later in Jerusalem, the evidence is not compelling that he thought of himself in this way. His ministry in the Galilee showed him to be a religious and moral idealist whose preoccupation was the coming kingdom. He was not ignorant of the political implications of his preaching, but he seemed rather aloof to the popular yearning for national independence. What best showed his indifference to politics was his answer to the question he was asked about payment of taxes to the Roman government. "Is it lawful to pay taxes to Caesar or not?" he was asked by some Pharisees.

"Should we pay them, or should we not?" Here was a specifically political question meant to expose his loyalty. If he answered
in favor of paying taxes, he would be branded a traitor to the
Israelite nationalist cause; if he answered negatively, Roman
authorities would be convinced he was a nationalistic rebel. He
escaped the snare with an evasive answer: "Render to Caesar the
things that are Caesar's and to God the things that are God's"
(Mark 12:17). Clearly his mind was less on politics than with the
coming kingdom, before which both Roman power and Israel's
cause seemed to pale in significance.

If Jesus was not a Jewish political zealot, was he in any event
the Messiah foretold by the prophets and long awaited by the
Jewish nation? Mark's Gospel makes it clear that Jesus' earliest
followers believed him to be the expected Messiah and that they
preached this message to both Jewish and non-Jewish converts
to the new Christian faith. But it is far from certain that Jesus
thought of himself as the Messiah—perhaps a divinely chosen
human instrument for proclaiming the redemption, but not *the
person* of the Messiah. We must remember that in the first
century the Messiah was popularly conceived as Israel's national
champion, a royal descendant of the Davidic house, a quasi-
military figure who was expected to strike down the wicked
gentile kings of the world.[6] In no way does Mark's portrayal of
Jesus comport with this Jewish expectation. The later Gospel
writers Matthew and Luke introduced nativity stories and attributed the title "Son of David" to Jesus in order to link Jesus to
the royal ancestery of King David, who was actually born in
Bethlehem. But this linkage was dictated by the need to defend
Jesus' messiahship in light of the Jewish expectation that the
Messiah would come from the royal house of David.

Toward the end of the year in which he preached and healed
in Galilee, at the age of about thirty-one, Jesus traveled to
Jerusalem a few days before the Passover. Mark has us believe
that Jesus quit the Galilee because he was disappointed by the
lack of faith among the people and by the opposition he
encountered from the Pharisees and political authorities. This
may be true, but it is also true that as a good Jew Jesus would
have felt an obligation to travel to Jerusalem as a pilgrim at the
time of the Passover. The Gospel of Luke records that Jesus'
parents came annually to Jerusalem at Passover, and one year
brought along the young Jesus (2:22).

Jerusalem was the logical place for Jesus to be at the time of the Passover. He shared the common belief that the redemption would commence in Jerusalem. Perhaps too he hoped for a success in Jerusalem that had eluded him in the countryside.

Given his sense of mission, we can well believe Mark's report that upon entering Jerusalem Jesus went straightaway to the Temple. As in Galilee, he preached, attracted crowds, and aroused the apprehensions of religious authorities, in this case the Temple priests. According to Mark, it was his prophecy of the destruction of the Temple that most offended the priests and eventually caused his arrest. He is reported to have said, "Do you see these great buildings? There will not be left here one stone upon another, that will not be thrown down" (Mark 13:2).

If Mark accurately reports Jesus' words, it is understandable that the high priest and the Temple hierarchy would have opposed him. It was their duty to safeguard this sanctuary of the divine which was also the symbol of Israel's national glory. But it is doubtful that Jesus spoke the words that Mark attributed to him. These would not be the words of an itinerant preacher of the kingdom, a religious idealist who avoided commitment to political causes.

In the prophecy of the Temple's destruction we seem to have not the words of Jesus but rather the attitude of the later church. We know that soon after Jesus' death, contacts between Jerusalem's Jews and the new Jewish-Christians became contemptuous and violent. The prophecy of the Temple's destruction seems to reflect these bad relations.

Jesus' idealism makes it plausible that he *did* preach against the commercialization of Temple practice. Mark records that he "began to drive out those who sold and those who bought in the temple, and he overturned the tables of the money-changers and the seats of those who sold pigeons; and he would not allow anyone to carry anything through the temple" (Mark 11:15–16). And then he condemned the priests and other officials for making the Temple "a den of robbers."

The picture presented is that of a country preacher, a rather unsophisticated moral absolutist, who arrives in Jerusalem when the city is teeming with Passover pilgrims and encounters a frenzy of commercial activity at the Temple. It is not surprising that such a man would be offended by the materialism, the tawdry sights all around him. Today, the Temple Mount area, adjacent to a thriving market, has much the same air.

In Jesus' day the Temple was not only the central religious shrine, it was also the major industrial and banking facility of the nation. It received the annual Temple tax payed by Jews throughout the world. Great sums of money were desposited at the Temple by wealthy families and by the hundreds of elderly Jews who had come to retire in the Holy City. The daily sale of sacrificial animals was routinely conducted in the Temple area. At the Passover, with the city's population bloated by pilgrims from its normal 25,000 to as many as 125,000, one can imagine the congestion of pilgrims, priests, beasts, blood, and money.[7] Conduits carried blood drained from the sacrificed animals down the southern side of the Temple into the Kidron Valley, where it was used as fertilizer for vegetable gardens.[8] The Temple itself gleamed from the sheer amount of gold, marble, and bronze used in its construction. And outside the walls of the Temple were artisan shops of gold and silver, and other shops of incense and shewbread catering directly to Temple needs. One need not have had so lofty a view of religion as Jesus to have found himself nauseated by such sights in a city whose ritual purity was promptly restored at sunrise each morning by an army of street cleaners.[9]

It was Jesus' preaching of the coming kingdom at the Temple that drew the adverse reaction of Temple officials, who may have warned Roman police authorities about him. Messianic preaching at the Temple site during the Passover would have been interpreted as an incitement to revolt. Jewish Temple officials guarded against nationalistic expressions, particularly at festival time, lest the permanently stationed Roman garrison act against people and priests alike. Possibly Jerusalem's Jewish leaders had heard of the troubles Jesus had encountered in the Galilee with the Pharisees and officials of Herod Antipas.

In any event, Jesus was arrested for commiting a civil offense of sedition, and was subsequently executed (a common punishment for this offense) according to Roman practice, by crucifixion. He was not the first nor the last Jew to be so arrested and executed. The tragedy of Jesus' death is that he seems to have underestimated the effect of his messianic preaching in Jerusalem at the Passover. He expected to be heard; he did not expect to be arrested, and he did not intend to die. The story of Jesus' sorrow at Gethsemane ("Abba, Father, all things are possible, to thee; remove this cup from me...") and the final words attributed to him on the cross ("My God, my God, why hast thou forsaken me?")—these expressions of human vulnerability suggest a man who went to Jerusalem in the same idealistic and innocent spirit that guided his ministry in the Galilee. In that respect it was understandable for the Gospel writer Matthew, in denouncing Jerusalem for the crime of executing Christ, to put into Jesus' mouth words of condemnation: "O Jerusalem, Jerusalem, killing the prophets and stoning those who are sent you!" (Luke 13:34).

If the arrest and execution were essentially political, what are we to make of the two dramatic scenes in which Jesus is interrogated about his messianic claim by Jerusalem's high priest Caiaphas, and later by the Roman procurator Pontius Pilate? The first thing to be said is that it is doubtful that either event, certainly in the form presented, ever took place. Both scenes were shaped by later Christian attitudes at a time when it was in the interest of the church to shift blame for Jesus' death from the Roman state authority to Jewish religious leadership.[10]

According to Mark, it is the charge of blasphemy which prompts Jewish officials to turn Jesus over to Roman authorities. But if it is unlikely that Jesus ever appeared before a Jewish court (Sanhedrin) in Jerusalem, it is equally unlikely that he was ever charged with blasphemy. The technical Jewish charge of blasphemy was directed not against a claim of messiahship but rather for using the sacred, unutterable name of God, the tetragram YHWH (Yahweh). Nowhere in the Gospels is Jesus depicted as so blaspheming.[11]

The point of the scene in which Pilate interrogates Jesus about his messiahship is to absolve Pilate of direct responsibility for Jesus' execution by the device of allowing a Jewish mob to make the decision.

> And Pilate again said to them, "Then what shall I do with the man whom you call the King of the Jews?" And they cried out again, "Crucify him." And Pilate said to them, "Why, what evil has he done?" But they shouted all the more, "Crucify him." So Pilate, wishing to satisfy the crowd, released for them Barabbas; and having scourged Jesus, he delivered him to be crucified.
>
> Mark 15:12–15

If there is a kernel of historical truth in this scene, it lies in the reference to Barabbas, who supposedly belonged to the anti-Roman revolutionary party of the Sicarii.[12] If so, it is conceivable that Jesus was arrested in a police roundup of any number of persons taken to be political agitators.

The belief in Jesus' resurrection took shape among the disciples soon after his death. They were convinced of the miraculous powers of God who in the messianic era would judge the wicked and rouse the righteous from their graves. The Pharisees held strongly to a belief in the resurrection, sharply disagreeing with the Sadduceean Temple priests who rejected it. Jesus believed in physical resurrection. And the disciples, convinced that Jesus was the messianic agent of God's redemption, could not accept his death as anything more than a prelude to his resurrection and second coming. With this attitude Mark, at the conclusion of his Gospel, provided reports of the apparitions of Jesus which appeared to the disciples after the discovery of the "empty tomb."

Upon the death of Jesus, the disciples, fearing arrest and a fate similar to their leader, now branded a criminal, fled Jerusalem. Undoubtedly they were disappointed that Jesus' prophecy of the coming kingdom had not immediately been fulfilled, and that the prophet himself had come to an ignominious end. We cannot be certain what made them overcome disappointment and return to Jerusalem to preach the message of Jesus' lordship and the coming kingdom. The magnetism of his personality, the authority of his teachings, the wonder of his healings, his personal courage in the face of opposition—all these must have played a role in keeping the memory of Jesus alive in their minds.

To the disciples, the Resurrection meant that the condemnation of Jesus by his fellow Jews and his death by crucifixion were not a human defeat but a divine revelation, stages in the fulfillment of God's plan to judge and forgive human sins through the suffering and death of his chosen son. As Saint Paul was later to preach to the gentile community of Antioch: "For those who live in Jerusalem and their rulers, because they did not recognize him nor understand the utterances of the prophets which are read every sabbath, fulfilled these by condemning him" (Acts 13:27).

At first it was only the confession that "Jesus is lord" that distinguished the Jerusalem community of Jewish-Christians from Orthodox Jews. The new believers retained Jewish ritual forms, including circumcision; they continued to worship at Jerusalem's Temple and, like good Jews, shunned gentiles as "unclean." But it did not take long before the message of the new faith reached the ears of gentiles who sought admission to the church. A question arose: Need a gentile convert fulfill the Jewish ritual law in order to be counted a true member of the church? The Jerusalem community led by Peter and James, Jesus' brother, said he did, but Paul said he did not. Had Peter and James prevailed, Christianity would have remained an obscure Jewish sect which would have died in the aftermath of the Roman-Jewish war of 66–70. History, however, favored Paul, with the result that Christianity was gradually transformed into a distinct religion with a mission to the gentile world.

The new theological interpretation that Paul gave to the message of Jesus' lordship was eminently suited to the gentile world and accounts for the success of Paul's own proselytizing missions to the pagan communities outside Jerusalem and Palestine. As his letters to the communities in Galatia and Rome make clear, Paul held that the Mosaic law, in both its moral and ritual aspects, could not "justify" the believer and place him in the right relationship with God. If it could do so, there would have been no need for Jesus to have appeared on earth as the Christ. The purpose of the Mosaic law was to reveal how deeply and unalterably sinful a human being was and therefore how great was his need of divine forgiveness. Forgiveness was a gift embodied in the person of Jesus Christ, whose suffering and death became a sacrifice for the "remission of sins." Thus *not* the law but faith in Jesus Christ justified the sinner, granting him forgiveness and a new relationship to God. This meant that the grace of Jesus Christ was offered to Jew and gentile alike, apart from the law.

From the beginning of their faith, Christians suffered persecution at the hands of both Jewish and Roman officials of Jerusalem. Their troubles were caused less by preaching faith in Jesus Christ than by their politically alarming prophecies of the coming kingdom which attracted unruly crowds. When the leadership of the Jerusalem church passed from Peter to James after the year 44, relations with the Orthodox Jewish leadership seem to have improved. This was due to James's insistence on scrupulous adherence to Mosaic law. But James's own popularity with the people of Jerusalem proved his undoing, and he was executed in 62 on false charges brought against him by the high priest of the Temple.

The Roman-Jewish war of 66–70 drastically changed the political situation in Jerusalem and fueled the conflict between church and synagogue which was to worsen in later decades. A Christian polemic against Jews and Judaism developed in the last decades of the first century and is reflected in many of the anti-Judaic elements of the New Testament. After 70 c.e. Christians "were modifying the stories in the Gospels to intensify the hatred against the Jewish leaders by portraying them as having assumed full blame for the death of Jesus."[13] The most infamous example of the polemic is when the Gospel writer Matthew has Jews cry out at Jesus' trial, "His blood be on us and our children" (27:25). On the Jewish side, the attitude toward Christians remained the same: Christianity was viewed by the rabbis as a heresy whose leader, Jesus, was the illegitimate issue of an adulterous union between Mary and a Roman soldier.

After 70 c.e. the Jewish-Christians of Jerusalem, fearing to be associated by Roman authorities with the defeated Jews and their discredited religion, fled the capital and took asylum in the gentile town of Pella in Transjordan. They continued to practice their own Hebraized style of faith, but in a short period they disappear from sight. The future of Christianity lay west of Jerusalem and Palestine, in the gentile world of the eastern Mediterranean which had been evangelized by Paul. The final break between Judaism and Christianity was sealed in the year 90 at the rabbinical council in Jamnia on the seacoast of Palestine. Responding to the threat of Christianity and its own scriptural claim to be the fulfillment of Hebraic prophecy, the rabbis for the first time determined the authorized books of the Hebrew Bible, which contained no reference to Jesus the Galilean and his followers.

After the defeat of the Bar Kochba Rebellion and the destruction of Jerusalem in 135, Emperor Hadrian decreed the rebuilding of a new Roman city. Using the pattern of the cross—that gruesome symbol of Roman justice—transversal streets were laid out, leading from the main gateways; the city was neatly divided into quarters, giving old Jerusalem its shape to the present day. The present Damascus Gate takes its Arabic name (Bab el-Amud) from the great column constructed there honoring Hadrian and Antonius Pius—the point from which distances were measured throughout the land. Great stone statues of Roman deities filled the forum, only a hundred yards from Golgotha, and statues of the god Jupiter and the Emperor Hadrian rose from the rubble of the Jewish Temple, reminding Jews and Christians alike of that "Abomination of Desolation" of which the prophet Daniel spoke.[14]

Of the Jewish-Christians who fled the city, there could not have been more than a few hundred who returned to it after 135. Well into the fourth century, Jerusalem continued to be inhabited predominantly by Greek-speaking pagans, and the biblical scholar Jerome (340–420) tells us that in his own day Jerusalem held more Jews than Christians. The small Christian community that developed in Jerusalem and Bethlehem practiced its faith quietly and inconspicuously so as not to antagonize Roman civil authority. The first church, located on Zion hill, just outside Aelia Capitolina, was thought to be the headquarters of James, Jesus' brother, the first bishop of Jerusalem, and came to be called "the mother of all the churches."[15]

The Roman government could not have paid much attention to what it perceived as a small, insignificant sect, one of many in the religious world of the ancient Near East. As a result, the Christians of Jerusalem and Palestine escaped most of the persecutions directed against their brethren in the western provinces of the empire during the second and third centuries.

The center of Christian activity in the first three centuries was not Jerusalem, with its Jewish majority, but Caesarea, the magnificent harbor town built by King Herod on the Mediterranean, which became the capital of Roman Palestine. The great third-century theologian Origen lived in Caesarea and accepted invitations from Jerusalem's bishop Alexander Flavian to lecture to the local Christian community. He was drawn to the city by its unique collection of scripture manuscripts.[16]

The church historian Eusebius (260–340) was bishop of Caesarea, and he too traveled to Jerusalem to use its library; he left us a vivid account of how the efforts of his contemporary, Emperor Constantine, transformed Jerusalem into a Christian capital. During the second and third centuries local traditions had developed about the sites of Jesus' teaching, suffering, and death in Jerusalem. Pious excavators needed no encouragement to discover a few bones or stones or other artifacts to confirm popular belief. In most instances, Christians had to contend over holy territory with pagans, whose shrines could be found throughout Palestine. In 325, when Constantine gave his permission to Jerusalem's Bishop Makarios to restore the site of Jesus' tomb, a temple dedicated to Venus had first to be removed. Christian tradition held that the temple was built by Emperor Hadrian to hide the Christian holy place. Similarly, a cave accepted by the faithful as the birthplace of Jesus in Bethlehem was discovered beneath a temple consecrated to Adonis. Were the pagan sanctuaries deliberate desecrations of revered Christian sites, or were the Christians drawn to holy ground by preexisting pagan sanctuaries? The latter was a distinct possibility, for well into the fifth century pagan temples could be found all over Palestine, particularly in Gaza where there were eight pagan temples and Christians numbered only 250 out of a pagan population of fifty thousand. Perhaps the sanctified lures all believers, irrespective of their gods. This was as true in the ancient Holy Land as it is today when we see Jews, Christians, and Muslims worshiping at shrines that lie one on top of another.

While Jerusalem was a city of recognized Christian holy places well before Constantine's personal conversion to the church's faith in 322, it was that conversion which led to the Christianization of the Jewish capital. Christianity in the two and half centuries before the emperor's conversion had risen from a small and despised sect to a formidable religious force which included among its adherents numerous members of the Roman ruling classes. In the first decade of the fourth century Christians withstood the last, major persecution under Emperor Diocletian, and in the Edict of Toleration, published in Milan in 313, they gained recognition as members of a legitimate religion. One generation later they were destined to rule the empire.

After defeating his imperial rivals in the second decade of the fourth century, Constantine took control of the empire and immediately laid plans for a new capital in the East. It was a fortunate decision, for in the next century northern European tribesman advanced into the lands of the Mediterranean and gained control of the principal cities of France, Spain, Italy, and

North Africa. In 330 Constantine dedicated the Second Rome on the shores of the Bosphorus, at the site of the ancient Greek colony of Byzantium, naming the city after himself, Constantinople.

If Saint Paul was the first apostle to the gentile churches of the West, then Constantine was the first emperor to bring the church back to all the Christian peoples of the East. From its base in Constantinople, the imperial army marched to every border of Syria, Palestine, Egypt, and Mesopotamia, and Constantine's architects followed the army with plans for new churches, monasteries, and pilgrims' hospices. No city, save Constantinople itself, could boast more proudly of the emperor's works than Jerusalem.

Jerusalem owed its new Christian face to Empress Helena's pieties no less than to her son Constantine's constructions. The emperor's devout mother induced him to accept the Christian religion for his own. In 320 she set out on a long and arduous pilgrimage from Constantinople to the land of Christ's birth. The sight of the old empress mother kneeling in prayer at every village church that fell on her itinerary was reported back to the capital, moving the noble, rich, and powerful in later centuries to undertake similar pilgrimages of Christian humility.

Shortly before Helena's pilgrimage, the emperor ordered the building of three great churches in Jerusalem: the basilica over Christ's Tomb (named *Anastasis* or "Resurrection," and later renamed by the Crusader Franks the Holy Sepulchre); the church in Bethlehem which enclosed the Cave of the Nativity; and the Church on the Mount of Olives (Eleona), on the site of Christ's ascent to heaven.

We do not know exactly what role Helena played in the building of these reputedly magnificent churches. But in the popular mind, if Constantine was the emperor who built the new Christian Jerusalem, his mother was the inspiration behind the great building. So closely was Helena identified with Christian institutions in the Holy Land that ultimate tribute was paid to her in the form of a legend which arose some sixty years after her death. It came to be believed that the empress, guided by the Holy Spirit, discovered the True Cross. One of the more fascinating aspects of the legend was that Helena was helped in her discovery by a Jew who later converted to Christianity and, under his Christian name of Cyriacus, became the last of the

Jewish-born bishops of Jerusalem. History shows that there was such a man, but he was martyred two hundred years before Helena's lifetime under Emperor Hadrian, when Roman authorities saw little distinction between Christians and Jews. His Jewish name happened to be Judas.[17]

It was also told of Helena that in discovering the cross she acquired two of the original nails that had pierced Christ's flesh. She bestowed the nails on her son as a gift, one for his crown, the other to be used for his horse's bridle—thus showing that in the person of the emperor, prophecy was fulfilled. For when, as the Hebrew prophet Zechariah foretold, the harnesses of the horses are inscribed "Holy to the Lord," the messianic age is upon us (Zechariah 14:20).[18] Considering the enormous ecclesiastical projects undertaken by her son, there was no doubt in Helena's mind that the messianic age had indeed arrived.

The constructions of Constantine and the pious example of Helena attracted pilgrims from all parts of the world, with the result that Jerusalem became even more an international city than it had been in the past. Every type of European could be found at the local shrines, kneeling in prayer alongside Ethiopians, Armenians, Copts, Persians, Syrians, and Indians.

What was life in Jerusalem like for those dedicated souls who often, at risk of life and certainly at great expense, journeyed to the land of their Savior's birth and death? Drawing from a pilgrim's diary left by a noble French lady named Sylvia of Aquitaine, the American author Norman Kotker offers a splendid description of the exhausting daily devotions in Jerusalem's churches.

> All the pious exercises are there, enough to satisfy the most intense spiritual hunger—psalms in the morning, psalms at the third hour, the sixth hour, the ninth hour or at vespers, the vigils through the night with hymns and antiphons, mass at the great church in Golgotha, mass at the square church of the Mother of God, mass at the sepulchre of Lazarus or at the Church of the Nativity; readings, processions, lighting candles, listening to sermons, kissing the cross, the stone of the tomb, the pillar of the flagellation, the holy cup, the holy lance. All this was to bring [Sylvia] and her fellow pilgrims to eternal life in the Jerusalem that hovered in the sky directly above the earthly city, instead of to the gate of hell that pilgrims could see in the valley beneath the city walls. "Go

every one of you home now to your cells and sit there for a little
while," the Bishop of Jerusalem urged pilgrims and local residents,
to rest after such strenuous devotions; and then refreshed, come
back "to gaze on the holy wood of the cross, trusting each one
that it will profit us for our salvation."[19]

The churches, monasteries, priests, and pilgrims made Jerusalem "a metropolis of Christendom," a development recognized in 431 at the Council of Ephesus when the city was raised
above Caesarea as a new patriarchate, taking its place alongside
the ancient patriarchal sees of Rome, Alexandria, Antioch, and
Constantinople.

The second era of Byzantine construction in Palestine was
due to the Empress Eudocia, who made a pilgrimage in 438,
stayed to rule the country, and used her own funds to pay for
new churches and monasteries and for a new, high, surrounding
wall for the city. Eudocia's piety was known throughout the
land, and behind her charity was seen the hand of God. According to Jerusalem scholar John Wilkinson, her rebuilding of the
city's wall was seen as a fulfillment of Psalm 51:18: "Do good to
Sion in thy good pleasure; building thou the walls of Jerusalem. . . ."[20]

The third and last great era of church construction was
carried out by Emperor Justinian (483–565). Historians are
agreed that Jerusalem in Justinian's day reached the pinnacle of
Byzantine Christian glory. The city was teeming with Greek-
speaking priests and traders; the monasteries had drawn monks
from every corner of Christendom; the churches were open
night and day, and pilgrims kneeled every hour at the shrines.

Building on what Constantine and Eudocia had left him,
Justinian made of Jerusalem a proud and powerful eastern
miniature of the imperial capital. No one is sure exactly how
many churches and monasteries were standing in Palestine in
this time, perhaps as many as two hundred. This may not be an
exaggeration, for on the Mount of Olives alone there were said
to be twenty-four churches.

An image of this city is given to us in the fascinating
sixth-century mosaic map on the floor of the Greek Orthodox
Church at Madaba in Jordan. The artist gives us a bird's-eye
view of the Christian city as an enclosed, rounded, neatly
planned, tight little island of a city—a picture which belies the

visionary's wish to see Jerusalem on its hill pointing upward to the heavens. In the Madaba mosaic the emphasis falls upon Eudocia's great fortification wall with its high towers and carefully situated gates, six of them (minus the later Herod's Gate and New Gate). With proper Roman order the city is neatly halved by the elegantly colonnaded *cardo maximus* running from the northern Gate of the Column (Arabic *Bab el-Amud* or present Damascus Gate) to the southern Zion Gate. The great stone pillar is shown inside Damascus Gate, opened to a graceful, spacious area, quite in contrast to the cramped, busy intersection this area became in later centuries. The four quarters visible in today's old Jerusalem are suggested by the location of the Church of the Resurrection—opening out to the cardo's midpoint and fixing the spot where the adjacent Street of David intersects the cardo east and west. The Church of the Resurrection dominates the upper city and its complex of buildings, housing Golgotha and the tomb, which extend to the northern side of the city wall, near the Jaffa or Hebron Gate. At the southern end of the enclosed city, not far from the original City of David, we are shown the immense "new" Church of Saint Mary built under Justinian and today being excavated in the area adjacent to the Jewish quarter. The Church of Holy Zion is also shown, looking even larger than Mary's, looming up from its hill and facing opposite the Church of the Resurrection. The Golden Gate is depicted, but prominence is given to Saint Stephen's Gate (later called Lion's Gate), where the artist has shown through the tightly fitted golden stones the beginning of Jesus' path of suffering (Via Dolorosa).

One of the most famous pilgrims to journey to the Holy Land was the Roman biblical scholar Jerome, who in 385 occupied a cave in Bethlehem, near where church tradition placed the birth of Jesus. Jerome had the pious wish to retrace the footsteps of Jesus and the scholar's desire to carry out scriptural research in the land that gave birth to the Bible. He spent his days translating the Old Testament into Vulgate Latin from the Greek Septuagint version and the original Hebrew, sometimes checking with local rabbis on proper renderings. When he was not studying or visiting shrines he was writing to fellow scholars and the noble and pious ladies of his acquaintance, urging them to forsake the Roman Babylon for pilgrimage to the blessed home-land of Christ. To one he described the spiritual delights in store: "We shall be able to enter with you the cave of the Saviour, weep at the Sepulchre, kiss the wood of the Cross, and ascend... the Mount of Olives."[21]

His words moved two aristocratic ladies from Rome, Paula and her daughter Eustochium, who soon joined the tiny Bethle-hem community and remained to found one of the first nunner-ies in Palestine, for which the church awarded them sainthood. Paula demonstrated a religious athleticism typical of many Holy Land pilgrims who followed her in later centuries. She began her sacred journey at Golgotha and Christ's Tomb, then walked to Bethlehem and the cave where Christ was born; from Bethlehem to Zion hill, then down the Valley of Jehosophat and up the Mount of Olives, walking, weeping, praying along the way as Christ had done. From Jerusalem she traveled into the Judean hill country to visit Hebron and the tombs of the Hebrew patriarchs. From Hebron she descended to the Jordan River where Christ was baptized. Then, following the Jordan, she slowly made her way north, fighting heat and exhaustion along the way, and finally reaching the Sea of Galilee, stopping at every site associated with Christ's ministry.

Jerome probably accompanied Paula on her pilgrimage, but on several occasions the learned scholar spoke out against the theological error of those who assumed that pilgrimage alone, without true faith, could win grace and guarantee the salvation of the soul. Jerome was an admirer of the ascetic Saint Anthony who never found it necessary to leave his cave in the Egyptian desert in order to pilgrimage to Jerusalem. Echoing the senti-ments of both Anthony and Saint Paul, Jerome asserted that the key to faith was not place but right conduct. A pilgrim, he thought, should not merely visit Jerusalem but live a holy life there.[22] All these church thinkers knew of the legitimate romantic and mystical impulses of faith which could lead pil-grims to Jerusalem or to one of the great shrine centers in Europe; but they knew too of how pilgrimage could degenerate into superstition and idolatry, as with those pilgrims who went hunting for a saint's bone and other sources of magical grace.

In cautioning against excessive reverence for holy places, the church's theologians seized an opportunity to disparage Jewish religion. Both Origen and Jerome argued that the Christian faith had replaced Jewish worship at the Jerusalem-based Temple "with a universal faith which demanded no resort to any holy place in Jerusalem" but rather required spiritual fellowship with Christ, irrespective of place.[23] For Christian thinkers, the destruction of Herod's Temple was demonstrable evidence of the illegitimacy of Jewish religion, a religion whose original meaning and purity were superseded by the church's worship of Christ. In roughly similar fashion the Roman destruction of the Jewish city of Jerusalem confirmed Christians in the belief that, as apostles Paul and John had said, the true Jerusalem was not on earth but in heaven. The subtlety of such theological distinctions, however, was wasted on most pilgrims. The pilgrim saw no contradiction between the Jerusalem of earth and heaven. He felt that to walk in Jesus' footsteps in the earthly city only brought him closer to the blessed Jerusalem-on-High.

Byzantine authorities in Constantinople ruled the eastern provinces of Syria, Palestine, and Egypt for three hundred years until the Persians mustered the strength to challenge the Greeks in 610. Two decades of war between Persians and Greeks weakened both peoples and made them an easy conquest for Muslim warriors who in the 630s laid claim to the civilized world in the name of an old God heralded by a new prophet. One of the most interesting developments in the defeat of the Byzantine Christians at the hands of both the Zoroastrian Persians and the Arab Muslims was the disloyalty shown by native subjects. Jews and Samaritans were treated with harsh intolerance in the Byzantine empire, so it was not surprising that they should welcome defeat of their Greek masters by the Asiatic conquerors. But what dismayed the Greeks was the sight of Syrians, Armenians, Copts, and other fellow Christians rushing to aid their enemies. What the Greeks should have known was that their three-hundred-year effort to impose their superior and haughty culture and theology on Eastern Christians produced only hostility and a yearning for independence.

The Byzantine empire had a highly centralized government, run almost exclusively by Greeks out of Constantinople—a small imperial clique which taxed heavily all subject peoples and showed little tolerance for cultural diversity among non-Greeks. The Emperor Theodosius (379–395) had in fact made conformity a legal requirement in the Byzantine state. The emperor was to be accepted as Christ's vice-regent on earth, and his policies took on the appearance of semisacred enactments. While Armenian, Aramaic, Syriac, Coptic, and Arabic were used throughout the realm, Greek was the language of administration and preferred by those who wished to rise in the state hierarchy. But the Eastern Christians not only had their own languages, over generations they had developed their own local church traditions in architecture and iconography, and in their warm, simple liturgies which were so different from the rich and showy ceremonies of the Greeks.

The area in which the Byzantine Greeks were most insistent on conformity was that of religious doctrine, and it was precisely in this area that the local Christians of the East proved most rebellious. No sooner had Emperor Constantine laid the basis for imperial rule in the new capital than trouble broke out in the form of a theological heresy fostered by an Egyptian monk named Arius. Constantine convened the First Ecumenical Council in Nicaea in 325 to combat Arianism. In the appearance of Arianism and in a number of other later heresies we can recognize the first deep and sure stirrings of nationalistic independence on the part of the different ethnic peoples of the Christian East against their Greek masters.

The conflict over heresy set the patriarchal sees of Rome, Alexandria, Antioch, and Constantinople against one another. Jerusalem, which did not become a patriarchate until 451, remained on the edge of conflict but felt every religious and political tremor in the realm. The city's church leaders were beholden to the patriarchate of Constantinople for their appointments and took the side of the emperor on most issues. But a majority of non-Greek, Aramaic, and Syriac-speaking lay Christians throughout Palestine resented the Greek bishops for their indifference to the needs of the village churches. It was the beginning of a wound in the Christian life of the Holy Land which festered through the centuries and has continued in the churches of Jerusalem to the present day.

What lay behind the charge of heresy was a theological disagreement over the person of Christ. The belief in Christ's resurrection inspired the Christian religion, but it was not long after the death of Jesus that Christians were debating the questions: Who was Christ? What was Christ's relationship to God?

What must a Christian believe to be certain of salvation? Answers differed; theologians contended; rival schools of thought developed, and the great patriarchal cities chose different sides. Today, few besides students of theology know what these controversies were about, and fewer still care; but during the early Byzantine period, theological speculation enjoyed the popular appeal we associate today with the daily horoscope or politics. The late fourth-century church father Gregory of Nyssa, while visiting Constantinople, recorded his surprise at ordinary people's absorption with abstruse theological reasoning:

> If you ask someone how many obols a certain thing costs, he
> replies by dogmatizing on the born and unborn. If you ask the
> price of bread, they answer you, the Father is greater than the Son,
> and the Son is subordinate to Him. If you ask is my bath ready,
> they answer you, the Son has been made out of nothing.[24]

The Egyptian theologian Arius, whose ideas captured the imagination of local Christians and spread northward in the empire, contended that Jesus was not identical to God in divinity but of a similar substance. He thus allowed the conclusion that the Son was subordinate to the Father in the Trinity. If Arius's view went uncontested, the Copts might influence other church communities to stand with them against the teachings of the bishops in Constantinople. Emperor Constantine, recognizing political trouble, convened the bishops in Nicaea in 325 to settle the issue. Accusing Arius of simplifying and distorting the profound metaphysical mystery of Christ's relationship to God, the bishops ruled that Christ was of "one substance" with God, the Son coequal in divinity with the Father. This ruling became a criterion—the "Orthodox" standard of faith against which every deviation was labeled heresy and promptly anathematized. For the next two hundred years the Christians of Palestine, Syria, and Egypt found themselves torn between the Orthodox view of faith defended by the emperor and the many heretical doctrines which at different times had the support of the patriarchates of Alexandria and Antioch and sometimes Constantinople itself. During this whole exciting, if troubled, period it was impossible for an ordinary Christian to know what to believe no less than whom to believe.

The greatest of the theological crises occurred in the fifth century with the emergence of the Monophysite heresy, which proved more successful than Arianism in winning adherents among Eastern Christians. Monophysitism came into being as a reaction to yet another heresy, Nestorianism, which took root in Constantinople, found favor in Antioch, and eventually spread eastward to become the dominant outlook of the Christians of Persia and Mesopotamia. Nestorianism stressed the human nature of Christ at the expense of divinity. The Monophysites took the opposite view—that Christ was of "one nature" (hence *mono-physis*), wholly divine, so that every human property of Christ was a mere appearance, not an essential part of his divinity. In a few decades Monophysitism became the dominant theological view of Coptic and Armenian churches. The great Syrian churchman Jacob Baradeus, in the fifth century, spread the Monophysite doctrine among the native Christians of Syria and the Arab tribesmen of the Banu Ghassan and Banu Taghib, all of whom came to be called "Jacobites." By the early seventh century, on the eve of the Arab invasion, the majority of Eastern Christians were Monophysites. If Monophysites were enemies to the Orthodox Christians, they found friends with Muslims. For Muslims came to believe (some think under the influence of Monophysite missionaries) that Christ on earth, as a prophetic forerunner of Muhammad, was God-sent, knowing no ordinary human limitation, experiencing no suffering and death.

The Fourth Ecumenical Council was convened in 451 in Chalcedon so that Orthodox churchmen could condemn Monophysitism. They did so by declaring that Christ was both human and divine, two distinct natures mysteriously united but unmixed. In Jerusalem the local Monophysites, hearing that their faith had been condemned, rioted, forcing the Orthodox bishop (just promoted by the Chalcedon Council to patriarch) to flee the city.

This was not the first time Jerusalem had been put in turmoil by heresy. In the second century the city had given no welcome to another heretical group, the Ebionites, spiritual descendants of the original Jewish-Christians, who continued to practice Jewish ritual and emphasized the ethic of Jesus above his messiahship. And in the third century the renowned Origen had provoked the Orthodox establishment with his rationalistic lectures which drew heavily from pagan Greek ideas and seemed to call the bodily resurrection of Christ into question. So controversial were Origen's lectures that his bishop, Demetrius of Alexandria,

A sixth-century mosaic map of Jerusalem
found at Madaba, southeast of the
Dead Sea, in 1897.

was compelled to recall him. A similar controversy was provoked by a fellow African theologian Pelagius, who visited
Jerusalem in the early years of the fifth century and made an
enemy of Jerome. Jerome, an arch conservative respected by
Orthodox bishops, attacked Pelagius for minimizing man's sinful corruption and exaggerating his moral freedom. The conflict
deepened when Jerusalem's maverick Bishop John sided with
the ideas of Origen and Pelagius, drawing down on him the
wrath of Jerome's circle in Bethlehem. It is said that for years
afterward Christians in Jerusalem and Bethlehem were not on
speaking terms.[25] Perhaps it was this controversy that prompt-
ed Jerome to say of Jerusalem that like all other cities in the
world, it was a place filled with prostitutes, actors, and jesters.

The Arian heresy must also have had many adherents in the
Holy Land. When the venerable monk Saint Saba, who lived in
a cave in the desert five miles east of Bethlehem, prevailed on
Emperor Justinian to drive the Arians out of the country, he was
careful not to condemn the many Monophysites in Palestine,

because the emperor's wife, Theodora, was sympathetic to their view of Christ. Theodora, in theological matters, followed in the footsteps of the devout Empress Eudocia, who, before she recanted, passionately promoted the "one nature" doctrine of Christ against its Orthodox detractors in Jerusalem.

The church in Jerusalem was in turmoil right up to the time of the Arab invasion. Patriarch Sophronius, who surrendered the city to the Muslim conquerors in 638, spent his last days fighting the Monothelite heresy, a refinement of Monophysitism widely accepted in Palestine and Syria.[26] Sophronius was something of a hero among his fellow Orthodox bishops for refusing heretics the right to worship at Jerusalem's shrines and jailing them whenever he could.

Clashes between Greek Orthodox and native Monophysites occurred in Jerusalem and in villages throughout Palestine and Syria; but the strategic coastal cities of Tyre, Acre, Caesarea, Jaffa, and Gaza were quiet. Here the emperor maintained military bases, and the native Christians had little choice but to conform to the emperor's faith—which led Monophysites to refer to them contemptuously as Melkites, or "the King's men."

In the spring of 614, after first conquering Antioch (611) and Damascus (613), the Persian soldiers of Sassanid King Khosroes II Purvis ("Victorious") invaded Palestine and in late April laid siege to Jerusalem. A thousand years earlier, Greeks and Persians had fought and the Greeks had bested their foe, preserving Western culture from those whom they considered "Asiatic barbarians." Now the Persians, in the eyes of Jews, Samaritans, Armenians, Syrians, and other "Asiatics," had come to liberate them from the intolerant Greeks. Jews and Samaritans reportedly put aside their ancient enmity and cooperated in guiding the Persians from Galilee to the Byzantine naval stronghold at Caesarea and from there inland to Jerusalem.

The Holy City paid a high price for its liberation. The Persian siege lasted nineteen days, and when it was over the city lay in ruins: churches looted and burned, monasteries destroyed, priests and people slaughtered where they were found. In all, 35,000 were killed and some sixty thousand taken into slavery. The Persians destroyed Constantine's most precious monuments, including the Anastasis Church. A legend states that the Church of the Nativity in Bethlehem was spared because the conquerors were moved by the sight of a mosaic over the church door depicting the Wise Men in Persian robes bringing gifts to the Christ child.

The humiliation of the Christians was deep and shocking. Christian captives were marched off to exile in Mesopotamia, with the Orthodox patriarch Zacharias leading them. The church's store of relics was seized along with (ultimate humiliation!) the True Cross. All these sacred objects were made a gift to the Nestorian Queen Meryem, whose community enjoyed security and prosperity in Persia under the Zoroastrian rulers.

There is a terrible story that Jews, seeking to revenge themselves on their former Christian masters, purchased Greek slaves from the Persians in order to massacre them outside the present Jaffa Gate, at the site of Mamilla Pool.[27] Knowing how well their own brethren were faring in Persia and Mesopotamia, Jerusalem's Jews petitioned the Zoroastrians to turn the management of the city over to them. Led by one with the illustrious name Nehemiah, Jerusalem for a few short years was again a Jewish capital. But the Persians, recognizing that control of Syria and Palestine required cooperation from local Christian communities, gave the city back to the local Monophysites. The treachery of the Jews in Palestine was not forgotten nor forgiven by the Byzantines in Constantinople, and they would soon get their revenge when a still powerful imperial army mounted a counteroffensive against the Persians.

The Persians eventually permitted the Orthodox Christians to rebuild their churches and monasteries, a task led by a monk named Modestos, who came to be called "Restorer of Zion" and later became patriarch of Jerusalem. Persians continued to rule the former Byzantine provinces, but they did so uneasily. They had won these areas in battle, but the central Greek power and authority in Constantinople remained undefeated. For the Greeks, the loss of Jerusalem and the theft of the True Cross by Asiatic infidels were blasphemous events begging for revenge. The aggressive new Christian Emperor Heraclius laid plans for a reconquest of the Christian East.

Launching a military campaign in 622, Heraclius skillfully penetrated Persian defenses and drove his imperial army deep into Mesopotamia. Nineveh was taken in 627, and the Byzantines continued fighting until the Persians had no choice but to agree to a peace which forced them to return Syria, Palestine, Egypt, and some areas of Mesopotamia. Jerusalem was reconquered in 630, Christ's cross was returned, and Greek pride was restored. The city celebrated the event with a solemn parade of Orthodox bishops bearing the cross from the Golden Gate, opposite the Mount of Olives, across the city to the remains of the Anastasis Church.

But the joy was not to last. Only eight years later Arab Muslims swept the Byzantine forces away, forever changing the future of the Middle East.

God Wills It!

Come forward to the defence of Christ,
O ye who have carried on feuds,
come to the war against the infidels.
O ye who have been thieves, become soldiers.
Fight a just war...
Set forth, then, upon the way to the holy Sepulcher;
wrest that land from the evil race, and keep it for yourself.
That land which floweth with milk and honey —Jerusalem...
—Pope Urban II, addressing the Council of Clermont in 1095

(Pope Urban's summons was interrupted by his enthusiastic
listeners with cries of "Dieu lo vult! God wills it!")

In 633 Arabs invaded Palestine near Gaza. Five years later the
fortress city of Jerusalem was starved into submission. Palestine
did not again see a Christian ruler for 350 years.

Greek Patriarch Sophronios refused officially to surrender
Jerusalem to anyone but the caliph Umar himself, and so the
caliph, acknowledging the religious importance which Jerusalem
had already acquired for the Muslim faithful, agreed to the
patriarch's request. Legend has it that the two men came
together on the Mount of Olives, the patriarch riding up on an
ass, his ecclesiastical robes trailing behind on the stone path,
while the caliph, in coarsely woven battle tunic, awaited him on
the summit, mounted on his favorite white camel. We do not
know what the two men said to each other, but it must have
been amicable, for when they descended together Sophronios
took Umar on a guided tour of the city, stopping first at the
Temple Mount. Other Christians resented the sight of the Arab

infidel standing before this holy place; recalling the prophet Daniel's words, they saw the Muslim leader as that "Abomination of Desolation standing where he should not."

But Umar was himself shocked at the sight of abominations on the Temple Mount. The gates were so filled with broken stones and debris remaining from the previous Persian destruction that it was impossible to enter the sacred enclosure. With his own hands the caliph cleared a narrow path through the rubble and, getting down on all fours, crawled to the Temple Mount; the patriarch, dressed in silk robes and dangling gold chains, obligingly followed him on hands and knees. Reaching the flat open area, Umar was further startled. To show their contempt for the discredited Jewish religion, Christians had made a practice of heaping garbage where the Temple's inner sanctum, the Holy of Holies, once stood. Umar immediately ordered the removal of the filth and won the respect of Jews forever after.

From the Temple Mount the two leaders proceeded north across the city, stopping outside the Anastasis Church just when the midday hour of Muslim prayer arrived. Sophronios, wishing to show his respect for the religious authority of the caliph (or Muhammad's "successor"), invited Umar to pray within the church. Legend states that Umar graciously refused, saying that if he were to do so his followers would immediately seize the church for a mosque. The caliph retreated a few hundred yards and laid his rug on the open ground for prayer. The spot was later made sacred by the dedication in 935 of the Omariya Mosque, a small building southwest of the Church of the Holy Sepulchre, which is guarded today by an immense Sudanese who bars entrance save for the Muslim faithful.

The legend of Umar's graciousness was repeatedly told to emphasize the fundamental Muslim tolerance toward Christians and Jews who, as "People of the Book," were accorded protective (*dhimmi*) status under Islamic (*Shari'a*) law. Both peoples were also required to pay the head tax (*djizya*) which the Koran stipulated was to be levied on all subject peoples "in recognition of their submissive status." Often the head tax went to pay for the army required to protect non-Muslim subjects. However much non-Muslims resented this tax, it seldom proved as heavy a burden as the tax imposed by previous Byzantine rulers.

The arrival of the Muslims brought a new religious authority to the Near East, but the basic pattern of life for Jews and Christians in Palestine was changed very little. As protected subjects they could not carry arms, but they were free to work, travel, and, most important, to worship in their own way without interference. For Monophysite Christians and Jews and Samaritans, Muslim rule meant freedom from the resented Greek Orthodox. It was also a gain that Muslim administration recognized each distinct ethno-religious group as a semi-autonomous "nation" (*millet*), free to conduct its communal affairs under its own elected leaders. For the first time in their history, Monophysites and other heretical Christians were accorded the status of a legally recognized community.

Muslim tolerance of Greek subjects can be explained by a realistic respect for the still powerful Byzantine military which might easily be provoked into trying to reconquer the Middle East. Apart from their fear, Muslim rulers genuinely admired the Greeks, particularly for their talents in commerce, art, law, and medicine. Greeks rose to high positions in the Umayyad royal court, and no caliph was without his Greek political adviser. The caliph Abd al-Malik (685–705) turned to Greek architects and craftsmen to build the Islamic shrine of the Dome of the Rock at the site of the Abramaic stone of sacrifice on the Temple Mount. What came of their efforts was an enlarged imitation of Constantine's Anastasis Church, its interior completed by finely wrought Byzantine-style mosaics bearing Koranic inscriptions.

Acts of persecution against Christians by Muslim rulers occurred from time to time, but they were more the result of the prejudices of individual caliphs than of any basic policy of the Muslim state. The first signs of serious trouble occurred in the late Umayyad period when Abd al-Malik introduced forced conversion of native Christians, particularly among the Monophysites of Syria and the Arabic-speaking desert Ghassan tribesmen. Within a hundred years of the Muslim conquest, Syria changed from a Christian to a Muslim country: Arabic replaced the native Syriac and Aramaic languages and began rivaling Greek as the language of administration.[1] Many native Christians in both Syria and Palestine found it economically and politically expedient to convert to Islam; and throughout the Muslim period large numbers of Muslims immigrated to Syria and Palestine from the eastern desert peninsula. Palestine, however, was inhabited predominantly by Greek Orthodox right up to the time of the first Crusade at the close of the eleventh century; Jerusalem, Bethlehem, and Nazareth remained almost exclusively Christian towns.

The Umayyad dynasty of Damascus held power until 750 when it was forced out by the rival Abbasids of Baghdad. The Abbasids were religious conservatives, less tolerant of cultural diversity than the cosmopolitan Umayyads. Ruling from distant Baghdad, the Abbasids showed little interest in the peoples of Palestine. The result for decades was chaos: Christians, Jews, and Muslims were exploited at the hands of unscrupulous local governors. The worst instance of systematic Muslim persecution of Christians occurred under the Abbasid caliph al-Mutawakhil (847–861), who prohibited Christians and Jews from riding horseback, forced them to wear distinctive clothes, seized churches, forbade any public display of the cross, abolished votive candles, and prevented the ringing of church bells. He also ordered the forced conversion to Islam of all native Arabic-speaking Christians. And he encouraged Orthodox Christians to flee north into Byzantine territory; many did so, feeding the appetite for revenge among Greeks in Constantinople.

Mutawakhil's rival as a persecutor was the later Fatimid caliph al-Hakim, who in his madness turned against the religion of his Christian mother and from 1004 to 1014 went on a fiery rampage against churches in Syria and Palestine, burning and looting some thirty thousand before he finished. When he was not burning churches he was compromising them by having mosques built on their roofs.[2] In 1009 he ordered the destruction of the Anastasis Church because, it is said, he took offense at the fraudulent Holy Fire ceremony performed there annually at Easter even by the Greek Orthodox. According to the historian Steven Runciman, "The persecution only stopped when al-Hakim became convinced that he himself was divine."[3] Thereafter the caliph had a change of heart, providing money for the rebuilding of churches and allowing thousands who had been forcibly converted to Islam to return to Christianity.

For every persecuting caliph there was also a Muslim ruler whom Christians could thank for his generosity. One of the most celebrated was the grandfather of al-Mutawakhil, the Abbasid caliph Haroun al-Rashid (ruled 783–809), who found in the French king Charlemagne an important ally against the ever-threatening Byzantines. A legend states that Rashid made Charlemagne a present of the keys of the Church of the Resurrection and encouraged him to make a pilgrimage to the Holy City. We know that the French king lavished money on Jerusalem and the Holy Land, rebuilding old churches and adding new ones, including the important Church of Saint Mary of the Latins in the Kidron Valley. He constructed numerous new hospices for Western pilgrims whose numbers were rapidly increasing in the ninth century.

Finally, in the late tenth century a resurgent Byzantium made good its threat to regain its former eastern provinces. Through the aggressive battle ability of the Macedonian emperor Nicephorus Phocas (963–969), known as "the white death of the Saracens," large areas of Syria, Armenia, and Mesopotamia were reconquered. Despite a declaration that the liberation of Jerusalem was a "holy obligation," the Greeks made no attempt to drive the Muslims out of the city; they preferred to concentrate on the lucrative coastal cities. When Jerusalem's Patriarch John asked the emperor to deliver the Holy Tomb from the Infidel, the local population, still preferring Muslims to the Byzantine Greek, seized the patriarch and burned him at the stake.[4]

Phocas was succeeded as emperor by an equally brilliant general, John Tzimisces (969–976), who also happened to be Phocas's cousin, murderer, and his wife's lover. In 975 Tzimisces continued where Phocas left off. He invaded Palestine from the north and seized Tiberias and Nazareth, but instead of going south to Jerusalem he then turned north to secure the strategically important coastline. The next year he died suddenly, and the Byzantine counteroffensive died with him. Instead of fulfilling the sacred obligation to drive out the infidel and restore the dignity of Christ's homeland, Palestine was left for another hundred years to the Muslims. Yet time had turned in favor of Christians. The Byzantine emperor Michael IV persuaded the Fatimid caliph in 1036 to allow the rebuilding of all the churches of the Holy Land; and, no less important, he won back from the caliph the right to appoint the Orthodox patriarch of Jerusalem.[5]

The seed of Christian holy war planted by Byzantines would bear fruit a century later under the Franks. Until the Franks invaded Jerusalem in 1099, the city remained under Muslim rule, exchanging hands between Egyptian Fatimid and Seljuk Turkish rulers for the last thirty years of the eleventh century.

If Arab rule of Palestine was a boon to native Eastern Christians, it was a bane to Western pilgrims. The pilgrim who was willing to bear the considerable expense of a sea voyage found his trip endangered by numerous Arab pirate ships which preyed in the eastern Mediterranean. If he succeeded in reaching the shores of Asia Minor, he found his overland journey to Palestine interrupted frequently by bandits or hostile Muslim officials who were suspicious of foreign travelers. If he arrived in Jerusalem he was safe, but the risk of returning home was so great that often he decided to spend his life in one of the local monasteries. One of the rare exceptions was the French bishop Arculf who went on pilgrimage in 670, spent three years touring holy sites in Palestine and Syria, and returned home to report how pleasantly surprised he was that the churches were in good condition and that Christians were left alone to worship in peace. But the hardships of the pilgrim traffic slowly took their toll. In 870 a Frenchman named Bernard the Wise "found [Charlemagne's] establishments still in working order, but empty and beginning to decay."[6]

In the late tenth century a Byzantine force eliminated Muslim pirate strongholds in the eastern Mediterranean and reopened the sea lanes to traders and pilgrims. Once again ships set sail from the port cities of Spain, France, and Italy, bound for Asia Minor and the Holy Land. A fresh motive for pilgrimage was provided by the belief that the rigors of pilgrimage to the Holy Land were an acceptable penance for the sinner and a source of indulgence against future sins. The jails of Europe were emptied, and criminals found themselves on the top deck of ships alongside hundreds of priests, peasants, titled lords, and fine ladies.

Another stimulation to pilgrimage was relics. Often the pilgrim went first to Constantinople to see with his own eyes the great collection of relics connected with Christ's life. The Crown of Thorns was there and the Seamless Garment; the cloth from Edessa which bore the image of Christ's face; and Saint Luke's portrait of the Virgin, and the hair of the Baptist, and the mantle of Elijah. Pilgrims could see all these precious objects and then travel to Palestine in the great hope of finding a bone or some remain from one of the numerous saints, martyrs, and holy men who had ended their lives there. If the pilgrim was successful—and many were successful by virtue of the sellers of relics who profited greatly from their trade—he took his precious possession back to the village church or local monastery where it was duly enshrined, inspiring others to make their own sacred journey to the land of Christ.

Steven Runciman describes the practice:

> When a lady of Maurienne brought back from her travels the thumb of Saint John the Baptist, her friends were all inspired to journey out to see his body at Samaria and his head at Damascus. Whole embassies would be sent in the hope of securing some such treasure, maybe even a phial of the Holy Blood or a fragment of the True Cross itself. Churches built in the West were called after eastern saints or after the Holy Sepulchre; and often a portion of their revenues was set aside to be sent to the holy places from which they took their names.[7]

What Runciman describes is seen in Jerusalem today among the Christian devout who, unable to find a sacred bone, grab eagerly for specially blessed candles or olive wood crosses, taking these symbols home to link them and their homes and their country permanently to the land of Christ's birth.

The practice of collecting memorabilia continued until the late eleventh century when a pope and a handful of barons and knights decided it was high time to recover the very land which had given their relics such precious meaning. Their actions—the Crusades—proved to be a spectacular epoch in the history of the Middle East. In successive waves for two hundred years, from the end of the eleventh century to the end of the thirteenth, the cream of Europe's nobility, hundreds of burghers, hordes of peasants "took the cross." Arming themselves with swords and metal helmets, they rode east to do battle with the infidel Muslim to retrieve the Tomb of Christ.

Never before (or since) was the blessed tomb so savagely fought for. The cross of the Crusader, it seems, became a sword to cut a path of blood from the cathedral towns of northern France to Constantinople, and from there to Antioch and finally to Jerusalem.

The Crusaders were called Franks because most came from

France, and they showed human traits common to their region—courage, piety, intolerance, and a streak of wanton cruelty. The Franks built castles in every land they conquered and designed hundreds of churches in Romanesque style; beyond these monuments there was little of cultural value they bequeathed to the Middle East which they ruled for generations.

Crusader conquests opened a wide road for masses of European pilgrims to voyage to the Holy Land, heightening the sanctity of Jerusalem's shrines and enriching Italian maritime merchants. From the point of view of Greeks, Armenians, Jacobites, and other Eastern Christians, it would have been better had the strangers stayed home. Those who lived in the Holy Land found the Western Latin Christians to be arrogant, boorish, brutal, and ignorant of Eastern Christians, whose distinct language, dress, and liturgy held little meaning for the Franks.

The truth is that the Christian East brought on its own troubles. The Franks would never have thought of marching so far from home if the Byzantine emperor himself, Alexius I Comnenus, had not first invited them. The invitation came in the form of a request to Pope Urban II for volunteer troops to strengthen the emperor's own army against the advances of Seljuk Muslims, the fierce Turkish tribesmen who in the late eleventh century had seized much of Byzantine Asia Minor and were threatening Constantinople. When the first Crusaders arrived in Constantinople in 1096, Alexius had already won a few battles on his own and had thwarted Turkish ambitions. But the pope's knights had not come so far merely to solve the Byzantine security problem; theirs was a nobler goal: the reconquest of Jerusalem.

The French Catholic pope had many reasons to go to the aid of the Greek Orthodox emperor. Ever since the Great Schism of 1054, Latin and Greek halves of Christendom had been torn apart by a doctrinal dispute in which Greeks had refused to recognize the supremacy of the pope, and the latter had in turn excommunicated the Orthodox patriarch of Constantinople. Urban reasoned that in helping to defeat the Turks, Emperor Alexius would be in his debt and more inclined to reconsider the question of papal supremacy.

Pope Urban was also anxious about the Muslim threat to the Eastern church. He was already supporting Christian armies to drive Muslims out of Sicily. Byzantine was the eastern, protective wall of Europe; were it to fall to the Muslims, Rome itself would come under attack by the infidel as it had once before in the ninth century.

The most important consideration in Urban's mind lay in devising ways to extend the church's power in Europe. For decades the continent was in perpetual turmoil because of petty wars between feudal barons. The pope reasoned that it would be vastly better if the barons directed their hostile energies against a real enemy, united as one Christian nation under the banner of the pope. The liberation of Jerusalem from Muslims was seen as the ideal war—a *holy* war which could bring a new spiritual and political order to Europe.

The pope also considered the pilgrimage problem. Seljuk control of Asia Minor had interrupted pilgrim traffic. When pilgrim groups were not directly attacked, taxes and other harassments were imposed on the defenseless travelers. The powerful French monastery of Cluny, which supported Urban and spearheaded the moral reform of Europe, advocated pilgrimage and was eager to see the reconquest of Jerusalem. The Cluniac monks were also strong believers in the penitential pilgrimage—an arduous journey to a Christian shrine in order to redeem the sinner. The Church of Saint James in Compostela, Spain, and a number of churches in Rome were popular pilgrimage centers, but no place quite so suited the requirements of the penitential pilgrimage as the Holy Land.

The pope's call for holy war was made quietly, without warning, in a routine church council in the small town of Clermont in Auvergne in 1095. We do not know how the pontiff imagined his words would be received, but the reaction was instant and overwhelming. It seemed that war against the hated Muslims was exactly what Europe's fighting lords had waited for. And for the peasants, barely surviving several years of famine, the call to join the pope's army bound for Jerusalem was like the voice of God speaking directly to their souls. Responding to the call "God wills it," thousands sewed on red crosses and prepared for the sacred journey.

Steven Runciman refers to the period of the first Crusade as the "age of visions."[8] Piety, poverty, and ignorance combined to convince masses of European Christians that they were living at the "end-time." People viewed the natural calamities of famine and flood as signs of the Last Judgment heralding the Second Coming of Christ and the appearance of the Kingdom of God. Now was the time of repentance, and there was no surer way of showing it than to sell one's goods in order to buy the provisions and arms needed to join the Crusader army.

Before the great armies were organized for the pope's Crusade, small peasant groups of zealous souls spontaneously marched through the Rhine and Danube valleys, headed for Jerusalem, a city which many confused with the Heavenly Jerusalem. The Israeli historian Joshua Prawer writes that these peasants "would ask on approaching each new city if they had finally reached 'Heavenly Jerusalem.'"[9]

The most famous leader of the peasants' Crusade was Peter the Hermit, so named because of the hermit's cape he wore. Peter went barefoot or rode a donkey, which was revered almost as much as himself. He eschewed bread and meat but ate fish and drank wine. If his appearance was forbidding, his preaching was magnetic. Calling for the liberation of Christ's Tomb in the same breath that he promised salvation, he attracted some twenty thousand souls from northern France and southern Germany and prepared to lead them through the Balkans to Constantinople. But very few ever arrived at their destination. The reason lay in fanaticism and greed. Even before the expedition began, Peter had threatened violence against local Jewish communities to extort financial support for his Crusade. This same technique of fund-raising had also been used by no less a person than Godfrey de Bouillon, the duke of Lower Lorraine, who led one of the pope's armies and became the first Frankish ruler of Jerusalem.

But where Peter and Godfrey merely threatened, other criminally minded leaders of the peasants' Crusade directed their hordes against the Jews. As their ultimate goal was to defeat the Muslims who had stolen Christ's Tomb, why not begin by punishing the Jews who were responsible for putting Christ in his grave? Ordinarily the Crusaders offered Jews the choice between apostasy or death, but often no choice was given. Hundreds were massacred, synagogues burned, and homes plundered at Worms, Mainze, and Cologne on the Rhine, in the city of Metz on the Moselle, and in Prague. Joshua Prawer views the destruction as the beginning of a thousand-year period of Christian anti-Semitism: "This was the 'Doom of 1096,' as it is called in Jewish sources (*Gzeroth Tatnu*), an event never to be forgotten by [Jews], perpetrated by those who claimed the Holy land . . . who went to liberate the sepulchre of a God of love and peace universal."[10]

Very few of the peasant Crusaders reached Constantinople, and fewer still—Peter the Hermit was one of them—realized the goal of entering a liberated Jerusalem. Most met their death at the hands of Hungarians who struck back at them for plundering the countryside. We are told that a contemporary historian, Cosmas of Prague, "regarded their extinction as God's just wrath and vengeance for the horrible massacre of the Jews."[11]

Urban and Alexius had agree that the Crusader armies should assemble at Constantinople and there together with the Byzantine forces begin the reconquest of Asia Minor. The Crusaders in successive waves began arriving in the summer of 1096; by spring 1097 sixty thousand to one hundred thousand Franks had collected in the great Byzantine capital.

Emperor Alexius greeted the Latin noblemen graciously with gifts, promising them guides through the treacherous wasteland of Asia Minor. In return he secured from the leaders a solemn pledge not to keep any imperial lands that were reconquered. The pledge was not extended to Palestine and Jerusalem. Here the emperor, deferring to the great goal set by Pope Urban, agreed to a suzerainty for the Holy City. The Crusaders failed to keep their promises in any event, so the healing between Latin and Greek churches which the pope had so earnestly hoped for never came about.

Trouble started as soon as the Franks began arriving. The sight of so many foreign soldiers, ill disciplined, contemptuous of the cultured Greeks, having little understanding of their customs and worship, provoked the Constantinopolitans and worried the emperor. The bulk of the Crusader army was encamped in the suburbs of the capital where the emperor had seen to feeding them. But in order to ensure against a repetition of the marauding that had gone on during the long journey, he dispatched his own police force to watch carefully over his guests.

The Franks resented the air of superiority which the Greeks affected, and the Greeks did not hide their distaste for the rudeness of the Westerners. The Franks had come to save the capital of Eastern Christendom only to find themselves awed and intimidated by Constantinople and its citizens. Runciman describes their reactions:

> Constantinople, that vast, splendid city, with all its wealth, its busy population of merchants and manufacturers, its courtly nobles in their civilian robes and the richly dressed, painted great ladies with their trains of eunuchs and slaves, roused in them contempt mixed with an uncomfortable sense of inferiority. They could not understand the language nor the customs of the country. Even the church services were alien to them.[12]

After invading Asia Minor in April 1097, a combined Byzantine-Frankish force met the Seljuk army and defeated it at a great battle in Dorylaeum two months later. The Turkish threat to the empire was ended, and the Crusaders had a clear road to Syria. The main Crusader force headed south for Syria, but a small company of knights under the leadership of Baldwin of Boulogne veered east to Armenian Edessa, beyond the Euphrates. Baldwin, answering a call to liberate the Armenian Christians from their Muslim overlords, won the country and promptly claimed it for himself, thus violating his promise to Emperor Alexius. The county of Edessa became the first Frankish state in the Middle East. It was to be followed by Antioch.

Antioch, the great capital of northern Syria, was holy to Christians as the place where they were first so named and where tradition held that Saint Peter established his first bishopric. It was a lovely and wealthy city, boasting an ancient Christian population. Here the Seljuks put up stiff opposition in the hope of reversing the defeat at Dorylaeum and driving the Christians out of Asia Minor. Fierce fighting ensued for several months, but the Franks finally prevailed. Their victory was deceptive, for no sooner was the siege ended when the Crusaders were themselves besieged in the city by a fresh Seljuk force. After withstanding counterattacks while suffering hunger and other deprivations, the Crusaders beat back the Muslims and took possession of Antioch in June 1098. But they did not boast of their victory. We are told that in the midst of the Muslim attack on the city, when things looked worst for the Christians trapped within the city walls, barely defending themselves and weak from hunger, the Holy Lance was found. The lance which pierced Christ's body on the cross became the instrument that aroused the Christian soldiers to beat back the infidel.

No sooner was the conquered city secured than the Crusader leaders set to quarreling among themselves over who should have it as his possession, a rivalry which threatened to postpone indefinitely the march to Jerusalem. The peasant soldiers, sickened at the sight of their leaders placing the spoils of war over the goal of faith, threatened to destroy Antioch altogether. The threat worked, and the Crusader force, now led by Raymond de Gilles, prepared to march south to Jerusalem.

It was during the battle for Antioch that the first major break occurred between Franks and Greeks. The Franks originally attacked Antioch in the expectation of help from Emperor Alexius. Seeing the terrible fighting for the city, the emperor decided not to risk his army. He paid a high price for his prudence. Feeling betrayed, the Franks refused to give Antioch back to the Byzantines, and the wily Norman nobleman Bohemond succeeded in winning the city for himself. Under his leadership Antioch became the second independent Frankish kingdom of the Middle East. After the conquest of Antioch, the Latin bishops, who accompanied the Crusader force, for the first time began replacing Greek priests with their own in the city's most important churches.

It took the Franks a year to advance from Antioch to Jerusalem. Once they began marching south down the coast of Palestine, they moved swiftly. Avoiding military engagements with the Muslims, they chose to save their strength and supplies for Jerusalem, knowing that once the Holy City was theirs, they could turn back and secure the coastline. It was the opposite strategy of the one pursued by the Byzantine John Tzimisces, who never reconquered Jerusalem. In the middle of June 1099 the pope's knights had reached the northern outskirts of the city. Encamped on Nebi Samwil, or Mount Joie, as they called it, they wept tears of joy staring down at the blessed city they had come so far to recapture for Christendom.

Jerusalem was heavily defended by a garrison of Egyptian soldiers who only a year before had driven the Seljuk Turks out of the city. Before the Crusaders' siege Jerusalem's Muslim population had doubled to forty thousand with the addition of villagers seeking safety within the city's walls. All the Greeks, and most other Christians, along with the patriarch Symeon, had been expelled as unreliable. The Jews, who numbered a few hundred, stayed to fight alongside the Egyptian soldiers.

The Crusaders facing them outside the walls were badly prepared for their formidable task. They lacked siege weapons and had little water. Worse, they believed their own theological myths: once the assault began they expected God to give them the victory. At one point they walked around the city walls barefoot and bareheaded, reciting prayers and carrying heavy wooden crosses, expecting the walls to tumble down as they had for the ancient Israelites. Their solemn entreaties to the Lord did not help them, but patience and intelligent hard work did. At once they set about opening a supply route to the port of Jaffa, where Genoese sea traders supplied them with food and the wood they needed to build assault towers.

After five weeks of frustrating combat, Jerusalem's walls seemed taller and more impenetrable than ever. But the Crusaders knew that Jerusalem always had one potential weak spot—its northeastern wall, near the present Damascus Gate, which overlooks an extended flat area, suitable for assault. It was from this angle that Titus had attacked in 70 (as did Yitzhak Rabin in 1967, leading a company of Israeli paratroopers). Led by Godfrey de Bouillon, the Crusaders finally pushed through on the 15th of July. In a few hours more forces under Tancred penetrated the city in the northwest corner, and Raymond de Gilles attacked from Mount Zion. Thousands of Crusaders stormed in and immediately took revenge for the frustrating defeats inflicted on them. Every Muslim soldier in sight was slain; women and children were massacred in their homes. The Jews who fled for refuge to their synagogue were burned alive in the building. The streets filled with blood, and the blood flowed downhill to empty into the Kidron Valley which Jesus had once graced with his footsteps. For the church bishop and historian William of Tyre, the horrifying sight of Christian knights slaying a whole city's people was a terrible omen for Jerusalem:

> It was impossible to look upon the vast numbers of slain without horror; everywhere lay fragments of human bodies, and the very ground was covered with the blood of the slain. It was not alone the spectacle of the headless bodies and mutilated limbs strewn in all directions that roused horror in all who looked upon them. Still more dreadful it was to gaze upon the victors themselves, dripping

with blood from head to foot, an ominous sight which brought terror to all who met them.[13]

The killing was followed by an orgy of looting to which even the Crusader lords succumbed. The intrepid knight Tancred was seen stealing eight golden lamps from the Golgotha Basilica, causing such a scandal that he was obliged to return them. The few prisoners taken were sold into slavery, including some Jews who escaped burning. Before being taken off they spent days carting bodies to be buried or burned outside the city walls.[14]

When the nightmare had ended and the city was silent, desolate, smelling of fire and death, the Franks did not forget to give thanks for their victory. In a great procession lords, bishops, burghers, and peasants walked solemnly to the foot of Christ's Tomb to kneel in turn and offer prayers to the God who guided them. The tomb was in Christian hands again; the dignity of Christ's homeland had been restored. When their prayers had ended, the Franks immediately began distributing Jerusalem's sturdy stone houses among themselves.

No sooner was Jerusalem theirs than the Franks reverted to their usual practice of quarreling over who should govern the city, this time with a difference. In the past church leaders, who had done none of the physical fighting, had little to say about who should rule conquered territory. But the Franks recognized that Jerusalem and Bethlehem were not like other cities, and so the church demanded and got a large hand in choosing Jerusalem's first ruler. It was the pious, brave, but not very bright Godfrey de Bouillon who rewarded the church with legal autonomy in the patriarch's quarter (today the Christian quarter) adjacent to the Anastasis Church. With genuine humility, Godfrey refused to accept a crown in the city where Christ alone was king; instead he took the more modest title of Defender of the Holy Sepulchre (*Advocatus Sancti Sepulchri*).

Godfrey lived but a year after his enthronement and was succeeded by his younger and shrewder brother, Baldwin de Boulogne, count of Armenian Edessa. Baldwin, a warlord to the core, immediately had himself crowned King of Jerusalem and set out to enlarge and strengthen the borders of his new kingdom. During his eighteen-year reign he fought continuously with the Turks, Egyptians, and bedouins, and on occasion with his own equally aggressive fellow Crusader princes. His successors to the throne took up where he left off, so that by the middle of the twelfth century the borders of the Latin kingdom of Jerusalem resembled those of David's monarchy. It was protected on the west by the Mediterranean seawall, a natural border which ran south of Gaza and north past Beirut to the edge of independent Tripoli, the last of the four Crusader states, established in 1109. The eastern border extended from the Lebanese Mountains southward through Transjordan to the port of Eilat at the northern tip of the Red Sea.

The conquest of 1099 left Jerusalem empty of its native inhabitants and with few water and food resources to sustain itself. After Jesus' Tomb was retaken, most of the Franks returned home, leaving only a few hundred knights and several thousand foot soldiers to guard the city. The first decade and a half was hard and lonely for the new rulers of Jerusalem, until 1015 when King Baldwin made the important decision to bring back to the city Greeks, Syrians, and other native Eastern Christians who had been exiled to Transjordan. They returned to live in the northeastern (formerly Jewish) quarter of the city, an area which came to be called the Syrian quarter until sometime in early Ottoman times when Muslims began replacing Christians (who moved to the patriarch's quarter) and the area became the Muslim quarter as it is known today.

The Syrian Christians provided the manpower for a revitalization of Jerusalem's age-old economy of small crafts of leather, wood, and metal. The main source of economic growth came from the activities of Italian trading colonies established in Acre, Haifa, and Jaffa. The Italians brought raw materials and took away finished products—and, most important, they supplied Jerusalem with pilgrims. As a result they gained trading monopolies which made Jerusalem and the Holy Land generally an immensely lucrative area for commerce. Although the Italians profited handsomely from trade with Jerusalem, few of them were willing to live in the city. Even the Genoese who owned numerous houses in a street of their own rarely lived in them. Jerusalem, it seems, was felt to be a city dripping with sanctity and tragedy. The Italians, like many Israelis today, preferred the warmer climate and relaxed atmosphere of the sea coast.

Within fifty years of its conquest, Jerusalem's population had grown to twenty thousand, as many as had lived in the city in Jesus' time. The Franks, like the Byzantines and Romans before them, prohibited Jews from migrating back into the city from their small communities in the Galilee and Ashkelon. The late twelfth-century Jewish traveler Benjamin of Tudela reported finding only three Jews in Jerusalem working as dyers. Jews approached the city only as far as the hill Nebi Samwil, where they would tear their garments and "recite a prayer for the deliverance of captive Zion" from Christians and "for its reestablishment as the glorious 'City of David.'"[15]

Muslims too were prohibited from entering Jerusalem, but Frankish hostility waned with the years and gradually Muslims took up residence again in the city they once proudly ruled. Slowly Jerusalem regained its international character. The pilgrim John of Wurzburg left us a list of the ethnic-religious mix in Jerusalem during the Crusader era: "For there are Greeks, Bulgarians, Latins, Germans, Hungarians, Scots, Navarrese, Bretons, English, Franks, Ruthenians, Bohemians, Georgians, Armenians, Jacobites, Syrians, Nestorians, Indians, Capheturici, Maronites, and very many others, whom it would take long to tell."[16]

As they had done at Antioch, the Latin bishops rushed to replace the Greeks in their churches with their own priests. The Greek patriarch Symeon's absence from Jerusalem had saved them the onerous task of evicting him. Poor old Symeon, he never gave up hope of returning to Jerusalem as patriarch. He hated what the Franks had done to his city, and he spent his last days "writing theological treatises against the use of unleavened bread in the Latin rite."[17]

The Greeks were utterly humiliated and wasted no time in taking unique revenge through the most famous spectacle in the city, the ceremony of the Holy Fire. This ancient Easter eve ritual consisted of the descent of fire into the darkened Tomb of Christ. For the faithful it was a heavenly manifestation of light, confirming the truth of Christ's Resurrection. The Orthodox patriarch of Jerusalem presided over the ceremony, enthusiastically supported by all the bishops of the Eastern churches. In 1009 the mad caliph al-Hakim burned churches because his advisers convinced him that the Holy Fire was a hoax. But years after the persecution, when relations between Christians and Muslims had improved, Muslim officials of Jerusalem were glad to accept seats of honor in the Anastasis Church to observe at close hand the God-sent flame.

The celebration of the Holy Fire was the greatest day in Jerusalem's festival-swollen yearly calendar. The Anastasis Church was packed with people, and hundreds were pressed together in the courtyard facing the church; everyone held an unlit candle, eagerly watching for the first sign of fire. A sudden flickering of light in Christ's Tomb announced the miracle. Immediately the patriarch stepped forward to light his candle from the Holy Fire, then passed his flame to bishops surrounding him, who in turn lit the candles of worshipers in the church. Within seconds the church and then the courtyard were ablaze with Holy Fire.

But in 1102, only three years after the Crusader conquest, it seemed that the Holy Fire might be extinguished by the sins of men. For in that year the Latin bishops expelled the Greeks, Armenians, Syrians, and Georgians from their monasteries. On Easter eve, for the first time in memory, the fire refused to descend. Panic spread in the church; angry accusations were hurled; bishops took counsel. The Armenian historian Matthew of Edessa tells us that the Armenians, Copts, and other Monophysite Christians decided to hold special prayers immediately. Apparently the prayers were heard, for in the church still crowded with the faithful, the fire finally appeared, a day late. The Latins heeded the message. Without delay the monasteries were restored to their former owners.

The behavior of the Latin clergy could not have pleased Pope Urban II. He had preached holy war in the hope of reuniting the Latin and Greek halves of Christendom. That hope was crushed by the barbarous manner in which the Frankish princes acted in Constantinople. The conquest of Jerusalem demonstrated beyond any doubt that the Franks had much less interest in Christian solidarity than in territorial domination. The pope died a disappointed man in August 1099, two months after the conquest of Jerusalem, never having visited the Holy City whose liberation he had so earnestly sought.

As the years passed, the Franks grew more tolerant of those Eastern Christians who had been brought back from Transjordan. But the Eastern Christians found that although Jerusalem was Christian once again, the French-speaking rulers of the city looked upon them with a haughtiness that reminded them of former Muslim governors. The Franks were seen as illiterate, coarse, and domineering, with tendencies toward physical violence and fanatical piety. The Coptic historian Saw-irus ibn al-Muffafa wrote that Christians from Egypt ended their annual pilgrimage to Jerusalem because of the hostility shown to them by the Franks.[18] It was true that the Franks left local Christians free to worship; but the Monophysite Armenian, Jacobite, and Coptic Christians, after suffering centuries of "second-class" status under successive Byzantine, Muslim, and Frankish rule, saw little future for themselves in the Holy City. Like the Jews, they gradually left for more flourishing centers in Egypt and Mesopotamia. It was a sad exodus. Save for the few who stayed to staff monasteries and churches, Jerusalem lost many of its most unique and vibrant Christians.

No groups in Crusader Jerusalem were more admired, feared, and hated than the Knights Hospitaller and Knights Templar, two religious orders of military-minded monks who mixed piety, finance, and warfare to forge a sanctified, un-challengeable power in the Holy Land. Members took vows of poverty, chastity, and obedience and adhered to them fanatically. As fighters the knights were skillful, experienced, courageous, and therefore indispensable to Baldwin II and his successors who were perpetually short of reliable men for their interminable skirmishing with Muslims. Both Hospitallers and Templars were nominally of the Benedictine Order, but in Palestine they functioned as independent organizations owing allegiance only to the pope, who held them in the highest esteem as his permanent foothold in the Holy Land.

The Knights Templar, founded in 1118, took their name from their headquarters in the Templum Solomonis, formerly the al-Aksa Mosque. They began as a society dedicated to the protection of pilgrims and holy places and influenced the older Order of Saint John of the Hospital (established in 1070 by Amalfi merchants as a charitable organization for the sick and poor) to accept similar duties. Through most of the twelfth century, members of both orders could be seen on the docks waiting for the pilgrim boats. The Knights Templar were distin-guishable by the red Maltese crosses sewn onto their white tunics, worn over metal battle vests; the Hospitallers wore black tunics bearing a white cross. Once the pilgrims had safely landed, they were taken in hand by the soldier-monks and escorted overland to Jerusalem. This was no mean accomplish-ment for the roads were constantly preyed upon by Egyptians,

Pilgrims paying tolls after landing in Jaffa
port on their way to Jerusalem.
(From a manuscript illumination)

Turks, and bedouin bandits. None of the pilgrims forgot the
kindnesses shown to him, and the wealthier among them often
sent gifts of money and property or remembered the orders in
their wills.

Grateful pilgrims were not the only source of wealth for the
military orders. The vow of poverty required that every monk
assign to the order all his earthly possessions and live on a
pittance, thus guaranteeing to the order a stable source of
income. It was rare when great lords renounced the worldly life
to take the habit of one of Jerusalem's orders, but any number
of lesser nobles were attracted to the ideals of the order and gave
over large and small fortunes.

The vow of poverty was so zealously kept that it was a law in
both orders that if any monk was captured by the enemy his
order would refuse to pay his ransom. A certain Odo of
Saint-Amand, one of the masters of the temple, was allowed to
die in captivity rather than violate the order's rule.[19]

Jerusalem's kings did not hesitate to reward the orders with
estates, houses, and castles for military victories which were
often directly due to the prowess of the soldier-monks. And the
Latin patriarch of Jerusalem, knowing how essential the Christian knights had become to the defense of the realm, did not

interfere when they claimed a share of all the tithes collected by the church.

Relations between the military orders and Jerusalem's Latin patriarch were never easy. The patriarch complained that the Hospitallers had built so many tall buildings south of the Holy Sepulchre, where the order had its headquarters, that the church was obscured and pilgrims had difficulty walking to it. The tension between patriarch and Hospitallers exploded one day at the Holy Sepulchre itself. Reacting to a new liturgical arrangement that slighted them, the Hospitallers stormed the church with swords drawn and chased out the priests. Today the tall buildings of the Hospitallers are gone; only the area's name, Muristan (Persian for "Hospital"), reminds us of the powerful men who once lived there.

However fanatical in faith and bloated with wealth, neither of these orders forgot its charitable ideals. Each organized an extensive system of hospices, hospitals, orphanages, and poor people's homes throughout the country. The Hospitallers had facilities to treat two thousand sick a day. Their example inspired a number of smaller orders such as the Teutonic Knights in southwest Jerusalem (today the site of the Jewish quarter) and the Order of Saint Lazarus, whose members cared for the city's numerous lepers in the farthest northwest corner of the city.

Given their charitable and military ideals, the soldier-monks looked with contempt on the self-indulgence of the secular knights of the first Crusade. Within a decade or two of the conquest of Jerusalem, most of the secular knights had returned home. Less than seven hundred remained, with several thousand foot soldiers. When they were not called out by the king for a battle, most of them settled down nicely to their Armenian or Greek or Syrian wives, and to the customary pleasures of drinking, gaming, and hunting.

Both Hospitallers and Templars particularly deplored marriages between Latins and native Christians, whom they regarded as in the same category as Muslims and Jews. The children of such marriages they contemptuously called *poulains*, "half-castes." (The blue-eyed, fair-skinned Arabs of today are the offspring of these half-castes, and the Israelis refer to them as "crusaders.") The soldier-monks did not hide their disgust at the showy dress, the long hair and effeminate manners of the worldly nobility. We have one eyewitness sarcastic account of the secular knight's appearance: "... The sleeves of their garments were fastened with gold chains, and they wantonly exposed their waists, which were confined with embroidered belts, and they kept back with their arms their cloaks, which were fastened so that not a wrinkle should be seen in their garments... and round their necks were collars glittering with jewels, and on their heads garlands interwoven with flowers of every hue...."[20]

Contrast this account to the description of the Templars by Saint Bernard of Clairvaux, a warm supporter of the military orders:

> They come and go at a sign from their commander; they wear the clothes which he gives them, seeking neither other garments nor other food. They are wary of all excess in food or clothing, desiring only what is needful. They live all together, without women or children. No idlers or lookers-on are to be found in their company; when they are not on active service, which happens rarely, or eating their bread or giving thanks to Heavens, they busy themselves with mending their clothes and their torn or tattered harness.... Insolent words, vain acts, immoderate laughter, complaints and murmurs, when they are perceived, do not go unpunished. They hate chess and dice, and they have a horror of hunting; they do not find the usual pleasure in the ridiculous pursuit of birds. They shun and abominate mimes, magicians, and *jongleurs*, light songs and foolishness. They crop their hair close because the Gospels tell them that it is a shame for a man to tend his hair. They are never seen combed and rarely washed, their beards are matted, they reek of dust and bear the stains of the heat and their harness.[21]

To the historian Joshua Prawer, the austere soldier-monks introduced a profound and disturbing change in Christian morality.[22] They were not the first Christians to practice holy war; that dubious distinction belongs to the Byzantine emperors Nicephoros Phocas and John Tzimisces, and even earlier to Emperor Heraclius in his campaign to drive the Persians out of the Christian East. But the Byzantine church understood that killing, no matter how warranted in a just war, was nonetheless a sin crying out for divine judgment and forgiveness. Jerusalem's monks of the Hospital and Temple had no such understanding. For them, armed warfare against the infidel, which involved all manner of killing and maiming, was viewed as *religiously wanted*, a practice pleasing to God.

We do not know precisely the condition of the Anastasis Church when the Crusaders reached Jerusalem. Constantine's original basilica was destroyed by the Persians and the remains fashioned into a version of the former Byzantine structure. This restored church was again destroyed by Caliph al-Hakim in the great persecution of 1009; forty years later the Byzantine emperor Monomachus received Muslim approval to begin another major restoration. The Crusaders in turn made drastic changes, producing a wholly new edifice. They were so busy defending their kingdom that it took them fifty years to complete the new church. Constantine's original church had been actually a complex of structures, with separate buildings for the Tomb and Golgotha. In place of these the Crusaders constructed a single massive Romanesque building over the sites of the Passion. Only the rotunda over the tomb was retained from the original Byzantine design. The church was dedicated in 1049 and, as befitted the pope's knights of death, the church's name was changed from Anastasis ("Resurrection") to "Sepulchre." This structure, heavily modified by later restorations, is today's Church of the Holy Sepulchre, a monument to the ideals and animosities of Jerusalem's Christians.

Over the centuries little has changed in the church. Entering it one has less a sense of a church than of a museum containing a bewildering collection of chapels dedicated to sundry saints—James, John, Michael, Longinus, Helena, Mary Magdalene, Abraham. In the church one can find earth's navel from which medieval cartographers drew their fanciful maps showing the continents of Europe, Africa, and Asia fanning out like petals from earth's stem, Jerusalem. Here too is the burial place of Adam under the Golgotha rock where, according to an ancient Greek legend, the Lord's blood first redeemed the father of mankind. A few feet from Golgotha is the marker showing the spot where the two Marys and Salome watched the Crucifixion and another showing the stone where afterward the women anointed the body of Jesus.

Pilgrims for centuries journeyed to this church to venerate Golgotha and Jesus' Tomb. They must have experienced a feeling of disappointment upon entering it for the first time. The building which stands over the places of Christ's death and resurrection ought to look no less regal than Saint Peter's in Rome, no less lovely than the cathedral at Chartres. Instead one is met with a cavernous stone hulk: dark, dank, airless, into which little light enters. There is little to delight the eye or move the heart. A feeling of disunity—so symbolic of Jerusalem's history—is immediate and depressing. The Church of the Holy Sepulchre is by no means a fine example of Crusader church architecture; that prize goes to the handsome Church of Saint Anne on the Via Dolorosa, built over the traditional site of the Virgin's birth. Nor is there archaeological evidence to support the contention that the Church of the Holy Sepulchre contains the Golgotha stone, or that Christ was buried in a cave lying today under the great rotunda. Little matter. The faithful come from every corner of the world to touch the holy stones that quicken the spirit. One sees them entering the church with pious excitement, singing hymns, closing their eyes so as not to be distracted by the motley sights.

Christians more than Jews or Muslims loved to parade in Jerusalem. During the Crusader era there were more religious processions than at any time before or since. Such processions were always a part of Christian tradition, but in Jerusalem they held a special meaning. Rome had power; Constantinople could boast of its relics and the Haghia Sophia Church; Antioch and Alexandria had venerable traditions; but Jerusalem had the most precious holy places on earth. The annual processions to each shrine associated with Jesus' Passion confirmed for the world the sacredness of these places.

Most processions began or ended at the Holy Sepulchre. Traditionally the Latin church showed more enthusiasm for the celebration of Christmas than for Easter; it was the opposite for the Greek and other Eastern churches. But in Jerusalem the Latins gave in to the Easterners and tried to outdo the Greeks in staging elaborate services for Easter, beginning with Palm Sunday.

At dawn a multitude would gather in the village of Bethany, a few miles east of the Mount of Olives, to retrace the footsteps of Jesus' fatal journey. Standing behind the True Cross, or what was left of it, the patriarch led the bishops of all the churches, followed by knights, monks, town merchants, village priests, peasants, and hordes of pilgrims from every nation—the whole of the city in one grand procession, minus the few Muslims and

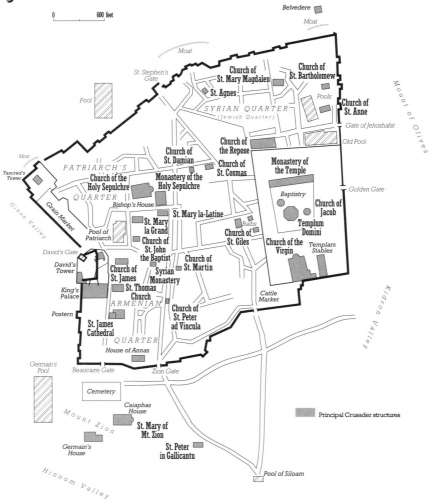

Jerusalem Under the Crusaders

0   600 feet

Belvedere

Moat

Moat

St. Stephen's Gate

Church of St. Mary Magdalen

Church of St. Bartholomew

St. Agnes

Pools

Pool

SYRIAN QUARTER
(Jewish Quarter)

Church of St. Anne

Gate of Jehoshafat

Church of the Repose

Old Pool

Mount of Olives

Moat

Church of St. Damian

Church of St. Cosmas

Monastery of the Temple

PATRIARCH'S

Tancred's Tower

Church of the Holy Sepulchre

Monastery of the Holy Sepulchre

Baptistry

Golden Gate

QUARTER

Bishop's House

St. Mary la-Latine

Church of Jacob

Gihon Valley

Grain Market

St. Mary la Grand

Baths

Templum Domini

Church of St. Giles

Pool of Patriarch

Church of St. John the Baptist

Church of the Virgin

Templars Stables

David's Gate

Church of St. James

Syrian Monastery

Church of St. Martin

David's Tower

St. Thomas Church

King's Palace

ARMENIAN

Church of St. Peter ad Vincula

Cattle Market

Kidron Valley

Postern

St. James Cathedral

QUARTER

House of Annas

Germain's Pool

Beaucaire Gate

Zion Gate

Cemetery

Caiaphas House

Mount Zion

St. Mary of Mt. Zion

Principal Crusader structures

Germain's House

St. Peter in Gallicantu

Hinnom Valley

Pool of Siloam

Jews who hid out during this week. Their path was cleared by white-robed boys incensing the ground to drive away demonic spirits. Slowly the procession walked to the Mount of Olives to pray at the stone which bore the footprints of Christ when he ascended to heaven. From there the column made its way downhill to the Garden of Gethsemane to witness to the Lord's sorrow. Then it marched up the Temple Mount through the

Golden Gate as Jesus had done; the gate was opened once annually for this occasion. The devout prayed first at the Templum Solomonis and then walked across to the Templum Domini for more prayers at the altar constructed over the Moriah stone. As they exited they knelt before the great picture of the Madonna which was affixed to the door of the former Muslim shrine of the Dome of the Rock. From the Temple Mount they went immediately to the Praetorium to follow Jesus' footsteps on the Via Dolorosa. They stopped at each of ten stations of the cross, which took them into the Church of the Holy Sepulchre and to the final four stations covering the Crucifixion and burial. Finally they would gather at the tomb to sing hymns of praise through the day, feeling the excitement that would fill them this entire week.

On Ash Wednesday the patriarch preached a sermon in the courtyard of the Holy Sepulchre Church, after which baskets of ashes would be strewn over the heads of the assembled. On Maundy Thursday, in imitation of the scene depicted in the thirteenth chapter of John's Gospel, the patriarch washed the feet of twelve of his bishops representing the disciples. Then he washed the feet of a few chosen poor, having previously checked for leprosy and other signs of infectious disease. On Good Friday the march up the Via Dolorosa was reenacted, ending with a midnight mass at the Holy Sepulchre lasting most of the night. The next day was the long-awaited ceremony of the Holy Fire. The week culminated the next morning with a great sunrise Resurrection service at the tomb, all of Christian Jerusalem gathering together to intone the words, "He is risen!"

Other special festival days were unique to Jerusalem. July 15 was one such day, the anniversary of both the conquest of Jerusalem and the dedication of the Church of the Holy Sepulchre. Another day was the third of May, celebrating Helena's discovery of the True Cross.

Jerusalem in Crusader times was a hierarchical city, where each group acknowledged the station of the other and each retreated behind the protective walls of its street, quarter, and compound. Frenchmen, Italians, Germans, Armenians, Syrians— each lived in their own area. Each family had its sturdy stone house, square-built in Middle Eastern style with an inner courtyard from which one seldom ventured. Only the marketplace brought people out and allowed them to mingle. Here, under the vaulted stone roofs, light streaming through the many windows in the vault, Greeks, Frenchmen, Germans, Italians came together to buy and sell from one another without much regard for who the other was and what he believed.

When the Franks were not fighting or praying, they indulged their taste for drink and dicing games. Many of the stalls in the central market were equipped with dicing tables which resembled the backgammon games seen today outside Arab shops. It was not uncommon for drunken knights to end their game with a stabbing.

Jerusalem has never been a city noted for its cuisine. During the Crusader era dishes were in fact done so poorly that one street in the market area was called the Street of Bad Cooking (Rue de Malquisin).

The successes of the first Crusade were only in part due to the skill and bravery of the pope's soldiers. The Franks were able to found and defend independent Christian states of Edessa, Antioch, Tripoli, and Jerusalem because of the disunity of the Muslim peoples in Palestine, Syria, Egypt, and Mesopotamia. Finally, under three successive leaders—Zengi, Nureddin, and Saladin—Muslim forces made common cause against the detested Franks. A counteroffensive was begun in the mid-twelfth century with the aim of expelling the Europeans altogether from the Middle East.

In 1144 the Abbasid caliph Zengi attacked and conquered the Christian principality of Edessa. The loss proved to be the beginning of the end of Christian domination of Palestine. The news of the Muslim conquest provoked the Christian leaders of Europe into organizing the second Crusade (1147–1149). Led by Louis VII of France and German Emperor Conrad III, the Crusaders marched off to recover Edessa only to lose most of their troops in the wastelands of Asia Minor. At this point the leaders changed plans. The spoils of Damascus looked more inviting than avenging Christian honor, so they attacked the great Arab capital. It was a terrible mistake. The attack failed, the Crusaders lost what was left of their army, and the myth of Crusader invincibility was broken. Worse, the Christians lost the strategic balance of power. Damascus, an independent Muslim power on peaceful terms with both Arab and Christian neighbors, had served the Franks well as a buffer against the powerful Abbasid caliphate in Baghdad. The treacherous attack on Damascus, while repulsed, weakened the kingdom and made its absorption by Zengi inevitable. Now there was nothing to keep the Crusaders safe from the ambitions of Muslim leaders who were rallying their people against the Franks under the banner of the *jihad*, the Islamic holy war.

The succession of leadership from Zengi to Nureddin and finally to Saladin marked the growth of Muslim power throughout the Middle East, resulting in the gradual encirclement of the kingdom of Jerusalem. In 1186, when Saladin was poised to strike against the Christian state, Crusader power was still something to be reckoned with. The Franks controlled the Mediterranean coastline and were well supplied by sea from Europe. The borders of the Latin kingdom were strongly defended by castles. The Crusaders had a mobile, well-equipped, battle-tested, and dedicated army which had repulsed Saladin's early forays into Frankish territory. Had the Crusaders at this point been willing to halt their own provocative plundering of Muslim towns and caravans, disaster might have been averted. Had the Crusaders been more willing to cooperate among themselves, they might have recognized the dangers they faced. Had they been less cruel in battle, more generous to their victims, more tolerant and less exploitive of all the native Muslim, Christian, and Jewish peoples, they might never have provoked the Muslim powers to rise up against them. But they were fighters first and last, with little regard for what life should consist of after the battle. The wanton destruction of the Muslim population of Jerusalem in 1099 showed the kind of men they were, and Muslim leaders waited for their day of revenge.

The end of the Crusaders came in a battle fought on a two-pronged hill, the Horns of Hittin, near Tiberias, overlooking Lake Tiberias. It is said that Saladin lost his patience with the Christian knights when they broke a peace agreement with him and attacked a caravan bound from Damascus to Cairo in which one of his sisters happened to be a passenger. In July 1187 the Muslim general crossed the Jordan with a force of twenty thousand and met a Crusader force of equal strength within sight of the famed lake. The Crusaders made the tactical error of deploying their entire army, leaving the defense of the kingdom to a token force. Exhausted and thirsty from a long

march through the dry Judean hills, they were forced immediately into battle. The result was devastating. The army was
destroyed and all the Frankish leaders killed or captured. Jerusalem's King Guy de Lusignan was taken prisoner and eventually ransomed.

After the victory, Saladin's forces swept down the Palestinian
coastline, easily taking towns and castles, and on October 12,
1187, conquered Jerusalem with little opposition. The Holy
City was once again in Muslim hands and, except for the brief
fourteen years in which Prussian King Frederick II ruled, it was
to remain so for more than seven hundred years.

Who Owns
Christ's Tomb?

*These Holy Places belong to the Sultan
and he gives them to whom he pleases.*
—Ottoman Grand Visier, 1757

The Arabs are rascals....They hate and defame us.
—Greek Archbishop Cyril of Lydda, 1843

After winning control of Jerusalem in 1187, the Muslim conqueror Saladin wasted no time in correcting the indignities suffered by the religion of Islam at the hands of the Latin Crusaders. The gold cross erected on the Dome of the Rock was taken down and melted for the mosque's treasury. All the mosques that had been converted to churches were turned back into mosques. And, adding insult to injured Christian sensitivity, Jews were invited back to Jerusalem.

But the Crusader spirit did not die with military defeat. The church's preachers issued fresh calls to regain Jerusalem. Saladin's victory was interpreted as a blasphemy against God. Pope Gregory VIII spoke of not "allowing this injury to Christ to remain unavenged." Cardinal Henry of Albano, a legate of Pope Gregory, saw in the fall of Jerusalem a vision of Christ recrucified. With perfect hyperbole he spoke of "the sacrilegious theft of the Cross of the Redeemer trampled upon by the infidels."[1] In the legate's mind, Jerusalem was a golden ladder leading to a glimpse of heaven. The ordinary peasant, lacking the subtle spiritual talents of meditation, had been given this ladder as the reward of pilgrimage. "The inscrutable wisdom of

The double-door entrance to the
Crusader-rebuilt Church of the Holy
Sepulchre. The eastern door was walled
up by the Greek Orthodox to hide
the tombs of the Latin Crusader kings of
Jerusalem. (Photographed by Adrien
Bonfils ca. 1860–1890)

God," Albano said, "desired to give to the Christians something
visible in order that those who cannot lift themselves to the
spiritual spheres may create for themselves through the visible a
ladder to the invisible."[2]

The infidel Muslims under Saladin had stolen the golden
ladder; it was high time to recover it. The liberation of the Holy
Sepulchre would expunge the sin against the True Jerusalem in
heaven. The new Crusaders were bidden to imitate the courageous Maccabees who recaptured Jerusalem from pagan Greeks.
It was God's wish. For was not the church the New Israel? Were
not Christians the inheritors of the all the promises made to
David, Jerusalem's king?

In the same spirit of piety and conquest, the Dominican
monk Stephan of Bourbon wrote:

> We are descendants of the Holy Land both according to the flesh,
> because our father Adam was created here and like the other
> patriarchs is buried in this country; according to the spirit because
> our father Christ and our mother the Holy Virgin were born,
> lived, died and were buried here; moreover here our fathers the
> apostles were born and brought up, and here our mother the
> Church had its origin. Likewise the land is ours by the right of
> succession as far as we are the true children of God. . . . [3]

So now, as Zengi's conquest of Edessa had provoked the

second Crusade, Saladin's capture of Jerusalem inspired Christian Europe into a third holy war, this time led by England's Richard I, the Lionhearted. In 1191 Richard fought with his customary bravery but failed to regain the Holy City, settling for a shrunken kingdom on a narrow coastal strip which included the port cities of Haifa, Caesarea, Arsuf, and Jaffa. Fortunately for the church, Richard was as good a diplomat as he was a soldier. He negotiated with Saladin the return of Jesus' cross and an agreement which allowed pilgrims free access to visit the Church of the Holy Sepulchre at any time, with a guarantee of safe passage from the coast.

The third Crusade proved a turning point. Successive waves of European soldiers found it more and more difficult to reach the Holy Land. Gradually with the years, the obsession to win back the cross, to restore Christ's dignity, faded and finally died. But not before the launching of several more massive military efforts. In 1199 French knights set out on a fourth sacred expedition which never reached Jerusalem. On this occasion the Crusaders were diverted to Constantinople which they seized from the Greeks in 1204 and then subjected to brutal plundering. It was an event which sealed the final break between the Eastern and Western halves of Christendom. The conquest of Constantinople proved to be a suicidal victory for the Latin Christians, for as the next three centuries were to show, a weakened Byzantium could not defend the Christian Balkans from the westward drive of a resurgent Islam.

Two more major Christian holy wars demonstrated to everyone that the pope's knights now fought less for the dignity of Christ than for the spoils of conquest. And then, in 1221, a most unusual event occurred in what was now the sixth major Crusade launched from Europe against the Muslim power in Jerusalem. Under the leadership of the German king Frederick II, the crusading army was able to take control of the Holy City—not by beating Muslim forces on the ground but through skillful diplomacy carried out by Frederick with Palestine's ruler, the Egyptian sultan al-Kamil. The Christians thereupon governed Jerusalem for fifteen brief years, during which time Frederick heard nothing but complaints from the pope. It seems that the Holy Father felt humiliated that a Christian king would negotiate with the infidel over Jesus' sacred tomb rather than waging a sacred battle until the stain on the dignity of Christ's name was cleansed. As punishment against Frederick, the pope began his own special Crusade to recapture the king's lands in Sicily; it was an action which discredited the concept of holy war in the minds of bishops, princes, and peasants alike.

After the defeat of the seventh and final Crusade in 1250, the whole of the Middle East came under the domination of the Mamluk sultans of Egypt, who ruled until the dynasty was ousted from power by the Ottoman Turks in 1517. In the nearly seven hundred years from the Mamluk conquest until the British ended Ottoman Turkish domination of the Middle East at the close of World War I, the Christian peoples resumed their customary status as protected but subordinate communities (*millets*) under central Muslim authority. As long as Christians paid their taxes and respected Islamic Shari'a law, they were free to worship according to their own traditions and to administer their domestic affairs.

Greek and Latin bishops in Jerusalem continued their usual quarrels, but now they fought for smaller stakes. Where once the two great branches of Christendom had contended over the truest meaning of the faith, over winning whole nations and extending their powers over entire territories of Europe, Asia Minor, and the Middle East, now they fought for control of a few square meters of hallowed ground in Jerusalem, Bethlehem, and Nazareth. This struggle, which began in the fourteenth century, ultimately extended beyond the rival churches and engulfed all the major European powers. The principal combatants were the Franciscan monks, supported by Venice and France, and the Greek Orthodox patriarchate in Jerusalem, a client of the powerful ecumenical patriarchate in Constantinople.

The Franciscans began arriving in Palestine around 1331, a hundred years after Saint Francis came to the Holy Land to retrace the footsteps of Jesus. With the conquest of Muslim-held Acre in 1291, the last of the Franks had been evicted from Palestine, and the Muslim rulers had seen to the return of shrines, churches, and monasteries to the Greek Orthodox and other Eastern Christians. The brown-robed, tonsured Franciscans wasted no time in waging a powerful campaign to regain what their church had controlled for two hundred years. In less than ten years, applying their scholarly and legal skills, they

The Greek Catholicon chapel of the Church of the Holy Sepulchre, showing the Greek patriarch of Jerusalem seated on his throne. (Painted by David Roberts in 1838)

persuaded Muslim authorities to recognize their own claims to the churches of the Holy Sepulchre and Nativity. The Greeks fought back, but they were no match for the Western monks who were "better educated and better disciplined" and "knew the value of title deeds and archives."[4] Moreover, the Franciscans were well supported from abroad. Venice and other mercantile cities held lucrative trade agreements with the Mamluk sultans of Cairo, and the Italians did not hesitate to use their influence to win concessions for their church. The success of the Franciscans was finally rewarded in Rome. In 1342 Pope Clement VI named the Franciscan Order the official guardian of Holy Land shrines in behalf of Catholics throughout the world. Meanwhile, the Greeks nursed their wounds.

The Turkish conquest of Palestine in 1517 intensified the competition between Greeks and Latin Catholics, a competition joined by Armenians, Syrian Jacobites, Ethiopians, and Copts. It was a recognized tradition among the different Christian communities that the repair, cleaning, and use of the shrines bestowed on the user the right of possession. Thus the Turks, who were able to sell to the highest bidder the right to repair a

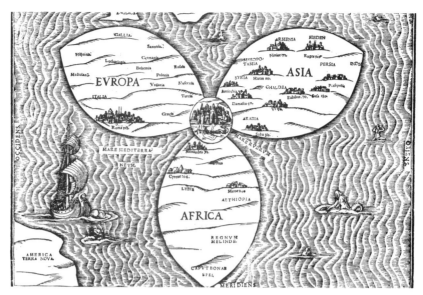

The late sixteenth-century "petal" map
which idealizes Jerusalem as the
center of all the earth's continents.

church roof or incense an altar or dust a lamp, profited from the
rivalry. For four hundred years the Sublime Porte manipulated
rival Christian claims on the holy places in order to enhance its
own political and economic relations with France, Austria, and
Russia.

From the beginning the Ottoman government favored Greek
interests above Latin because the ancient Orthodox patriarchal
sees of Constantinople, Alexandria, Antioch, and Jerusalem
were under Turkish authority. The Turks made the Greeks
trusted advisers, and the Greek patriarchate was given immense
authority over all the Eastern Orthodox churches in the empire,
including the patriarchate of Jerusalem.

The change of fortune for the Franciscans can be seen in the
manner in which they were evicted from their headquarters on
Mount Zion, Jerusalem's southwest hill. For two hundred years
they had occupied a tall stone building, the Coenaculum, containing what many believed to have been the site of the Last
Supper. They had purchased the building from the Egyptian
sultan Melek al-Nasr for thirty thousand ducats. The Franciscans were evicted from it in 1552 when Ottoman officials
determined that King David was buried there; they immediately

erected a mosque over his presumed tomb. The Muslim expulsion of the Franciscans set the pattern for interreligious quarrels for the control of Zion hill, even to this day.

Upon their eviction the homeless Franciscans crossed the hill one hundred meters into the walled city and were taken in for a time by the Armenian Orthodox. In gratitude the Franciscans for years celebrated a special mass in the Armenian Cathedral of Saint James. Eventually they were able to purchase the Monastery of Saint Savior from the Greeks, who were eager to make money from the misfortunes of their fellow Christians. Indeed so. For the Greeks had earlier bought the same monastery from the Georgian Orthodox church which went broke paying off tax debts to the Turks.

The Greeks made more advances. In 1605 they gained the northern part of Calvary in the Holy Sepulchre Church. And in 1637 they extended their control over the Basilica of the Nativity in Bethlehem, the Tomb of Christ, the Stone of Unction, and the southern chapel on Calvary. Further, in 1656 Greek bishops succeeded in evicting Ethiopian Christians from their properties, a victory which was capped only two years later when the Greeks forced the Armenians out of the magnificent Church of Saint James in the Armenian quarter.

In 1690, however, the tide turned Latin. The Ottoman government, now at war with Austria, Poland, and Venice, was desperate for the help of Catholic France to save many of her colonies. The French price for aiding Turkey included returning to the Catholic church the rights lost in 1637. In 1735 the same pattern was repeated when Turkey was involved in a losing war with Austria and Russia. Again Turkey turned to France, which in turn demanded a decree strengthening Latin rights in the shrines. In the Capitulations of 1740 (so named for the *capituli* or "chapters" in the Franco-Turkish agreement) the decree of 1690 was reconfirmed, bestowing on the Catholic church preeminent rights at the shrines in Jerusalem and Bethlehem.

The Greeks were furious. In Jerusalem, Christian quarreling led to fighting. Greek and Franciscan monks took after each other with candlesticks and crosses. To Ottoman officials who were caught in the middle, the internal stability of the empire suddenly posed a greater challenge than cultivating relations with Catholic France. A new decree in 1757 restored to the Greeks preeminent rights in the holy places.

When he heard of this decision, the French ambassador in Constantinople was apoplectic. He rushed to the sultan's palace where the Grand Vizier, with an oriental's exquisite disdain for Western moral logic, explained to him, "These [holy places], Sir, belong to the Sultan and he gives them to whom he pleases; it may well be possible that they always were in the hands of the Franks, but today His Highness wishes that they belong to the Greeks."[5]

Later, in 1808, the Greeks saw their cup of joy overflow when the decree of 1757 was reconfirmed. At this time they were also granted imperial permission to repair the roof of the Holy Sepulchre Church which had been destroyed by fire. By tradition such a repair meant virtual ownership of the church and thus total control over Christ's Tomb. Greeks accused Armenians of setting fire to the church, but later it was discovered that drunken Greek priests "had accidentally set some wood on fire and tried to extinguish it by dousing it with brandy, thinking it was water."[6]

The Latins (joined by Armenians, Copts, and Syrian Jacobites) were in despair to see church and tomb go to the Greeks. Bishops and diplomats were dispatched to confer with the sultan's advisers. They succeeded in persuading the sultan to agree that the Greeks could repair the roof without prejudice to the worship rights of the other church communities.

But the right to repair the roof over Jesus' Tomb was clearly a Greek victory. After that there was no question that the large Catholicon chapel with its immense altar, the spot at which medieval Christian tradition had placed "the center of the world," belonged to the Greeks. But the victory was not cheap. The Greeks could pay for the repairs only with the help of the Russian church, which had gone to the aid of the Greeks against the French-backed Franciscans. The repairs were said to have cost 1.5 million roubles, a sum which fell short of the bribe to Turkish officials—that amounted to 2.25 million.

The final insult was administered to the Latins (who had never been forgiven by the Greeks for the Crusades) when, at the beginning of the nineteenth century, instructions were given to the Muslim guards of the Holy Sepulchre Church to wall up the tombs of Godfrey de Bouillion, Baldwin I, and other Latin kings of Jerusalem buried there.

In 1850 the disappearance of the silver star in the Grotto of

The site revered as the Tomb of Christ, an imposing structure of brown and reddish marble. The ownership of its crypt, lamps, and candlesticks is in perpetual dispute among all the oldest churches of Jerusalem. (Photographed by Adrien Bonfils ca. 1860–1890)

the Nativity in Bethlehem stirred the ever-boiling pot of inter-Christian resentment; it also provoked the Crimean War. The Latin inscription on the star persuaded the Franciscans that the Greeks had stolen it, while the latter accused the Latins of removing it in order to blame the Greeks. As accusations flew, France seized the opportunity to demand from Ottoman authorities that the Catholic church be given back rights at the shrines guaranteed to her in the 1740 Capitulations. Russia vigorously protested any change that would prejudice the interests of Greek and other Eastern Orthodox Christians. The Turks, seeing a chance to slip out of past obligations, announced that they were withdrawing "protector" status from both France and Russia. France acquiesced, but Russia and Turkey fought the Crimean War, and after that met in battle a second time in 1878.

Following the war of 1878, the Treaty of Berlin was signed in which it was decided that "no alteration can be made in the status quo in the Holy Places." It was a prudent decision. The quarrels between Greek and Latin churches had drawn in the great nations of Europe—to their regret—and they were now looking for ways to end destructive confrontation with one another. They failed. The Treaty of Berlin froze the question of Christian holy places, but after the collapse of the Ottoman empire following World War I, European nations again confronted one another over Palestine and the whole Middle East. Although Europe's preoccupation with Christian holy places had ended, attention was now drawn to the new forces of Zionism and Arab nationalism, each with its own sense of holy place, and each with a powerful resentment of how the other had desecrated it.

For two hundred years Franciscan claims to the holy places posed one kind of threat to the Greeks; a different kind of threat was posed by their own Arab Orthodox. While Arab Christians comprised the vast majority of the Orthodox laity in Palestine in the nineteenth century, they had no influence over church policies and came to protest their exclusion from the church's leadership. Relations between Greek clergy and Arab laity in the Orthodox church in Palestine had never been good during the four hundred years of Ottoman rule. Greeks looked on the Arabs as ignorant and untrustworthy; Arabs viewed the Greeks as arrogant and corrupt. There was truth on both sides.

The typical Greek attitude was expressed by the Greek bishop Cyril of Lydda (who was later to become patriarch of Jerusalem) in a conversation in 1843 with the Russian Orthodox archmandrite Porfiry Ouspensky, who defended the Arabs.

CYRIL: The Arabs are rascals.... They hate and defame us. You have no affection for us and defend them.

PORFIRY: God knows the extent of my love towards you, but I

CYRIL: pity the Arabs and I am prepared to defend them before anyone.

CYRIL: They have no faith; they are barbarians, villains.

PORFIRY: You must teach them faith for you have fostered their unbelief.

CYRIL: They will not listen to us.

PORFIRY: That is not surprising, for you do not love but despise them. They are a martyr people. They are persecuted by the Muslims yet receive no protection from you. They even have nowhere to pray. The village churches are in a most miserable condition.

CYRIL: You forget that we are under the Turkish yoke.

PORFIRY: That does not prevent you from repairing and . . . decorating the churches. . . . The priests do not understand their duties. They keep their cattle in church. When they ask for help you refuse to see them. . . .

CYRIL: We do not accept Arab priests among us so as not to lower our episcopal dignity. . . . Nor do we understand their language.

PORFIRY: Why not learn Arabic, or if you are too old why not have an interpreter to forward their requests?

CYRIL: We cannot introduce new customs.

PORFIRY: So you cling to your old habits. There will be no school for the sons of Arab priests; Arab widows and orphans will receive no shelter in convents; no Arab will be a bishop or head of a monastery.[7]

What lay behind this exchange was a long list of charges of Greek corruption. According to the Arabs, Greek priests had no sense of the sanctity of their vocation. They drank and fornicated without shame. Arab villagers near monasteries were filled with children who were the issue of the illicit union between monks and village women. Bishops commonly made mistresses of their housekeepers. Bishops loved money more than discharging their duties at the patriarchate. Church offices were regularly bought and sold, and money derived from pious donations at the shrines went into the pockets of the priests. Little money was used to meet the needs of Arab churches in the villages. Arab priests were paid no salaries and were forced to beg from the poor communities which they served. And they were denied opportunities to attend seminaries. The Orthodox hierarchy, staffed solely by Greeks, was closed to Arabs. Arab priests were discouraged from remaining celibate and thus eligible for promotion to bishop. Arabs further charged that if they were ignorant it was because the patriarchate responsible for their education under the Turkish *millet* system would not build adequate schools or hire qualified teachers.

The root of the Greco-Arab conflict could be traced back to the administrative organization of the Ottoman empire which transferred power from Arab Orthodox to Greek bishops. In the three hundred years from Saladin to the Turkish conquest of the sixteenth century, Arabs had made inroads into the hierarchy of the Greek Orthodox church. The office of patriarch in the ancient patriarchates of Alexandria, Antioch, and Jerusalem was held in a majority of instances by Arabs. Out of political self-interest the Ottoman government reversed that trend.

A central element in the reversal was the *millet* system which conferred governmental powers on the religious leaders of non-Muslim communities or "nations." From the beginning of their rule the Turks favored Greeks over Arabs in the leadership of the Orthodox church, particularly favoring the influential Greeks at the ecumenical patriarchate of Constantinople, which was recognized as "first of equals" by the other Eastern patriarchates. From 1517 the Greek clergy began to exercise responsibility for the internal affairs of all the Orthodox peoples of the empire— Greeks, Arabs, Syrians, Bulgarians, and Serbians. In a relatively short time the Greek-held ecumenical patriarchate acquired immense wealth, power, and influence, so much so that the patriarchates of Alexandria, Antioch, and Jerusalem became dependent on it. Major decisions affecting these patriarchates and the Orthodox peoples living under them were made only in distant Constantinople. So great was the power of the Greek church in Constantinople that the patriarch of Jerusalem, Germanos (1534–1579), was forced to move his residence permanently to the Turkish capital in order to be closer to the source of support of his own church in Palestine.

It was Germanos who first took steps to exclude Arabs from the hierarchy of the church by refusing Arab priests admission to the Brotherhood of the Holy Sepulchre, from which the governing synod was elected and candidates nominated for patriarchal elections. With this decision the Arab Orthodox

were effectively shut out of the leadership of the Eastern Orthodox church of Palestine. It did not take long before Arabs
complained that the Greek bishops cared more for the holy
places and for money derived from pilgrims than for the welfare
of the Arab communities under their spiritual care. The Orthodox clergy responded by sanctimoniously stressing their primary
responsibility to safeguard the holy place for all the churches of
Christendom.

The alienation of Arab Orthodox from the Greek-led church
of Palestine opened the door to missionary conversions.
Throughout the eighteenth and nineteenth centuries, significant
numbers of Arab Orthodox left their church and joined the
Greek Catholic "Melkite" church in union with Rome. Conversions were encouraged by Catholic leaders in Rome who, earlier
in 1622, had established a special Middle East office ("Propa-
ganda Fide") for this very purpose. The Catholic missionary
effort was immediately successful, for in 1723 all four Eastern
partriarchs, led by Jerusalem, prevailed on the Sublime Porte to
issue a decree forbidding Catholic evangelizing efforts aimed at
the Orthodox. Despite the decree, the Greeks continued to lose
Arab Orthodox to other churches.

During the regime of Ibrahim Pasha (1831–1840), the fortunes of all Christians changed for the better. For the first time
in centuries the *dhimmis* status of Christians was abolished.
Christians were officially regarded as equal to Muslims in political rights. They were exempted from the army without having to
pay an exemption tax. Both Jews and Christians were encouraged to repair their sanctuaries and build new ones. This freedom was intoxicating to Arab Christians who began to demand
that the Greek bishops reform the patriarchate of Jerusalem.
Helping the Arabs press their demands were the Russian Orthodox officials. Led by the archmandrite Porfiry Ouspensky, the
Russians came to the Holy Land in the middle of the nineteenth
century to aid the Greek hierarchy and then found themselves
encouraging the Arab Orthodox to turn against their Greek
overlords.

The involvement of Russian churchmen and politicians with
Jerusalem and Palestine lasted seventy-seven years, from 1840
until the Russian Revolution of 1917. What drove the Russians
was a combination of power and piety: a lust for imperial
expansion and a mystical sense of Russia's messianic role in the

Christian world. Throughout the eighteenth and early nineteenth centuries, Russia was continually at war with Turkey in the hope of destroying the Ottoman empire. After the defeat of Russia in the Crimean War of 1854–1856, the policy of the tsarist government shifted to that of keeping Turkey a weak southern neighbor. The penetration into the Middle East in the mid-nineteenth century was part of that strategy. Millions of Eastern Orthodox peoples lived within the Ottoman empire, and ever since the fall of Constantinople to the Turks in 1453, Russian tsars had seen themselves as successors to the Byzantine kings. The Byzantine imperial emblem of the double eagle was added to the Russian royal coat of arms. Russian royalty declared Moscow as the Third Rome and made no secret of its ambition to liberate Constantinople, the Second Rome, from the infidel Turk. Now the Russians were the true protectors of their fellow Orthodox Christians living under Muslim rule.

In the treaties of Kuchuk Kainardy (1774) and Jassy (1792), Russia won from Turkey the important concessions to represent all Orthodox peoples within the Ottoman empire, paralleling the right enjoyed by France in behalf of Catholics. Tsarist officials had also to consider the welfare of thousands of Russian pilgrims who in the late nineteenth century were journeying to the Holy Land. The Russians contemplated their own holy war to win back to the Orthodox fold a country which they felt belonged to them. Derek Hopwood describes the attitude:

> For the Russian believer, accustomed as he was through the liturgy to a deep reality of God's presence, pilgrimage to the Holy Land, baptism in the waters of the Jordan, Easter in Jerusalem with its reiterated refrain of "Christ is risen—risen indeed!"—these experiences were the very essence of his faith, so much so that the idea developed that Palestine was an extension of Holy Russian territory.[8]

The deterioration of the Greek patriarchate in Jerusalem and the discontent among the Arab Orthodox laity throughout Palestine deeply disturbed Russian religious leaders. They persuaded tsarist officials to send representatives to Syria and Palestine to examine possibilities for establishing a permanent Russian presence in the region. In the latter half of the nineteenth century several missions were sent, the first in 1843, led by Archmandrite Ouspensky, whose sharp exchange with Bish-

The Russian Orthodox Church of Mary
Magdalene, built in Muscovite style
in 1888 on the Mount of Olives.
(Photographed by Adrien Bonfils ca.
1860–1890)

op Cyril paints a clear picture of the problems which the
Russians faced with both Greeks and Arabs.

Through a combination of hard work, money, and intrigue,
the Russians succeeded in establishing a powerful presence in
Palestine. On the Mount of Olives were built the Russian
Church of the Ascension (1866) and the five-domed Muscovite
Church of Mary Magdalene (1888); the Church of Alexander
Nevsky was constructed (1890) adjacent to the Church of the
Holy Sepulchre. North of the old city, on a former Turkish
parade ground, the Cathedral of the Holy Trinity was built
(1872) at the center of what was to be called the Russian
Compound: a huge complex of chapels, schools, hospices,

clinics, and consular offices. The Russians built another church compound in Ein Kerem, northwest of Jerusalem, at the lovely hillside village where it was believed that John the Baptist was born.

The Russians conducted archaeological and charitable work through the newly endowed Imperial Orthodox Society, established in 1882. Russian archaeologists began to look for their own roots in the Holy Land by reviving scholarly interest in the history of the Georgian church in Palestine. One of the magnificent monuments of the church was the Monastery of the Cross in west Jerusalem's valley, itself a holy site where legend placed the tree from which Christ's cross was cut. Because they could not pay their taxes to the Turkish government, the Georgians lost this monastery to the Greeks, who later refused all Russian offers of payment to return the site to its original owners.

After the Crimean War, Russo-Greek relations began to deteriorate, especially when Russia shifted her strategy against Turkey. The idea developed in Moscow that in order to weaken Turkey it was necessary to foment internal disorder within the Ottoman empire, particularly among minority Christian peoples. Initially this was accomplished by encouraging Bulgarian Orthodox to declare their independence from the ecumenical patriarchate in Constantinople. Part of the same strategy called for supporting Arab Orthodox in their grievances against the Greek hierarchy in Jerusalem.

With regard to Jerusalem and Palestine, Russia recognized that she was in a competition with France, chiefly, and with other European powers as well. While French pilgrimage to the Holy Land had slowed in the nineteenth century, France's ability politically to influence Palestinian affairs had not declined. Her position was improved in 1847 when the Vatican decided to send the Latin patriarch (Joseph Valeria) to reside in Jerusalem where no Latin patriarch had lived since the end of the Crusades. Meanwhile, the awakened interest of both Great Britain and Prussia in the Holy Land was signaled by the establishment in 1841 of the combined Anglican-Protestant bishopric of Jerusalem. The Russian church also took careful notice of the missionary work by Anglican and Catholic churches.

In the last half of the nineteenth century, until 1917, the Russian goal was set: to encourage Arab Orthodox independence as a way of undermining Greek authority in the church.

Beggars, merchants, and passersby on the stone staircase leading from the Christian quarter to the courtyard of the Church of the Holy Sepulchre. (Photographed by Adrien Bonfils ca. 1860–1890)

Russian bishops sent to Palestine worked energetically to wrest control of the patriarchate from the Greeks and wherever possible to replace Greek with Russian priests as custodians of the holy places. The strategy failed, partly because Arab strength was overestimated and partly because Greek resolve was underestimated. The revolution of 1917 ended all efforts to enlarge Russian church influence in the Middle East.

But the Russian campaign had important and lasting consequences in awakening the political consciousness of Arab Christians, a development which directly contributed to the rise of nationalistic thinking among both Arab Christians and Muslims. To appreciate this connection one must recall 1870 when Bulgarian Orthodox Christians, encouraged by Russia, expelled the Greek bishops who presided over their church and declared their independence of the ecumenical patriarchate in Constantinople. It was a momentous event in the Ottoman empire. The ecumenical patriarch tried but failed to persuade the Ottoman government to suppress the schismatic church. Attention then shifted to the church in Palestine where the Greek bishops expressed apprehension about Russian efforts to encourage independence among the Arab Orthodox. Arabs, like the Bulgarians, resented the Greek hierarchy ruling a church consisting overwhelmingly of local non-Greek peoples with different nationalistic aspirations. Thrown together with Greeks as members of the Orthodox *millet*, Arabs were persecuted in reprisal for the Greek rebellion of 1822; after that event Arabs had less reason to see themselves as loyal members of the Greek "nation." They preferred to see their church headed by one of their own who would live among them, not a Greek patriarch of Jerusalem residing in distant Constantinople, begging money from Turks.

The issue between Greeks and Arabs came to a head in 1872 over what Greeks regarded as betrayal by their own patriarch Cyril. Cyril, perhaps influenced by the very words of Porfiry Ouspensky quoted above, had finally come to share the Russian view of the Arab Orthodox. Provoked by the growing European presence in the Holy Land, he made the crucial decision to move his residence to the Holy City soon after his election as patriarch of Jerusalem—the first Greek patriarch to do so since the sixteenth century. Moreover he supported the Russians against his fellow Greeks on the issue of independence for the Bulgarian church. The Greeks in Constantinople, along with the Brotherhood of the Holy Sepulchre (to whom Cyril was answerable), retaliated by ousting him as patriarch in 1872. It was a fateful decision. From that moment the all-Greek Brotherhood of the Holy Sepulchre openly showed its antagonism to the Arab Orthodox. The conflict between Arabs and Greeks continued through the years, and in 1908 Patriarch Damianos was also ousted by the church hierarchy when he showed pro-Arab tendencies.

In encouraging Arab opposition to oppose the Greek hierarchy, Russia had in fact acted as midwife to Arab nationalism. As Derek Hopwood writes:

> What Russia *had* done was to encourage the creation of a conscious Arab Orthodox opinion and to awaken a strong desire for greater

participation in the affairs of the patriarchate. The Orthodox
Arab national movement dates from this moment. Its echoes
resounded during the remainder of the nineteenth century and until
the first World War and its problems remain unsolved today.[9]

Indeed, Arab national problems remain unsolved not only
because of internal church politics but because the Ottoman
government ruling the country for more than four hundred
years preferred that they stay unsolved. Turkey had gotten a bad
taste of Arab Palestinian independence during the reign of
Ibrahim Pasha, who governed the country for his father, the
rebellious Sultan Muhammad Ali. When his rule ended in 1840,
the Turks were quite reluctant to see more expressions of Arab
Christian independence and supported the Greek hierarchy against
the Arab laity. After the Turks, the same pro-Greek strategy
guided Britain, then Jordan, and today Israel in coping with the
small but explosive world of Christian politics in Jerusalem.

The nineteen hundred years of Christian life in the Holy Land is
a history of warriors, pilgrims, politicians, and monks; they
conquered the land, colonized it, and erected churches and
monasteries to honor the memory of Jesus Christ whom they
believed had made this land earth's stepping-stone to heaven. We
can never know if Jesus, a Galilean Jew who showed little
interest in sacred sights and rituals, would have approved of
their works. His mind was on the coming kingdom, which he
believed would put an end to the earthly Jerusalem.

But the kingdom did not arrive. Jerusalem remained, and it
was this one small place that focused the energies of conquest
and consecration of all the nations in Christendom. The emperors, theologians, and architects of Byzantium established the
Christian presence in the Holy Land. The Latin Crusaders
showed what courage and brutality could accomplish in preserving it. The English, French, and German missionaries of the
nineteenth century, moved by the romance of the Crusades,
brought an ironic humanism to the land: failing in their original
mission to convert the Jews, they stayed to open schools and
found hospitals in the hope of winning Arabs. And the Greeks,
sometimes aided by their fellow Orthodox Russians, combated
the encroachments of European missionaries. Always willing to

negotiate with Muslim leaders, the Greeks clung to their holy places in the belief that as the true successors of Christ's disciples they were the lords of the Holy Land.

Conquest and consecration have mixed deeply among the Christians in this land. The mentality of conquest persists today in Jerusalem's church communities: in the wealth and power of the bishops, in the autocracy of the patriarchs, in the disdain of church leaders for the laity, and in the insulated religious compounds where monks and nuns stay close behind fortress walls, exactly as in Crusader times. One has only to see Greeks bargaining with Israelis, and Latins maneuvering with both Israelis and Arabs to undermine the Greeks, to know that the mentality of conquest is very much alive among Jerusalem's Christians.

The end of Christian military conquest in the late twelfth century did not spell the end of pilgrimage. Christians never stopped journeying to the Holy Land, and today they continue to arrive by the thousands. What draws them to the Holy Land is what has always drawn them: a desire to unite with the source of their religion. Christianity had its beginning in Galilee and Jerusalem. To journey to these places, to walk the land, to descend into sacred caves and climb up hallowed mountains, to dip one's hands in the River Jordan and gaze out on the Sea of Galilee, most of all to kiss the marble surface of Christ's Tomb—these acts of seeing and touching continue to be the pilgrim's communion with the sacred source of his faith.

For pilgrim Paula of the fourth century, the holy places made the scriptures come alive. Worshiping where Christ had stood, taught, prayed, and suffered was like walking on a spiritual bridge connecting past, present, and future. To see and touch the places which Christ had touched was to join the earthly life of the pilgrim to the glorious scriptural past. John Wilkinson points out that to Paula and to all pilgrims it is a short step from seeing a holy place to "visualizing the events of the history of salvation."[10] Wilkinson adds that we should not be "overprecise in marking the boundary between visualizing and receiving a vision." For "Paula pictured the Lord on the Cross, and actually sees him in the manger." Since Paula, centuries of pilgrims have descended into the Cave of the Nativity and mounted Calvary, and in the ecstasy of the moment not a few report seeing the form of Christ.

It was precisely the pilgrim's visions and other temptations to superstition that made Jerome so uneasy. He understood Christianity to be a spiritual, intellectual religion and reminded his fellow Christians that the heavens were open equally over Jerusalem and Britain. Save for archaeology and scriptural study, Jerusalem and the Holy Land do not appeal to theologians and to the leaders of world church organizations. It is to the pious, to those of direct, simple, emotional faith that Holy Land pilgrimage has its greatest appeal. Pilgrims are indeed prone to pious exercises and crude superstitions: all-night vigils; buying specially blessed water, candles, and crosses; wearing unashamedly the miniature crown of thorns sold in souvenir shops and carried past the doors of the Church of the Holy Sepulchre.

There is humor in the sight of Christian pilgrims in Jerusalem. But there is no mocking the pilgrim. The pilgrim has come here to see and touch and kiss the sacred stones. Never mind how badly tended are the shrines, how motley the crowds around the churches, how obscured the site of Calvary with encrustations of gold, emerald, and ruby; if the pilgrim can see the wood and touch the stone, it is enough. Thus the earthly city bestows a vision of the City on High.

One should add that to the Christian pilgrim it matters little whether Turk or Arab or Jew rules Jerusalem. What matters is that he is free to come to the holy places and free to worship in his own language once he arrives there. All the rest is politics, symbols of a broken world which the pilgrim would gladly leave behind in his devotions. And if the monks who tend the shrines seem officious and often contemptuous of the pilgrims praying at them, that too for the pilgrim is part of a broken world sooner forgotten.

Jerusalem holds a different meaning for Christians than it does for Jews. For Christians, Jerusalem is not a national center, uniting land, people, religion. Christians, unlike Jews, are not one ethnic-national people sharing a single historical experience. Diversity, not commonality of nation, land, language, and ritual, characterize Christians. Jews had only Jerusalem to unite them as a nation people; Christians, consisting of many national groups, had Rome, Constantinople, Geneva, Canterbury, and more. When Christians came to Jerusalem as conquerors or pilgrims or missionaries or merchants, they came to a city whose shape resembled their mind's ideal and the places they left behind. And so, like the Italian merchants who re-created Genoa and Pisa in the neighborhoods of Jerusalem, what one found in this city was a piece of Constantinople, a part of Mainz, a bit of England.

Jesus could never have anticipated the development of Christianity in Jerusalem. The Gospel writers portray him as expressing contempt for the practices of his own Jewish religion in this city. Considering the record of bigotry and bloodshed, it is doubtful that Jesus would have had much use for Jerusalem's churchmen. Jesus' eyes were on the coming kingdom, whose appearance would put an end to the earthly city as he knew it and as we have known it through history.

PART THREE

Jerusalem's Holiness in Islamic Tradition

CHAPTER 7

Islam's Triumph
in Jerusalem

Glorified be He who carried His servant [Muhammad]
by night from the masjid al-haram *[Mecca]*
to the masjid al-aqsa *[Jerusalem?].*
—Koran, 17, 1

[Nothing] could rival in grace this Dome of the Rock.
—al-Mukaddasi, *Muslim geographer, 10th century*

The construction of a magnificent shrine on the site of the
ancient Jewish Temple confirmed the holiness of Jerusalem for
Muslims. The shrine, an imposing octagonal building named the
Dome of the Rock (*Qubbat as-Sakhra*), was constructed in 685
over the outcropping of limestone rock which Jewish tradition
held to be the place of Abraham's intended sacrifice of Isaac and
of the Holy of Holies of Solomon's Temple. Later Islamic
tradition pointed to this sacred rock as the place from which
Muhammad began his Ascent to Heaven to receive Allah's final
revelation.

In building the Dome of the Rock, the earliest Arab rulers of
Palestine expressed their reverence for Jerusalem, city of the
prophets from Abraham and Moses to Jesus, culminating with
Muhammad, the "seal of the prophets." Thus the Dome symbolized both Islam's inheritance from and triumph over Judaism
and Christianity.

Jerusalem's sanctity was reinforced for centuries by millions
of Syrian and Palestinian Muslim pilgrims who, unable to make
the obligatory *hajj* to Mecca, settled for a visit to the Dome of

the Rock in Jerusalem. There all the prayers and other pilgrimage rituals were performed, including circumambulation around Abraham's stone as if before the Ka'ba, the sacred cube-shaped building housing the black meteorite in Mecca.

Although the religious importance of Jerusalem in Islam was unquestioned, the city never became a capital for Muslims as it had earlier been for Jews and briefly for Latin Christians. Even when Muslim rulers had the chance to designate Jerusalem a regional capital, that honor fell to the newly endowed Muslim town of Ramla, a few miles inland from the Mediterranean Sea. The lack of economic resources in Jerusalem explains its lack of political significance. The first Muslim conquerors recognized from the beginning that Jerusalem was a city which made religion, not money. For profitable export the city produced olive oil and handcrafts, and little else that could interest profit-minded Muslim raiders and traders.

A second reason which explains Jerusalem's political insignificance is that for a very long time after the original Muslim conquest of the city in 638, Jerusalem was seen as a preeminent Christian city whose skyline was dominated by dozens of church spires. While this view challenged the Muslim conquerors to rebuild Jerusalem, it also made them feel that this city was not their own, that they had come here as alien conquerors. Their world was east and west of Jerusalem, in the great caliphal cities of Damascus, Baghdad, Cairo, and Istanbul. Throughout the long period in which Muslim imperial power shifted from Syria to Iraq and Egypt, and then to Turkey, Jerusalem and Palestine remained on the periphery of Muslim struggles. Jerusalem was repeatedly the object of Muslim conquest, but it remained in Muslim eyes a remote place of little importance beyond its religious significance as the place where it was believed Muhammad stopped on the Night Journey before ascending to heaven.

Undoubtedly Jerusalem was known and revered by Muhammad's followers before the city was conquered, but the conquest itself was motivated by nothing so noble and fanatic as "holy war," certainly not the ferocious holy wars practiced in earlier centuries by Byzantines and Franks. Nor was territorial conquest precisely the reason the first Muslims entered Palestine. Their motive was more mundane: to loot the country in a series of raiding adventures which had begun in Syria. The first of these raiding expeditions occurred in 629, in the month of September when Greek bishops joyously celebrated mass daily at Christ's Tomb to thank the Almighty for the return of the True Cross stolen by the Persians only nine years earlier. While the Christians were at prayer, a small party of Arab bedouins crossed the Jordan River and clashed with local Byzantine border troops at a tiny hamlet called Mu'ta at the southeastern tip of the Dead Sea. Historian Philip Hitti eloquently describes this skirmish as "the first gun in a struggle that was not to cease until the proud Byzantine capital [Constantinople] had fallen [in 1453] to the latest champion of Islam and the name of Muhammad substituted for that of Christ on the walls of the most magnificent cathedral of Christendom, St. Sophia."[1]

The purpose of the Arab raid was to loot sword-making shops for weapons needed by the prophet Muhammad to carry out his planned attack on Mecca. Muhammad got his swords, conquered Mecca, and purified its sacred stone of pagan idols, after which he subdued and converted to his own faith most of the native peoples of the Arabian peninsula. Then, in 632, he abruptly died, one year before Syria and Palestine were invaded. It is doubtful that this remarkable prophet-warrior of Islam sat down to plan the conquest of the rich fertile lands northwest of his desert home; there is even less reason to think that he saw this region as promising for missionary conversion. What we know with certainty is that bedouin tribesmen from the Arabian peninsula, Muhammad's earliest followers, continued their raiding in the northwest; they were forced to do so because the Prophet's teachings had called a halt to the ancient desert practice of intertribal plundering. Muhammad had convinced them that because all Muslims are united as brothers in the *umma*, the "community of faith," it was an offense against Allah to attack a brother's camp to steal his gold, camels, and women.

Fortunately for the fledgling Islamic nation, Syria and Palestine were a plunderer's paradise: easy to reach, rich with treasure, and guarded by native garrisons of slow-moving, unreliable foot soldiers who hated their Byzantine Greek officers. When the fighting started, the Byzantines were pitted against skilled Arab camel and horse cavalrymen who knew they would be handsomely rewarded for a good fight in the desert where they had the natural advantage. In the next four years hit-and-run raids gradually expanded into major military engagements, and in 633 the conquest began in earnest. The initial target was not Jerusalem, which lacked commercial value, but Gaza, the ancient market town on the great coastal trade route from Syria to Egypt. Rushing troops to the area, the Byzantines stood off their Muslim foes who now grew anxious about their own fate in the alien land. The turning point in Arab fortunes occurred months later when Abu Bakr, elected caliph (or Muhammad's spiritual and political "deputy"), ordered the brilliant general Khalid ibn al-Walid to go to the rescue of fellow Muslims in southern Palestine. Employing a bold strategy, al-Walid, whom Muhammad himself had originally dubbed "sword of Allah," led a forced march across the waterless Syrian desert, reaching Damascus in the astonishingly short time of eighteen days (a feat still studied in desert warfare). The surprised Byzantine forces proved no match for the swift-riding Muslim warriors and temporarily lost Damascus, some say by the treachery of Jews and disaffected Syrian Christians within the city walls.

A little more than a year later, in July 634, Arab troops under al-Walid won a second important battle at Ajnadyn near Lydda in southern Palestine, which gave them control of the countryside. The pressure of the Arabs was felt in Jerusalem where Greek Patriarch Sophronius complained in his Christmas sermon that because of Arab marauders he was prevented from making the ritual pilgrimage to the birthplace of Christ in Bethlehem, only five miles away. After Christmas the situation deteriorated, particularly for the church. These were Sophronius's pained words to describe Arab actions in his January Epiphany sermon:

> Why is there no end to the bloodshed? Why are churches being destroyed and the cross desecrated? The Saracens, "abomination of desolation" foretold by the Prophet Daniel, are passing through lands forbidden to them, plundering cities and destroying fields, burning villages and razing holy monasteries... and priding themselves that they will finally conquer the whole world.[2]

The Byzantine emperor Heraclius retaliated. Drawing from his huge reserve of manpower in Asia Minor, he sent a force which regained Damascus for a short time, only to lose it to the Muslims again in September 635, this time for good. The storied capital did not see Christian rulers again until French officials arrived under a League of Nations mandate in the early twentieth century.

The death knell was sounded for Byzantine control of Palestine in August 636 in a hot, dry, dusty valley of the Yarmuk River, a northern tributary of the Jordan, where Muslim cavalry decimated their opponents, leaving the country wide open to the new conquerors. The Muslims took their time sweeping down through central Palestine, easily taking selected towns, often helped by the local inhabitants who viewed them as liberators from the Greek yoke. Avoiding stationary warfare for which they had little skill and patience, Arab generals decided not to storm Jerusalem's towers and chose instead to starve the city into submission. This they achieved in 638. It was an anticlimax, for in the previous year the vastly more important capital of Ctesiphon had fallen, breaking the back of the Sassanid empire and leading to the mass conversion to Islam of thousands of Zoroastrians of Iraq and Iran. The strategic Palestinian port city of Caesarea, supplied by sea, held out until 640 before it too surrendered. In the same year the entire country of Egypt capitulated. Thus only eighteen years after Muhammad's humiliating flight (*hijra*) from Mecca to Medina, the whole of the Middle East was in the hands of a few thousand Arab warriors united in the Prophet's faith.

No one grieved more at the loss of his provinces than the Byzantine emperor Heraclius. His forces and those of the Persians had exhausted themselves in unrelenting combat for more than thirty years and could not stave off the Arab advance into their respective lands. Heraclius, who had rushed to the defense of his beloved Syria, which region included Palestine, knew that all was lost at the battle of the Yarmuk; he fled north to the safety of his capital Constantinople, his parting words a bitter prophecy of the country's destiny: "Farewell, O Syria, and what an excellent country this is for the enemy."

Seized by the momentum of conquest, the intrepid Muslim fighters struck out in every direciton. By the year 700, only sixty-eight years after the death of Muhammad, they had seized lands stretching from the Atlantic Ocean to the western mountain range of China, creating a new empire larger than any preceding it.

Historians are agreed that during the seven years (633–640) from the initial invasion of Syria to the fall of Caesarea, the lives of the native peoples of Palestine were little changed by the coming of the new conquerors. This was chiefly because the caliphal inheritors of Muhammad's mantle were little interested in the conquest of territory per se. Those who controlled Syria and Palestine for more than a hundred years were raiders and traders, exactly what Muhammad himself had been. After subduing the population, they had no wish to cultivate the land and so left this inferior activity to the native peoples. Muslim leaders were chiefly interested in taxing their subject peoples in order to generate income for continuing military operations and the construction of mosques and palaces, and for their own family treasuries. Property taxes were the primary source of revenue. In addition, a head tax was levied on all non-Muslim subjects to defray the cost of the military protection provided them, as non-Muslims were forbidden to bear arms. Having paid their taxes, all subjects were free to live their lives, to work, and to worship without interference. To the native Christians and Jews of Palestine, these changes were a qualitative improvement over former Byzantine times when the Greek governor taxed heavily and often interfered in local community life without reason or apology.

Many of the Muslim conquerors stayed to live in Palestine; avoiding the native population, they formed a small, exclusive military elite living in the new camp town of Ramla on the coastal plain. A hundred years after the conquest, the Arab Muslim population was a mere 200,000 out of a total Syria-Palestine population of 3.5 million. The social hierarchy was clear and rigid: Muslims at the top and, in descending order: converts to Islam who were called *mawali*, or tribal "clients"; Christian and Jewish *dhimmis*, or the "protected ones," required to pay the head tax; and finally slaves, mostly blacks from the conquered African territories.

Contrary to popular depictions of armed zealots clutching a Koran in one hand and brandishing a sword in the other, Arabs did not invade Syria and Palestine to spread the gospel of their new faith. Quite the opposite was true. The early Muslim leaders neither sought nor desired converts to the faith, for every convert meant a loss of the head tax imposed on non-Muslims. When it was clear that a number of native Christians were converting to Islam in order to escape this tax, Muslim officials actively discouraged conversion. The notable exception to this practice was the fifth Umayyad caliph Umar II (717–720), who earned his sobriquet the "pious caliph" because he thought no obstacle should stand in the way of spreading the faith to the ignorant and unbelieving. Once, his advisers complained that the state treasury was jeopardized by his religious ideals and suggested a test of sincerity for the new convert—ascertaining whether he had undergone required ritual circumcision. Upon hearing this Umar protested, "Verily God sent His Prophet as a missionary and not as a circumcisor."

The early Muslim conquerors of Syria and Palestine and the Umayyad rulers who followed them were Arabs first and last and viewed their religion as a precious vessel entrusted to them by Muhammad, a vessel defiled in the hands of non-Arabs. For that reason they took the attitude that the Shari'a religious law was too holy to apply to non-Muslims. Here the Arabs merely repeated the ancient pattern of ethno-religious exclusivity common to peoples of the Middle East. The Byzantines of Constantinople, in their contempt for native Syrians and Palestinians and in their implacable hostility toward the Church of Rome, thought of the Christian faith as irreducibly Greek. And well before the rise of Byzantium, the early Israelites believed that the Torah-based covenant of God and the circumcised-elect people were one, setting Israel apart from the *goyim*, the foreign nations of the world.

In the spring of 638 starved and exhausted citizens of Jerusalem, all of them Christian because of the Byzantine ban against Jewish residence, begged for peace but insisted that the caliph Umar come in person to accept their surrender. Demonstrating that Jerusalem was revered by Islam well before the Arab conquest, Umar agreed to the request. What made Jerusalem holy to Muslims? What was the relationship of Jerusalem's holiness to the Ka'ba sanctuary in Mecca? What was Muhammad's own view of Jerusalem? We begin to find answers in examining the fascinating details of Umar's visit to Jerusalem.

The visit itself is legend, a story based less on historical fact than on the Arab chronicler's esteem toward the caliph. The chronicler stresses Umar's moral superiority over those he had conquered, particularly the Greek patriarch of Jerusalem Sophronius, who personally surrendered the city to the caliph. When the two leaders met for the first time, the simple rough battle garb worn by the Muslim seemed to rebuke the ecclesiastical finery of the Christian prelate. By contrast to the Greek, whose mind was a cauldron of hot intrigues and manipulations, Umar is described as one who "did not glide about and whisper like the hippocrites, but was sincerely God-fearing and never indiscreet."[3]

Umar's first request was to be led to the Temple Mount, an acknowledgment of Islam's acceptance of the Hebraic prophetic tradition. Reaching the Temple Mount, the caliph found himself disgusted on seeing that Christians had heaped garbage in the sacred enclosure to express their contempt for the Judaic faith; deliberately included in the garbage was an added touch of ritual defilement—menstrual cloths. The caliph, out of respect for Jews, ordered the cleansing of the area, an act which also prepared the sacred Jewish site for Muslim worship. But the legend includes a bit of malice. In retaliation for befouling the Temple Mount, Muslims deliberately began mispronouncing the Arabic name for the Church of the Resurrection (kiyama or "resurrection") as al-kamama, or the Church of Shit.

Another expression of Umar's superior Muslim morality occurred when the caliph and patriarch arrived at the Church of the Resurrection at the noon hour for Muslim prayer. Deferring to his guest, the patriarch invited him to pray in the church, but the Muslim, not wishing to see the building turned into a mosque by his followers, declined and walked outside into the courtyard to perform his devotions.

Umar fulfilled the hopes of Jews by refusing the church's request to continue the ban against Jewish residence and inviting them back into the city. To the oldest lovers of this city, Umar was the fulfillment of prophecy: "...Jerusalem is not handed over other than to a king who is fit to be called a mighty one."[4]

For Arab writers there was no greater symbol of Muslim tolerance than the contract which Umar made with the people of Jerusalem. Offering physical protection and freedom of worship in exchange for a mere tax, the contract was a model of practical wisdom in the treatment of defeated peoples by Muslim conquerors. But to Jerusalem's Christians, Umar's contract was demeaning. The head tax was a symbol of their inferiority in the new Islamic empire, and the assurance of protection for their churches was offset by a ban against building new ones. Yet so seriously did the Muslims take the exchange of protection for taxes that when Sophronius briefly regained Damascus in 634, Muslim leaders returned the Damascenes their taxes. Here is one account of Umar's contract with Jerusalem's people.

> In the name of Allah the Merciful, the Compassionate. This is what Umar the servant of God, the Commander of the Faithful has offered to the people of Aelia [Jerusalem] by way of security. He has given them security for their persons and for their property, for their churches and for their crosses. . . . It is obligatory on the people of Aelia to pay the poll-tax according to what is paid by the people of Medain [the Persian capital]. They must expel from the town the Byzantines and the robbers, but whoever among them goes out is guaranteed in the matter of his life and property until he reaches a place of safety, or whoever stays will be safe and have the same obligation as is upon the people of Aelia with regard to the poll-tax. Again whoever of the people of Aelia prefers to depart with his life and property along with the Byzantines, but giving up their churches and crosses, they will be guaranteed safety for their persons until they arrive at a place of safety. . . . And pertaining to what is in this document there is the convenant of God and the guarantee of his Prophet as well as that of the Caliphs and the Faithful, provided they pay the poll-tax which is imposed on them.[5]

Included in the legend about Umar is also a conversation between Jerusalem's conqueror and one of his most trusted advisers, a converted Jew, Ka'b al-Akbar, whose name in Arabic combined the sacred meteorite in Mecca with the exalted power of Allah. The reported conversation between the two men helps suggest not only the reverence which Muslims held for Jerusalem but also their feelings of insecurity in this centuries-old Jewish and Christian city.

The adviser Ka'b suggests to the caliph that he should pray on the Temple Mount behind Abraham's Rock of Sacrifice. In this way the caliph will have both the holy Abrahamic stone and Mecca's Ka'ba before him. Suddenly the caliph recognizes a trick from the converted Jew who has not entirely stopped believing in the superiority of his former religion. "O you clever Jew," Umar seems to say, "you are clinging to the faith of your forefathers." Umar then reminds Ka'b that the prophet Muhammad himself, infuriated with Jews for rejecting him,

changed the *qibla*, the "direction of prayer," from Jerusalem to
Mecca. To the caliph this meant that Jerusalem and Mecca, the
Abrahamic stone and the Ka'ba, could never be placed on the
same level of sanctity.

There were other, more obvious implications in Umar's
rebuke of his adviser. Acknowledging that Jerusalem was the
City of the Prophets, and granted that the prophetic tradition
took shape with Abraham, the vastly superior truth in Umar's
eyes was that the prophetic tradition culminated in Muhammad.
Therefore it was the cities of Muhammad, Mecca, and Medina
that were to exercise religious superiority over Jerusalem.

Fully to appreciate the way in which Jerusalem, while sacred,
began to be seen as subordinate to Mecca and Medina, we
should examine for a moment Muhammad's esteem for Hebrew
and Christian scriptures, and further his antagonism toward
both Jews and Christians for rejecting his apostolic authority.

Scholarly study of the Koran shows that the main principles
of Islam were derived from Hebraic scriptures with certain
additions from the New Testament. Muhammad himself made
no claim for originality. He made it clear from the beginning of
his ministry (which began in 610 C.E., when he was forty years
of age) that he was not delivering a new prophecy but rather
seeking to reunite human beings by the message of the One
Creator God of the universe. It was a message which had been
voiced by all the biblical personalities from Abraham and Moses
to Jesus—prophets upon whose shoulders he stood.

The message which he taught came to be called Islam,
meaning "confident submission" to God, a religious practice
which consisted first and foremost in the confession of the
Oneness of God and concurrently in the rejection of all idolatrous worship. Following Jewish scriptures, Muhammad interpreted the purpose of human life as righteousness under
God-given moral law. He accepted the Jewish fast days and the
Sabbath day of prayer as models for Muslim devotion. From the
outset, in imitation of Jewish synagogue ritual, he ordered his
followers to pray facing Jerusalem, the symbol of prophecy and
moral law. Further, he believed in a Final Judgment and the
resurrection of the dead; and he acknowledged the messianic
misssion of Jesus. Certainly one of his greatest achievements was
the setting forth of these theological principles in the majestic

cadences of the Arabic language, an act which eventually produced the written Koran.

Sometime before his death in 632, with utter sincerity and high expectation, Muhammad called out to all his tribal kinsmen who practiced paganism to quit their idols and heed the message of the one spiritual God of heaven; and to the Jews and Christians of Arabia he issued an invitation to accept his prophecy of God as their own and to accept his (Muhammad's) apostolic authority. In all these hopes he experienced sharp disappointment. His kinsmen would not turn about, and his fellow monotheists would have nothing to do with him. What followed underscores a truth learned from all religious history: rejection, far more than acceptance, provides the energy to transform an ideal vision into a concrete reality. One need only remember that if Jerusalem's Jews had accepted Jesus' apostolic authority, the church would have remained an obscure Jewish sect.

The crucial moment in the early career of Muhammad's ministry occurred in 621 when he was driven out of Mecca by the powerful Quraish Arab tribesmen who would not allow his anti-idolatry sermons to interfere with their lucrative trade with pagan pilgrims to the sacred meteorite in the Ka'ba ("cube") in Mecca. These pilgrimages had made Mecca a regional center for idol worship. The next year, as resistance to his message grew more violent, Muhammad and his few followers fled to the city of Yathrib (it later came to be called, in Muhammad's honor, Medina, "City of the Prophet").

In Yathrib, Muhammad found a wealthy and influential Jewish community whose leaders he immediately sought out for support. To the Jews, Muhammad appeared a strange, repellent figure who proclaimed his belief in God, the moral law, and the prophets, but who seemed to have little scholarly skill in interpreting biblical passages and who often misquoted scriptures. Further, he was not prepared to agree that God had chosen the nation of Israel as his eternal vessel for proclaiming the moral law to the world. Worst of all, he acknowledged Jesus as an authentic prophet.

Nor would the Christian monks in the neighboring monasteries pay any attention to him. What little they knew of him convinced them that he was an ignorant heretic. For while this self-proclaimed prophet accepted Jesus, he would not call him the Son of God, stubbornly insisting that the One God could have no son. To the horror of the theologically sophisticated monks, Muhammad branded the dogma of the Trinity as a false teaching.

Despite these reactions, Muhammad persisted in his teaching, attracted followers, and they together with him became in time a united group which turned increasingly to military means to achieve their goals. After crucial victories against local Arab tribes in the vicinity of Yathrib, enlarging the Muslim treasury, Muhammad found himself in a position to return to Mecca and enforce his religious authority.

In 630, nine years after his humiliating flight, Muhammad appeared in Mecca with a skilled and experienced army. He went straightaway to the Ka'ba to cleanse the sanctuary of idols, destroying all statues and pictures save a portrait of the Virgin Mary and child which moved him. In this one action he instilled in Islam forevermore that iconoclastic hatred of images that would later challenge Christians into rethinking the propriety of icons in the church's worship.

After disposing of the idolators, Muhammad turned to his Jewish detractors. According to one story, he ordered the systematic slaughter of eight hundred Jewish men, then sold their wives and children into slavery. It was an ugly stain on Islamic history which plagued Muslim apologists centuries later. It also qualified as an early instance of *jihad*, or "holy war," later authorized by the Koranic passage, "The infidel is more serious than killing" (Surah 2:214). But here, too, Muhammad was not original. The concept of holy war, deriving from the Hebrew *herem* and reinforced by the Christian concept of "God's war," was a well-established practice in the ancient world.

Jews and Christians were not, strictly speaking, infidels or unbelievers; but in their resistance to the authority of the prophet Muhammad they were clearly seen to be an obstacle to the spread of the religion of Islam. What should Muslims think of them? Muhammad answered with a special category, *Ahl al-Kitab*, "People of the Book": those who had received the true revelation of God but, unlike Muslims, did not share the privilege of having accepted the final revelation of God's truth vouchsafed through Muhammad. The implication was clear: Jews and Christians were socially acceptable but religiously inferior. How should that inferiority be symbolized? The answer was clear and practical: taxes. In one Koranic passage (9:29) Muslims are warned not to follow Jews and Christians "to whom scriptures were given until they pay tribute out of hand, being brought low." Muslims were even prepared to believe that the smell of idolatry and moral corruption continued to linger around Jews and Christians, for the passage cited continues in this manner:

> The [Jews and Christians] choose their rabbis and monks as lords instead of God and the Messiah the Son of Mary. But we are ordered to worship one God alone. There is no God but He. He is far above what they associate with Him. . . . O believers, many rabbis and monks devour man's wealth wantonly and debar men from the way of God.

In the Islamic state, Jews and Christians were assigned a place above that of slaves but below that of Muslims, the symbol of their inferiority being payment of the required head tax. But since so much of Islamic belief was rooted in Hebraic scriptures, did not the inferior status of the Jews reflect poorly on the truth of the Prophet's message? Muhammad replied with a theological maneuver. He circumvented both the question of Islam's historical roots and the Jewish rejection of his ministry by the simple act of claiming the patriarch Abraham as his own, an act of "filching" the historian J. Wellhausen called it.[6] The basis of the theft was already laid in the traditional acknowledgment of Abraham's son Ishmael as the spiritual ancestor of the Arab people. The bond was deepened with the claim that both Abraham and Ishmael were founders of the Ka'ba, and as Abraham led pilgrimages there, he was therefore the first Muslim.[7] Thus in one bold, imaginative stroke Muhammad declared Islam to be the original, underived truth of God, a faith "independent of, and prior to, both Judaism and Christianity."[8]

Had the Medinese Jews shown more sympathy for Muhammad's ministry, Islam might not have developed as an independent religion. And had Arabia's Christians accepted the Meccan preacher, whose unswerving monotheism bore some resemblance to Monophysite doctrines (which may have influenced him), it is also conceivable that Islam would have died the death of an obscure desert sect. Fortunately for the champions of Islam, the message of the Prophet was rejected by both Jews and Christians. He lived to give birth to his own religion which united the disparate tribes of the Arabian peninsula, substituting "faith for blood as the element binding the community together."[9] In time the military prowess of his closest followers produced a world empire.

The antagonism which developed between Muslims on one side and Jews and Christians on the other cost Jerusalem its preeminence. Muhammad made the decision to change the direction pf prayer (*qibla*) from Jerusalem to Mecca.[10] Did the city then lose its sanctity? What happened is best described as a reordering of sanctity. Once Muhammad had taken control of Mecca, carried out his cherished desire of cleansing the Ka'ba of idolatrous images, and rededicated the sacred black meteorite there in the name of Allah, there was no question that Mecca was for all Muslims the shrine center of their faith. After Mecca in order of sacral importance came Medina, the city where the *hijra* took place and where Muhammad founded Islam as a distinct religious community. Jerusalem, more particularly Abraham's Moriah stone and the great Muslim domed shrine later built over it, while never ceasing to be a place of pilgrimage, did not become an obligatory *hajj* like the pilgrimages to the mosques of Mecca and Medina. Throughout the Muslim centuries, Jerusalem remained a *desirable* pilgrimage place of visitation (*ziyara*) for those already on *hajj* to Mecca and Medina. And for those who could not make the long, arduous, expensive journey to the Arabian cities, a pilgrimage to Jerusalem was seen as a much desired alternative—and this included the Muslims of Syria and Palestine. Thus, in an informal system of pilgrimage worship, Jerusalem was ranked ahead of all other Muslim cities but distinctly behind Mecca and Medina.

The year 661 marks a major turning point in the history of Islamic Jerusalem, for in that year Muawiya, the military governor of Syria and Palestine, was solemnly installed as caliph by his fellow Muslims in a small mosque on the Temple Mount. The ascension of Muawiya, a member of the old aristocratic Umayya clan of Mecca, launched a dynasty of caliphs which would greatly expand the boundaries of an empire that would last for a hundred years, until the Persian Abbasids brought it down.

Muawiya did not attain his exalted position easily. He succeeded Ali ibn-abu-Talib, the Prophet's cousin, who became the fourth caliph after the murder of the incompetent and nepotistic third caliph, Uthmann, the latter an Umayyad kinsmen of Muawiya. The personal animosity between Ali and Uthmann was fed by an older continuing tension between Muhammad's humble Hashimite family clan and the wealthy and powerful Umayya clan of Mecca. The Hashimites resented the Umayyad for first opposing the Prophet's faith and then accepting it when it proved militarily and financially successful. The supporters of Ali rejected the election of Uthmann as caliph; to them the legitimate basis of succession to the Prophet's mantle was heredity, not the traditional desert tribal democracy. Of all the Muslim leaders, they believed, only Ali could truly succeed the founder of Islam as his caliphal deputy, for he stood closest in family to Muhammad as his cousin, son-in-law, and the father of Hassan and Husayn, the Prophet's only grandsons.

As Ali's party rejected Uthmann's claim to the caliphate, so the Umayya clan rejected Ali; the dispute in 656 led to the first Muslim civil war, pitting Ali's Shi'ites (or "partisans") against their opponents, called Sunni (or "orthodox") Muslims, and opening a wound in the body of Islam that remains unhealed to the present day. Ali won the war, but his troubles had only begun. When Ali was declared caliph, he moved the caliphal headquarters from Medina, where the older Muslim leaders lived, to the new military camp town of Kufa in Iraq, where he had gained many new Shi'ite followers. From that point, the power center of Islam, originally in the Arabian peninsula, gradually shifted northward to Iraq and Syria.

Muawiya did not wait long to avenge his cousin Uthmann, in whose murder Ali was implicated. In 657 their respective supporters came to blows on the banks of the Euphrates River in a battle which greatly weakened Ali's power and prepared the way for Muawiya to realize his own political ambitions. Four years later, following the fate of his predecessors Umar and Uthmann, Caliph Ali, walking to prayers in Kufa's mosque, was felled by an assassin's dagger. After first bribing Ali's son Hassan not to press his right to the title of caliph, Muawaiya proclaimed himself the Prophet's deputy not in Arabia or Iraq, where he and his family were detested by the Shi'ites, but in Jerusalem, the central city of the province he had ruled effectively for the preceding twenty years.

Muawiya was crowned caliph in Jerusalem but he ruled from Damascus, the newly selected capital of the enlarging Islamic empire. With the choice of Damascus as the new imperial capital, neighboring Jerusalem was favored with architectural works, becoming something of a personal shrine city of the House of Umayya. At the same time both Mecca and Medina, while remaining cities of central religious importance, lost much of their political influence in the affairs of the empire.

Damascus, sitting on green hills at the foot of snow-covered Mount Hermon, was the oldest continuously inhabited city on earth—a town whose gates Muhammad declined to enter because "he wished to enter paradise but once." "Paradise" lay in the human scene no less than in the natural. Philip Hitti sketches a delightful portrait of Damascus's public face in the early Muslim era that could serve accurately for Jerusalem in those days.

> . . . In its narrow covered streets the Damascene with his baggy trousers, heavy turban and red pointed shoes rubbed shoulders with the sun-tanned Bedouin in his flowing gown surmounted by the *kufiyah* (head shawl) and *iqal* (head band). Occasionally a European-dressed [Christian] passed by. A few women, all veiled, crossed the streets; others stole glimpses through the latticed windows of their homes overlooking the bazaars and public squares. There was no right or left rule of way, no part of the passage reserved for riders or pedestrians. Amidst the confused crowd an aristocrat might be seen on horseback cloaked in a silk *aba* and armed with a sword. The screaming voices of sherbet sellers and sweetmeat vendors competed with the incessant tramp of passers-by and of donkeys and camels laden with the varied products of the desert and the town. The entire city atmosphere was charged with all kinds of smell. The demand on eye, ear and nose was overwhelming.[11]

Soon after Umar's conquest, Muslim settlers began arriving in Jerusalem from Arabia. Some fled the impoverishment of the infertile desert peninsula; others, mostly from Medina, were attracted to the city's aura of sanctity. Among the luminaries were Simeon, the father of Muhammad's Jewish concubine Rayhana; he took up residence on the Temple Mount and delivered sermons from the first mosque built there. The Muslims followed the example of Jews and Christians and engaged in works of charity among the poor. The wife of Damascus's *cadi* (religious judge) would spend six months each year helping Jerusalem's poor. One philanthropic practice begun by Caliph Uthmann, only eight years after the conquest, was to dedicate "the revenue from the rich vegetable gardens of Siloam [the village now called Silwan, south of the city walls]... to the poor of the city."[12]

Muslims mixed well in the city, and Christians had no complaints about the new masters of the country. Indeed, one high-ranking Greek bishop went out of his way to compliment Muslim officials, saying "... They are not enemies of Christianity. On the contrary, they praise our faith and honor the priests and saints of the Lord and confer benefits upon the churches and monasteries."[13]

When Muawiya arrived, Damascus and Jerusalem were Greek cities managed by thousands of native Christians, fluent in Aramaic, Syriac, and Greek, many speaking Arabic. The caliph needed these people, for the illiterate bedouins he commanded were incapable of managing a bureaucratic organization. To pay for new palaces, castles, and mosques, and to subsidize the ambitious military expeditions directed against the still-powerful Byzantine forces in Asia Minor, the caliph required vast sums of money. Money was raised from taxes imposed on the non-Muslim subjects of the empire, the vast majority of whom were native Christians of Syria and Palestine; and the caliph relied upon priests, monks, and other trusted Christian subjects to collect the taxes. The eminent church theologian John of Damascus, when he was not writing polemical anti-Islam sermons, was faithfully serving the caliph as a high treasury official, as had his father before him. Since Arabic had not yet been introduced into the official bureaucracy, Greek continued to be used as the language of public affairs, with the result that many native Syrians, Greeks, and Jews attained positions of immense influence within the empire.

So intimately was Muawiya involved in the Christian life of the conquered provinces he ruled as governor and caliph for forty years that Jacobite Christians would bring their disputes to him for mediation. The caliph's physician and court poet were Christians, and his wife was a Jacobite.

Muawiya was not handsome: a short, physically repulsive man with a fat belly and huge buttocks—but his skills as a politician and administrator were undeniable. He organized a motley fighting force into a disciplined professional army, which native Christians entered in great numbers. He established the first Muslim navy, operated by Greek seafarers who resisted the temptation to flee north to Byzantium. We do not know whether it was an Arab or a Greek who gave the order to dismantle the Colossus of Rhodes, one of the ancient wonders of the world, and sell it as scrap metal when the island was seized by Muawiya's fleet in 653; it was one of the few acts of desecration which the culture-conscious Umayyads had to live down. Muawiya installed an extensive and efficient postal service and a land registration system. Like his caliphal predecessors, he was a dedicated desert fighter who, having helped Khalid al-Walid drive the Byzantines out of Syria, could not resist the temptation of trying to capture Constantinople himself. His repeated efforts proved unsuccessful, but he kept at it, making the campaigns training exercises for his army and navy.

The Byzantines, safe in Asia Minor, nonetheless remained a power to be reckoned with throughout the one hundred years of the Umayyad caliphate. The emperor and the church in Constantinople insisted on acting as patrons of the Greek Orthodox peoples of Syria and Palestine. Byzantine power was so feared that caliphs at times were obliged to pay a bribe to keep the Greeks from reinvading their former provinces.

Even before the Arabic conquest of Jerusalem, the Jewish Temple area was revered by Muslims, a feeling reflected in the original Arabic name for the city, Bayt al-Maqdis, "House of the Temple." But it was not until Muawiya's decision to lay plans for the construction of a grand Islamic shrine that the Jewish sacred site was gradually transformed into al-Haram esh-Sharif, the "Noble Sanctuary," as it came to called later in Ottoman times.

Muawiya planned the construction of the Dome of the Rock shrine, but it was left to one of his successors, the Caliph Abd al-Malik, to complete the building in 691. The Dome is not strictly speaking a mosque or place of congregational prayer (a function exercised by the later-built al-Aksa Mosque) but a memorial honoring the sacred gray Moriah stone upon which

Abraham undertook to obey the divine command to sacrifice Isaac.

Well before the building of the Dome, a mosque stood on the Temple Mount, a large structure of brick and wood, said to be an imitation of Muhammad's own family mosque in Medina. In 670, during the reign of Muawiya, the French bishop Arculfus journeyed to the Holy Land and left us an eyewitness account of this mosque:

> ...In that renowned place where once the Temple had been magnificently constructed, placed in the neighborhood of the wall from the east, the Saracens now frequent a four-sided house of prayer, which they have built rudely, constructing it by raising boards and great beams on some remains of ruins: this house can, it is said, hold three thousand men at once.[14]

Legend attributes the Dome's modest predecessor to Umar, who desired to see the Jewish Temple site resanctified for Islam. Umar and his caliphal successors interpreted their military conquests as proof of the superiority of Islam over Judaism and Christianity. But the conquest of Jerusalem presented a special problem: for centuries after the conquest, Jerusalem remained a predominantly Christian city, and local Christians, particularly monks and priests, did not behave like conquered subjects. The Muslims were impressed by the many beautiful churches dotting the hills of the city; the shrines were all sites from Jewish and Christian scriptures; great monasteries lay only a few days' journey from the heart of the city; the caves in the hills surrounding Jerusalem were alive with the prayers of hundreds of ascetics. The Christians, coming from every part of the world, made the city truly international. A list of hermits dwelling in huts on the Mount of Olives informs us that "eleven said their psalmodies in Greek, six in Syriac, five in Latin, four in Georgian, two in Armenian, and one in Arabic."[15] The power of Christianity in the Holy City was sounded from church bells every day. Remarkably, only one Umayyad caliph, Umar II (717–720), inclined toward persecution. He forbade bells and forced the church to use wooden clappers, a set of which is still used today outside the Church of Saint James in the Armenian quarter. In the space of two hundred years, three famous Christian pilgrims (Arculfus, 670; Willibald, 770; Bernard the Wise,

870) found the churches in Jerusalem in good repair and their brethren well treated by Muslim authorities.

The aura of church sanctity hovering over Jerusalem impressed the early Muslim leaders, but it also challenged them. After Muawiya was installed as caliph in the city he went to pray at Golgotha, at Gethsemane, and at the Tomb of Mary in the Kidron Valley. This was more than a show of respect for the Christian shrines; it demonstrated the triumph of the Prophet's faith in the Holy Land over both Christians and Jews whose religious wisdom Islam had raised to a higher level of truth.[16] What could emphatically, visibly show all peoples of the empire simultaneously this inheritance, this transcendence, this triumph? The caliph answered with plans for the construction of a monument commensurate with his pride, power, and wealth. The result was the Dome built over Abraham's Moriah rock, the symbolic foundation of monotheism.

The construction of the Dome was left to Caliph al-Malik, who in 685 employed Greek architects, Armenian artisans, and Syrian laborers to erect a spectacular, eight-story, octagonal structure in the Byzantine style, a more sumptuous imitation of Constantine's original Church of the Resurrection two hundred yards west. To recognize the likeness one must ignore the façade of the present-day Crusader-built Church of the Holy Sepulchre and enter the octagonal rotunda, which is reminiscent of Constantine's building or what was left of it after the Persian devastation in the early seventh century. The Dome copies the rotunda, but it outshines it in every way. In contrast to the darkness and disorder within the church, the interior of the Dome invites the worshiper with the calm symmetry of its lines, with its rich warm colors and subdued light—which explains why a loud sound is seldom heard in its main chamber. Here is the oldest existing Islamic monument in the world and for most still the greatest; certainly its sanctuary (along with the courtyard of Saint Anne's Church nearby) is the perfect place today for meditation in a busy, loud, and troubled city.

As the Dome's form was inspired by Constantine's Golgotha church, so it in turn gave birth to Christian imitations, such as the Temple Church in London and the sanctuary in Aix la Chapelle. The rounded shell that is the dome itself was made of lead and gold, and in the winter a hood of animal skin was placed over the structure to protect it against ice and Jerusalem's

The shrine of the Dome of the Rock seen
through the arches, or "scales,"
upon which, according to Muslim belief,
all human deeds will be weighed on
Judgment Day. (Photographed by Adrien
Bonfils ca. 1860–1890)

fierce winter winds. When the spring came the hood was
removed and the dome sparkled in the sun, moving the famous
Jerusalem Muslim geographer al-Mukaddasi to record this impression in the tenth century:

> At the dawn, when the light of the sun first strikes on the Cupola,
> and the Drum catches the rays; then is this edifice a marvelous
> sight to behold, and one such that in all Islam I have never seen its
> equal; neither have I heard tell of aught built in pagan times that
> could rival in grace this Dome of the Rock.[17]

Tremors shook the foundation of the building repeatedly
through the centuries until the original dome collapsed in 1016.
A major reconstruction was carried out by the Mamluk caliph
An Nasr Muhammad in 1319, giving us the structure as we see it
today, not much different from the building erected by al-Malik.
Today the shrine, with its gold-lacquered aluminum dome (the
original gold leaf disappeared centuries ago), sparkles over the
city like an enormous gem, pointing the way to heaven which,
according to a medieval Muslim tradition, is located only twelve
miles above the shrine.

In the sixteenth century, inspired by the mosaic façade of

Venice's Church of San Marco, Muslim artisans decorated the outer surface of the Dome with Persian (Kashani) porcelain tiles of yellow, blue, green, black, and turquoise set in geometric and floral designs which are the finest of their kind in the world. The essential principle of Islamic art was brilliantly enunciated for the internal surface: the even covering of every inch of space with color and design which cause the eye to wander with delight over the whole space. Kufic inscriptions from the Koran were woven into the interior and exterior walls of the building. The interior is upheld by handsome columns of gray-veined white marble, topped with gold-leafed Byzantine capitals. Well-spaced windows of richly stained glass permit entry of a soft, roselike light, deepening the aura of sanctity in the rounded central chamber.

The dome protects Abraham's Moriah, *Even Shetiyah*, the Hebraic "Foundation Stone" at which Islamic tradition places Muhammad's Heavenly Ascension. The massive outcropping of rough-faced limestone appears in sharp contrast to the splendid artistry surrounding it. Yet there is nothing brute or ugly in the stone; quite the opposite. Because it is attached to the earth in only one place, the giant object seems suspended in air—an effect which gave rise to a charming legend. When Muhammad began his Heavenly Ascent, the stone in reverence tried to follow him. But the angel Gabriel, who was the Prophet's guide, pressed the stone back with his own hands, shouting to it, "Your place, O Stone, is on earth. You have no part in the Prophet's Garden of Eden."[18] Today Muslim guides are pleased to point out the imprint which one of Gabriel's hands made on the holy stone, not far from the place where Muhammad's footprint can be found.

The legend about the stone's hovering in the air persisted, and the belief spread that if the stone should fall to earth it would signal the coming of the Messiah, bringing the redemption of Israel.[19] The Ottoman Turks believed the legend. They sought to prevent the entry of the Messiah Jesus by walling up the Golden Gate, and they also hoped to prevent the appearance of Israel's Messiah by constructing a firm support to prevent the stone's fall.

On the underside of the mysterious stone lies a cavern which is especially precious to Muslims as the place where Muhammad

The Abrahamic stone of sacrifice within the Dome of the Rock. It is the "foundation stone" of the earth according to both Jewish and Muslim beliefs. (Photographed by Adrien Bonfils ca. 1860–1890)

prayed before his journey to heaven; a depression in the ceiling marks the spot where his head inclined during his prayers. In the recesses lining the walls of the cave are tiny chapels dedicated to the Prophet's predecessors—Abraham, David, Solomon, and Elijah. It seems that the layers of sanctity in this shrine have no end: the dome covers the rock, and the rock sits over the cave, and the cave hides a well beneath it. It is the terrible fathomless well where the souls of all the departed lie, anxiously awaiting the Judgment Day in Jerusalem when the righteous and wicked will receive their just rewards. Muslims and Jews share the belief that the center of the world—the point at which earth is separated from heaven above and hell below—is located not at the foot of Christ's Tomb, as Christians hold, but at the mouth of the well below the Foundation Stone. And here in the well, too, is "the source of all the springs and fountains from which the world drinks its water"[20]—a description which touches on truth, for we know that beneath the stone floor of the Haram are numerous vast cisterns for catching rain water.

Encircling the stone are two wide ambulatories to be used in the sacred walk (*tawaf*) performed by pilgrims who cannot travel to Mecca to perform the obligatory encircling of the Ka'ba. The Persian traveler Nasir-i-Khosrau tells us that, unable to make the *hajj* to Mecca, as many as twenty thousand would gather in Jerusalem at Ramadan to pray at the Dome.

In the courtyard facing the Dome in all directions are tall, decorative, open-air stone arches, like slender hands clasping the shrine with fingers pointing skyward. Arabs call the arches *mawazeen* (scales), because they believe that on Judgment Day moral scales will be hung from the arches to weigh the good and evil deeds of every human being.

Small groves of cypress and olive trees offer shade to the hot and weary in selected corners of the vast esplanade of the Haram. A lovely sight after noon prayers are Muslim families sharing picnic lunches under the graceful branches of the cypress trees. Another tree in the Haram which is looked on with affection by Muslims is the tall nettle tree, whose leaf wards off the evil eye. Solomon himself first planted these trees to protect his sacred Temple; today young Muslim women can be seen with fresh garlands of nettle leaves gracing their necks.

Caliph al-Malik spared no expense in constructing this shrine. It cost him the fortune of seven years' revenue from Egypt. But he must have treasured his creation, for he himself performed a ceremonial cleaning of the shrine, "sweeping and washing it with his own hands," establishing a ritual custom for all the caliphs who would follow him.[21] For daily cleaning, however, he employed over fifty cleaners who washed the rock with a mixture of saffron, musk, and rose water. Most of the jobs were taken by Jews, who also made lanterns to light the shrine at night and looked on their work as a *mitzvah*; for they "viewed the renewed use of the Temple site as the beginning of the Redemption."[22] The lamps in the Dome held a further meaning for Jews. Legend says that on the ninth night of the Hebrew month of Av, which commemorates the destruction of the Temple, the lamps will go out and nothing can light them until the next day.[23]

Why was such a large and expensive structure built in Jerusalem and not in the Umayyad capital of Damascus or in the religiously more important cities of Mecca and Medina? The old theory that Caliph al-Malik wished to divert pilgrims from Mecca to Jerusalem in order to undermine a rival, Caliph Abdallah Ibn al-Zubayr of Mecca, was refuted by S. D. Goitein on the ground that had al-Malik acted so foolishly, he would have been branded a *kafir* (infidel) against whom the Imams would have been right to preach *jihad* (holy war).[24] The political struggle between the two leaders was another stage in the long drawn-out conflict of succession between the descendants of Muawiya and their opponents, including the Shi'ite followers of Ali. If this struggle influenced al-Malik's decision to build his monument in Jerusalem, it was to demonstrate that he, not his rival, was the true champion of the Prophet's faith.

Al-Malik's wish was not to displace Mecca with Jerusalem but to foster the sacral significance of Jerusalem for Muslim worshipers so that they would accept the city on the same level of veneration as Mecca and Medina. The caliph's political motive was not difficult to fathom. Mecca was in the hands of the old Muslim aristocracy, which never ceased to look on the Umayyads as wealthy and worldly upstarts whose power stemmed from the luck of their military successes. While during the hundred years of the Umayyad caliphate (650–750) Mecca and Medina never lost their preeminence, the city of Jerusalem, because of al-Haram esh-Sharif, became something of a family shrine center for the Umayyad caliphs of Damascus.

As we have noted, the building of the Dome was a symbol of Islamic inheritance from and triumph over the religions of Jews and Christians, and equally an expression of the insecurity of Muslims in a city dominated by Christians from the initial Arab conquest in 638 until Saladin drove out the Crusaders in 1187. In making the Dome a taller, more imposing copy of the Holy Sepulchre, Caliph al-Malik was making visible to all Jerusalem's Christians the power and permanence of Islam in the Holy City. Christians had splendid churches in Jerusalem, Lydda, Damascus, and Edessa, but none would be more sumptuous than the Muslim shrine. Further evidence of al-Malik's thinking is provided by the decorative motifs in the tiled wall mosaics. The caliph's artisans deliberately adopted Christian crosses and Persian crowns, symbols of imperial majesty and sanctity, to express the point that these empires had been defeated, and in the case of Persia its unbelievers converted to Islam.[25]

The Temple Mount drew Muslim pilgrims in large numbers from throughout Palestine and Syria. To make certain that the pilgrims were not shaken in their faith by the sight of so many handsome churches in the area, the caliph saw to it that explicitly anti-Christian sentiments from the Koran were inscribed on the upper inner walls of the Dome. The major inscription, an incredible 240 meters long (the oldest contemporary piece of Islamic writing extant), denounces Christ's Incarnation and the Trinity. Asserting repeatedly *la sharika lahu* (God has no companion), it states:

> ... He is God, the One; God the Eternal; He has not begotten nor was He begotten; and there is none comparable to Him (Koran 112:5). ... Praise be to God, Who has not taken unto Himself a son, and who has no partner in Sovereignty, nor has He any protector or account of weakness (Koran 17:11). Believe in God and his apostles, and say not Three. ... God is only one God (Koran 4:169–171).

The popular appeal of the Dome of the Rock and the Haram esh-Sharif to Muslims explains how the Koran's stories of Muhammad's Night Journey and Ascension to Heaven were connected with this sacred area. Years after its construction, it came to be believed that the Dome commemorated the fabled night in which, according to the Koran, Muhammad was transported from Mecca to a place called the "Farthest Mosque" and then to heaven to receive the final revelation of truth from God. The passage in translation reads as follows: "Glorified be He Who carried His servant [i.e., Muhammad] by night from the *masjid al-haram* [i.e., Mecca] to the *masjid al-aqsa* [i.e., the farthest place of worship]" (Surah 17, verse 1). The "farthest place of worship" was erroneously taken to be Jerusalem; recent scholarship has shown that the "place" refers to a sanctuary at the small town of al-Jiranah, near Mecca, where Muhammad lived for a short time in the eighth year after the *hijra*.[26] In fact, there is no explicit reference to Jerusalem in the Koran, and only one reference to the Holy Land (*al-Ard al-Muqaddosa*, Koran 5:21). But folk tradition is usually more powerful than historical accuracy. Muslim pilgrimage to Jerusalem undoubtedly influenced interpretation of the Koranic stories. Once the connection between Jerusalem and Muhammad's Night Journey and Ascension had been made in popular belief, Jerusalem officially gained its place as a "holy city" in Islamic theology.

Sometime after the Dome was completed in 691, the Night Journey of Muhammad was wonderfully embellished. Escorted by the angel Gabriel, Muhammad was borne through the skies from Mecca to Jerusalem, with intervening stops at Sinai and Bethlehem in honor of Moses and David. The Prophet rode a magical white horse named Buraq (lightning), which had a woman's face and sported a peacock's tail. As he was about to begin his Ascent to Heaven from Moriah, Muhammad tethered Buraq to the west wall of the Temple Mount; thereafter the wall was called al-Buraq, thus to become an object of twentieth-century contention with the Jewish "Wailing Wall." With Gabriel as his guide, Muhammad ascended the heavens on a ladder of light to meet and talk with Adam, Moses, Abraham, Solomon, John the Baptist, and Jesus. Finally he was conducted past the Seventh Heaven where Allah himself awaited his chosen servant to bestow on him the final revelation, "including injunctions as to the prayers his followers were to perform."[27] After he descended to earth at the very spot on Moriah from which he had earlier ascended, he returned to Mecca on the back of Buraq before the dawn. In later centuries the story of the Prophet's Night Journey proved so captivating that the poet Dante used it as the paradigm for "Paradiso" in *The Divine Comedy.*

The handsome silver-domed al-Aksa Mosque, standing on the extreme south end of the Haram, would dominate the Temple Mount were it not for the more lustrous beauty of her sister, the Dome of the Rock. Taking its name from the Koranic account of Muhammad's Night Journey, al-Aksa, the "farthest mosque," was built in the period 709–715 over the site of Justinian's Church of Saint Mary and incorporated much of the church in its own construction. The mosque's builder, Caliph al-Walid, al-Malik's son, rivaled King Herod in commissioning numerous great monuments such as Medina's central mosque and the great mosques of Damascus and Cairo. Upon completion, al-Aksa became Jerusalem's central congregational mosque. According to English scholar John Gray, "Al Aksa is a classic example of how close the two faiths of Christianity and Islam may be on the level of popular tradition, for the prayer-niche (*mihrab*) giving

The silver-domed Mosque of al-Aksa,
with cypress and eucalyptus trees in
the foreground, at the extreme south
end of the Haram esh-Sharif.
(Photographed by Adrien Bonfils ca.
1860–1890)

the worshippers the orientation towards Mecca is associated in
Muslim tradition with the Annunciation to Mary, and a stone
basin is reputed to be the cradle of Jesus where he spoke to the
people...."[28]

Most visitors to the Haram, attracted by the sparkling presence of the Dome of the Rock and al-Aksa, overlook the lovely
array of smaller domes, minarets, and ancient *madrasas* (religious schools) which made Jerusalem in the late Middle Ages a
favored city for Muslim scholars and mystics. The large graceful
fountain in front of al-Aksa, named *El Kas* (The Cup), is
noticed, but few know it is there for the faithful to engage in
the ritual of washing their hands and feet before entering the
mosque for prayers. All these smaller structures are delightful
ornaments in the Haram, noticed only when the eyes tire of
gazing on the more famous buildings.

Perhaps the most interesting of the dozen or so smaller
domes is one called Qubbat al-Silsilah (Dome of the Chain)
which is a scaled-down replica of the Dome of the Rock and

originally served as a treasury for the larger building. As with so much at the Haram/Temple Mount, Silsilah symbolizes an act of ultimate judgment. One of the many legends venerated by Muslims states that once a chain hung where the smaller dome now stands. King David used the chain "to test the honesty of the people who stood before him for judgment."[29] If a person lied, a link would fall from the chain, exposing him. It must have made for a very long chain in Jerusalem.

We cannot leave the Haram without recalling one particular legend. It concerns the crescent on the top of the Dome of the Rock. The crescent always points south to Mecca, and Muslims believed that if the crescent should ever face in any other direction it would signal disaster. The Crusaders disposed of the legend by removing the crescent and replacing it with a cross. After Saladin's conquest the crescent was returned to its rightful place, facing south. And so it faced until the present day, when one of the Muslim gatekeepers of the Haram in 1980 told me that for the first time in his life he noticed that the crescent was inclining to the east. "What does this mean?" I asked him. "Is the Haram about to be lost?" "Yes," he replied. "We lost the city to the Jews in 1967. Now the Haram itself is threatened."

CHAPTER 8

A Golden Bowl
Filled with
Scorpions

*One prayer in Jerusalem
is worth forty thousand prayers elsewhere.*
—Popular Muslim saying

*In Jerusalem the oppressed have no succor;
the meek are molested; and the rich envied.*
—al-Mukaddasi

The Umayyad princes who ruled Jerusalem for more than a hundred years (638–750) were courageous fighters, splendid builders, and dedicated Muslims of the Sunni tradition, but to their Shi'ite rivals in Iraq and Iran they were secularists, sensualists, and racial elitists. The accusation was continually heard that the ideals of sympathy and modesty embodied in the life and teaching of Muhammad had been abandoned by the caliphs of Damascus in favor of the megalomania of the old Byzantine or Persian kings. It was true that Muawiya, the short, ugly genius of empire management, had adopted some flamboyant symbols of the foreign monarchs. He chose to wear royal garments, installed a throne in his palace, and, worse, delivered the Friday sermon in Jerusalem without standing, as was traditional. He instituted the practice of cursing Caliph Ali (Muhammad's son-in-law) from the pulpit. It was even said that only on formal occasions in the mosque was Muawiya religious, that he often ignored the obligatory five daily prayers. Like his cousin the Caliph Uthmann who was rich from usury, "loved perfume, thoroughbred horses, and young slave girls," Muawiya had self-indulgent tastes which enraged the more pious among his brethren, particularly in Iran where Shi'ite fanaticism was taking root.[1] Nearly all the succeeding Umayyad caliphs, in their love of drink, sport, games, and concubines, resembled Uthmann and Muawiya.

In the eyes of religious zealots in Mecca and Medina, Muawiya had committed the sin of changing the caliphate into a kingship, of cutting the spiritual bond with the Prophet in favor of imitating a model of Western secular power. Functioning as king, Muawiya had broken the democratic tradition of the Arabian desert clan, where the leader, the sheik, is chosen as "first of equals" by the elders of the clan. This was a terrible irony, for Muawiya had opposed Ali's own claim to a hereditary caliphate only to found a royal dynasty of his own. In place of the elected sheik, Muawiya had practiced a cult of personality, abrogating the Koran's injunction that a man's highest loyalty was not to another man but to Allah.

It was also true that the Umayyad princes had made mistakes which hastened their downfall, none worse than their haughtiness. They never missed an opportunity to remind imperial subjects of their own Arab ancestry and aristocratic beginnings. Descended from the wealthiest and most powerful merchant family of Mecca, they viewed native Arabic-speaking Syrians and Palestinians as ignorant, of little value beyond army service and farm work, which they as Arab military men disdained.

After the conquest of Palestine, thousands of south Arabians, "Yamanites," fleeing the poverty of their arid homeland, emigrated westward and soon became the majority of the Arab population. The Yamanites were loyal to the Umayyad rulers, yet Damascus never saw fit to assign them imperial offices, preferring their own north Arabian "Qaysites," who proved much less loyal.

The Umayyads also made the mistake of practicing a form of racial superiority inconsistent with Muhammad's democratic vision of Islam. Umayyad rulers frequently elevated talented or influential *dhimmis* ("protected" Christians and Jews) to positions of power, but for the *mawali* (converts to Islam) they did very little, viewing them as non-Arab "outsiders" who had converted to Islam in order to escape the head tax levied on all non-Muslims. An added discrimination was the insistence that *mawali* build their own mosques and avoid praying in those used by Arabs. With the passing of years and despite official discouragement of conversion, the *mawali* multiplied in number, particularly in Iran where many became Shi'ites and learned to hate the Umayyads.

The Umayyads lavished attention and money on Jerusalem, but they also insulted it by making Ramla the administrative capital of the country in 718. Ramla was originally a military garrison town set up by the Muslim conquerors as they had set up Kufa and Basra in Iraq and Fustat (later named Cairo) in Egypt. The town, in the strategic coastal plain, controlling the trade route from Damascus to Egypt, was a shrewd choice. But the Jerusalemites were incensed that this hot, stinking place should be chosen over their own lovely, historic city. One complained bitterly of Jerusalem's fall from ancient splendor: "Jerusalem is a provincial town attached to Ramla after having been the seat of the government in the days of Solomon and David."[2]

But the choice of Ramla proved of immense benefit for the spread of the Arabic language among the people living in the countryside who would come to Ramla to buy and sell goods. By contrast, Jerusalem was the Greek-speaking *dhimmis* city par excellence. It was in the late seventh century, during the caliphate of al-Malik, that the decision was made to introduce Arabic as a second administrative language, alongside Greek. A humorous tale illustrates the dependent but often delicate relationship between Arab and Greek peoples in Jerusalem, as in Palestine and Syria generally. As the story goes, one day the caliph decided to introduce Arabic for official purposes when it was discovered that a high-ranking Greek scribe, disgusted at one of the caliphal decrees, had urinated in his ink well....

During the hundred years in which the Umayyad caliphs reigned supreme, the Shi'ites multiplied in the eastern lands of Iraq and Iran. Nursing their wounds, they waited for the moment to avenge the wrongs done to their beloved Ali. They found a ready vehicle to strike back against their enemy through the Persian Abbasid family of Iraq, which shared Sunni orthodoxy with the Umayyads but questioned the legitimacy of the Damascus caliphate and, unlike the Umayyads, could trace its lineage back to the Prophet's own family. Reckoning day occurred in January 750 when the Iraqi leader Abu-al-Abas, with the backing of thousands of Iraqi and Persian Shi'ite Muslims, led an army composed mostly of *mawali* against a Umayyad force whose ranks were filled with Syrian Christians. Abu-al-Abas won a decisive victory at the Upper Zab River, a tributary of the Tigris. There he earned his title al-Saffa ("bloodshedder") for exterminating all the Umayyad princes he could catch; then he went on an orgy of mystical sadism by exhuming the corpses of dead Umayyad caliphs in order to whip, crucify, and scourge the skeletal remains.

Umayyad rule ended tragically in Jerusalem. Citizens revolted against the incompetent and corrupt governor appointed by the last Umayyad caliph Marwan II; in retaliation the caliph sent a force which demolished the city walls and dealt harshly with the inhabitants. This was followed by a series of earthquakes which boded ill for the city during the next two hundred years of Abbasid rule. Umayyad names were effaced from Muslim monuments and replaced by Abbasid. One of the most notorious changes occurred at the Dome of the Rock where the name of al-Malik, the Dome's builder, was replaced by that of the Abbasid caliph al-Mamun, who, neglecting to change the erection date inscribed on the building, exposed his dishonesty.

The victory of the Abbasids over the Umayyads was a major turning point in the history of the Islamic Middle East. The new regime called itself *dawlah*, a "new era." The center of power shifted from Damascus to Baghdad, the new capital founded by Caliph al-Mansur, brother and successor of Abu-al-Abas. With the change, Syria and Palestine, shaped by the rich, sensuous Greek cultural tradition, were relegated to secondary status in the new empire which favored the more devout Persian Shi'ite religious tradition of Iraq and Iran. The poets, musicians, and philosophers of the glittering Umayyad court were banished, and for the first time theologians, mystics, and doctors of Shari'a law found favor with the throne. Royal drinking, gaming, and whoring gave way to a new spirit of sober-minded and circumspect government run largely by the very *mawali* whom the Umayyad princes had rejected as unworthy of high position in their empire. At the same time the Abbasid leaders successful-

ly converted to Islam the Arabic-speaking Christian Taghlib and
Tanukh tribesmen of the Syrian desert, whom they viewed as
native kinsmen separate from nonnative Greek Christians.

Unlike the Umayyads who were Arab elitists, the Abbasid
princes made a deliberate effort to cultivate relationships with all
the different convert peoples, with the result that the Baghdad
caliphate acquired an international character it was never to lose.
The de-Arabization of the Islamic empire which occurred during the period of Abbasid rule affected the central Muslim
pilgrimage cities of Mecca, Medina, and Jerusalem. Mecca and
Medina had begun to lose their political significance once the
Umayyads made Damascus their new capital; the emergence of
distant Baghdad as the capital of the Abbasid empire isolated the
two Arabian cities, leaving them, with Jerusalem, as places
merely of annual pilgrimage significance. Jerusalem had an
additional stigma in Abbasid eyes: it was the city not of *mawalis*
but of *dhimmis* (Christian pilgrims and priests) who were the
majority population and who never stopped boasting of their
magnificent churches and looking upon Jerusalem as their own.
The Abbasids, like the Umayyads before them, left the Christians and the few local Jews alone, but they were adamant about
collecting taxes. There must have been a great many *dhimmis* in
Jerusalem in the middle of the eighth century, for to make
certain that none of them evaded the required head tax, the
Caliph Mansur ordered their hands to be tatooed. The Christians' tax was often paid by church communities from abroad,
whose leaders continued to look upon Jerusalem as the capital
of Christendom. Certainly this was the case with French Emper-
or Charlemagne who exchanged embassies with Abbasid Caliph
Harun al-Rashid in 800 and who, with the permission of the
caliph, built new churches, hospices, and hospitals in Jerusalem.
Charlemagne's son and successor Louis "ordered each estate in
his empire to contribute one denarius for the needs of Christian
Jerusalem."[3]

Of the thirty-seven caliphs of the five-hundred-year-old
Abbasid dynasty, only two ever visited Jerusalem; the most
notable was al-Mansur (745–775) who journeyed there it seems
out of respect for the centennial of Muawiya's installation as
caliph. The Abbasids largely ignored Jerusalem, but they were
willing to repair monuments. Seeing the damage done to al-Aksa
in the devastating earthquake of 747, Caliph Mansur in 771

decreed the repair of the mosque but insisted that the gold and silver plates on the great entrance door be melted down and sold to pay the expenses. But few new mosques were built in Palestine, nothing to symbolize the importance of Jerusalem as an Islamic shrine city. Jerusalem's glory passed with Damascus; and with the centuries, as Baghdad was replaced by Cairo and Constantinople as political centers of the Islamic Middle East, Jerusalem joined Mecca and Medina as places of mere religious significance. It is revealing that in Philip Hitti's book *Great Arab Cities*, individual chapters are devoted to Mecca, Medina, Damascus, Baghdad, Cairo, and Cordova, but none to Jerusalem. The few pages in which Jerusalem is discussed are devoted entirely to the Dome of the Rock and al-Aksa.

The Abbasids maintained control of their empire for about a hundred years, reaching a high point during the reign of the Caliph al-Mamun (813–842). After that, corruption, poverty, and unceasing warfare ravaged the empire, nowhere worse than in the western provinces of Syria and Palestine. In the reign of Mamun's successor al-Mutasim (833–842), economic conditions went from bad to worse. Under normal conditions Palestine was a productive country, able to feed itself; but several years of unexpected drought led to famine, which in turn led to a peasant revolt with telling political consequences. Palestinians were never happy under their Abbasid overlords, whom they looked upon as alien intruders from the east, and the sudden denial of bread sparked a move for independence. Involved in this fascinating event was the lingering hope of many native Muslims that Umayyad rule might be restored to Palestine through the appearance of a *Sufyani* or Messiah of the Umayyad family. Such a leader did appear, one Abu Harb al-Mubarka, who rallied the peasants by promising to abolish land taxes; both Jews and Christians joined his movement because he promised to reduce the head tax. The movement failed when the caliph sent a special force from Baghdad to put down the rebellion. But al-Mubarka eventually proved a false messiah to his own followers. He did nothing to improve the lot of Muslims; the entire Jewish, Christian, and Muslim population of Jerusalem turned against him, and the Greek patriarch had to pay a ransom to keep him from burning the Church of the Holy Sepulchre.[4]

The Umayyad obsession to defeat Byzantium ended with the removal of the caliphal capital to distant Baghdad, safe from the

Greek menace. But Muslim fear of the Byzantines was revived in the late tenth century when the emperor Nikephorus Phocas II swore to invade the Holy Land and reconquer Jerusalem. He made good on his threat, and his successor, John Tzimisces, might very well have retaken the Holy City if he had not died. The Greek action led to an important architectural initiative in Jerusalem. A portion of the courtyard of the Church of the Holy Sepulchre was seized for the construction of a small mosque, named Omariya, in honor of the Muslim conqueror's legendary act of kneeling for prayer outside the church. It was an ironic reversal. Umar, it is said, refused to pray in the church because his followers would turn it into a mosque; three centuries later, to demonstrate their power over the city, Muslims seized a portion of the Holy Sepulchre's courtyard for a mosque.

The peasant revolt in the middle of the ninth century marked the beginning of a dark age for the Holy Land. The Abbasid rulers in Baghdad began to feel the threat of two emerging powers in the Middle East: the Seljuk Turks from central Asia, and the Shi'ite Fatimid Egyptians who established a new dynasty in the name of the Prophet's daughter which would control North Africa, Arabia, Syria, and Palestine.

The Abbasid caliphate lasted five centuries, but its real power did not extend much beyond a hundred years, 750–850. What caused the decline of the Iraqi princes from Baghdad after 850 was their decision to make use of the superb fighting skills of central Asian Turcoman and Seljuk tribesmen. These Turks, entrusted with state security, served so effectively as palace guards that in time they took control of the palace, making virtual house prisoners of a number of Abbasid caliphs. Originally acquired as the human spoils of conquest, the Turkish slave-soldiers rose to positions of eminence in the Abbasid state bureaucracy, serving as governors, administrators, tax collectors, and military officers. In the middle of the ninth century they organized small mobile armies and struck out on their own. From that point on, the fate of Syria and Palestine was decided by a series of wars between the Turks and their Abbasid overlords and the Egyptian Fatimids, the latter a regional power contesting the Abbasids for control of the Middle East. Jerusalem played no prominent role in these wars, but it was often the victim of the devastation they caused. Adding to troubles in

Palestine was the condition of virtual lawlessness which seized the country in the last two hundred years before the Crusader conquest of 1099. Bedouin marauders made it almost impossible to travel with safety to any part of the country. People were really safe only within the walls of the major cities. Often the bedouins received financial aid from the Byzantines in Constantinople who saw them as a force to undermine the Muslim government of the country.

We have testimony about the spirit of life in Jerusalem during this long dark period from two remarkable men. The first is Muhammad al-Mukaddasi, a native citizen who lived when Jerusalem and Palestine were under the Turkish Ikhshidid family (935–969), which ruled from Cairo. Al-Mukaddasi, who took his name from his native city (*Mukaddasi* means "sanctuary," a reference to the Temple Mount), was a man of broad interests: geographer, writer, skilled observer of places, plants, and people, a tireless traveler of twenty years in the Middle East, North Africa, and the Iberian peninsula. His love of culture and his scientific bent of mind came from his grandfather, a renowned architect who was commissioned by the earlier Egyptian ruler of Palestine, Ibn Tulunid, to design a new harbor for Acre.

In 967, at age twenty-one, al-Mukaddasi went on *hajj* to Mecca; he continued his travels for the next two decades and in 985 completed a book whose dry title utterly belies its lively contents—*The Best Clarification for the Knowledge of Climates.* Al-Mukaddasi speaks of a "land of blessing, a country of cheapness, abounding in fruits," from which he makes a shopper's guide of produce: olives, oranges, almonds, dates, figs, lemons. He shows a special fondness for bananas, "which is a fruit of the form of the cucumber, but the skin peels off and the interior is not unlike that of the watermelon, only finely flavored and more luscious." He mentions the quantity of milk, honey, and sugar so necessary to a typically Middle Eastern country which delights in sweets. The grapes are sweet and enormous, he tells us, and "there are no quinces equal to those of the Holy City."[5]

What then is there to complain about in Jerusalem? "A lot," answers our native observer. He is sarcastic about the pilgrims who have made the Holy Land "a mine of profit both for this world and the next." The country is filled with holy men, but

real doctors of Shari'a law are hard to find and "preachers are
held in no kind of consideration"; further, "people show neither
zeal for the Holy War, nor honor to those who fight against the
infidel." The mosques are empty and "Christians and Jews have
the upper hand," laments al-Mukaddasi, reminding us that after
the fall of the Umayyads the development of Islamic law and
theology bypassed Palestine and Syria in favor of Iraq and Iran.

Who, then, were the holy men of whom al-Mukaddasi
speaks? They were the dervishes, the Qarmatians, Sufi mystics,
and other spiritualists, mostly from Iran, who were attracted to
Jerusalem for its sanctity; they settled in and around the Haram
to study their books and meditate in the madrasas. The most
famous to come to Jerusalem to engage in lonely contemplation
was the great Muslim mystic Ghazzali in 1095. The mystics
came mostly from Iran, and after their studies and spiritual
exercises they would enjoy eating bananas in the shade of the
Dome of the Rock.[6] The Muslim population of the city was
increased overall by immigrants from Morocco, who settled at
the west end of the Haram, beside the Western Wall, giving their
name *Mugrabi* to this area to the present day.

Al-Mukaddasi was sensitive to the treacherous politicians of
his day. Paraphrasing the Hebrew Torah he speaks of Jerusalem
"as a golden bowl filled with scorpions." Like a good citizen
outraged by inefficient government, he denounces the filthy
public baths in town, the high hotel rates, and the steep taxes
which reduce profit on retail goods. He states flatly that in
Jerusalem "the oppressed have no succor; the meek are molested, and the rich envied."[7] Jerusalem was beautiful but not
pleasurable; it was a serious city, and no one knew it better than
a contemporary of al-Mukaddasi, a silk merchant who, writing
to his friend in Cairo, said that in Jerusalem "black and sky-
blue silk are worn, not crimson as in Ramla and Ascalon."[8]

But al-Mukaddasi took heart by remembering a great tradition. Jerusalem was the divinely chosen city, from whose blessed
rock the Prophet ascended to heaven. To al-Mukaddasi this
meant that the city's destiny lay not with men on earth but with
Allah in heaven. Allah decreed that the Last Judgment would
take place in Jerusalem, just east of the old city gates, down in
the Valley of Jehosophat. At that time, a second miraculous
event would also occur. The sacred cities of Mecca and Medina
would rise up like obedient servants and journey to Jerusalem to

pay homage to the Lord. Al-Mukaddasi writes: "Verily Makkah and Al Madinah have their superiority by reason of the Ka'abah and the Prophet—the blessing of Allah be upon him and his family—but verily, on the Day of Judgment, they will both come to Jerusalem, and the excellences of them all will there be united."[9] None heeded al-Mukaddasi's words more than the Iraqi Shi'ite sect, the Qarmatians, who ravaged the Syrian and Palestinian countryside but who revered Jerusalem and chose to ignore the Prophet's injunction by facing not Mecca but Jerusalem in their prayers.

The belief in Jerusalem as the scene of the Last Judgment and Resurrection gained strength in succeeding years, becoming a central theme in the observations of a second Muslim world traveler, the Persian Nasir-i-Khosrau. Khosrau traveled throughout Persia and India before visiting Jerusalem in 1047, when the Holy City was under the rule of the Fatimid caliph al-Mustansir. Like al-Mukaddasi, Khosrau was a devout man who went on pilgrimage to Mecca and decided to make a special trip to Jerusalem as a penance to atone for his love of wine. How different the history of Jerusalem might have been if the Umayyad caliphs had followed the Persian's example.

Khosrau observes that Muslim parents brought their children to Jerusalem to celebrate their circumcision. Further, the old and sick from every corner of the globe came to Jerusalem as a final resting place, "in order that when the day fixed by God ... shall arrive, they may thus be ready and present at the appointed place."[10] Here Muslims followed the traditional Jewish practice of burial in the holy soil of Zion. The most prized Muslim cemetery was just outside the Golden Gate, overlooking the Valley of Jehosophat, where God would judge the righteous and the wicked. So prized were these Jerusalem cemetery plots that many Muslim rulers and noblemen were buried there, including the Ikhshidid caliph of Egypt, the famous black eunuch Kafur.[11]

If Khosrau was drawn to Jerusalem as the place of divine judgment, he seems also to have been fascinated by the city of "living waters." He was deeply impressed that a city with scant natural water resources could build hundreds of cisterns for rainwater which he describes as sweeter and purer than that of any other place. He observes that the streets of Jerusalem's bazaar are made of large stone slabs, so that when it rains the city is washed clean. He further notes the wonderful curative properties of the water from the Virgin's Spring in Silwan, so "that when anyone washes from head to foot in this water he obtains relief from his pains, and will even recover from chronic maladies."[12]

The air of depression and danger hovering over Jerusalem in al-Mukaddasi's time continued in the days of Khosrau's writing. But the air was not so heavy that the Persian visitor could overlook the simple, direct kindness shown daily to the Muslim pilgrims, whose numbers during the *hajj* could swell to twenty thousand, doubling Jerusalem's population. In the following lines he describes food given to pilgrims who would walk from Jerusalem to neighboring Hebron to pray at the tomb of the patriarch and prophet Abraham:

> ... There are slave girls who during the entire day are engaged in baking the bread. The loaves they make here are each a mann weight [about three pounds], and to every person who arrives they give a loaf of bread daily and a dish of lentils cooked in olive oil, also some raisins. This practice has been in use since the days of [Abraham] the Friend of the Merciful—peace be unto him—down to the present, and there are some days when as many as five hundred pilgrims arrive, to each of whom this hospitality is offered.[13]

In 969 Palestine came under the control of the Fatimid caliphs of Cairo who had earlier conquered all of Egypt. For the next 130 years the city of Jerusalem continued to be a soccer ball kicked between contending Muslim powers—with one difference. The Fatimids began to see that Palestine had strategic value as a buffer between Cairo and the westward march of Turkish Seljuk tribesmen. For this reason the caliphs in Cairo made the decision to defend Palestine and Jerusalem. They took action against Qarmatian pillagers and marauding bedouin tribes who had made life hell for Christian and Muslim pilgrims, threatening the one reliable source of the country's economy. Ramla, the designated capital of Palestine, suffered earthquakes in 1033 and 1068, and because of its location on the flat coastal plain was an easy target for bandits. In the middle of the eleventh century Muslims began leaving Ramla for the safety of the high walls protecting the natural mountain fortress of Jerusalem, with the result that Jerusalem began replacing Ramla as the center of Muslim affairs in the country. Fatimid officials responded to the development by reinforcing the city walls in 1033 and 1063, and building new mosques in and around the Haram. The governor of the country also acted to insure pilgrim traffic. He organized special police escorts to take the pilgrims from the port cities of Jaffa or Acre up through the mountains to Jerusalem. The assurance of protection paid dividends in 1065 when, to the delight of Jerusalem's merchants, some twelve thousand Christian pilgrims arrived from Germany and Holland.

Save for the period of Caliph al-Hakim's rule (996–1021), Christians and Jews were treated well during the Fatimid caliphate, as during the earlier caliphates. But it seems that in each of three great caliphal dynasties there was at least one caliph who turned a deaf ear to the Prophet's command that the *dhimmis* should be taxed but also protected. The aim of the persecutors, it seems, was the same: physical humiliation to remind the *dhimmis* of their inferior station.[14] The Umayyads produced Umar II (717–720), who barred Christians from public office, forbade them to wear turbans, and ordered them to cut their forelocks and to wear a girdle of leather that would distinguish them as non-Moslems; he further forbade them to ride with saddles and insisted they hush their voices in prayer. In the mid-ninth century the Abbasid caliph al-Mutawakkil (847–861), who continued the discriminatory policies of his grandfather Haroun al-Rashid, destroyed churches and demanded that Christians and Jews nail "wooden images of devils to their homes" and "level their graves even with the ground." Legal discrimination was also practiced. The testimony of Jews and Christians was not permitted in court; if a Muslim murdered a *dhimmi* he was merely fined, but any non-Muslim murdering a Muslim was automatically executed. Fatimid Caliph al-Hakim reintroduced all the old persecutions, including the wholesale destruction of two thousand churches throughout the empire, most notoriously the church of the Holy Sepulchre in 1009. But he added some bizarre persecutions of his own. Phillip Hitti states that al-Hakim ordered Christians in public baths to "display a five-pound cross dangling from their necks, and Jews an equally weighty frame of wood with jingling bells." Hating wine and remembering the Koran's injunction against it and how wine had ruined many a good caliph, al-Hakim ordered all the vineyards in the empire destroyed. Even in his own day al-Hakim was thought mad; some believed his brain had dried up, but, as Norman Kotker describes it, "No one dared pour rose-oil into his nose to moisten it again and restore him to sanity."[15]

It was only a few years after Jerusalem's walls were repaired and enlarged in 1063 that the first of five small wars took place for control of the city. Turks and Egyptians fought each other in a contest that would last thirty years and end only when the Franks seized the city from the Fatimids in 1099. The Fatimids were so intent on defending Palestine against their Muslim rivals that they were oblivious to the greater danger represented by the Christian knights, who for the preceding year had cut a path of blood from Constantinople to Jerusalem. Had the Egyptians known what was coming, they might have rushed to the Holy City with an adequate force. It took fifty years for the Muslim powers to awaken to what they eventually perceived as the foreign Christian menace in their midst.

Yet there were some in Jerusalem who anticipated the oncoming catastrophe. Sickened of the never-ending fighting, the Jewish gaon, leader of the city's rabbinical academy, fled the city for the lovely Lebanon seacoast town of Tyre; he was followed by Nasr b. Ibrahim, Jerusalem's leading Muslim scholar.[16] And many Greek Christians fled the country for the safety of Byzantine Asia Minor.

With the conquests of Edessa and Antioch in 1098, Jerusalem in 1099, and Tripoli in 1102, the Franks established four small Christian states, each bordering on another, a territory mostly occupying a narrow strip of Mediterranean seacoast and extending from Armenian Edessa in the north to Gaza and Aqaba in the south. The European barons believed they had created of Jesus' homeland a new Christian bastion, but what they had actually done was to lie down beside a sleeping giant who would eventually arise in irritation at the alien intruder.

The original Crusader successes were due as much to Muslim disunity and ignorance as to the Christians' fighting skills and bravery. The various caliphs and sultans of Baghdad, Cairo, and Damascus were engaged in their customary quarrels and were largely indifferent to the entry of the knights into Syria and

Palestine—areas which were not highly esteemed in their eyes for their political or strategic value. In addition, Muslim leaders underestimated the dedication with which the Franks would fight for and defend the Holy Land. The Muslims' old common enemy had been the Byzantine Greeks, and since the failure of Emperor John Tzimisces to recapture Palestine and Jerusalem more than a hundred years earlier, the region had been theirs, passing back and forth between Egyptian and Turkish hands. By and large the Muslims looked on the new Christian invaders as adventurers and plunderers who would return to their distant homes once they had filled their wagons and tired of battle.

The Crusaders, of course, were determined to stay in the Holy Land forever. They might have done so if a united Muslim force, powered by its own religious ideals, had not driven them out of Jerusalem nearly a hundred years after their arrival, and out of the Middle East entirely a hundred years after that.

The Franks won all their battles, established their tiny principalities, and built mighty castle-fortresses to defend them; but as long as the Crusaders remained in the Muslim East they were vulnerable to attack and defeat. Their lifeline was the Syrian-Palestinian coastline whose seaports made possible the regular supply of men and money from Europe. Once Muslim pirates began interfering with the lucrative Christian sea trade, the survival of the Crusader kingdoms was thrown into doubt. The situation on the ground was no less treacherous. So close were the knights to their enemies in the east that in most places a day's ride put them on the edge of a Muslim encampment. This explains why the pope's cross-bearers knew no peace and were perpetually riding out to do battle with marauding Muslim bands.

For more than forty years the pope's knights exercised dominion over their principalities until a succession of three Muslim leaders, all bearing names playing on the word "faith," rose up to evict them. In 1144, Imad al-Din Zangi ("Pillar of the Faith"), Turkish emir of Mosul and Aleppo, attacked and conquered Edessa, the first Christian state to be established, then died two years later after laying plans for the reconquest of Jerusalem. It was said that Zangi was so incensed when he heard that the Knights Templar had established their military barracks on the sacred ground of the al-Aksa Mosque that he promptly declared a *jihad* against the infidel. It was time to "purify Jerusalem from the pollution of the Cross!"

Zangi's son, Nur al-Din ("Light of the Faith"), took up the cry of *jihad*. In the meantime the knights contributed to their downfall by committing the colossal strategic mistake of attacking Damascus, an independent Muslim state of no threat to the Crusaders, which functioned as a buffer between the Christian states on the Syraeo-Palestinian coast and the aggressive Turks threatening to move west from Mesopotamia. When they were attacked by the Christians, the Muslim leaders of Damascus saw the bloody writing on the wall and decided to abandon their neutrality and cast their lot with Nur al-Din and his *jihad* against the Christians. Eventually Damascus was absorbed by the sultan, who embarked on a policy of reuniting the Muslim world against the Crusaders, a policy which could not succeed without winning over Egypt, still in the hands of a Shi'ite Fatimid caliph.

Nur al-Din died in 1174 before realizing his goals of Muslim unity and evicting the Franks, but the cause of *jihad* was continued by a great Kurdish general named Saladin ("Soundness of the Faith"). He was instrumental in eliminating the schismatic Shi'ite Fatimid government of Egypt and then uniting Egypt with Iraq and Syria under his own Sunni banner. Thus, for the first time in centuries the Muslim world was politically and religiously united. With planning, patience, and daring, Saladin managed to draw the Crusaders into a monumental battle which decided the fate of Palestine and Jerusalem for Muslims until the twentieth century. Moving across the Transjordanian desert in 1187 and crossing the Jordan River at the southern edge of the Sea of Galilee, he took Tiberias, then met the main Crusader force in the hills above the city. At a hill called the Horns of Hattin, he decimated the large but ineptly led Christian force. After that it was an easy march south to Jerusalem where the local Latin knights and bishops threatened to destroy the city's mosques, including the monuments in the Haram, if Saladin did not propose surrender terms. The sultan heeded the warning and allowed Christians to ransom their freedom. The stories of his magnanimity are legion; it is said that he offered the ransom money himself for poor nuns and monks.

On October 2, 1187, Jerusalem formally surrendered. The

date confirmed for the faithful the divine significance of the conquest. It was the anniversary of the prophet Muhammad's Ascent to Heaven.

Immediately Saladin acted to purify the mosques of Christian symbolism. The cross and Christ's portrait were removed from the Dome of the Rock. Muslims were enraged when they discovered that chips from the sacred stone had been broken off by the Franks, who sold them in Constantinople and Europe for their weight in gold. The military barracks at al-Aksa were removed and the vast stone chambers beneath the mosque, where the Franks had stabled their horses, were cleaned of accumulated filth. A fine symbol of renewed Muslim pride was brought from Aleppo: the handcarved *minbar*, or pulpit, ordered by Nur al-Din specially for the recovery of al-Aksa.

Saladin took revenge on the Latin prelates who had seized churches for mosques: he turned the elegantly built Crusader Church of Saint Anne into a college for the study of Shari'a law. He also took the ancient Church of Zion for his private residence. To the dismay of all Jerusalem's Christians and Jews, he declared the Mount of Olives Muslim sacred (*waqf*) property, which of course meant that Christians were no longer free to worship there and Jews no longer allowed to be buried in its soil. The Tomb of David on Mount Zion, sacred to Muslims no less than to Christians and Jews, was seized for a mosque, and a minaret was built above the Church of the Holy Sepulchre. After spurning advice to destroy the Holy Sepulchre altogether, the sultan arranged to resume religious services with the Greeks, who were overjoyed at the eviction of Latin bishops. We do not know how many Latin Christians remained in the city, but the bishops and the patriarch fled. Jerusalem did not know another Latin patriarch until the pope appointed one in 1847. Latin shrines and churches fell into Greek hands until the arrival in Palestine in the fifteenth century of the Franciscans who, following the visit of their illustrious leader, became the custodians of all the Latin properties.

Saladin, who was said to have hated "philosophers, heretics, materialists, and all opponents of religious law," was especially generous to the Arabic-speaking native Christians. He made a special decree of protection for the Armenians. He returned the Monastery of the Cross to the Georgians, who unfortunately later had it snatched from them by Greeks in Ottoman times.

The Syrian Jacobites received funds to repair their beautiful Church of Saint Mark and were rarely bothered again by Greeks or Latins. As happened so often before, Jews were welcomed back to their homes in the Holy City. Upon returning they moved across the walled city to the southwest corner, near the Western Wall, creating a new quarter for themselves which exists to the present day.

The forty-year period of the reconquest marked an important change in Muslim attitudes toward Jerusalem. The presence of the Latin Crusaders in the city, occupying the mosques, disgracing al-Haram esh-Sharif with weapons and horses, enraged Muslim leaders and reminded them of the traditional status of Jerusalem as the city of the "third mosque" sanctified by Muhammad's Night Journey and Heavenly Ascension. No one was more aware of this tradition than the Turkish sultan Zangi, who shrewdly used it to advance the cause of *jihad* against the Franks. In a brilliant essay the Israeli scholar Emmanuel Sivan explains a special genre of literature, "Praises of Jerusalem" (*Fada'il al-Kuds*). Exercising the rhetorical skills of Arab poets and pietists, it aroused popular support for *jihad* and the reconquest of Jerusalem from Zengi's time to that of Saladin.[17]

The spirit of the "Praises" is conveyed by a local Palestinian who, in 1185 after Saladin's victory at Hattin, wrote to the conqueror: "Soon we will march to Jerusalem. For too long the night of error has enveloped this city. Here comes the dawn of salvation which will shine on Jerusalem." What confirmed his faith in the "dawn of salvation" was the fact that Saladin's victorious entry into the city turned out to be the anniversary of Muhammad's Ascension to Heaven from the Temple Mount. This remarkable conjunction enhanced the prestige of Jerusalem throughout the Muslim world and strengthened the resolve to eliminate the Crusaders entirely from the Middle East.

To the native Muslim Palestinian lovers of Jerusalem, the reconquest of their sacred capital was long overdue. For them the city of the "farthest mosque" was scarcely less sacred than Mecca and Medina. A journey from the countryside to the Dome and al-Aksa was a virtual *hajj* to Mecca, and certainly no less deserving of spiritual merit than a visit to the Prophet's mosque in Medina. We already glimpsed an expression of this local religious patriotism when the tenth-century Jerusalem

geographer al-Mukaddasi repeated the widely known saying that
on Judgement Day both Mecca and Medina would travel to
Jerusalem, so that the three cities together would magnify the
divine glory. To the Muslims of Syria and Palestine, Jerusalem's
special place in the divine scheme was assured by the universal
recognition that Judgment Day and the Resurrection would
occur in their city and nowhere else. So it was only fitting that
both Mecca and Medina pay their respect to Jerusalem.

The local tradition extolling Jerusalem inspired a number of
other sayings: "God looks toward Jerusalem twice a day"; and
"Judgment Day will not come until Allah leads the best of his
bondsmen to live in Jerusalem and the Holy Land." Another
high-blown praise, reminiscent of Hebraic psalms, was: "One
day in Jerusalem is like a thousand days, one month like a
thousand months, and one year like a thousand years. Dying
there is like dying in the first sphere of heaven. . . ." There was
special praise for the city to encourage pilgrimage: "Allah pays
heed to [the pilgrim's] prayer, removes from him all sorrow,
cleanses him of his sins as on the day he was born, and if he asks
Allah to grant him [the privilege of] a martyr's death, he will
receive his wish."[18] One frequent local saying about Jerusalem
was adapted from the Jewish Talmud where ten levels of sanctity
are named, beginning with Palestine and reaching the highest in
the Holy of Holies within the Temple: "The sanctuary of the
earth is Syria; the sanctuary of Syria is Palestine; the sanctuary of
Palestine is Jerusalem; the sanctuary of Jerusalem is 'the Mount';
the sanctuary of the Mount is the Mosque; the sanctuary of the
Mosque is the Qubbat as-Sakhra [the Dome of the Rock]."[19]

Singing its praises of Jerusalem fueled the Muslim reconquest
of Jerusalem and encouraged local Palestinians to believe that
their city and country were divine gifts. But not all saw it that
way. Muslim legal scholars in Baghdad, Cairo, and other capitals
did not always share the popular adulation of Jerusalem shown
by the Palestinians themselves, nor did they feel the compulsion
to journey to the mountain-top city as many Sufi and other
Muslim mystics were doing. In fact, scholars and mystics differed sharply on the religious importance of Jerusalem. The
most famous critic of excessive praise for the city was the early
thirteenth-century Damascene Ibn Taymiyya, who especially objected to the Palestinian practice of modifying Islamic ritual in
venerating Jerusalem. He found distasteful the local practice of

kissing the Rock, which was an illegitimate imitation of the solemn act of the pilgrim kissing the Ka'ba; nor did he take kindly to the practice of circling the Rock as was done on *hajj* to the Ka'ba, even when the Jerusalem ceremony, out of deference to the Ka'ba (which is encircled seven times), limited the circumambulations to three. Many champions of orthodox Muslim tradition applauded Taymiyya's condemnation of the local Palestinian superstition which decreed that when a Muslim urinated or defecated, he or she had to face away from both Jerusalem and Mecca.

Criticism of the local pro-Jerusalem tradition at times suggested that the city might enjoy no sanctity at all. Some questioned whether Muhammad really made the Temple Mount his stepping-stone to heaven; others wondered if the hair found on the Rock and kept in an urn in the sanctuary for centuries was actually from the beard of the Prophet. This hostility found expression in a famous saying which rejected altogether any spiritual value in pilgrimage to Jerusalem: "If [the whole distance] between me and Jerusalem were two parasangs [seven miles] I would not go there."[20]

While Jerusalem had both its admirers and its detractors among Muslims, neither group altered the basic perception of the city's place in the traditional hierarchy of sanctity. The holiness of Jerusalem exceeded that of all other cities on earth save that of Mecca and Medina which came before it. When necessary, Syrian and Palestinian Muslims could regard pilgrimage to Jerusalem as a worthy alternative to the sacred *hajj* to Mecca; but even they knew there was no substitute for this *hajj* required of all the faithful once in a lifetime. Accordingly, the meaning of *hajj* was restricted to the sacred pilgrimage to Mecca and Medina, whereas the journey to Jerusalem was deemed not a *hajj* but a *ziyara*, a spiritual sojourn or visitation. The city's religious ranking in orthodox tradition was virtually formalized in a famous saying which ranks Islamic cities according to the value of prayer in them. As the saying goes: One prayer in Mecca is equal to 100,000 prayers elsewhere; one prayer in Medina is equal to 50,000 prayers elsewhere; one prayer in Jerusalem is equal to 40,000 prayers elsewhere; and one prayer in Damascus is equal to 30,000 prayers elsewhere.[21]

✳   ✳   ✳

Because of Saladin's reconquest, Jerusalem was closely linked to his Ayyubid family successors, each of them inheriting the conqueror's title "Protector of Jerusalem." But not all of Saladin's successors lived up to their glorious heritage. The Ayyubid dynasty lasted slightly more than seventy years (1186–1260), and not long after the death of Saladin in 1193, his royal descendants set to quarreling. The internal feud between the sultans of the Syrian and Egyptian branches of the family gave the Latin Crusaders an opportunity to regain some of the territory they had lost to Saladin; but they were never able to take Jerusalem until the year 1229, when an unexpected event took place. The Egyptian sultan Kamil, a nephew of Saladin, fearing the territorial ambitions of the new Crusader, German King Frederick II, and wanting the king's support against his own nephew, Sultan Nasir of Damascus, ceded Jerusalem to the Christians for ten years. Frederick accepted the deal, entered the city, and crowned himself King of Jerusalem in a near-empty Holy Sepulchre Church. Pope Honorarius III, who had sent the German king off on Crusade, was furious that he did not engage the Muslims in battle. For the pontiff, the dignity of Christ could be regained only through the blood of slain Muslim infidels. He punished Frederick by calling for a local crusade against the king's estates in Italy; at the same time he called a halt to all pilgrimage to the Holy Land. Meanwhile, in Jerusalem the Hospitallers and Knights Templar refused to serve in Frederick's army—an act which disgusted the monarch, who quit the city for Europe only six weeks after his diplomatic triumph.

The treatment of Frederick showed that the old Crusader passion for Jerusalem had waned at about the time the Ayyubid princes also began to lose interest in the city. Few of them after Saladin deserved the title "Protector of Jerusalem," for in the eyes of local Palestinian Muslims they had betrayed the sacred trust borne in that great sultan's title. How different was Saladin, who refused Richard the Lionhearted's request for Jerusalem in exchange for a much needed peace treaty. Kamil defended his deal with Frederick, saying that the German king had given his solemn word to permit Muslims free access to al-Haram esh-Sharif, which of course he did not keep. It was a pathetic excuse, because according to Shari'a law only a Muslim can exercise government over sacred Muslim property. When the

Muslims of Nablus and Hebron heard the news of the gift of Jerusalem to the Crusaders they came as a mob to the city and were driven off by the local garrison. And when Frederick arrived and, like Caliph Umar before him asked to be escorted to the Temple Mount for a ceremonial visit, the chief muezzin of the Haram seized the occasion to express the resentment of the country's Muslims by intoning from the minaret the most striking of the Koran's anti-Christian expressions: "Allah did not bear a child."

Sultan Kamil humiliated all Palestinians, but they had had a foretaste of humiliation ten years earlier. Kamil's brother, Sultan Muazzam of Damascus, when he ruled the city, decided to demolish Jerusalem's walls and stone houses in order to deny a fortified city to the threatening Crusaders. The resentment of Palestinians to the sultan's action was voiced by the cadi Magd al-Din, whose own castle housing Muslim contemplatives on Mount Tabor was destroyed in 1217. With lament he wrote:

> I have passed in front of noble Jerusalem, saluting the remains of its houses. My eyes pour burning tears remembering our glorious past. Here is a barbarian who wants to erase the past; he raises a criminal and impious hand. I said to him: Let your right hand wither! Respect this city for those who pray and meditate in it. If human life could serve as a ransom for Jerusalem, I would give my life and so would all its Muslim inhabitants.[22]

Jerusalem remained in Christian hands until 1239 when another Ayyubid prince, al-Nasir Daud, seized the city, only to lose it in 1244 to his Egyptian cousin Sultan Salih, who paid a brigade of fierce Khwarazmian Turks to conquer the Holy City. The arrival of the Khwarazmians, who came from central Asia and were driven west by the equally fierce Mongols, was a portent. For it was not long before the Mongol hordes of Hulagu and later of Tamerlane came west in periodic waves which struck terror in the hearts of all Muslim leaders. The Khwarazmians lingered long enough in Jerusalem to devastate the city, rape women and boys, burn churches, including the Holy Sepulchre, and drive the final nail into the coffin of Ayyubid rule and reputation in the Holy Land.

The dynasty of Ayyub fell, but the glory which Saladin imparted to Jerusalem stood. He had rescued the Dome of the Rock from the infidel Christian, converted churches into mosques, and reminded the entire Islamic world that not Mecca or Medina but Jerusalem was the original city of the prophets—the city which Muhammad had uniquely graced by his Night Journey.

To be sure, the glory of Jerusalem was religious, with little political significance. It was a place of pilgrimage and prayer, not a place in which to seek one's fortune or to plan great conquests. But remembering Saladin, no Muslim conqueror could ignore Jerusalem or risk losing it again to an alien intruder. None proved more loyal to the sacred memory of Saladin's liberation of Jerusalem than the Mamluks, the Turkish slave-soldiers who became the sultans of Egypt, and who in 1250 replaced the Ayyubids as rulers of Syria and Palestine. They built well on what Saladin had left them in Jerusalem.

Ottoman Indifference

To see its destroyed walls, its debris-filled moat,
its city circuit chocked with ruins,
you would scarcely recognize this famous metropolis which
once fought against the most powerful empires in the world;
which for a moment held Rome at bay....
In short, you would scarcely recognize Jerusalem.
—Constantin Volney, 1784

When I have money to spare I lay it on a house,
a slave, a diamond, a fine mare, or a wife;
but I do not make a road up to [Jerusalem]
in order to invite strangers to come that way.
Jerusalem is the Jewel after which
all the Europeans are greedy;
why should we facilitate access to the prize they aim at?
—Arab Jerusalemite notable, mid-nineteenth century

The powerful clique of Egyptian-based military men who took control of Palestine and Syria in 1250 were descendants of Turkish pagan slaves whom the Abbasid caliphs had converted to Islam and trained for their armies. Called Mamluks (or "owned"), they rose in the Muslim hierarchy of the Abbasid and later Ayyubid empires to become sultans themselves, and to rule the Middle East for two and a half centuries until another Turkish tribe, the Ottomans, defeated them for control of the Muslim world.

The Mamluks had little political interest in Palestine and

Syria; they ruled these countries through semi-autonomous district governors who were ultimately responsible to Cairo for taxes and military matters. Their rule was as inefficient and corrupt as many of the Muslim regimes that preceded them. Centuries of earthquakes, disease, and bedouin marauders had ravaged the country, so much so that the Jewish sage Nachmanides (coming to Palestine for the first time in the 1260s) wrote, "Palestine is destroyed more than the other countries, Judaea is the most devastated in the whole of Palestine and Jerusalem is the most destroyed of them all."[1]

But the early Mamluk rulers also recorded real achievements. Under the leadership of the superb general Baybars, who later became a sultan, the Mamluks defeated the Crusaders in a series of battles which reduced their hold on the Palestinian coastline and hastened their exit from the country with the loss of Acre in 1291. Baybars, along with Sultan Qutus (whom he later assassinated), turned back the first great Mongol invasion of Palestine in 1260 in a famous battle at Ain Jalut in the foothills of Mount Gilboa, near Nablus. It was a momentus event which preserved the power of Islam in the region. For the Mongols, nominally pagan, were led by a vigorous Nestorian Christian general named Kitbugha; had he prevailed, Christian conversion might have resumed among the Arab-speaking peoples of the region. But the Mongols did not prevail and in fact gradually converted to Islam, recognizing in its teachings a power more superior than they had known before.

Despite the incompetence of their rule, the Mamluks built well in all the cities of their realm, and nowhere more beautifully than in Jerusalem. A succession of Mamluk governors built mosques, hostels, and hospitals; wonderful inlaid stone archways and ornate fountains; religious colleges; and new houses for the many important generals and politicians who fell out of favor with the sultan in Cairo and were banished to Jerusalem as an isolated place where they could do no harm, contemplate their sins, and relax in peace and security against the day when the sultan might recall them to duty.

During the Ayyubid-Mamluk times and during the long period of Fatimid rule before the Crusader interlude, Jerusalem became a Muslim religious city where any number of dervishes, sufis, theologians, and other spiritualists could be found, all of them living close by their Christian and Jewish counterparts, all subsisting on charitable contributions sent from mother communities in other parts of the world. For these communities to provide financial support for a rabbi, a monk, or a dervish in Jerusalem was an act of righteousness which would please God and assure one's place in heaven. From Saladin's time through the Mamluk period, the face of Jerusalem gradually changed from Christian to Islamic as Muslim pilgrims from Yemen, Morocco, and Spain, fleeing poverty or political crisis, began immigrating to the city.

But for all its religious significance, Jerusalem was merely a subdistrict of seven larger Mamluk districts, one of which was Damascus, Jerusalem's capital. Historian Joseph Drory sums up the status of Jerusalem in the Mamluk empire:

> Mamluk Jerusalem was a town of limited political importance. It was not there that the political affairs of the state were determined. No significant political event occurred in Jerusalem. Its rulers were not directly subordinate to the center of the state, but rather to some other administrative capital; the town governors were low-ranking officers; there was no proper wall surrounding the city; and only a small military force occupied its citadel. The rulers saw no reason to build a state communications line to it, and emirs who lost their positions found calm refuge in its streets.[2]

If the Mamluks built handsomely, they did not govern well. At times city and country fell into virtual chaos, with the omnipresent bedouins marauding at will. In the sixteenth century, not long before the Ottomans dethroned the Mamluk sultans, the regular pilgrimage route from Jerusalem to Mecca via the Red Sea was blocked by bedouin bandits for ten years.

Anyone who has lived for long in Jerusalem knows that wealth and influence there are monopolized by a handful of Muslim and Arab Christian families. When one inquires about this today he is told that it was always this way. Actually this concentration of power began in Ayyubid-Mamluk times, when a group of families, with the blessing of officials in Damascus and Cairo, to whom doubtless they paid a tribute, began acquiring large land holdings and monopolizing appointments to the most important political and religious offices in the country.

Despite the presence of these families, the city was depressed—in fact, there were few times under Muslim rule when the city was not depressed. It is a sad fact that under medieval

Christian rule and ancient Jewish rule the city was economically secure and sometimes prospered, but under the Muslims, with the exception of Umayyad times, Jerusalem was usually impoverished. The only native industry was the production of soap from olive oil and the steady but modest income from the sale of religious objects to pilgrims.

Of the immense number of Mamluk constructions, some ninety monuments are present in the city today.[3] Most visible are the archways, several of which can be found at the openings to al-Haram esh-Sharif: high-vaulted structures with layers of inlaid stone decorations, striking the eye like open spring flowers, welcoming signs to enter the buildings that lie behind them. Perhaps the most impressive of all these façades is the one which leads into the Haram from the Bazaar of the Cotton Merchants, a splendid stone arcade built by the Crusaders which the Mamluks restored and which recently was again put into use by local Muslim authorities.

Two other beautiful Mamluk works are worth noting. The great ablutions al-Kas, or "the Cup," in the Haram, was built by the Damascus-based governor of Palestine Tankiz to collect water piped from the so-called Solomon Pools near Bethlehem. And in the Haram, the jewel-like fountain was built in the fifteenth century by Sultan Qait Bay and known by his name.

One must also mention Jerusalem's bathhouses. The Mamluks constructed fine bathhouses in a city unprotected by walls and daily covered with dust. The civilized atmosphere in these bathhouses continued with the passing of years. The following account of a Jerusalem bathhouse in the early twentieth century could well describe the same facility in Mamluk times.

> ...Bathrooms with tubs and showers were unknown in Jerusalem in those days. Mothers bathed their small children in basins and then used the bathwater for washing the floor. On Fridays, men took their older sons to...ritual baths [near synagogues]. Before holidays, they would go to one of the Old City's three bathhouses.... Upon reaching such a bathhouse, one enters a large hall with a round dome some twelve meters. In the center is a pool, and lining the walls are many couches where the bathers may relax. Large towels hang in mid-air, four or five meters from the floor. The bathing rooms are windowless, with ventilation holes around the circular domes. Next to the walls are small pools, into

which hot water flows from a hole in the wall. The bather sits on the stone floor beside the pool, draws water in a tin can, and pours it on his body, scrubbing himself with sponge and soap. If he can afford to pay (more money), he hires the bath attendant to lay him on the floor and scrub him with sponge and soap. After bathing, he enters the steam room, sits for a few moments on a stone shelf, and absorbs the invigorating vapor until the bath attendant arrives with a large towel to wrap him in. Escorted into the spacious hall, he lies down on a soft couch and enjoys total relaxation. If he wishes, he orders a cup of coffee and a nargila (a bottle for smoking tobacco). When he leaves the bath, he feels renewed and refreshed.[4]

What motivated the energetic building program of the Mamluks? The answer, according to Joseph Drory, is that, like the Ayyubids before them, they saw themselves as "successors to the Crusaders." It was an attitude which "obligated them to work energetically to glorify Jerusalem as a Muslim city, by adding religious places to the town, renovating and maintaining existing shrines, and destroying any offensive remnants of the previous Crusader culture."[5] It was also true that being converts to Islam, Mamluk leaders demonstrated through their monuments their deep and abiding commitment to their new faith.[6]

One further fascinating reason for Mamluk building zeal was wholly personal. It seems that as lifelong members of an exclusively military elite, the Mamluks were forbidden to bequeath their positions and wealth to their sons, who by the strict orders of the caste could not become Mamluks. In order then to ensure for the well-being of their offspring, the Mamluks constructed religious buildings and appointed their sons as trustees and treasurers to them. It was a position that could be handed down by the sons to their sons without interference from the sultan. As Drory explains, "The ruler dared not confiscate such holy endowments, and the son responsible for them was legally guaranteed a regular monthly income."[7]

The Ottomans were the last wave of the hardy central Asian Turkish people to migrate west in search of good pastures and rich conquests. At the beginning of the fourteenth century they came to Anatolia hard on the heels of the Tartar Tamerlane and took control of the lands his Mongol tribesmen had conquered and then abandoned when he died. The Ottomans were tribal cousins of the Seljuks, who initially employed them as herdsmen and mercenaries until they became masters of their former bosses' empire, extending its limits into most of the Islamic world and into the eastern Mediterranean and northeastern Europe.

Only the stubborn Persians were never subdued. In their western migration the Ottomans passed slowly through the lands of Iraq and Iran, acquiring Persian habits of speech, dress, etiquette, and food; whatever serious moral or theological reflections the Turks engaged in, whatever artistry they developed, were learned from the older culture of the more civilized Persians. But the Persians were Shi'ite Muslims and the Ottomans were devout observers of the Sunni faith; so when the Turks failed to conquer the Persians and win them back from their Alid heresy, they simply let them withdraw to their lonely but secure Iranian mountain plateaus, the last permanent bastion of Shi'ite religion in the Islamic world.

The Ottoman quest for empire began with a series of clashes against a weakened Byzantine government in Asia Minor. The Turks were skilled horsemen who loved to fight as much as the first Arab conquerors, and victory came almost as easy for them as it did for the Arabs. The Greeks could not withstand them, and in 1453 Constantinople fell to the Muslims.

With the Ottomans in Asia Minor controlling all the northern territory east of Baghdad to the borders of the Persian kingdom, and the Mamluks of Cairo continuing to hold sway in Egypt, Arabia, south Mesopotamia, Syria, Palestine, and Lebanon, it was inevitable that the two would clash for control of the Arab East. The crucial battles were fought in 1516 in northern Syria, at a town called Marj Dabiq, and one year later at a place near Cairo. The Turks won resounding victories because the Egyptians, clinging proudly to their swords and bows, were easy prey to the new black-powdered muskets and artillery pieces used by the Ottomans. Within a few months, Syria and Palestine were under Turkish rule.

The ruler of the new Ottoman empire was Salim I, the first of thirty-six consecutive sultans, all directly descended from him, each inheriting the all-important title of caliph which Salim had the shrewdness to garner for himself from the last Abbasid caliph who was languishing in Baghdad. Combining both military and religious powers of rule, as the Umayyad and Abbasid caliphs did before them, the sultans enjoyed a long and stable four hundred years' rule. Indeed, the empire might have continued indefinitely had western European powers in the late eighteenth century not spied the Middle East as a lucrative commercial market and as a vehicle for their own imperial ambitions.

One cannot read about the Ottoman period without recognizing in it a profound tragedy for all the Arab-speaking peoples of the Middle East. How different it was in the West. From the fifteenth to the twentieth centuries, peoples of western Europe experienced the cultural creativity of the late Renaissance and the religious freedom of the Reformation, the sea exploration of new continents, modern scientific discovery, and liberal political movements and revolutionary change leading to the formation of modern states. While all these extraordinary changes were occurring, the Arab East under the Ottoman sultans sank more deeply into ignorance and apathy. Beyond their skill in the military arts, it is difficult to find any political, cultural, or religious achievement that can be credited to the Turks. Through the four hundred years of their rule, the sole preoccupations of the Sublime Porte, as the Turkish government was called, were to maintain peaceful order and to collect taxes. The vast empire was organized for no other purposes, as we can see by the way in which Palestine and Jerusalem were treated.

Jerusalem fell to the Ottomans in 1517. Despite the Ottoman respect for the well-established status of Bayt al-Maqdis as Islam's most important shrine center after Mecca and Medina, Sultan Salim I did not see fit to make the city a district capital. The Ottomans retained the administrative structure which the Mamluks had earlier set down. Thus Jerusalem was relegated to a mere provincial town (*sanjak*) in a larger district whose capital was Damascus. And Damascus was one of several such capitals in the greater Syrian area—others being Aleppo, Tripoli, Sidon, and Gaza. The key to the stability of Ottoman rule was flexibility. The leaders in Constantinople—or, as the Turks called it, Istanbul—delegated authority widely if not wisely. The governor of Damascus, with the title of pasha, was responsible for civil order but was free to keep whatever taxes he could collect from his subjects. This made the office of district governor a lucrative one, awarded by Istanbul to successful generals or simply to the highest bidder. And because of its location in a country with a large non-Muslim taxable population, the pashalik of Damascus was much prized. The Damascus pasha drew income from Jerusalem as an important stopover place for Muslim pilgrims on *hajj* from northern Syria to Mecca and Medina. The Christian pilgrims continued to make annual visits to Jerusalem at Christmas and Easter times and to pay the required toll to enter the Nativity and Holy Sepulchre churches, a fee used to pay the salaries of the Koran readers in al-Aksa. In addition, native non-Muslims had to pay an annual head tax of one gold piece, which for most was their annual savings.

Tax farming was like a snake extending from Istanbul to Damascus to Jerusalem. Each tax authority got its share, which created great wealth for Jerusalem's Muslim elite families, who further increased their wealth by buying huge tracts of agricultural land and operating them as feudal estates. All the notable Muslim families—the Khalidis, Nusseibis, Alamis, Husseinis, and Dajanis—grew rich and powerful by dominating the money-producing areas of the society: tax collection, farming, commerce, and trade, and by monopolizing appointments to the lucrative religious positions of cadi, imam, and Koran reader.

To the Muslim rulers the non-Muslims were *raya*, flocks of sheep to be herded and periodically fleeced for their tax money. But Arab Muslim subjects did not fare well either in the Ottoman empire. The sultan deliberately excluded them from civil administration, and virtually all the military, legal, and civil business of the empire was run by the Janissaries, the grownup children of Christian slaves converted to Islam and specially trained to serve only the sultan. With the Janissaries the sultan had an efficient bureaucracy, utterly loyal to his own person, which at the same time shielded him from the often ambitious Muslim elite of the imperial provinces—a system designed ultimately to preserve the absolute despotism of the Ottoman ruler. It was also true that the Turks, precisely because they looked on themselves as inheritors of the haughty culture of the Persians, tended to look down on Arabs as inferiors. This was a curious throwback to Umayyad caliphs who were also racial elitists and relied on Greeks, Jews, and other "foreigners" to run their empire.

The one certain Turkish accomplishment in Jerusalem was

Muslims at prayer within sight of the
Dome of the Rock. Painted by
British royal court artist David Roberts
in 1838 with all the romantic
impressions of the Western Christian love
of Palestine as "the Land of the
Bible."

the rebuilding in 1537–1541 of the great defensive walls under
Suleiman I ("The Magnificent"). Fearing that the Mamluks
might try to reconquer Palestine, the Turks took what was left of
the walls after Muazzam's destruction and built a magnificent
high stone structure which gave Jerusalem its distinctive face.
Only one mistake was made. According to legend, the sultan's
architects neglected to extend the southwestern edge of the wall
to incorporate the Tomb of David on Zion hill, a site no less
sacred to Muslims than to Jews and Christians. Pleased with
their wall but incensed at their omission, the sultan ordered the
architects beheaded and buried with all honors inside Jaffa
Gate.[8] Their tombs can be glimpsed today in a small stone niche
above the gift shop called The Gate.

    In addition to the new wall, the sultan had the façade of the
Dome of the Rock redecorated with lovely green and blue
Persian tiles. A few public fountains were built, including a
finely chiseled one (commemorating the twenty-fifth anniversary
of the reign of Abdul-Hamid II) which stands on the extreme
west end of the Birket Sultan ("The Sultan's Pool"), today

a convenient receptacle for the gum wrappers of indifferent tourists.

At the beginning of the Ottoman period the population of the city, ravaged by war, famine, and disease, had shrunk to four thousand, mostly Muslims. Most of the Greek Christians had fled north to Lebanon or west to Greece. The Christians who remained were native Arabs who paid their taxes, kept quiet, and tried to get along with the Muslim leaders of Jerusalem. There were not many Jews living in Jerusalem; most of the Jewish population of Palestine lived in Hebron, Tiberias, and Safed.

The *raya* were taxed but they also had to be protected, and here the Ottoman government and their venal pashas in Damascus proved wretched failures. Jerusalemites were fairly safe once the city walls were rebuilt, but one could not wander out from the walls at night without encountering bedouin desert pirates. Nor were properties entirely safe even within the walls. At one point it was known that the city police chief was the leader of a burglary ring. The smaller towns lived in perpetual fear of bedouin raids. Pilgrims quite literally took their lives in their hands in making the long journey from the coast to Jerusalem. The most notorious brigand family was the Abu Ghosh family, which settled in the green hills west of Jerusalem. So powerful was the Abu Ghosh in controlling the area that in late Turkish times the Sublime Porte simply bought off the family and used it to police the pilgrim route. Ironically, Jerusalem was the beneficiary of the prevailing chaos, for the city's Muslim population tripled in the sixteenth century as a consequence of Palestinian peasants fleeing the dangers of the countryside.

The first attempts to upgrade the status of the *raya* came about in the reform measures introduced by Sultan Salim III (1789–1807), followed by Muhammad II (1808–1839). The sultans wished to guarantee security of life and property, to reform the tax regulations which discriminated against non-Muslims, and to establish a system of equal justice; but none of these reforms really became effective in Syria and Palestine because officials responsible for administering them lacked will and money.

Substantive reform occurred only in 1831, when a powerful rebellion rocked the empire, opening it to the political, economic, and social forces of the twentieth century. The rebellion was led by the brilliant and audacious viceroy of Egypt, Muhammad Ali.

Ali was an Albanian tobacco merchant from the eastern Greek town of Kavala, a superb Janissary who rose in the ranks of the Turkish army and gained fame by crushing a group of Mamluk dissidents in Egypt. After that he ruled Egypt with exemplary efficiency as a semi-autonomous state under his own banner. But, anxious to maintain good relations with the imperial rulers in Istanbul, Ali did not hesitate to help put down a dangerous rebellion in 1811 when the Wahabi sect threatened to seize Mecca and Medina; ten years later his troops dealt a blow to the Greeks in their struggle for independence. The pasha of Egypt expected to be rewarded for these acts of service by an invitation to extend his authority to Syria and Palestine, but he was disappointed. Istanbul had no wish to see competent and ambitious provincial generals draw closer to the sultan's palace. Ali was offered the island of Crete as a token of appreciation. Angered at the Sublime Porte, he simply ordered his large and experienced army into Syria, shocking the Turks who could do little to stop him. After winning a series of battles, Syria and Palestine were securely in his possession; continuing his drive into Asia Minor, he soon threatened Istanbul and began to dream of toppling the Ottoman empire itself. That distinct possibility moved European powers to rush to the aid of the sultan by forcing Ali to withdraw his army from the conquered province in 1840.

In the nine years in which Palestine was ruled by Ali's stepson, Ibrahim Pasha, the country underwent dramatic changes. Ibrahim began by abolishing tax farming, that great source of corruption throughout the country. Taxes were collected by Egyptian army officials, whose troops put a stop to the bedouin raids and imposed a new peaceful order on the land. The several pashaliks were abolished, and over the vast Syraeo-Palestinian region one governor-general was appointed, answerable directly to Cairo. The new centralized administrative structure aimed at eliminating the ignorance, neglect, and apathy that had prevailed under the former highly decentralized Ottoman administration. Jerusalem was not officially elevated in administrative status, but everyone knew that a new day had dawned for the ancient sanctified city.

None benefited more from the reforms than Christians. Overnight they ceased to be treated as *raya*. For the first time in Islamic history their testimony was accepted in a court of law on the same basis as that of Muslims. Christians were appointed to administrative positions once closed to them.[9] The head tax—that hated symbol of inferiority in the Muslim state—was abolished. Christians were permitted to run for election to the Jerusalem town council, hitherto an exclusive Muslim body dominated by wealthy pro-Ottoman family elite. The reforms extended also to the practice of the Christian religion. Christians could discard the distinctive black garments (and Jews red ones) which they had been required to wear as an ignominious symbol of their religion, and the ban against wearing the Prophet's color green was lifted.[10] The new regulations allowed Christians to ride horses, ring church bells, and display the cross in public ceremonies. They could repair their churches without special permission, and they could build new churches as well. The reforms extended also to Jews, who for the first time felt they need not hang their heads in fear and shame whenever they appeared on the public streets. They could repair synagogues and pray at the Western Wall without special government permission. For the first time in centuries, the life and property of all the inhabitants of the region were guaranteed.[11]

Most of these decrees were not well received by the country's Muslims, particularly in Jerusalem where the addition of Christians to the town councils was seen as a direct threat to the power and influence of the family notables. Muslims were incensed that the abolition of the head tax put both Christians and Jews on the same level with them, particularly when the wealth of the monasteries made it evident how easily the church could pay its taxes.[12] Muslims were also offended when the new government began to conscript local Muslim youth into its army while continuing exemptions for Christians. The apprehension felt about the new reforms was emotionally expressed by the Palestinian Muslim who complained, "O my brother, the state has become a Christians' state, the Islamic state has ended."[13] Muslim anger finally surfaced in 1834 and 1835 when riots occurred in the major towns. In Jerusalem, Muslim urbanites joined forces with peasants from the surrounding villages who had "infiltrated the city through ancient underground sewage channels."[14] But Ibrahim Pasha and his father in Cairo would brook no interference. The rioters were ruthlessly punished and the reforms energetically pressed forward.

As part of the Egyptian strategy to open up the country to European commerce and culture, special consulates were established in Damascus and in Jerusalem in 1838. Britain and France led the way, and soon almost a dozen European countries sent representatives. The consulates were intended to facilitate trade, but it was not long before they were deeply involved in representing the interests of their nation's minority community in Palestine. To counteract growing European involvement in the Middle East, Russia made its own aggressive moves to represent the sizable Eastern Orthodox community in the Holy Land. The European consulates were also left free to help Protestant and Catholic clergy in their educational and missionary work among Muslims and Arab Orthodox.

All these developments were watched with continuing resentment by Jerusalem's Muslims, who began for the first time to lose the demographic struggle to Christians and Jews. By the mid-nineteenth century, Jews fleeing poverty, disease, and earthquake in the north of the country began migrating to Jerusalem; so many migrated that by the mid-1860s they constituted the largest of the city's three main communities. The Arab Christian community also prospered as a direct result of the Egyptian reforms. By the opening of the twentieth century, Jerusalem's Jews and Christians outnumbered the Muslims, though the town council (originally founded in 1863) was still dominated by Muslim notables with only token representation from the other two communities.

In 1840, fearing that Ibrahim and Ali might succeed in toppling the Ottoman government, a combination of European powers led by Britain forced the Egyptian leaders to withdraw from the region. France, which alone supported Ali's rebellion in 1831, would have strengthened its hand in the Middle East through an Egyptian victory over the Turks; and Britain, along with Russia, Austria, and Prussia, did not wish to see French interests advanced at the cost of their own—and so opposed Ali's ambitions. It was one of the many stages in the Europeans' unending game for commercial profit and political influence in the Middle East. The game had begun in the sixteenth century when Sultan Suleiman I granted civil and tax privileges to the city of Venice with the understanding that the Venetians could also look after the welfare of their ethnic minority living in the Ottoman empire. From the Turkish perspective it was a noble gesture by a strong and wise ruler. Similar privileges, or "Capitulations" as they were called, were later extended to France and Britain, and eventually to Russia. The Capitulations became the basis for inter-European rivalry for money and power in the Middle East, each nation supporting or opposing the Sublime Porte depending on where its own best interests were served.

So purely out of European self-interest, Ibrahim and Ali were forced out of Palestine; but it was a very different Palestine than the one which the Egyptians had wrested from the Turks in 1831. European economic and political interests, Jewish immigration, and resurgent Christian missionary activity—all these forced the Ottoman government to take a new look at the long neglected country, and particularly at Jerusalem. From the new look came the decision to continue the reforms which the Egyptians had introduced.

The Ottoman sultan Abdulmecid in his decree (Hatti Houmayoun) of 1850 promised civil rights for all the inhabitants of the empire. But the Turkish spirit of reform was short lived. Once again the Turks failed to keep their promises. The old malaise returned to Palestine: tax corruption set in, bedouin bandits returned, travel became unsafe, and Christians and Jews began to worry about their relations to Muslims. They had reason for worry. Muslims punished the *raya* in Nablus in 1856 when a number of local Christians were massacred and in 1860 in Damascus in an even bloodier slaughter.

Religious rivalry over pilgrimage also contributed to the deterioration of communal relations in Jerusalem. Muslims were provoked by the sight of Christians flooding Jerusalem at Easter time. Jerusalem's Muslim governor (1876–1888), described as a "zealous upholder of Islam" and "an opponent of Jewish colonization," developed the custom of Muslim pilgrimage to Jerusalem and Nebi Musa, the latter being the site (on the road from Jerusalem to Jericho) where Muslim tradition placed the tomb of Moses.[15] It was a custom that continued into the twentieth century and became an important symbol in the rise of Arab Palestinian nationalistic feeling. Each year, under instructions from Rauf Pasha, thousands of Muslim villagers were summoned to Jerusalem to gather for the walk to Nebi Musa precisely in the week when as many as fifty thousand Russian peasants would be in the city celebrating Easter. Confrontations were inevitable. The British explorer Claude Conder left us a memorable sketch of one confrontation in which violence was avoided.

> In 1875 the pilgrimage to Nebi Musa was going on at the same time, and parties of wild fanatical Moslems paraded the streets of Jerusalem, bearing green banners surmounted with the crescent and inscribed with Arabic texts. A bodyguard armed with battle-axes, spears, and long brass-bound guns accompanied each flag, and a couple of big drums with cymbals followed. It speaks well for the Turks that with all the elements of a bloody riot thus ready to hand, with crowds of fanatics, Christian and Moslem, in direct contact, still no disturbances occurred.[16]

When chaos returned to Syria and Palestine, there was a difference: Muslims, no less than Christians and Jews, began to resent the ignorance, neglect, and cruelty of Ottoman administration. For throughout the nineteenth century, Muslims as well as non-Muslims were influenced by Western ideas and values in believing that life could be better than what the Ottoman Turks allowed. The first political meetings held by Arabs in the late nineteenth century in Damascus, Beirut, Baghdad, Cairo, Paris, and London were the direct consequence of this growing Western influence in the Middle East. No meetings were held in Jerusalem because the city retained its traditionally conservative character, where Muslim notables enjoyed good economic and political connections with the officials in Istanbul. And had there been meetings, there was not a single Muslim printing press in all of Palestine to publish the minutes of the meetings.[17]

The goal of the Arab meetings was to persuade the Sublime Porte to grant local autonomy or self-government. The members, mostly Arab Christians, wanted Arabic to replace Turkish as the official language of their province, and they wanted a greater voice in the appointment of district governors. They insisted that tax moneys be used for the benefit of the people and not disappear into the pockets of officials as had often happened in the past.[18] Syrian and Palestinian Muslims took part in these meetings, but the bond of Islam felt by Muslims generally dampened whatever secessionist thoughts they had and kept them obedient to the sultan, however much they may have personally resented him.

The major break in the wall of Ottoman power occurred in 1908 when a group of army officers, the Young Turks, exasperated by the incompetence of the government of Abdul-Hamid II, led a successful coup and demanded a constitutional parliament. Arabs were elated because the Young Turks promised full Arab participation in the new parliament and responded favorably to the questions of local self-government and the use of the Arabic language. But once again the Turks did not live up to their promises.

The failure of the Young Turkish rebellion to result in a better life for Arabs in the Ottoman empire finally turned Arabs away from demands for local autonomy and toward the plotting of national independence. The drive for independence in the early twentieth century was led by King Hussein, sharif of Mecca and father of Faisal and Abdallah who would eventually become kings of the new states of Iraq and Transjordan. The revolt instigated by Hussein against the Turks aimed to create a single vast Arab nation which would include all of Palestine on both sides of the Jordan River, and be led by him. The specific nationalistic movement for an independent Arab Palestine did not begin until after Sharif Hussein's ambition was frustrated, and as a direct consequence of Zionist colonization of Palestine.

The Arab-Turk issue came to a head in 1914 when World War I erupted. To no one's surprise, Turkey supported Prussia, which cultivated good relations with the Ottoman empire. Prussian Kaiser Wilhelm I had visited Istanbul, Damascus, and Jerusalem in 1901, when he received as a reward commercial concessions, notably the contruction of the important Aleppo-Baghdad railroad. Jaffa and Jerusalem were later linked to this rail line, shortening the distance between these cities from five days on camel back to five hours in a carriage.

Receiving promises that the British government would reward him with the leadership of an independent Arab nation, Sharif Hussein agreed to aid the British war effort by launching a rebellion in June 1916 against the Ottoman army in Arabia. It was a courageous decision, for the Turks enjoyed military supremacy in the region and with their new railroad could provide supplies and reinforcement for their troops. Moreover, the sultan was also the caliph and therefore the spiritual head of Islam, to whom Hussein was subject by Shari'a law. In that respect the rebellion was heresy, and this troubled the devout Arab mon-

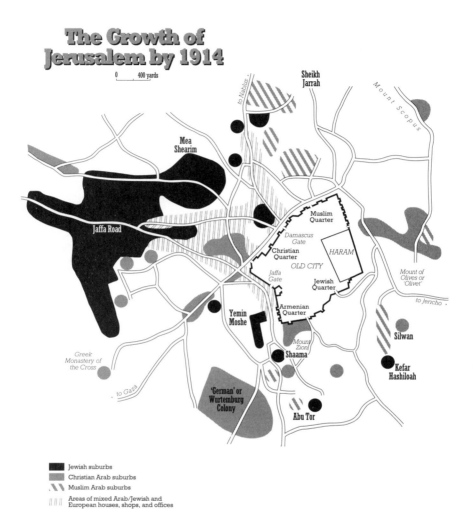

The Growth of
Jerusalem by 1914

0   400 yards

Sheikh
Jarrah

Mount Scopus

to Nablus

Mea
Shearim

Muslim
Quarter

Jaffa Road

Damascus
Gate
Christian
Quarter   HARAM
OLD CITY

Jaffa
Gate
Jewish
Quarter

Mount of
Olives or
'Olivet'

to Jericho

Armenian
Quarter

Yemin
Moshe

Mount
Zion
Shaama

Silwan

Greek
Monastery of
the Cross

Kefar
Hashiloah

to Gaza

'German' or
Wurtemburg
Colony

Abu Tor

■ Jewish suburbs
▪ Christian Arab suburbs
☒ Muslim Arab suburbs
▥ Areas of mixed Arab/Jewish and
European houses, shops, and offices

arch; but he made his decision in spite of it. Hussein also had
personal resentments against the Turks. The Sublime Porte had
kept him and his family in elegant house arrest in Istanbul for
more than thirty years precisely to avoid any possibility of
secession. To appease Arab cries for autonomy, the Ottoman
government permitted him to return to his palace in Mecca; he
was cautioned to avoid politics and merely to assume his role as
protector of the Muslim holy places in Arabia. It was a costly
mistake. No sooner did Hussein return to his homeland than he

entered into the plot to remove the one obstacle to the fulfill-ment of his dream to rule an independent Arab nation.

Aided by the Arab rebellion, the British force drove north from Gaza and reached the gates of Jerusalem on the 9th of December, 1917, after its Turkish garrison had fled. Two days later the chief of the British expeditionary force in the Middle East, General Edmund Allenby, arrived formally to take com-mand of the city. As an expression of reverence for the city of Abraham, Jesus, and Muhammad, he dismounted outside Jaffa Gate and walked on foot through the gate and up to the top step of Herodian citadel. There he delivered a message whose open-ing words were:

> To the inhabitants of Jerusalem the Blessed and the people dwelling in the vicinity. The defeat inflicted upon the Turks by the troops under my command has resulted in the occupation of your city by my forces. I therefore here and now proclaim it to be under martial law, under which form of administration it will remain so long as military considerations make it necessary. However, lest any of you be alarmed because of your experience at the hands of the enemy who has retired, I hereby inform you that it is my desire that every person should pursue his lawful business without fear of interruption.[19]

The British made good on Allenby's promises of physical safety for all Jerusalem's peoples and the safeguarding of shrines. But the general could not have foreseen that in making contradictory promises of national independence to both Arabs and Jews, his government planted the seeds of conflict that have ravaged Palestine and Jerusalem from the day Allenby entered Jerusalem to our own day. The events that followed Allenby's speech are the subject of Part Four of this book.

A City Divided and United

CHAPTER 10

Birth and Betrayal: The Struggle for Jerusalem, 1917–1967

*Jewish Palestine without Jerusalem
would be a body without a soul.*
—Jewish Agency, 1936

These palaces should have been built in Jerusalem.
—Arab Jerusalemite, 1962

The modern struggle for Palestine and its most treasured city began in 1917 when the British drove the Turks from the Fertile Crescent and inaugurated three decades of rule under a mandate granted by the League of Nations in 1921.

There were anticipations of the conflict before the British came to power. According to Israeli historian Yehoshua Porath, in 1891 "the leaders of the Muslim and Christian communities in Jerusalem petitioned the sultan to prohibit Jewish immigration to Palestine and the purchase of land by Jews."[1] Twenty-six years later the Turks, withdrawing in the face of the British advance in Palestine, "warned the Palestinians and general Arab public that the British conquest meant Jewish rule."[2]

But Zionists, too, were aware of the potential for conflict. Ahad Ha-Am, the eloquent spokesman for cultural Zionism, wrote a warning in 1891.

We abroad have a way of thinking that Palestine today is almost desert, uncultivated wilderness, and that anyone who wishes to buy land there can do so to his heart's content. But that is not in fact the case. It is difficult to find any uncultivated land anywhere in the country.... We abroad have a way of thinking that the Arabs are all savages, on a level with the animals, and blind to what goes on around them. But that is quite mistaken. The Arabs, especially the townsmen, see through our activities in their country, and our aims, but they keep silence and make no sign, because for the present they anticipate no danger to their own future from what we are about. But if the time should ever come when our people have so far developed their life in Palestine that the indigenous population should feel more or less cramped, then they will not readily make way for us. . . . [3]

British policies from 1917 set the stage for the Arab-Jewish conflict, and the withdrawal of British government forces from Palestine in 1948 opened the curtain on the first of a succession of wars. Britain left behind in Palestine a thirty-year legacy of contradictory promises and calculated betrayals. While these policies laid the groundwork for war, the real cause was the refusal of major Arab leaders, including the Palestinian leadership, to tolerate in their region a Zionist-led Jewish nation. Having for thirty years rejected compromise or cooperation with the Zionists, Arab leaders were determined to eliminate by force of arms the newly declared state of Israel. In this they failed.

Zionists succeeded in building and defending their nation-state because they were able to absorb their own factional differences and unite behind a single political goal. By contrast, Arab leaders were seldom able to join in pursuit of any clearly conceived goal, save for the defeat of Zionism—which often became a surrogate for developing the national institutions necessary to a future independent Arab state in Palestine.[4]

As one reviews the history of British rule in Palestine before the first Arab-Israeli war, a single event deserves to be called the watershed. This was the Arab rejection of the United Nations Resolution of 1947 for the partition of Palestine. That plan was intended as a logical and fair solution to the Arab-Zionist dispute over the historic land, including Jerusalem. Its rejection produced ceaseless military confrontation for the next forty years. The plan, accepted by a majority of UN member nations, called for the creation of both Arab and Jewish states; it also designated Jerusalem a *corpus separatum* to be governed by an international administration. Zionists did not like the geographic split which awarded prized fertile land to Arabs and withheld Jerusalem as a Jewish capital; yet, led by David Ben-Gurion, they were prepared to accept the plan as the price for international support of their new state. Arab leaders were not as pragmatic. Believing that they need not settle for half a loaf when the whole loaf belonged to them, they gathered the armies of five nations for war.

The Zionists did not attain their goal without help, and the Arabs did not fail alone. The British were intimately involved on both sides. They came to Palestine as conquerors and remained to develop the country and rebuild Jerusalem; but when the nationalistic rivalry between Arabs and Zionists drained their resources, they left both country and capital, a common object of contempt to both Arab and Jews.

The bright side of British mandate government rule centered on Jerusalem. With generations of Bible-reading love of the Holy City in their hearts, British officials were determined to alter the social order. The lash, the bribe, and the venal tax collector were replaced by the trained civil servant. The city rose from an ill-kept, neglected backwater town in one of the lesser provinces of the Ottoman empire to become for the first time in centuries the administrative capital of Palestine. Major economic development occurred in the coastal cities of Haifa, Gaza, Jaffa, and Tel Aviv; but Jerusalem, the inland seat of government, also benefited from the general prosperity. Jerusalem took fresh breath with investment money, housing construction, and new immigration.

The World War I years had devastated Jerusalem with famine and disease; people were stinking in untreated sewage, suffering from lack of clean water, unable to move around because of the absence of usable roads, and shut in at night by the breakdown of the electrical system. Responding to the crisis, the military government brought grain from Egypt, opened hospitals, developed sources of clean water, installed new roads, repaired the electrical system, and improved the Jerusalem-Jaffa railway which for the first time connected Jerusalem to the main Cairo-Damascus commercial route.

Foreign investment led to construction of office buildings, hotels, shops, and restaurants. The tourist and pilgrim trade, Jerusalem's sole source of wealth, was revitalized. New schools and libraries were opened, and cultural centers for Jews, Christians, and Muslims were funded.

During the mandate era three important new churches were built; the Roman Catholic Church at the Garden of Gethsemane (1924); the Scottish Presbyterian Saint Andrew's Church across the Hinnom Valley west of the old city (1927); and the Saint Peter in Gallicantu Catholic Church on the southern slope of Zion hill. The Hadassah Hospital was constructed on Mount Scopus, along with the Jewish National Library and later the Hebrew University, which was opened in 1925. The sumptuous King David Hotel was built in 1930, and across the street from it three years later the imposing American YMCA building was constructed. Also new were the central post office, the Rockefeller Archaeological Museum, and Government House, which first housed mandate officials and was later used by representatives of the United Nations.

This flurry of building which occurred during the early period of British administration in Jerusalem provided work for both Arab and Jewish peoples, thus solving the unemployment problem left over from the Turks. Building activity also led to the opening of new residential areas. New Arab housing created the Wadi Joz district, and the building of rental homes for British families provided development in the American colony and Sheikh Jarrah areas of east Jerusalem.

New areas of Jewish settlement developed in the western sections of the city: Romemah (1921), Talpiyot (1922), Rahavia (1924), Bayit Vagan (1925), Kiryat Shmuel (1928), Geula (1929), and Tel Arza (1931). Beit Hakerem, the first suburban settlement on the western edge of the city, was established in 1923. Under the British some of the most important Jewish institutions were established: the Jewish Agency, the Chief Rabbinate, Vaad Laumi (the National Council), the Hadassah Hospital, and Hebrew University. After the Arab riots of 1920–1921, the Haganah, the Jewish defense force, was established with British approval.

The British not only built up Jerusalem, they saw to its beauty. Sir Ronald Storrs, the first military governor of Palestine, decreed that all constructions in the city should use the local pink stone, which accounts for the beauty of the city to the present day. Storrs also founded the Pro-Jerusalem Society, whose aim was to raise money from abroad to maintain the many shrines that bestow on the city its unique cultural and religious significance.

In no area was the thirty years' record of British government in Palestine prouder than in the area of religion. On December 11, 1917, General Edmund Allenby, breaking military custom, reverently walked on foot through Jaffa Gate officially to take command of Jerusalem. The last words of the speech he made that day showed that the *holiness* of the Holy City was uppermost in the government's mind.

> ...Since your city is regarded with affection by the adherents of three of the great religions of mankind, and its soil has been consecrated by the prayers and pilgrimages of multitudes of devout people of these three religions for many centuries, therefore do I make known to you that every sacred building, monument, holy spot, traditional shrine, endowment, pious bequest, or customary place of prayer, of whatsoever form of the three religions, will be maintained and protected according to the existing customs and beliefs of those to whose faiths they are sacred.[5]

The British were concerned to maintain good relations with both Arabs and Jews, despite clashes at the Western Wall–Haram esh-Sharif area commencing in the early 1920s. While their efforts to arrange cooperation between Muslim and Jewish leaders almost always failed, British officials sought through their policing powers to reduce strife. In 1921 the government established both the Supreme Muslim Council to preside over internal Muslim affairs and the Chief Rabbinate which represented the Jewish community.

With the Christian population of Jerusalem and Palestine, mandate officials had more success. They encouraged the development of native Arab churches, particularly among their fellow Anglican adherents. They solved the financial problems of the large and influential Greek Orthodox church. Their support of traditional Roman Catholic privileges and powers reassured France, the principal European defender of Latin interests in the Holy Land. By endorsing the earlier Turkish *firman* (decree) of status quo (1852), which fixed the rights and responsibilities of the different churches as regards the holy places, the British government showed it would not play one church off against another.

British administration succeeded in making Jerusalem a clean, efficient, and prosperous city. But in May 1948 the government was forced to withdraw from Palestine because it had failed at the task of mediating between rival Arab and Jewish political claims on Jerusalem and Palestine. The reasons for the failure are common to the anxious self-concern of great nations: preoccupied with her own power, security, and prestige in the world, Britain was late to appreciate the potential for conflict in Arab and Jewish nationalism.

The deterioration of the British position must be traced first to the diplomatic crisis that Britain faced after defeating Turkish forces in the Middle East in 1917 and, second, to the original contradictory promises made to Arabs and Jews before war's end.

The central question faced by the European allies at the close of World War I was how to dispose of the Arab lands that fell under their control as a result of the collapse of the Ottoman empire. France and Britain were in a dominant position to answer that question, but their respective imperial ambitions made them eye each other warily. Britain, through her navy, enjoyed control of the eastern Mediterranean, but France's influence in Lebanon and Syria was expanding, and if it extended south to Palestine, British power in Egypt and the Suez Canal would be threatened. Palestine and the Sinai Desert were seen by British leaders as a strategic buffer safeguarding the Suez Canal entry to the Persian Gulf and the Indian Ocean, where vital economic and political interests lay. The need for compromise overcame rivalry, forcing France and Britain to draw a new map of the Middle East. Joined by Russia, which also had competing interests in the region, the European allies entered into secret negotiations which produced the Sykes-Picot Agreement of May 1916, wherein France's predominance in western Syria was acknowledged in return for British control of Iraq. As part of the agreement it was decided that no single nation would have exclusive control of Palestine; rather, the allies would share power in the country within an unspecified international framework. The arrangement was never carried out, for shortly after the Sykes-Picot Agreement, in exchange for British support of further French claims in Lebanon and Syria, France gave Britain a free hand in Palestine, much to Russia's regret. The prevailing Russian strategy in the secret talks had been to limit the expansion of British power in the Middle East while also seeking ways to establish a firm Russian presence. The French concession to Britain in Palestine later influenced the League of Nations in awarding to Britain a mandate for governing Palestine, thus legitimizing Britain's presence in a country which she had already taken from the Turks by military conquest.

The promises of political independence to Arabs and Jews served strategic interests but eventually proved Britain's undoing. For in committing herself to support nationhood in Palestine, Britain fueled the nationalistic ambitions of both Zionists and Arab leaders, with the result that soon after taking control of Palestine in 1917, Britain found herself drawn into developing local conflict with no means to resolve it.

What was the promise made to Arabs? During the war with Turkey the British government negotiated with the Hashemite monarch Hussein, sharif of Mecca, to lead a rebellion against Turkish forces in the Hejaz. The negotiations took the form of a correspondence between Sharif Hussein and Sir Henry Mc-Mahon, British high commissioner for Palestine. In exchange for Arab assistance against Turkey, Britain promised to help realize Hussein's great dream of ruling a unified and independent Arab nation. The Hashemite king envisaged a nation which would have the Red Sea and the Mediterranean as its southern and western borders; it would be bounded by the Lebanese Mountains in the north and stretch east to include Iraq—thus incorporating the whole of "Greater Syria." There was no doubt in Hussein's mind that this nation would include Palestine, for the country was looked upon throughout the Arab world as southern Syria. Moreover, Palestine at that time referred to *both sides* of the Jordan River, that is, Transjordan and western Palestine.

Keeping his part of the bargain, Hussein led a rebellion in the Hejaz against his former Turkish rulers which diverted Turkish forces and in turn aided the British in their conquest of Palestine. But the one great Arab nation never came into being. Instead of giving Hussein a free hand to rally the Arab world around him, Britain acted to extend her own power in the Middle East, first through the Sykes-Picot Agreement which divided the Arab East between France and Britain, and then through the League of Nations mandate which gave Britain authority over Palestine. The mandate proved to be a double blow to the Arabs of Palestine: it not only denied them independence but specifically called for British support of a Jewish national home in a country they considered their own.

British leaders were not unaware that they had shown bad faith in their dealings with the Hashemite royal family, without whose support they could not expect friendly relations with the Arab world. They did nothing to prevent the expulsion of Sharif Hussein from Mecca by the rival Saudi clan which took control of the Arabian peninsula; but consolation prizes were awarded to Hussein's sons Abdallah and Faisal. Transjordan was "detached" from Palestine and awarded to Abdallah in 1920 to rule as an independent emirate with British supervision. After the French had evicted Faisal from Damascus when he had tried to establish an independent Arab kingdom of Syria, the British named him King of Iraq, where he ruled until his death in 1933.

The creation of an emirate in Transjordan in 1920 infuriated the Zionists who considered the action a betrayal of the agreement that the Jewish national home would be established in the whole of Palestine, meaning Transjordan as well as western Palestine. What then of the British promise to the Zionists? Just a month before the military conquest of Palestine, on November 2, 1917, Britain pledged support to Chaim Weizmann and other Zionist leaders for the establishment in Palestine of a Jewish national home, with these words:

> His Majesty's Government view with favour the establishment in Palestine of a national home for the Jewish people, and will use their best endeavors to facilitate the achievement of this object, it being clearly understood that nothing shall be done which may prejudice the civil and religious rights of existing non-Jewish communities in Palestine or the rights and political status enjoyed by Jews in any other country.

For years there had been a favorable climate of opinion in Britain toward the Zionist cause. It was influenced by a number of Englishmen, "Christian Zionists" they were called, who believed that the reestablishment of the Jewish people in their ancestral homeland was biblically prophesied. There were also humanitarian considerations. Anti-Semitism was on the rise in eastern Europe after the Russian pogroms of the 1880s and 1890s, and the Zionist proposal of a Jewish national home as a solution to the problem of anti-Semitism sounded convincing to many British leaders.

But the decisive reason for Britain's support of the Zionist cause lay in Britain's own strategic situation in the Middle East. When Britain was contemplating sharing rule in Palestine with France, it was thought that encouraging Jews to settle in the country would favor Britain's claim to govern the country exclusively. The Balfour Declaration, promising Jews a national home in Palestine, was seen in the same light. Eugene Bovis explains the British reasoning:

> ... Some British statesmen came to believe that, if given a chance, many Jews would flock to Palestine after the war to settle and that if Great Britain supported the idea of a Jewish national home in Palestine, it might be able to establish a British protectorate over the country, thus assuring exclusive British control rather than international control. The Balfour Declaration would thus give moral weight to a British claim to be the protecting power, just as the military conquest then in progress would give the British claim a material basis.[6]

The Balfour Declaration served British interests, but it left unclear what was meant by "national home." Did this entail a Jewish state or did it not? In all Palestine or parts of it? Which parts? And what relation would Jerusalem bear to the "Jewish national home"? No one could answer these questions.

Some thought the crucial reference to the Jewish national home was left deliberately unclear to allay Arab suspicions that the British government had sold out to the Zionists. Certainly Britain had pledged herself to support Jewish settlement in Palestine, and while the establishment of cultural and political institutions was envisaged, the pledge did seem to fall short of explicit support for the founding of a sovereign state. British leaders stressed this to Arab critics. But most Zionists shared the attitude of Chaim Weizmann who was not discouraged by the vagueness of the British pledge. He viewed it, as he said, as "no more than a framework, which had to be filled in by our own efforts." And he confidently concluded, "It would mean exactly what we should make it mean—neither more nor less."[7] There was little doubt among Zionists as to the goal of their struggle. Weizmann's words expressed the common attitude: "Palestine is to become as Jewish as England is English." If this was so, what then of that curious clause in the Balfour Declaration: "... it being clearly understood that nothing shall be done which may prejudice the civil and religious rights of existing non-Jewish communities in Palestine"? To Arabs, the words meant that any Jewish expansion in Palestine meant Arab extinction.

Jewish immigration to Palestine before 1917 was resented by Arabs, but they did not actively oppose it until the increases of the 1920s, and even more when the mass migration of the 1930s made them feel, in Ahad Ha-Am's word, "cramped." But the statistical facts of immigration make one question whether Arabs were justified in feeling cramped. Certainly the rate of Jewish influx did not threaten to change the traditional Arab character of the country or of its capital.

Before 1840 the entire Jewish community in Palestine numbered fewer than 24,000, a minute fraction of the total population estimated at half a million. These Jews, living in ghetto-like neighborhoods in the traditional holy cities of Safed, Tiberias, Hebron, and Jerusalem, were mostly poor, pious souls dedicated to religious study and subsisting on charitable gifts from abroad. At this time Jerusalem had a population of only 11,500, including 4,500 Muslims, 4,000 Arab Christians, and 3,000 Jews.

As a direct consequence of pogroms in Russia and eastern Europe in the 1880s and 1890s, immigration to Palestine more than doubled the Jewish community to 50,000 by 1900. Now Arabs began to take notice, particularly in Jerusalem—the favored place of Jewish settlement—where for the first time since the Bar Kochba Rebellion Jews had become the majority community. By 1896 the total population was estimated at 45,000, including 28,000 Jews, 8,600 Muslims, and 8,400 Arab Christians. Throughout the mandate period the total population of Jerusalem increased steadily and the trend favoring a Jewish majority in the city continued. In 1948, before the outbreak of war, the city counted 100,000 Jews, 40,000 Muslims, and 25,000 Arab and European Christians.[8]

The Jewish majority in Jerusalem was an exception to the prevailing demographic pattern in the country as a whole. Jewish immigration, despite the intensity of Zionist efforts, failed to realize Weizmann's vision of making Palestine "as

Jewish as England is English." From 1917 to 1932 the Jewish population of Palestine increased steadily but slowly, adding about 10,000 each year, reaching a total in 1932 of 174,000—thus disappointing Zionists who expected the issuance of the Balfour Declaration to ignite mass immigration from Europe. At that point Jews represented only 23 percent of a total Palestine population estimated at 760,000. The mass migration did come in the 1930s because of Jews driven from Europe by Hitler's anti-Semitic laws. Here was the single instance of a dramatic expansion of the Jewish population in the pre-state period. From 1933 to 1936 the population doubled to 370,000, representing 28 percent of a total population of about 1,355,000. In the next twelve years Jewish population doubled again, standing at 600,000, or 32 percent of a total settled population of 1,900,000, in 1947.

Yet it is important to note that while Jewish population increased in the 1917–1947 period, the total Arab population in the same period, mainly through natural increase, dramatically doubled from 630,000 to 1,300,000.[9]

Arab opposition to Zionism was led by the old Muslim patrician family-clans of Jerusalem, whose wealth, power, and prestige derived from extensive agricultural lands acquired during late Ottoman times and during the entire period of British dominance. The British, who were eager to gain support for their rule in Palestine, cultivated the heads of such families as the Husseinis and their arch rivals the Nashashibis, along with the prominent Dajanis, Alamis, and Jarallahs. At an earlier time the Muslim aristocracy of Jerusalem was united behind King Faisal's "Greater Syria" scheme for Arab independence, but unity ended when Faisal was evicted from Damascus by the French in 1920. After that the Husseinis, joined by the Khalidis, entered on a militant course to secure Palestinian independence, while the more conservative Nashashibis, in alliance with the Dajanis, Alamis, and Jarallahs, transferred their allegiance to Emir Abdallah of Transjordan in the belief that the emir's connections with Britain would ultimately result in independence.

A turning point in local Arab politics came around 1920, when the mandatory government made several decisions which both enhanced the power of the Jerusalem Muslim aristocracy and intensified clan rivalry. A young member of the Husseini clan, Haj Amin al-Husseini, was maneuvered by the British into the religious position of grand mufti of Jerusalem; then, in 1922, they appointed him president of the newly created Supreme Muslim Council, responsible for Muslim institutions throughout Palestine. The local balance of power was thus tipped in favor of the Husseinis, who now controlled appointment of judges to the Shari'a courts and commanded the Waqf, or charitable trust. In the fifteen years that Haj Amin held power he made the treasury a financial resource to fight Zionism as well as to promote the importance of Jerusalem throughout the Islamic world.

Ironically, Haj Amin was the personal appointment of the first high commissioner of Palestine, Herbert Samuel, an English Jew who believed that Arab militancy would be curbed by assigning major administrative responsibility to its most important firebrand. It was not to be. Haj Amin wasted no time in rallying Palestinian nationalists around him and leading them in public demonstrations against Zionism.

Jerusalem's Muslim elite continued quarreling among themselves, but they never stopped making common cause against Zionism; nowhere was this more evident than in the struggle for control of the Jerusalem municipality, where Muslims for generations exercised hegemony. The municipality as an organized civil administration came into being in 1863 by special Ottoman decree. It consisted of an elected council of six to twelve members, who in turn elected one of their own members to serve as mayor. The duties of the council lay mainly in the area of road, sanitation, and water services, paid for by municipal taxes. Voting for council was restricted to "male Ottoman citizens over age 25 who paid a certain minimal sum in taxes on their property."[10] This qualification barred as voters a high percentage of Jerusalem's majority Jewish population (who were foreign nationals) and virtually guaranteed Muslim control of the council until the British came to power. Ottoman councils had token representation from both Arab Christian and Jewish communities but, as the Israeli journalist Daniel Rubenstein observes, "the first municipal elections (1908) showed that the Jewish votes could affect the election of Muslims because of the principle whereby all voters cast ballots for all candidates, although representation was denominational and communal."[11]

Support of the Jerusalem Muslim aristocracy did not prevent

British authorities from ending Muslim control of the municipal council by equalizing representation. Throughout the mandate period the council consisted of more or less equal numbers of Muslims, Arab Christians (both Catholic and Orthodox), and Jews (from both Sephardic and Ashkenazi traditions). While Muslims maintained their hold on the mayor's office, for the first time Christian and Jewish deputy mayors were appointed. From the beginning of the mandate, Jews complained that Muslim council members were abusing their office by promoting the Arab national cause at the expense of Jewish citizens. Muslims controlled patronage with the result that most of the city jobs and construction contracts went to Arabs. Moreover, Muslims ignored the British regulation that as one of the three official languages of Palestine, Hebrew had to be used, along with Arabic and English, in official council communications. And Muslims opposed any alteration of the property-owning qualification for voting that might enfranchise more Jews.

Despite the Arabs' opposition to Zionism, their internal clan rivalry sometimes led to unusual alliances with Jews. It was known that members of the Husseini clan, seeking to gain advantage over the Nashashibis, approached Zionist leaders with the proposal that "the Arabs refrain from voting for Agudat Israel [the extreme anti-Zionist Jewish religious party] candidates if the Jews would refrain from voting for al-Nashashibi."[12]

Tensions between Jewish and Muslim members of council came to a boil in 1931 when four Jewish members, protesting the anti-Zionist nationalism shown by Mayor Nashashibi, boycotted the council for almost four years. The tables were turned after 1937 when Muslim council members, reacting to the growing numerical strength of Jewish voters and to the appointment of a Jew as acting mayor, refused to participate in council meetings, which action effectively ended joint Muslim-Jewish administration of the city.

In 1917 the British proclaimed their support for the Jewish national home, but after that they heeded Arab opposition to Zionist settlement. In 1921, responding to Arab petitions and demonstrations, high commissioner Samuel, who emotionally endorsed the return of Jews to their ancestral homeland, ordered a temporary suspension of Jewish immigration. His action was forced by the first full-scale anti-Jewish riot in Palestine. In April 1920 in Jerusalem, six Jews were killed and 110 wounded; a year later in Jaffa a second riot claimed forty-seven Jews and forty-eight Arabs. Throughout the 1920s, as Jewish settlement expanded and Arab complaints mounted, the British government, while never officially repudiating the Balfour Declaration, left it free to local mandate administrators to ignore its provisions. As a consequence, Arabs, led by Haj Amin and the militant Arab Higher Committee, were emboldened to increasingly violent actions.

After 1920 the flash point of riots was the Western Wall area beneath the mosques on the Temple Mount. Muslims had repeatedly complained to mandate officials about the Jewish practice of bringing to the wall benches and chairs and other objects considered prohibited under earlier Ottoman decrees regulating worship at the sacred site. While to Jews the "offending objects" had a practical purpose, Muslims believed they were being used to establish a kind of squatter's claim at the sacred wall, whose ownership had for centuries been acknowledged to be Muslim. For in Islamic tradition the Western Wall is named al-Buraq after Muhammad's magical horse, who it is believed was tethered at the wall when the Prophet began his Heavenly Ascent.

Even under the best of circumstances it was never easy for Jews to gather at the wall for prayers. They would make their way to the wall from a street at the south end of the Arab market in the old city. As they did so they would be pelted with rocks from rooftops. When they arrived at the wall they had to wade through garbage which was habitually thrown there by Arabs living in the neighboring Mugrabi quarter. Often animals were driven down the narrow passageway in front of the wall. At times worshipers had to wipe animal excrement from the face of the sacred structure, recalling the practice of the medieval Christians who would "empty their slop pails [on the Temple Mount] as a special token of contempt for the Jewish religion."[13]

The Supreme Muslim Council under Mufti Haj Amin al-Husseini succeeded in preventing Jews from bringing the proscribed benches and chairs in 1922, 1923, and 1925. After that the mufti began an international campaign to discredit Zionism by charging that Jewish innovations at the wall were part of a Zionist plot to seize control of the mosques on the Temple

Mount and replace them with a rebuilt third Temple. The organized opposition to Jewish practices at the wall, begun in 1922, ended in 1929 with Arabs killing one hundred Jews in the towns of Hebron and Safed.

Significantly, none of the Arab actions persuaded the British government to renounce the Balfour Declaration and end Jewish immigration, which sharply increased after 1933. The armed Arab general strike of 1936–1939 was called partly because of Arab frustration with British policies. The strike leaders, speaking in behalf of the Arab Higher Committee, announced to the mandatory government that no taxes would be paid until Jewish immigration and land purchases were brought to a halt. When it became clear that the British were resisting their demands and were doing little to facilitate an independent Arab government in Palestine, the mob took to the streets against both Jews and Britishers. After a year of rioting the government had had enough. The Arab Higher Committee was declared illegal and Haj Amin was removed as president of the Supreme Muslim Council. In late 1937, fearing arrest, the mufti, disguised as an old woman, fled to Beirut where he continued to direct revolutionary activities. The Muslim mayor of Jerusalem, Husayn al-Khalidi, an ally of the Husseini clan who had supported the rebellion, was exiled to the Seychelles Islands. But the strike continued and became increasingly bloody. Hundreds of Arabs and Jews were killed; the British, caught between them, lost the most lives. Except for sporadic acts of vengeance, Zionist leaders organized no counteroffensive, preferring to do nothing to provoke the British into heeding Arab demands.

During the months of rebellion the government officially addressed itself to the crisis of Arab-Jewish relations in Palestine. A royal commission (the Peel Commission) was sent out in April 1936 to investigate the situation and recommended that the country be partitioned into two separate and independent Arab and Jewish states, and that the Jerusalem-Bethlehem area and Nazareth be set aside as a special enclave under mandate administration. For the first time it was officially admitted that in fact a struggle for control of the country was taking place, and further that Jerusalem was the most heatedly contested prize in the struggle, bringing to boil the frustrations and resentments felt by the two peoples for each other. The commission recom-

Members of the 1936 British royal
commission, headed by Lord Peel, in
Jerusalem. The commission recommended
the partition of Palestine into Arab
and Jewish states.

mended that the government abandon hope of mediating between the conflicting parties.

It was clear from these recommendations that British leaders
wished to avoid international criticism. In proposing partition of
the country they were yielding to the control of Muslims and
Jews the most hallowed places of the Christian tradition. Thus
the report noted unctuously:

> The partition of Palestine is subject to the overriding necessity of
> keeping the sanctity of Jerusalem and Bethlehem inviolate and of
> ensuring free and safe access to them for all the world. That, in
> the fullest sense of the mandatory phrase, is "a sacred trust of
> civilization"—a trust on behalf not merely of the peoples of
> Palestine but of multitudes in other lands to whom these places,
> one or both, are Holy Places. . . . [14]

Predictably, the Peel Commission report received a mixed
reaction. Most members of the League of Nations favored its
recommendations as a rational solution to a political impasse.
Arabs were disappointed because the commission awarded state-

hood to the Zionists. Zionists approved it, for, as Eugene Bovis writes:

> Many, like Dr. Chaim Weizmann, believed that the immediate creation of a Jewish state, although not as large as the Jews would like, would be preferable to continuation of the mandate under the alternative proposals of the Royal Commission. At least, a Jewish state would be able to control its own immigration policies, whereas the Peel Commission had recommended restrictions on Jewish immigration if the mandate was to continue.[15]

In a counterproposal brought forth by the Jewish Agency, in which the Jewish new city of Jerusalem and Mount Scopus were retained in the Jewish state, Jews took the occasion to remind the world of the centrality of Jerusalem in Jewish religious and cultural tradition.

> It has been said that Jewish Palestine without Jerusalem would be a body without a soul. Jerusalem has throughout the ages been the spiritual center of the Jews, dispersed as they were over the face of the earth. . . . It is a symbol of Jewish national life and practically synonymous in the minds of Jews with Palestine. Throughout the ages, Jews have persisted, in spite of all obstacles, in attempting to reestablish themselves in Jerusalem. In this latest phase of the Return to Zion, Jews have built the greater part of the new Jerusalem outside the city walls. . . . The separation of this Jerusalem from the Jewish State is an injustice to both.[16]

The special connection between Jerusalem and the Jewish people was emphasized in later years as pressure was applied for internationalization of the Holy City.

King Abdallah of Transjordan responded favorably to the Peel Commission's recommendations, recognizing them as an opportunity to press for the inclusion of Palestine in his kingdom. At this point the split widened between the Hashemite monarchy in Transjordan and the more militant Palestine leadership. The split widened still further as the issue of Palestinian independence deepened in succeeding years.

The report also displeased many leaders throughout the Arab world who for the first time began to interest themselves in the question of Palestine. Most expressed support for the Arab Palestinian nationalist movement and supported Jerusalem's grand mufti against King Abdallah.

Events overtook the Peel Commission report. Mounting troubles between Arabs and Jews in Palestine, and the possibility of war with Nazi Germany, forced the British government to abandon partition. The British reasoned that the safest way to reduce tensions in Palestine was to back off from complete commitment to the Zionists and to introduce measures that would pacify Arabs. At a time when Britain's attention was drawn to Europe, it was necessary to avoid further troubles in the Arab East. In a major restatement of policy, the government in May 1939 issued a White Paper which called for severe restrictions on both Jewish immigration and land purchases. Seventy-five thousand new immigrants would be permitted over a five-year period, after which immigration would cease unless Arabs agreed to its resumption. Once this period of immigration ended, the total Jewish population of Palestine would be fixed permanently as one-third of the total, thus assuring Arabs of a continuing majority.

As expected, Jews were enraged at the White Paper, judging it a betrayal of the Balfour Declaration. They were especially incensed at the British restrictions on immigration which came precisely at the moment when thousands of Jews were fleeing from Hitler-dominated Europe. The British government responded with a clever self-justification. It argued that the national-home provision of the Balfour Declaration did not obligate the government "to transform Palestine into a Jewish state against the will of the Arab inhabitants." It was further stated that the Jewish national home had in fact been established through the immigrations which had already taken place. The government took the view that it had honored its promise and felt no further responsibility to the Zionists under the Balfour Declaration.

Arabs were encouraged by the White Paper, which they interpreted as a vindication of their struggle against Zionism. But the White Paper also galvanized Jewish leaders into organizing elaborate procedures for illegally transporting to Palestine thousands of European Jewish refugees.

The outbreak of World War II in September 1939 confronted Zionists with a dilemma. In the war against Hitler, Jews saw themselves as allies of the British; but in Palestine, given the White Paper, the British government was seen as the enemy. David Ben-Gurion, then head of the Jewish Agency, solved the dilemma when he urged Zionists "to fight with Britain against

Hitler as though there were no White Paper and to fight against the White Paper as though there were no war."[17]

World War II introduced a period of calm in Palestinian affairs. Jews raised volunteers to fight for the Allies under British command. Haj Amin al-Husseini, forever scheming, took up residence in Berlin in the hope that after the war Hitler would solve the Arabs' own "Jewish problem." It was of no help to Palestinian delegates attending the British-sponsored Arab League meetings in Cairo to be reminded that their most inspired leader had become a Nazi collaborator.

At the close of the European war in June 1945, Jews and Arabs resumed their conflict for control of Jerusalem. A portent of the troubles to come occurred in August 1944 with the death of the Muslim mayor of Jerusalem, Mustafa al-Khalidi. Jews insisted that, given their majority in the city, one of their own should now be appointed mayor. Muslims strenuously objected. The ensuing conflict made cooperation on the council impossible, forcing the British to appoint their own people to run the city's affairs until their mandate ended in May 1948.

The thirty-one years of British rule served the strategic goal of controlling the vital Suez Canal entrance to the Persian Gulf and the Indian Ocean. The strategy succeeded. Britain was predominant in the region and successfully defended herself in the face of the threat launched by Nazi Germany. But postwar developments forced a reevaluation of imperial policy. The cost of World War II, plus mounting political and financial problems in India as part of a shaky empire, persuaded British leaders to resign the mandate and give up Palestine. It was at this point that Britain turned to the United Nations to provide solutions to the problems of Palestine and Jerusalem. The UN response was the Palestine Partition resolution of November 1947 which, influenced by the earlier Peel Commission report, recommended the division of the country into an Arab state, a Jewish state, and a third area, a *corpus separatum*, including Jerusalem and Bethlehem, to be governed by an international regime. European nations and the United States supported the plan as a way of handling an explosive set of problems. The Soviet Union supported it because it meant the diminishment of British influence in the Middle East and created an opportunity for Soviet penetration. The Vatican and Roman Catholic countries especially favored the provision for internationalizing Jerusalem, which effectively maintained Christian control over the holy places. The Zionist leadership, led by David Ben-Gurion, endorsed the plan, viewing the loss of Jerusalem's new city as a price to be paid for international recognition of the Jewish state. Transjordan's King Abdallah, as expected, signaled his approval of the plan which he believed would increase his kingdom; later, under Arab pressure, he denounced the resolution. Other Arab leaders opposed the UN plan as they had the earlier Peel Commission's recommendations, both because it would bring the Jewish state into being and because it would expand the power of King Abdallah. Local Arab nationalists, still guided by the policies of Grand Mufti Haj Amin, violently protested the partition scheme since it meant the triumph of everything they had opposed. The more moderate pro-Hashemite Arab party, led by the Nashashibi family of Jerusalem, went along with King Abdallah in supporting partition. But subsequent events were to show that Palestine was partitioned not because of the UN partition plan but as the result of war between Arabs and Jews.

The British government had made its official decision to terminate the mandate on May 15, 1948. Zionist leaders, anticipating the British withdrawal and ensuing chaos, particularly in Jerusalem where Arabs and Jews were engaged for weeks in guerrilla combat, proclaimed the statehood of Israel a day before the mandate ended and immediately geared for war. Within hours of the British withdrawal, the armies of Egypt, Syria, Iraq, Lebanon, and Transjordan invaded Palestine with the aim of destroying the new Jewish state. Thus began the first of five major Arab-Israeli wars. The outcome of the 1948 war determined the fate of Palestine and Jerusalem for nineteen years.

The siege of Jerusalem lasted almost two months, from April 22 until June 11, 1948, the beginning of the first truce. Some of the most intense fighting occurred in the Jewish quarter, inhabited by some two thousand devout Jews preoccupied with religious study and devotions, housed in compact, closely situated dwellings. Minor damage was done to the buildings when the regular defense forces of the Jewish Haganah took up positions in some of the synagogues and schools and exchanged fire with the enemy. But the real devastation occurred afterward when the Jewish defenders surrendered to the victorious Arabs who eventually took control of the whole of the old city.

Jewish soldiers were taken prisoner, and the original inhabitants of the quarter were moved out by their own people to the Katamon area of west Jerusalem. No sooner had they departed than the Arab forces looted synagogues, schools, and homes and made a fire of religious articles and anything else they could not use. Then, acting under orders, they set about dynamiting the synagogues and schools in the area. In total, twenty-seven synagogues and some thirty schools were damaged or destroyed. The Porath Yosef, Hurva, and Tiferet Israel synagogues were destroyed. The famous Yochanan ben Zakkai Synagogue was devastated from within and survived only as a shell. The synagogue founded by the great biblical scholar Nachmanides in 1267 was also devastated. The loss to the Jewish heritage in Jerusalem was irreplaceable. But the destruction did not end there.

Over the nineteen years of Jordanian rule of east Jerusalem, the most hallowed Jewish cemetery on the Mount of Olives suffered a similar fate. Gabriel Padon describes what happened: "Graves had been ripped open and bones scattered; thousands of tombstones had been smashed or removed by the Jordanian Army to build fortifications, footpaths, army camps, and latrines. The Arab Jerusalem Municipality had granted concessions to merchants who destroyed graves and sold the gravestones to building contractors."[18] It is said that the original foundation stones of the Intercontinental Hotel which stands on the Mount of Olives includes pieces taken from the Jewish graveyard.

The Jewish quarter was so thoroughly destroyed, according to news reporters, that it had the look of Stalingrad or Berlin in World War II. The quarter was emptied of its Jews and turned over to squatters, mostly Arab refugees from the Hebron area who used the remains of the synagogues as "stables, hen houses, rubbish dumps, and even latrines." When Israeli soldiers regained the territory in June 1967, and entered the Yochanan ben Zakkai Synagogue complex, they found garbage piled to the ceiling.

The Israelis complained repeatedly to the United Nations about Jordanian treatment of the Jewish quarter and the cemetery on the Mount of Olives, treatment which violated the provisions of the truce agreement between the nations guaranteeing the safety of shrines and holy sites in their respective areas. But the complaints went unheard. The Jordanians countered by citing desecration to Muslim graves by Israelis in the Mamilla Cemetery in west Jerusalem. The Israelis heatedly denied this. There is little doubt that the provision of the truce agreement allowing for free access of peoples between the two halves of the city was flagrantly violated by the Jordanians when they erected a wall of concrete and barbed wire to keep Jews from reentering west Jerusalem and the old city, thus denying them access to the Western Wall and to the synagogues. The barrier also prevented Muslims residing in Israel from visiting the mosques on the Temple Mount. So severe were the Jordanian restrictions against Jews gaining access to the old city that visitors wishing to cross over from west Jerusalem (at the Mandelbaum Gate) had to produce a baptismal certificate.

Despite their losses, both Israel and Transjordan were winners in the 1948 war. In the fighting for Jerusalem, Israelis, battling both the Jordanian Arab Legion and irregular Palestinian soldiers under the command of Mufti Haj Amin al-Husseini, retained control of the new city and a small enclave on Mount Scopus, where Hebrew University and Hadassah Hospital were located. All of Arab east Jerusalem and the old city were taken by the Arab Legion, including the ancient Jewish quarter, west of the Wailing Wall. And in May 1949, King Abdallah signed an armistice agreement with Israel fixing the boundaries of Jerusalem and Palestine and effectively dividing the country between the two nations. A year later the king formally annexed Palestine, including east Jerusalem, incorporating it into his country as the West Bank of the newly named Hashemite Kingdom of Jordan. The annexation was protested by the Arab League which had decided in April 1948 that at war's end Palestine would be returned to the Palestinians.

The Israelis gained greater territory as a result of the 1948 war than they would have enjoyed under the UN partition plan. They obtained the port city of Jaffa which originally had been designated for the Arab state. In addition, large Arab neighborhoods in west Jerusalem, such as Katamon and Baka, became part of the new Jewish capital.

As soon as the armistice agreement in Jordan was signed, preparations were made to declare west Jerusalem the capital of

Israel, which was formally done by the Knesset in December 1949. It was an action which did not meet with official approval by European nations and the United States, any more than Jordan's annexation of the West Bank in 1950 met with international approval. The U.S. and other countries officially recognized the statehood of Israel but refused to acknowledge the legitimacy of Israel's incorporation of west Jerusalem as a national capital and declined to locate their embassies in Jerusalem. The official position taken by Western leaders was that the UN resolution affecting the internationalization of Jerusalem was still valid, and that both the Israeli and Jordanian actions to alter the status of Jerusalem were, from their point of view, illegitimate. The Vatican in particular stressed the point that only the carrying out of the UN resolution on internationalizing Jerusalem would safeguard the holy places and ensure Christian interests throughout the Holy Land. Israel countered by expressing its willingness to cooperate with any body to provide international supervision of all Christian and Muslim holy places in Israel, an offer continually ignored.

Both Jordan and Israel ignored outsider complaints and concentrated on governing their respective halves of Jerusalem. The Israelis undertook extensive building projects designed firmly to establish their half of the city as the capital of the new nation. A new university campus went up in Givat Ram, and a major hospital complex was established in the hillside suburb of Ein Kerem, the traditional birthplace of John the Baptist. The foreign ministry was moved from Tel Aviv to Jerusalem.

The conquest of the West Bank and east Jerusalem was as close as King Abdallah came to leading an independent Arab nation in the Fertile Crescent—a dream he shared with his father and brother. But it was a sweet victory nevertheless. More than half of Palestine was added to his kingdom, and 900,000 Palestinians became subjects of the Hashemite monarchy. Islam's third holiest city, the al-Aksa Mosque, and the Dome of the Rock shrine were under his protection, thus mitigating the humiliation suffered by the Hashemite family when it was expelled from Mecca and Medina by King Ibn Saud in the early part of the century.

In certain important ways, Abdallah extended a gracious welcome to his new subjects. All Palestinians were issued Jor-

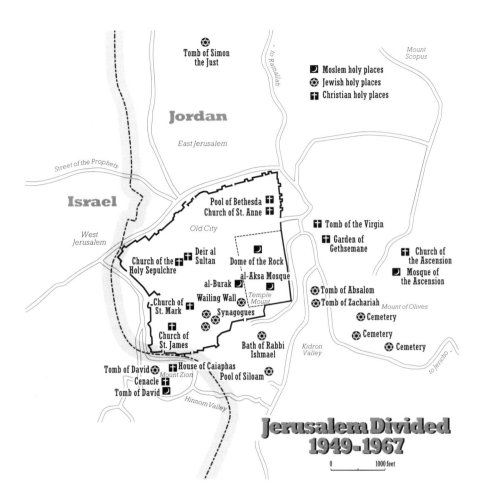

Tomb of Simon
the Just

to Ramallah

Mount Scopus

◨ Moslem holy places
✡ Jewish holy places
✝ Christian holy places

Jordan

East Jerusalem

Street of the Prophets

Israel

West Jerusalem

Old City

Pool of Bethesda ✝
Church of St. Anne ✝

✝ Tomb of the Virgin

✝ Garden of
Gethsemane

✝ Church of
the Ascension
◨ Mosque of
the Ascension

Church of the ✝✝
Holy Sepulchre

Deir al
Sultan

Dome of the Rock ◨

al-Aksa Mosque ◨

al-Burak ◨

Wailing Wall ✡   *Temple Mount*

Church of
St. Mark ✝

✡ Synagogues

✝ Church of
St. James

Bath of Rabbi
Ishmael

Tomb of David ✡   ✝ House of Caiaphas
   Mount Zion
Cenacle ✝
Tomb of David ◨   Pool of Siloam ✝

Hinnom Valley

✡ Tomb of Absalom
✡ Tomb of Zachariah   *Mount of Olives*

✡ Cemetery

✡ Cemetery

✡ Cemetery

Kidron Valley

to Jericho

Jerusalem Divided
1949–1967

0 _____ 1000 feet

danian passports. The Jordanian parliament was reconstituted
with half its seats set aside for Palestinians. During the succeeding years, any number of Palestinians rose to high positions
in government and became leaders in business and education.
Culturally more advanced than the original bedouin stock of
Transjordan, Palestinians actively participated in Jordanian commerce, industry, and education. So dramatic was the impact of
Palestinians on the life of Jordan from 1948 to 1967 that many
said that Jordan could not survive as a modern nation without
this people who constituted somewhere between one-half and
two-thirds of its population.

In stark contrast to Abdallah's reception of the Palestinians was his (and later King Hussein's) neglect of the Palestinians in their own country, particularly in Jerusalem. A concerted effort was made to build up the city of Amman at the expense of Jerusalem. In 1962 a Jerusalem candidate for election to the Jordanian parliament expressed his resentment: "See the palaces which are being built in Amman . . . these palaces should have been built in Jerusalem, but were removed from here, so that Jerusalem would remain not a city, but a kind of village."[19]

Housing and office construction boomed in Amman; very few new buildings appeared in Jerusalem. The construction of the Intercontinental Hotel on the Mount of Olives—an eyesore—was a rare exception. After the 1948 war the Christian organization behind Saint John's Ophthalmic Hospital, originally located in the German colony area of west Jerusalem, was relocated in the Arab side of the city against the wishes of the Jordanian government which wanted the hospital moved to Amman.

All government offices were transferred to Amman, and Jerusalem ceased to be the administrative capital for Palestine—thus reversing the British policy which had done so much to revitalize the city. Only minor clerks remained to handle local affairs. If one wanted to arrange a bank loan, order a telephone, apply for a business license, or register a parcel for mailing he had to travel thirty miles to Amman. Only the Ministry of Tourism remained in Jerusalem, because the government encouraged pilgrimage to the Holy Land as a steady source of foreign currency.

The Jordanian government set out to break the back of the Muslim aristocracy of Jerusalem and succeeded. The Nashashibi clan was rewarded for its continuing loyalty to the crown, but the more revolutionary-minded Husseinis were purged. Through emigration, intimidation, or cooption, the family clans lost the power and prestige they had once enjoyed in the city. The Supreme Muslim Council, the power base of the Husseinis, was abolished, as was the Arab Higher Committee, the political organization founded by Mufti Haj Amin in 1936 to fight the British and the Zionists. In time all local Palestinian political parties were officially abolished, forcing them to go underground. The treasury of the Palestine Waqf was removed to Amman, and thereafter Muslim officials complained that little money found its way back to Jerusalem for upkeep of the mosques. All Muslim judges were appointed from Amman.

Where Haj Amin sought to promote the religious importance of Jerusalem to Muslims, Hashemite officials sought to diminish it. To Muslim Jerusalemites it was insulting that "Friday prayers were broadcast from the Great Husseini Mosque in Amman instead of from the world's third most holy mosque in Jerusalem."[20]

From the beginning of their rule, Jordanian officials encouraged the immigration of Hebronites to Jerusalem as a way of loosening the hold of the old Muslim elite in the city. The strategy succeeded, for in time the Hebronites, known as the frugal, industrious "Scotsmen" of Palestine, controlled some 40 percent of Jerusalem's commerce. Jordan also dealt a blow to Jerusalem by diverting the city's own tax revenues for projects to help Nablus and Hebron. Plans for an Arab University of Jerusalem, drawn up by the city's notables, were abandoned when the Jordanians came to power. Politically and culturally Arab Jerusalemites were isolated, and the wall erected by government to divide the Arab side of town from the Jewish only served to remind them of this isolation.

The marginal improvement of Jerusalem showed up in population growth. Whereas from 1948 to 1967 the population of Amman increased fivefold, from 61,000 to 311,00, Jerusalem's increased from 50,000 to 75,000.

Palestinians rose high in government service, but they rarely entered the prime minister's cabinet which advised the king, nor did they find advancement in the all-important army. Only two Palestinians became prime minister, Hussein Fakhri al-Khalidi in 1957, and General Muhammad Daoud al-Husseini in September 1970; in both instances the appointments presaged government campaigns to suppress the Palestinians.

The fiercely loyal bedouin Arab Legion was much in evidence in Jerusalem, arresting, deporting, or imprisoning anyone who showed signs of disloyalty. The Palestinians' resentment of the native Jordanians, whom they regarded as uncultured bedouins, preceded the 1948 war but was intensified by the war's outcome. In Palestinian eyes, the Jordanians had not won the war against Israel but merely seized the opportunity to grab more territory for the monarchy—this contrary to the agreement at the Arab League meeting in 1947 to turn Palestine over to its people at war's end. Fearing rebellion after the battle for Jerusalem, the forces of Abdallah disarmed the troops under the command of Mufti Haj Amin. Yet the Palestinians were reluctant to give up the torch of freedom.

In September 1948, only four months after the war, the Palestinian leadership, under the aegis of the Arab Higher Committee, met in Gaza to establish the "All Palestine Government," naming Haj Amin al-Husseini as president. The action was endorsed by all Arab states save Transjordan. Abdallah reacted by letting loose the Arab Legion on the mufti's supporters, arresting and jailing many of them. Haj Amin once again fled to Beirut, and his position as mufti of Jerusalem was filled by the pro-Hashemite Husam al-Din Jarallah. After quashing the rebels, Abdallah called his own meeting in December 1948 in Jericho, where, through bribery, coercion, and flattery, he arranged for two thousand Palestinian notables to declare their wish to have Palestine united to Transjordan and to proclaim him "King of all Palestine." It was significant that powerful Sheik Muhammad Ali Ja'aburi of Hebron, who had been an opponent of Abdallah, now supported him as did the influential Jerusalem personalities Anwar Khatib and Anwar Nusseibeh, both of whom were rewarded with high government positions. Haj Amin was to get his revenge on Abdallah; in July 1951 the king was assassinated by the mufti's agents as he was about to enter al-Aksa Mosque for Friday morning prayers.

The Palestinians also resented the Arab Legion for not fighting hard enough in the 1948 war to win Ramla, Lydda, and Jaffa. Further they suspected that collusion with the Israelis led to the loss of Arab neighborhoods in west Jerusalem. They detested Jordanian leaders for their willingness to sign an armistice agreement with Israel which was de facto recognition of the Jewish state; one Palestinian called the agreement "a new Balfour Declaration."[21]

CHAPTER 11

The Future of Jerusalem

...The dove came back to Noah in the evening, and lo,
in her mouth a freshly plucked olive leaf,
so Noah knew that the waters had subsided from the earth.
—*Genesis 8:11*

For centuries Jerusalem has been a city where Jews, Christians, and Muslims have exchanged roles as conqueror and subject. Is there is any reason to think that the pattern of Jerusalem's past can be broken in favor of a new future without domination and subjugation?

If so, it is because Jerusalem is no longer a small, isolated hilltop town in a backward province of some vast impersonal empire. After many centuries Jerusalem has become the capital of a nation of military and political importance. For that reason Jerusalem is a world capital. What happens in this city instantly draws the attention of the world press. Leaders of the world's religions, races, and nations want a say in Jerusalem's future. Jerusalem has come close to realizing the medieval cartographer's vision of the Holy City at the juncture of all the world's continents.

British mandate officials lifted Jerusalem out of the dust, administered a face cleaning, and removed her from provincial obscurity by naming her the capital of Palestine. But the credit for elevating this city to world status must be given to the Israelis and to their late-nineteenth-century Jewish forebears. Hurting for space in an old Jerusalem owned and dominated by Muslims and Christians, Jews settled outside the old walls and proceeded in fifty years to build a modern, bright new Jerusalem; it was a city they would defend as their nation's capital in 1948 and again in 1967. As a result of its battle victories in 1967, Israel found itself in control of the historic old city for the first time in eighteen hundred years. Promptly the old city and the Arab-populated eastern half of town were annexed to the new city to form a united Jerusalem, the nation's sovereign capital. From that point, the Israelis worked to enlarge and build this united Jerusalem. And they seized every opportunity to proclaim to the world that Israel ruled in "united Jerusalem" not by might but by right.

Since 1967 a "united Jerusalem" has become in the Israeli mind the symbol of national sovereignty. With it Israelis face a formidable challenge. For all future questions of war and peace in this city will be answered not only by how well Israel governs a "united Jerusalem" but by what compromises she is willing to make with the Arab Palestinians who assert their own historic, religious, and nationalistic claims to the city. As Jerusalem has become a potent emotional symbol to Jews, so also has it become one to Muslims and Christians.

The oldest truth about this city is that Jerusalem consumes her conquerors; the city rises taller on the wreckage of her history. Past patterns of conquest and domination will be broken when Arabs and Jews together agree on territorial compromises in Jerusalem, the West Bank, and Gaza.

If compromise proves impossible, a settlement imposed by the major powers is always mentioned as a logical alternative. Such a settlement would establish an internationally sponsored government for Jerusalem, thus taking the city out of the hands of contending Arab and Israeli politicians. Internationalization is an idea especially favored by Christian and Muslim organizations who resent the sight of a Jewish government presiding over a city that contains the Church of the Holy Sepulchre, the Dome of the Rock, and al-Aksa Mosque.

But here we should remember that every reference to internationalization recalls the ill-fated United Nations resolution of 1947, a decree which designated Jerusalem a *corpus separatum*. That resolution, approved by Israel, was defeated by the unwillingness of Arab nations to accept a Jewish state in Palestine.[1] Today, when the whole of Jerusalem is under Israeli control, the idea of internationalization seems less a solution to a problem than a device to weaken Israel's hold on Jerusalem.

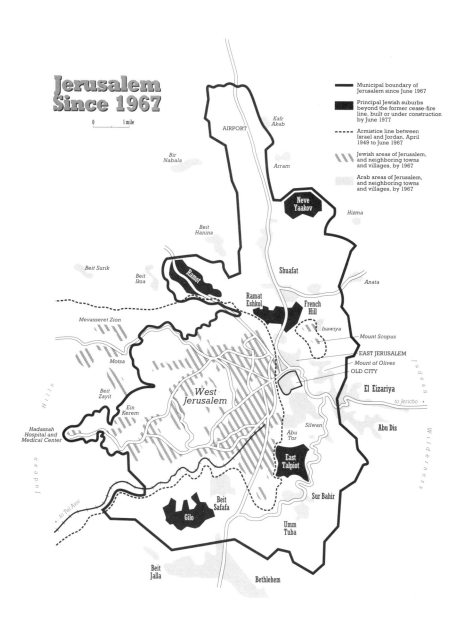

Jerusalem
Since 1967

0   1 mile

Municipal boundary of
Jerusalem since June 1967

Principal Jewish suburbs
beyond the former cease-fire
line, built or under construction
by June 1977

Armistice line between
Israel and Jordan, April
1949 to June 1967

Jewish areas of Jerusalem,
and neighboring towns
and villages, by 1967

Arab areas of Jerusalem,
and neighboring towns
and villages, by 1967

Kafr
Akab

AIRPORT

Bir
Nabala

Arram

Neve
Yaakov

Hizma

Beit
Hanina

Beit Surik

Beit
Iksa

Ramot

Shuafat

Anata

Ramat
Eshkol

French
Hill

Mevasseret Zion

Isawiya

Mount Scopus

Motsa

EAST JERUSALEM

Mount of Olives

OLD CITY

El Eizariya

Beit
Zayit

West
Jerusalem

to Jericho

Ein
Kerem

Hadassah
Hospital and
Medical Center

Silwan

Abu Dis

Abu
Tor

East
Talpiot

Sur Bahir

Beit
Safafa

Gilo

Umm
Tuba

Beit
Jalla

Bethlehem

Judean Hills

Judean Wilderness

to Tel Aviv

Thus it is inconceivable that Israel would agree to yield
control of the city to an international regime when she has had
to defend both state and capital repeatedly in the past forty
years—precisely because of Arab rejection of the UN resolution
calling for partition of Palestine and internationalization of
Jerusalem.

The single most important question facing the future of Jerusalem is whether the whole of the city will remain governed by Israel as its "united capital" or whether the Arab-populated parts of Jerusalem will be partitioned from the Jewish parts to allow for an Arab capital of a Palestinian state. All the other issues affecting the holy places, municipal administration, town planning, and security for ethnic and religious minorities can be resolved once an answer is found to the vastly more important question: Jerusalem—united or divided?

Division of Jerusalem? It is a question which causes Israelis anguish. First hear Jerusalem's Jewish mayor Teddy Kollek:

> Let me be perfectly candid. The thing I dread the most is that this city, so beautiful, so meaningful, so holy to millions of people, should ever be divided again; that barbed-wire fences, mine fields and concrete barriers should again sever its streets; that armed men again patrol a frontier through its heart. I fear the re-division of Jerusalem not only as the mayor of the city, as a Jew and as an Israeli, but as a human being who is deeply sensitive to its history and who cares profoundly about the well-being of its inhabitants.[2]

Teddy Kollek speaks for the overwhelming majority of Israelis who, despite their domestic political differences, are one in saying that Jerusalem must never again be divided. Reinforcing his point, he refers to the bond of history and national soul evoked in the words of the Israeli paratrooper who helped conquer Jerusalem's old city in the Six Days War of 1967.

> In 1967, when attacked by the Jordanians, the Jews were willing to sacrifice their lives for Jerusalem. They would again. Some would give up . . . the Golan, the Sinai, the West Bank. But I do not think you will find any Israelis who are willing to give up Jerusalem. This beautiful golden city is the heart and soul of the Jewish people. You cannot live without a heart and soul. If you want one simple word to symbolize all of Jewish history, that word would be Jerusalem.[3]

But Palestinians, too, have their feelings about Jerusalem. Consider now the words of Harvard professor Walid Khalidi, a native Jerusalemite:

> ...[Jerusalem] is the site of the holiest Muslim shrine on
> Palestinian soil. Muslims first turned to it in prayer before they
> turned to Mecca. ... Within its precincts are buried countless
> generations of Muslim saints and scholars, warriors and leaders. It
> evokes the proudest Palestinian and Arab historical memories. It
> contains the oldest religious endowments of the Palestinians, their
> most prestigious secular institutions—the cumulative and priceless
> patrimony of a millennium and a quarter of residence.
> Architecturally it is distinctively Arab. In ownership and property,
> it is overwhelmingly so. It is the natural capital of Arab Palestine.[4]

Khalidi's reference to "Arab Palestine" reflects the attitude of
the Arab and Muslim worlds that Jerusalem cannot be excluded
from any future solution to the problem of the Palestinian West
Bank and Gaza. So just as Israelis claim that for historical and
religious reasons Jerusalem is the heart of the Jewish nation, so
Arabs insist that for equally compelling historical and religious
reasons Jerusalem is at the center of the Palestinian demand for
national independence.[5]

Arab nationalistic demands on both Jerusalem and the West
Bank weigh on the minds of Israeli politicians and planners.
They are aware that the West Bank's 1.7 million Arabs, increasing at a rate double that of Israelis, will result in an Arab
majority in the land in twenty years. They are also aware that the
doubling of the Arab population of Jerusalem, from 65,000 in
1967 to 125,000 today (out of a total population of 450,000),
poses a formidable problem for Jewish government in a city
where one of every four citizens rejects that government. An
additional 300,000 Arabs in villages and towns adjacent to
Jerusalem makes the number of Arabs in the metropolitan area
(Ramallah to Hebron) equal to the Jews.

When the Arab population of Jerusalem is added to the
predicted increase of the Arab population of the West Bank and
Gaza (now 1.7 million), it is certain that the Arabs will exceed
the Jewish population of the country in the early decades of the
twenty-first century.

What is the Israeli response to the question of Arab political
self-representation in a Jerusalem governed by Israel? Many
Israelis reject any Arab self-representation while others would
preserve Israel's sovereignty over all Jerusalem but allow for
some form of Arab administrative autonomy within Arab neigh-

borhoods. This scheme calls for the reorganization of Jerusalem along the lines of the London municipal borough system. Arabs would be free to administer their own boroughs under an overarching Israeli political and security authority.[6]

Another proposal calls for the "Vaticanization" of Muslim holy places in Jerusalem, whereby the Haram esh-Sharif would be granted extraterritoral status. Within the framework of Israel's sovereignty, Arabs would be permitted certain symbols of political self-expression, such as flying an Arab flag over the mosque on the Temple Mount, wielding postal and taxing powers, and employing Arab security guards as the Vatican has the Swiss Guard.[7]

Not surprisingly, Palestinians have summarily rejected these proposals on boroughs and Vaticanization. They continue to believe that since the Jerusalem problem is one with the West Bank problem, both problems can be solved only by an end to military occupation which opens the door to a Palestinian state with Arab east Jerusalem as its capital. In that respect the outbreak of Arab rebellion (*intifada*), coming as it did after twenty years of Israeli military occupation in the West Bank, Gaza, and east Jerusalem, has dramatically underscored Palestinian frustrations over their failure to win political independence and their determination to do so in the future.

Teddy Kollek speaks for most of his fellow Israelis in rejecting divided sovereignty in Jerusalem. Thus a major question for Kollek and others is how to govern thousands of Arab Jerusalemites who look upon the Israelis as alien conquerors and occupiers of their half of the city? The first thing to be said here is that very few Israelis see themselves as "occupiers" and "conquerors" of Jerusalem. Certainly not Teddy Kollek himself, a skilled and moderate Zionist politician who, after serving as west Jerusalem's mayor for two years, found himself in charge of the whole city after the 1967 war. Old Jerusalem, including the Jewish quarter and the Western Wall, were once again in Jewish hands.

To Kollek, as to all Israelis, the unification of Jerusalem represented a healing of a centuries-old wound in the body of the Jewish nation. Redeemed was the humiliating memory of the expulsions enacted by Emperors Titus, Hadrian, and Heraclius.

But what to do about the 25,000 Arabs who lived in the old city, not to mention another fifty thousand in east Jerusalem? From the beginning, Teddy Kollek and other Israeli officials found themselves confronted by a contradiction: the "united city" was in fact two cities of radically different cultures and conflicting political aspirations. To promote the image of unity, Kollek and other Israeli leaders embarked on a campaign to convince Palestinians, Israelis, and the world that Arabs and Jews could live together in the One Jerusalem, albeit under Israeli sovereignty.

And the campaign succeeded for a time. For years following the unification of the city in 1967, Mayor Kollek ran a peaceful and prosperous city in which Jews and Arabs mixed freely and even exchanged home visits. I attended many such visits, always warm, where expressions of love were common. But never once did I hear a Palestinian tell an Israeli that he accepted government sovereignty over Arab Jerusalem. Just the opposite. At these gatherings, politics were avoided until the last hour. Palestinians would always refer to a "peaceful settlement," by which they meant the removal of Israeli forces from every part of Palestine and from Jerusalem.

Yet for a time there was coexistence. In the aftermath of the 1967 war, Arabs felt humiliated and were responsive to Israeli expressions of good will and generosity. Recalling hardships under the previous Jordanian regime (1948–1967), Arabs were eager to accept the bounty of goods and services rained down on them by the Israelis.[8] Municipal and national governments extended to Arab Jerusalemites a number of social programs, including health care, family allowances, and retirement. Vocational schools, day-care centers, youth clubs, and libraries were opened. Arab workers found new jobs in the Jewish part of town in construction, maintenance, restaurants, and as workers in the Jewish municipality and as domestics in Jewish homes.

At the outset, Kollek and his advisers adopted the strategy enunciated by Moshe Dayan, Israel's defense minister during the 1967 war. Dayan, who did not wish to repeat the mistake made by the "Americanization" of the Vietnam War, urged that nothing be done to interfere in the lives of the Arabs; rather, he said, do everything to let the Arabs feel free to lead their own lives.

Following that strategy, a number of important policies were put into effect whose goal was the preservation of Arab self-identity. Arabs were declared "permanent residents" of Jerusalem but were allowed to keep their Jordanian passports; they were encouraged to vote in municipal elections and to stand for elected office. In fact, few voted, and no one ran for elected office. Nor did anyone accept the standing government offer to apply for full Israeli citizenship.

In the important area of religion, the application of the Dayan strategy of self-government was especially effective. Where both the previous British and Jordanian governments had banned the Supreme Muslim Council for revolutionary activity, the Israelis allowed the council to be reestablished as an important vehicle for Palestinian self-expression. In addition, the Muslim trust, the Waqf, which administered the mosques in the Haram esh-Sharif, became a virtually autonomous agency. To fund the Waqf, the Israelis allowed millions of dollars annually to come into the country from Jordan; these funds helped to pay for the restoration of the al-Aksa Mosque and the salaries of West Bank teachers and mayors. Further, despite the fact that the Haram esh-Sharif also happens to be the sacred Jewish Temple Mount, Israeli officials, in deference to Muslim feeling, prevented Jews from entering the Haram for the express purpose of holding prayer services near the site of Solomon's Temple.

For some fifteen years following the war of 1967, Israeli "good works" and an occasional expression of Arab gratitude convinced Kollek and others that they were not "occupiers" and "conquerors" but rather benefactors of the Arab society in the so-called "united city." What confirmed Kollek in his belief in coexistence was the sight of several thousand Arabs every five years voting for him as mayor, giving him just the margin he needed to maintain a majority of "coexistence-minded" Israelis on the city council. Kollek's confidence in Jerusalem's future was richly expressed in a number of public utterances. In 1977 he wrote in *Foreign Affairs*:

> We have given the Arabs independent education; we have allowed
> them to preserve their Arab citizenship, in this case
> Jordanian.... They have the right to vote for their country,
> whatever it would be, although they live in Jerusalem; they have
> the management of their Holy Places; they have free access from
> the outside and 150,000 people have come every year from Arab

countries to the Holy Places; there is an absolute use of the Arab
language in the city and you can find arrangements for
self-government either through a borough system or a combination
of both.

Within this framework you can find self-rule for Arabs. . . .

[But] despite all our efforts, it is obvious that the Arabs in
Jerusalem still do not accept being included within Israel's
frontiers. But then it must not be forgotten that the city's Arabs
also complained about occupation when the Turks, the British and
the Jordanian Bedouin were in control. They called it occupation
even then.[9]

Kollek concluded with these words:

I believe that if the Arabs of Jerusalem are encouraged to feel
secure, it should be possible for all to live together in reasonably
neighborly relations.

The bottom line is that Jerusalem must never again be
divided. . . . Within an undivided city, everything is possible, all
kinds of adjustments can be made, all kinds of accommodations
can be considered, all kinds of autonomy can be enjoyed, all kinds
of positive relationships can be developed.[10]

For Kollek, the success of his social programs and the
absence of violence ensured the future of the "united city." Thus
he wrote:

The city administration of Jerusalem cannot solve the political
problems of our area. However, I feel that by creating in Jerusalem
an infrastructure of tolerance and coexistence, in spite of the
absence of a political consensus, we ensure the future of our city
and we may be creating a model for emulation, once the
conditions conducive to peace are in sight. In this respect, I feel
we can claim a certain measure of success in spite of the existing
political tensions from which Jerusalem . . . is not immune. Ours is
a peaceful and tranquil city, and terrorist outrages are fortunately
few. . . . In short, Jerusalem is once again an open city and a good
place in which to live.[11]

"A good place in which to live." Kollek made this statement
in 1980, when he still had some reason to believe that the Israeli
administration of a "united city" could overcome Arab feelings
of resentment about the occupation. Two years later, Israel went

to war against the forces of the Palestine Liberation Organization in Lebanon with the express purpose of eliminating that organization as a political voice for the Arabs of the West Bank.[12] But Israel left Lebanon following the death of eighteen thousand Palestinian soldiers and civilians and seven hundred Israeli troops, having failed to destroy the PLO. In succeeding years the PLO remained the most powerful political voice of the Palestinians in the West Bank, Gaza, and east Jerusalem.

Six years after the war in Lebanon, rebellion, *intifada,* broke out in Gaza and spread to the West Bank, Jerusalem, and even to the Israeli-Arab communities of the Galilee. Today, because of *intifada,* the Arab old city market of Jerusalem has become a ghost town, and Israelis are afraid to travel anywhere in east Jerusalem as Arabs are afraid to enter the Jewish new city. The tensions in Jerusalem resemble the situation in 1947 when terrorism between Arabs and Jews was a prelude to the outbreak of a major war a year later.

The seeds of the developing turmoil were planted at the very beginning, shortly after Israel had consolidated her victory in east Jerusalem in June 1967.[13] Despite the desire they later expressed for "coexistence," Teddy Kollek and other Israeli leaders ruined any genuine possibility of Arab-Israeli coexistence in Jerusalem when they dismissed the Arab municipality three weeks after the Israeli takeover. The Palestinian mayor of east Jerusalem, Rauhi Khatib, was later deported to Jordan.

Immediately after the war, Palestinian officials made it clear to the Israelis that they, the Arabs, wished to continue functioning as a municipality in behalf of Arab inhabitants in east Jerusalem and the old city. While they wanted administrative autonomy, they felt no reluctance in cooperating with their new city counterpart, the Jewish municipality headed by Teddy Kollek. But the government's decision to annex east Jerusalem and Kollek's personal opposition to a separate Arab municipal council made this impossible. In a brief meeting marked by rude insensitivity, the former Palestinian-Jordanian municipal council as a body was formally dismissed; its members were invited as individuals to join the Jewish municipal council, which now exercised administration over the entire city. It was an invitation which all the Arab council members refused, fearing to be charged as "collaborators." Several hundred Palestinian municipal workers were effectively integrated into the Jewish munici-

Jerusalem today, looking northeast across the old city. In the distance is the Hyatt Hotel and behind it a complex of high-rise apartments built by the Israeli government—examples of the massive Jewish residential constructions ringing east Jerusalem.

pality, however, having heeded Arab Mayor Rauhi Khatib's advice to go on working so as "to preserve the Arab presence in Jerusalem."

It was Mayor Khatib's suggestion that water, electricity, sewage, and other services be integrated throughout the city while the Arab municipal council be left intact to deal as an equal with the Jewish council in jointly administering Jerusalem. But the personal ambitions of Teddy Kollek ruled out any scheme for dual municipal government. According to Meron Benvenisti, once Kollek's deputy mayor, it was Kollek's ambition "to take upon himself, and upon the municipality he headed, total responsibility for the reunited city, a goal that had guided him in all his steps since the end of the war."[13]

Arab Jerusalemites were also angered by the Israeli government's decision to construct massive high-rise apartment complexes on expropriated Arab lands on the eastern fringes of Jerusalem. The goal of the government housing program in east Jerusalem was the demographic reinforcement of Israel's sovereignty over the total city. To accommodate this new Jewish presence, the municipal boundaries were extended 200 percent beyond the limits of the original undivided pre-1948 British-governed city. Beginning in 1970, after the annexation of east Jerusalem and the expansion of the city's borders, thousands of acres were expropriated in the Arab-populated half of the city. It was an enormous area amounting to "half the size of Israeli Jerusalem before '67, and almost twice the area of Arab Jerusalem at that time."[14] The apartments built on the expropriated land were intended to house a Jewish population of 150,000. Today about 100,000 live there.

About 70 percent of the expropriated land was under private Arab ownership; the balance was state-controlled, passing from Jordan to Israel after the 1967 war. The Israeli government offered financial compensation, but Arab owners viewed the offers as minimal, scarcely true market values; and all the owners rejected compensation because, as one put, it "We do not want to sell our homeland."

On August 20, 1970, a day after the first acts of expropriation were announced, the Arab daily *al-Kuds* condemned the government action with these words:

> Respect for private property is a human law, which should be
> implemented everywhere... even if the land is in occupied
> territory.... What kind of peace will there be if land is expropriated
> in the Holy City?... It is clear that this entire initiative shows no
> consideration for the rights of the Arab inhabitants and will leave
> them in inferior conditions. The Arab community will work in
> Jewish concerns, it will build houses for new immigrants, and will
> not find [enough] space on its land to build homes for the next
> generation.[15]

When the last building project is completed, a wall of Jewish neighborhoods will come between 125,000 Arab Jerusalemites and the 300,000 Palestinians who live in the towns and villages surrounding Jerusalem. Their fear of isolation was expressed to me by the Palestinian journalist Mohammad Abu Shilbaya when he said, "It is disheartening to realize that Jews who fled the ghettos of Europe should now be creating Arab ghettos in Palestine... here in the holy city which we cherish no less than they."

The Israeli government's vast and controversial building projects did satisfy Jewish housing needs, but the deeper reasons for them were political. In June 1967, days after the conquest of east Jerusalem, former Prime Minister David Ben-Gurion urged the creation of physical facts which would strengthen the Israeli hold on east Jerusalem. His words were: "Jews must be brought to East Jerusalem at all costs. Tens of thousands must be settled in a very short time. Jews will agree to settle in East Jerusalem even in huts. One shouldn't wait for the building of regular neighborhoods. The importance is that there should be Jews there."[16] Later Prime Minister Levi Eshkol, Ben-Gurion's successor, created the desired facts, and all subsequent Israeli prime ministers have added to them.

The government hoped to create such a large and visible Jewish presence in east Jerusalem as to make impossible any future redivision of the city. The Israeli aim in expropriating Arab-owned land was not to drive Palestinians off the land but to enlarge the Jewish presence in the Jerusalem area. The Israeli demographer Michael Romann points out that the expropriation of Arab lands was guided by one consideration: "maximum territory—in particular one with strategic value—but only with a minimum Arab population."[17]

As Romann suggests, strategic concerns also influenced the location of the housing estates. The 1967 war gave Israelis the opportunity to reduce the geographic vulnerability of the nation's capital to Arab attack on its eastern border. The map of Israel before June 1967 shows that Israeli west Jerusalem lies at the end of a narrow corridor reaching deeply into the center of the Arab West Bank. The annexation of east Jerusalem after the Six Days War, and the subsequent enlargement of the city's eastern border, extended Israeli control to the valuable high ground at the edge of the Judean wasteland. In building clusters of fortresslike apartment buildings on this high ground, the government sought to protect the eastern approaches to the city.

The government's housing policy in east Jerusalem also involved a contradiction. In order to unify Jerusalem under Israeli sovereignty, the apartment complexes were built in the Arab part of town; but the remote and insecure location discouraged new immigration and therefore worked against Israeli control of the city. Romann explains:

> In view of the many political... difficulties in realizing major
> Jewish housing projects in such a sensitive area [as east Jerusalem],
> it seems that the rate of Jewish population growth in Jerusalem
> was probably held back on the whole, and that it might have been

somewhat accelerated had the new Jewish housing schemes mainly been realized in West Jerusalem and in the purely Jewish sections of town.[18]

Romann also criticizes the government's housing policy as "one-sided," for "no public housing projects for Arabs were undertaken in the Jewish sector of town, and East Jerusalem Arabs were not permitted (for political reasons) to reclaim their abandoned assests in West Jerusalem."[19] Israeli demographers estimated that the rate of Arab population increase in Jerusalem called for a minimum of four hundred new housing units annually. Yet the government did little to meet these needs. Only a few hundred units were built by government funds and private Arab contractors.

Were the Jewish housing estates an obstacle to a settlement between Arabs and Israelis over Jerusalem? When the question was asked of a Jordanian spokesman, he replied: "No, it's a problem which can be solved in the framework of the compensation payments that we shall have to make to each other."[20]

To the aesthetically minded, the Israeli housing projects are a disfiguration of an incomparable desert landscape. One Israeli condemned the government's politically motivated housing policy in plain words: "If a Jewish presence means an ugly blot, that isn't a Jewish presence. It is even bad politics to forgo the aesthetic aspects of Jerusalem, for whose preservation the British made such great efforts."[21]

Indeed, the beauty of Jerusalem was a serious consideration for British mandate officials. When Governor General Ronald Storrs decreed in 1917 that every house and public building be constructed of the handsome pink "Jerusalem stone," the result was architectural symmetry within the city and a visual balance between the modern city and the ageless desert surrounding it. In order to preserve the balance between city and desert, a ceiling of four stories was placed on all constructions.

When the Israelis became the major builders of Jerusalem in 1948, gestures toward beauty were made by using the local stone as facing to hide concrete pillars. But in time the combination of haste, cost, and profit overtook proportion and restraint. The local stone was used, but high-rise buildings rose which marred the city's appearance and upset the natural balance between earth and sky.[22] Compare the British-built YMCA and King

David Hotel with the first Israeli skyscraper, the Omariya Tower and with later, more monstrous constructions such as the Hilton, Plaza, and Sheraton hotels. In the early morning light, the apartment complexes and the hotels appear on the horizon as massive clusters of naked, faceless, and forbidding buildings; they seem to loom above Jerusalem and to dwarf her.

If this judgment seems harsh, test it by walking up the Mount of Olives to the Church of Dominius Flevit, named for the traditional site of Jesus' weeping over Jerusalem. Had Jesus actually climbed the hill with us and looked out at the city from the great window facing west, he would have reason enough to weep. In past years the view from this window was so breathtaking that it was a favorite perspective for painters and photographers. Today one looks out the window and still sees the old city, the Temple Mount, and the skylight; but now, staring back is a thick granite phallus of a hotel called the King Solomon Sheraton—an ironic naming for the Israelite king who was condemned by the prophets for desecrating Jerusalem's hills with pagan temples.

The massive apartment complexes, the high-rise hotels and office buildings are a modern form of idolatry worked on Jerusalem's landscape. With their height and girth they fragment and disfigure the city. What a pity. Amidst all the political, religious, and ethnic forces that divide this city, the energy uniting the place comes from stone, light, and hills. When God chose to dwell in this city, he also chose good collaborators in the Canaanites and early Israelites who built small and beautifully. They constructed Jerusalem below the sacred hill where the Temple would be located—the Temple that looked directly up at the movements of the morning and evening sun. The buildings of today's Jerusalem tower over the Temple site and seem to interfere with the sun itself.

At least one wise policy of the Israeli government in administering "united Jerusalem" was to turn the mosques in Haram esh-Sharif over to Muslim authorities. Yet it was a decision that did not reassure Muslims.

In the early twentieth century, Jerusalem's grand mufti Haj Amin al-Husseini played on Muslim fears of a Zionist takeover of the Haram to rally support for Palestinian national independ-

Jaffa Road, the main Israeli shopping
street in west Jerusalem's "new
city."

ence. The symbolic bond between the Dome of the Rock and
Palestinian independence deepened with the decades. I recall a
young Arab Roman Catholic schoolteacher from Bethlehem
who said to me, "When I look at Qubbat esh-Sakhra [the Dome
of the Rock] I don't think of Muhammad's Heavenly Ascent or
anything specifically religious. I think of Palestine and our
dreams for a state of our own."

No one was more aware of Muslim feelings about the
monuments in the Haram than Defense Minister Moshe Dayan.
Following the conquest of 1967, Dayan allowed Muslims to
police the Haram and, in order to avoid Arab-Jewish clashes,
prevented Jews from gathering for prayer in the area revered as
the site of Solomon's Temple. Dayan's decisions were reinforced
by the state rabbinate which interpreted Jewish religious law
(*halakah*) as prohibiting Jews from entering the Temple Mount
lest they inadvertently tread where the Temple's inner sanctum,
the Holy of Holies, once stood.

The delicate balance was upset in 1969 when an Australian
sheep rancher and Christian fundamentalist named Denis
Michael Rohan set fire to al-Aksa Mosque causing extensive
damage, including the destruction of the renowned *minbar* (pulpit) donated by Saladin. Muslims charged that Rohan was an
agent of the Israeli government bent on destroying the Muslim

monuments in order to rebuild the Jewish Temple. Embarrassed by the incident, Israeli authorities imprisoned Rohan, whom they found to be a lonely psychopath.[23]

Since the al-Aksa fire, a series of incidents have renewed Muslim fears and challenged Israeli authority. In 1974, defying the government prohibition, a small group of ultranationalistic Jews succeeded in holding a service in the Haram/Temple Mount area; they were arrested but released by a Jewish magistrate on the technical grounds of not having violated an official law. It was an action which revealed the curious dilemma faced by the Jewish state with regard to Judaism in Israel. For Israel's Knesset cannot guarantee to Muslims *exclusive* control of the Haram. To do so would mean passing a law barring Jewish worship on the Temple Mount and thus insulting the extremist Jewish Orthodox groups that view the rabbinate's ban as wrong.

The Muslim reaction to the magistrate's decision was swift and loud. Interpreting it as "legalizing" Jewish worship in the Haram (despite government assurances to the contrary), Muslims throughout the city marched through the streets, waved Palestinian flags, and burned tires; it was the first disturbance of its kind in Jerusalem since the 1967 war.

As after the arson fire of al-Aksa Mosque, Jewish authorities spent months reassuring Muslims that despite the absence of an explicit law barring Jews from praying in the Haram/Temple Mount, Israeli police would prevent Jews from gathering there for religious purposes. But many observed that after the 1967 war the Temple Mount and the Western Wall had become religio-political symbols for Jews. The process was hastened by the rise to power in 1977 of Menachem Begin's ultranationalistic Likud coalition party. Sensing the mood of the government, the chief Ashkenazi rabbi Shlomo Goren (today retired) broke with his rabbinical colleagues and government policy by declaring that the location of the Holy of Holies can be determined. In Goren's opinion, Jews might be allowed to pray on the fringes of the Temple Mount.

Goren's finding enraged Muslims who saw it as a first stage toward seizing the Haram, destroying the monuments, and rebuilding the Jewish Temple. Their fears were exacerbated by physical threats voiced by the Jewish Kach ("Thus") movement, led by the late extremist American rabbi Meir Kahane who openly called for the rebuilding of the third Temple. Another threatening group was the "Temple Faithful," who continually pressed the government to alter its prohibition against worship in the Haram.

Muslim fears about their monuments were aroused again in April 1982 when a second psychopath named Alan Goodman, a recent American recruit in the Israeli army, "shot his way past Arab guards and into the Dome of the Rock, whose walls were nicked by a hundred bullets from his machine-gun."[24] Goodman killed two Muslims and wounded eleven others. When asked why he did it, he told the court that by "liberating the Temple Mount" he could become "King of the Jews."

Just two years after the Goodman incident, the worst fears of Muslims were realized when the Israeli police uncovered a conspiracy to blow up the Dome of the Rock on the Temple Mount. The conspirators had gone as far as to plant explosives in the Haram. This time psychopaths were not involved but rather eighteen young Jewish men, religiously Orthodox, from the "best" families, including several decorated war veterans, who had plotted for four years to carry out a terroristic campaign against Muslim monuments. According to the writer Naomi Shepherd, "Their attack on the Temple Mount, their hatred of the mosques, was related to messianic doctrines and the belief that the Mount had to be 'purified' of the Muslim presence before the Third Temple could be built."[25]

While a few fanatic Jews were planning the third Temple, Muslim officials of the Haram were restoring al-Aksa Mosque. Wanting to see the progress, I met in 1986 with Issam Awad, the chief architect, who conducted me through the building. When we entered the great hall of the mosque, evidence of restoration was everywhere: great slabs of new marble were piled neatly in corners; long beams of wood lay on the floor, along with enormous curtains of stained glass waiting to be fitted into the empty windows of the building. One of the Arab nations had made an offer to provide an exact replica of Saladin's minbar, which was politely refused. A new and different one was being fashioned from local materials by Palestinian artisans.

After the tour we retreated to the back of the mosque, where Awad seated me in his office, an enormous room with a vaulted ceiling held up by pillars dating from the eleventh century. I was offered Turkish coffee.

"Issam, there is one question which fascinates me. It is this matter of the Muslim regard for Jerusalem's sanctity. I know the mosques are sacred to Muslims, but what about the city itself? Is the city itself also viewed as sacred?"

"Certainly we consider it sacred. We call it al-Kuds, the Holy One. But why are you concerned with this?"

"Teddy Kollek and others say that while the Haram is a Muslim sacred place, Jerusalem is not.[26] What I want to know is whether the city as a whole is sacred to Muslims."

"I will tell you. My answer is that Kollek can say what he likes...he is not a Muslim. It is a bit silly of him to divide mosques and city. Will he divide synagogues and city, or churches and city?"

"The two are inseparable?"

"Yes, you can can see that. Jerusalem for Muslims is holy not just because of the mosques or because of religion. It is holy because the people live here."

"Please explain."

"Look, people have their homes here, their lives. I am not from Jerusalem. I was born in Jenin in the north. But my wife is from Jerusalem, and although I work here in Jerusalem, we live on the road to Ramallah. But I don't have to be born in Jerusalem or have my house here to believe Jerusalem is my home."

"Is this the feeling of all the West Bank people? Do they regard Jerusalem as their second home?"

"Absolutely. Not second home. Just home."

"Does that make Jerusalem sacred?"

"I don't care about sacred...the word. The mosques don't make Jerusalem holy. Perhaps they make it more holy or show its holiness. But the city is holy to Muslims because they live in it or, like me, they are a part of it all their lives. This is our home. The Jews say it is their home. For some it is, but not for the Russian Jews who arrived here last week. But for me, a Palestinian, it is my home, my city. If there were no mosques, it would still be a holy city to us."

As Arab and Jewish extremists multiplied and incidents of terrorism mounted throughout the 1970s and 1980s, there was reason to wonder if the Israeli government had begun to lose

This unfinished hotel in east Jerusalem fell victim to inter-Arab competition and is now a convenient target for *intifada* graffiti.

control of Jerusalem. The anti-Zionist ultra-Orthodox Jews of Mea Shearim had become more vocal, more willing to resort to violence in demanding strict observance of the Sabbath. Against violations of the Sabbath and other rules of the religious law, they had succeeded in closing public roads to Sabbath travel, shutting down Saturday cinema performances, preventing the building of a soccer stadium in the Holy City, and eliminating sexy public advertisements.

The secular Zionist population of Jerusalem had much to worry about when contemplating religious trends in the city. More Jewish children were going to religious schools than to the state-supported secular schools. Further, when the present population of 100,000 ultra-Orthodox Jews of Mea Shearim were added to the 125,000 Arab Jerusalemites, fully half of Jerusalem's population actively opposed the Zionist-based municipal and national governments.

An incident on Good Friday, April 11, 1990, aroused the worst fears of Israeli officials: an alliance of Christians and Muslims against Jews in the old city.[27] The incident was sparked by the sudden appearance of Jews in a Greek Orthodox building, Saint John's Hospice, adjacent to the Church of the Holy Sepulchre. The Jewish "settlers," 150 men, women, and children, went by the exalted name of Ateret HaCohanim ("Crown of the Priests"), a reference to the Solomon's Temple priests.

Parading to Saint John's Hospice in a festive mood of singing and handclapping, they made no secret of their goal to use Saint John's as a base to make Jerusalem's old city completely Jewish. The vision of the Ateret HaCohanim was identical to that of Gush Emunim ("Bloc of Faithful"), the extremist nationalistic movement sponsoring Jewish settlements in the heart of the Arab-populated West Bank.

The settlers moved into Saint John's without incident and immediately engaged in the ritual of reconsecrating the building Neot David ("Dwellings of David"). Toward evening they welcomed their honored guest, General Ariel Sharon, supernationalist who caused a major riot in the old city in 1989 when he took an apartment in the Muslim quarter.

Something had to be done about the Christian symbol sculpted into the stone lintel above the door. That symbol, a Greek Tau placed over a Phi, stood for the first two letters of the Greek word for tomb, tafos—the insignia of the local Greek Orthodox patriarchate which exercises rights as the custodian of Christ's Tomb. The Greek patriarchate is the recognized legal owner of Saint John's Hospice. As it happened, a local Christian tenant had subleased the building (illegally, said the Greek church) to the Jewish settlers.

Thus began a conflict which took on major political implications when the Israeli government first denied and then admitted it had helped fund the Jewish group's penetration into the Christian quarter. Prime Minister Yitzhak Shamir, remembering that Jews historically had been stoned and spit upon when they appeared in the Christian quarter, announced that Jews had the right to live anywhere in Jerusalem. In response, the Hebrew press was quick to remind the prime minister that non-Jews were forbidden by Israeli law to purchase any residence in the Jewish quarter, only a couple of hundred yards south of the Christian quarter.

Mayor Teddy Kollek condemned the settlers for breaking the unwritten law of status quo. This informal agreement, observed for centuries, achieved a measure of peace in Jerusalem by dictating that each ethno-religious community will live in its own recognized space and not intrude into the space of another. With status quo in mind, Mayor Kollek chastised his fellow Jews with a rhetorical question: "How would [Jews] feel if singing and dancing Christians and Muslims moved into the Jewish quarter on Passover?"

After taking residence in Saint John's, the Cohanim decided to take a cardboard cutout of the Star of David and place it over the Greek Tau-Phi insignia. The next day Greek priests mounted a demonstration to evict the Jews. Local PLO leader Faisal Husseini appeared at the demonstration alongside Greek Patriarch Diodorus I, a juxtaposition of Muslim and Christian, politics and religion, which had Israelis very worried.

Israeli solders were on the scene to keep the Christians from storming the building and to prevent Jewish settlers from shooting at the demonstrators. The patriarch gave the order to have the Star of David removed from the Greek Tau-Phi, whereupon Bishop Timothy was hoisted on the shoulders of his fellow priests and succeeded in tearing away the star. Palestinian youths howled in delight. Someone threw a rock at the building; more rocks followed. The Palestinian flag was unfurled. Suddenly the Christian demonstration became a PLO rally. Israeli soldiers lost patience and exploded tear-gas canisters. Priests ran for cover. The patriarch fell to the ground in the melee; his great pectoral cross tore loose from his neck. Faisal Husseini, surrounded by Palestinian youths, was led away in safety. The windows of Saint John's were shut against the rising clouds of tear gas. Bishop Timothy was seen hobbling away in the direction of the patriarchate holding a wet handkerchief to his face. Also scurrying away were members of the Israeli dovish "Peace Now" movement; they had come to show support for the Christians against the settlers.

The next day the battle for Saint John's moved to the Israeli courts where each side, represented by the country's most skilled Jewish lawyers, fought for control of an old pilgrim's hospice. The case is not likely to be resolved for years.

Six months after the occupation of Saint John's Hospice, during a Jewish holiday, Muslim youths on the Temple Mount rained down rocks on Jews worshiping at the Western Wall. The Muslims said they had been provoked by reports that the extremist Jewish sect, the Temple Mount Faithful, had planned to lay a cornerstone near the mosques in preparation for the building of the third Temple. After worshipers were cleared from the Western Wall, Israeli police stormed the Haram, and in the riot that followed nineteen Arabs were killed and 140 injured. Immediately Muslim preachers called for the killing of Jews throughout the land.[28]

Jerusalem, says Mayor Kollek, is not a melting pot but a mosaic. If the principle of aesthetic unity is invoked, then the city is scarcely a mosaic. Rather we should think of Jerusalem as a veteran of a thousand wars, a worn and wounded body held together by surgical tape, a body still moving on a hundred crutches. No one has done more to keep the body intact and moving than Teddy Kollek himself, a man energetic, charming, shrewd, and fundamentally fair. Even his critics agree that he has accomplished more for Arab-Jewish coexistence in this city than anyone could have expected. In a city of political and religious extremists, Kollek is the pragmatist. The only solution is the one that works; when that fails, look for another. He meets with every group, listens to all complaints, makes changes. Put in a street here, plant a garden there. Make sure we get full taxes from the Jewish side of town, but don't press collecting from Arabs—"We don't want to anger them, and we may need their votes."

It is a commonly held belief in this city that on the day Teddy Kollek ceases to be mayor the deluge will follow. Meanwhile, Kollek hunts for more surgical tape to keep the body moving. In retaliation for violating the religious ban against Sabbath travel, the ultra-Orthodox are stoning cars on the Ramot road: Kollek responds by building a bypass. The limousine of a Greek bishop is seized at the Jordan River bridge with smuggled gold in the boot: Kollek rushes to the military authorities and pleads that for the sake of Jewish-Christian relations, all charges be dropped. A Jewish extremist has just taken a machine gun and mowed down Muslims at the Dome of the Rock: Kollek rushes to the Waqf offices to assure the mufti that the government was not involved and will punish the killer. The Arab shopkeepers in the old city are losing business because tourists are afraid of *intifada* rocks and bombs: Kollek reacts by setting up a temporary office at a coffee house inside Damascus Gate and chats with passersby two hours each morning.

And yet the effectiveness of Kollek's managerial talents seems to end where the basic Arab-Israeli struggle for this country and capital begins. Kollek believes that good Jewish government can be a substitute for Arab self-government: "...One of these days—in fifty or a hundred or two hundred years—the Arabs will accept this as the capital of Israel."[29]

Can Israeli "good works" dampen the Palestinian desire for independence? I took this question to Meron Benvenisti, who was once Jerusalem's vice mayor and Kollek's own intended successor until the two men had a falling out. Benvenisti is a distinguished author and a tireless investigator of the social conditions of Arab life in the West Bank, Gaza, and east Jerusalem. He is overweight and chain smoking, wears thick glasses, and has masses of gray curly hair. He smiles readily but does not seem to enjoy humor. He often responds to a question with a question, and he seems incapable of lying. His public quarrels with Kollek over how to plan Jerusalem, his resistance to high-rise constructions, and his undisguised ambitions to replace Kollek as mayor—these made Benvenisti the *enfant terrible* of Jerusalem politics and a national celebrity.

I met Benvenisti at his house in the Abu Tor hill area, a mixed Arab and Jewish neighborhood of Jerusalem. Climbing the many stone steps leading up to his house on a hot July day, I was instantly sweating and thirsty. My host met me at the top of the steps, shook hands brusquely, and led me wordlessly into his house. Without benefit of water or rest, without giving me a moment to remark on the gorgeous view of the Hinnon Valley from the window in his living room, he gestured for me to sit down and told me to begin with the most important question.

"Despite the fact that Palestinians will not vote in large numbers or run for municipal office, don't you think that Kollek's administration is meeting Arab needs and gaining good will in the Arab community?"

Benvenisti replied in monosyllables: "Some needs, yes. Good will, no."

He paused and then said more thoughtfully, "Look, Jewish money cannot buy Arab good will. We are no better at playing the colonial administrator than the British were."

"So the economic argument that Kollek repeats...that the Arabs are better off..."

Benvenisti interrupted me. "Kollek deludes himself into

thinking that because Arabs will take money for widowed
mothers and sing his praises because he opens a day-care center
in east Jerusalem—that they feel better about our occupation of
them."

"The economic argument is self-serving?"

"Yes, self-serving. So what if the Arabs have it better under
us than under the Jordanians? Does anyone really think that the
Arabs of this city, or the West Bank, prefer our rule to that of
the Jordanians merely because they make more money from the
jobs that we provide?"

"So Kollek is not as popular with the Arabs as the press
says he is."

"I didn't say that. He is popular. But his popularity is the
popularity of the colonial administrator, the effective, benevo-
lent, and secretly despised colonial administrator. Don't forget
that before us the Arabs were ruled by Jordanians, then the
British, and then the Turks—all colonial administrations."

As there are Israeli right-wingers who refuse to consider any
peace-for-territory negotiations with the Arabs of this country,
so there are Israeli left-wing politicians, writers, professors,
students, and generals who accept such negotiations as inevitable
and necessary. One such left-winger is Meir Pa'il, former member of Israel's Knesset, a reserve army colonel, and a military
strategist. Pa'il is one of a handful of left-wingers, ignored at
home but heralded abroad, who is willing to make a redivision
of country and capital a part of future negotiations with Jordan
or with the PLO.

Pa'il is a large, round-shouldered man in his late fifties with a
wide-open face, black curly hair, and a pixie wit. I met Pa'il
when he agreed to take me on a walk to Jerusalem's old city,
where he wanted to show me how he would politically divide
Jerusalem in order to allow for an Arab capital of a future
independent Palestinian state. We walked through the old city,
descended into the Valley of Jehosophat, and then slowly made
our way up the Mount of Olives, headed for the open space in
front of the Intercontinental Hotel, where the whole of old
Jerusalem stretched out before our eyes.

When we reached the top of the hill, Pa'il extracted an
ordinary tourist map of Jerusalem and began to draw a line of

red ink across the city, beginning at the summit of the Mount of Olives.

"The key to partition," he said, "is this sacred hill. I believe that God chose this hill to solve the Israeli-Palestinian problem. After all, is not the summit of this hill the place where the Messiah is to appear?"

I looked at Pa'il skeptically and replied, "I thought that religious rhetoric was reserved for the right-wing nationalists." Pa'il smiled his pixie smile and continued.

"Yes, God provided the solution on this hill. This hill divides Arab-populated Jerusalem from the Jewish new city. He gestured outward toward the city, the map in his hand. Everything east of the city should be under Arab sovereignty, he proclaimed, and the Jewish part of town to the west should remain under Jewish sovereignty.

With more skepticism I said, "Meir, what about the Mount of Olives on which we're standing, and what about the old city below us? Both places are exactly between the Arab and Jewish halves of the city. Can you divide them?"

Another pixie smile. "Here we have a big, big problem. Everyone wants the old city. The Christians want their churches; Muslims want their mosques; Jews want their Wall—so let each community have its own places, let each community govern itself. Let the old city be the one place in all Jerusalem where the three peoples are forced to cooperate in shared government."

"And sovereignty?" I asked. "To whom will sovereignty go?"

"Shared sovereignty between Arabs and Jews. Dual sovereignty, a condominium in which each people exercises sovereignty over its place in the old city. But the old city itself should be administered by Jews, Christians, and Muslims together."

"Meir, is this practical?"

He replied instantly. "Practical? It was intended by God. God put the Mount of Olives and the old city between the two peoples so that they are forced to live together in peace."

Pa'il took my arm and led me to the edge of the observation area. "You see," he said, pointing with his map to the old city below us. "Everyone thinks Jerusalem is too complicated a problem. Everyone living in one small space surrounded by walls; the shrines all squeezed together—mosques, churches, synagogues, one next to the other, some on top of each other.

Impossible to separate. Impossible to settle conflicting claims to this city. No solution to the Jerusalem problem, everyone says. Rubbish. The old city is a challenge from God for all of us to live together in peace."

I listened carefully and remembered the lack of popular support for the political left wing in Israel. "Meir, critics of your way of thinking say that yielding any part of Judea, Samaria, and Jerusalem is nonsense. The land and its capital belong to Israel. And even those Israelis who don't necessarily accept the Jewish biblical claims to the land will say that if Arabs are given sovereignty in any part of the country, they will use their sovereignty to gain more land, either through diplomacy or terrorism. What do you say to those arguments?"

"Listen, professor, the reason we should settle the problem of the West Bank and Jerusalem is not for the Arabs but for ourselves. The Arabs will go on hating us no matter what we do. Jerusalem is not that essential to them. They ignored Jerusalem until we built the new city and until we reunited the whole city in 1967. No, it is not for them that we must solve the problems. We must solve them for ourselves. Israel needs peace. We cannot afford to continue fighting and killing Arabs, because we lose our own people and weaken our country. Each war weakens us."

"But Meir, aren't you afraid of trusting the Arabs in any treaty that involves returning land to Arab sovereignty?"

"No, I am not afraid. I believe we have superb fighting forces that can defend the nation and deal with any Arab threat in the territories."

Later that evening, Pa'il showed me a draft of an essay he had composed detailing his plan for the return of Arab sovereignty to the West Bank and east Jerusalem in a peace treaty with any Arab partner, including Jordan and the PLO. Pa'il's argument was that Israel must not wait for an Arab initiative to make peace; Israel must announce its own plans for settling the questions of territory and sovereignty. One of the most striking suggestions was that Israel should follow the British example and make a "Balfour Declaration" in behalf of Arab nationalistic aspirations as follows: "The Government of Israel looks with favor on the establishment of a national home for the Palestinian people alongside the State of Israel, with peaceful relations and mutual recognition being maintained between the two nations."[30]

To ensure that Arabs will not gain a military advantage that would undermine Israel's security, Pa'il proposes a phased withdrawal of Israeli forces from lands now occupied, with treaty rights allowing Israel to enter the Arab area with force at any moment that Israeli security is threatened by unlawful troop concentrations or buildup of weapons. The West Bank would be demilitarized and would be patrolled only by local police or militia. To counter the argument that the West Bank is needed as a security buffer between Israel and its Arab neighbors, Pa'il contends that an occupation force in the West Bank is not needed as long as Israel can militarily control the West Bank. And this would be the case when the West Bank is demilitarized under conditions favorable to Israel.

What Pa'il makes clear in his essay is that the Jerusalem problem cannot be solved alone. It is an integral part of the West Bank problem. The problem is not only self-determination for the Palestinians; it is also the future of the Jewish state. As long as the military occupation continues and the Palestinian determination for national independence remains strong, then *intifada,* as we know it today in the form of demonstrations, strikes, rock-throwing, shootings, and killings, will continue indefinitely into the future.

Save for Meir Pa'il and other left-wingers who are willing to negotiate with the PLO over the West Bank and Jerusalem, every Israeli proposal for territorial compromise has assumed that Jordan's King Hussein would be Israel's partner. This assumption has had a label: the "Jordan Option." It has been assumed that eventually King Hussein would address himself to the question of negotiating with Israel for the return of his rule to the West Bank. But secret negotiations between Hussein and Israeli prime ministers, beginning with Golda Meir, came to nothing. The reason was clear: Hussein insisted that nothing less than *all* the occupied territories, including east Jerusalem, be on the bargaining table. He was adamant about not leaving east Jerusalem under permanent Israeli sovereignty. "If I were to sign away Arab Jerusalem," he said, "the whole of the Arab world would cry out against that signature."

Even before the loss of the West Bank and east Jerusalem to Israel in 1967, King Hussein had seen his country become more

A Jewish foreman with an Arab worker,
planting trees and flowers in
Jerusalem.

than half Palestinian in population. He has watched the growth
of the PLO, whose power so threatened his kingship in 1970
that he launched the Black September massacre of Palestinian
leaders and fighters. Over the years he has borne witness to the
emergence of a Palestinian nationalist movement which not only
seeks to establish an independent state in the West Bank and
Gaza but which may turn against him and claim Jordan for
itself.

Hussein needs the Palestinians to maintain the infrastructure
of his country, but his needs are hedged by fears of their
nationalistic aspirations and anti-Jordanian resentments. It was
with a mixture of regret and fear that he cut his ties to the West
Bank in 1988, only six months after the outbreak of the *intifada*.
The action made it clear that Hussein will support no Palestinian
rebellion that could endanger his own kingship.

Anyone who has studied Hussein's thinking over the past
thirty years recognizes a pattern that runs so: "I, King Hussein,
will sit down with the Israelis to discuss peace only when they
are prepared to discuss the return of the West Bank and east
Jerusalem. I am aware of their security needs; but these needs
can be met within the framework of joint Palestinian-Jordanian
sovereignty in the West Bank and Arab Jerusalem. I can ask for

no less than what Sadat asked in the negotiations over the Sinai Desert. Israel met Sadat's conditions because Egypt is the most populous and strategically important state in the Arab world; Israel knew that to sign a peace treaty with Egypt meant future security for Israel. For, as Sadat reminded Israel, 'Without Egypt there can be neither peace nor war.'

"Now, everyone knows that Jordan is not Egypt and I am not Sadat. The Israelis know that Jordan alone can never be a threat to her security. Moreover, for more than twenty years I have maintained cooperative relations with Israel, symbolized by the 'open bridges' policy which serves my needs. Save for radicals like Ariel Sharon who want to destroy my monarchy in order to seize my country and hand it over to the Palestinians, I can trust to the moderation of the Israeli leaders. But until they are willing to negotiate the return of Arab Jerusalem to joint Palestinian-Jordanian sovereignty, I can never seriously contemplate a formal peace treaty with Israel. And no one should forget that Jerusalem has an emotional meaning for me. My great-grandfather, Hussein the sharif of Mecca, who led the Great Revolt, is buried within the Haram esh-Sharif; and my grandfather, Emir Abdallah, was assassinated at the entrance to al-Aksa Mosque. Yes, Jerusalem is of great significance to me.

"From another point of view, my interests are best served by *not* having a peace treaty with Israel—which would require me to accept more Palestinians in my kingdom. In this respect, the uncompromising line of such leaders as Begin and Shamir actually serves my interest. Their policy makes Israel look bad in the West, including the United States. The future demographic trends favor the Palestinians, and within a decade or so Israel will be more isolated than ever: facing a large interior Palestinian lake and surrounded by a vast Arab sea.

"Let Israel have the Palestinians and all the problems of *intifada*. As long as the Israelis do not try to transfer masses of Palestinians to the East Bank, I need not do a thing. If the Israelis want peace in the West Bank, they will come to me with east Jerusalem in their hands. Until that happens I will propose nothing. I will stay put."

If this is the pattern of Hussein's thinking,[31] we can then ask if there is a reasonable compromise that Israel might make with Jordan. The answer is yes. Israel can share sovereignty with Palestinians and Jordan in Jerusalem, and Jordan can accede to

Israel's annexing the specifically Jewish parts of east Jerusalem, which include the Jewish quarter, Neve Yacov, and Mount Scopus. The Western Wall, Haram esh-Sharif (Temple Mount), and Mount of Olives areas can be jointly administered by a commission of Israeli-Muslim authorities.

The keys to compromise are two: Israel must agree to the return of Arab sovereignty to both Jerusalem and the West Bank, and both Jordanian and Palestinian authorities must agree to Israel's extension of boundaries into both east Jerusalem and the West Bank, consistent with security needs. In sum, Israel need not return to the pre-1967 borders in Jerusalem and the West Bank, but it can restore to Arab sovereignty the bulk of the land conquered in the 1967 war. Moreover, just as Jewish west Jerusalem is Israel's capital, so Arab east Jerusalem is the logical capital of Palestine.

No one knows whether the parties to the Palestinian-Israeli dispute will make this wise compromise. Certainly they will be helped to do so if other Arab states, such as Syria and Iraq, end their hostility and further the Palestinian cause by signing a peace treaty with Israel. Should that happen, good things will follow. The crushing burden of the Palestinians will be lifted from Israel's shoulders, and the Palestinians will be set on the road to self-determination.

To those who rally around the election slogan "One Jerusalem," favored by Teddy Kollek, and argue that the resumption of Arab sovereignty in the city will lead to a new wall isolating Jews once again, it can be said that this is always a possibility. But the alternative to compromise is far worse. Should Israel not lift the Palestinians from its shoulders, should it continue to dominate the West Bank and Gaza, then a dissolution of the peace with Egypt and more war are probable.

It should also be pointed out, as Meir Pa'il argues, that just as Israel would have the right to intervene militarily in the West Bank should its security be threatened, the same right would obtain in Jerusalem. When Jordan erected the wall in 1948, Israel was capable of attacking Jordanian troops in Jerusalem in order to remove the wall—but it did not do so. However insulting the wall, Israel wished to live in peace with Jordan, and it wished to have the new city internationally accepted as Israel's legitimate national capital. The Israeli restraint spoke volumes of wisdom; Israeli leaders have been willing to forego control over a maximum amount of Jerusalem in order to realize the greater goals of national independence and security. Today it is the Palestinians in the midst of *intifada* who are a distinct threat to the independence and security of the Jewish state. The question now and for coming years is whether Israeli leaders will recognize the need to compromise over Jerusalem in order to preserve their own national independence and security.

The Lions' Fountain at the south end of King David Street is Teddy Kollek's most visible contribution to coexistence in Jerusalem; he encouraged West Germany to commission this delightful piece of statuary for Jerusalem.

Lions sit regally around the water fountain, bronze depictions of the mighty beasts that roamed the Judean desert in King David's time. Every day one can find Jewish, Muslim, and Christian families at the fountain, their children splashing water together amidst the lions.

I go often to the Lions' Fountain, usually in the early morning hours before the families arrive. I always notice the tiny metal bird which crowns the fountain. After a long flight, it seems, the bird has landed, an olive branch in its mouth. The question in my mind is, who will take the branch from the bird's mouth and plant it? Who will make the compromises that could reverse the three-thousand-year-old cycle of conquest that mocks the "city of God"? Who will break the chain binding Jerusalem to a dreadful history? Who will decide for the future and not the past? Who will not only pray for but act in behalf of the "peace of Jerusalem"?

Who indeed!

> Awake, awake, O Zion! Clothe yourself in splendor....
>
> Isaiah 52:1

Notes

Chapter 1: Zion, City of David

1 Kibbutz Members, eds., *The Seventh Day* (London, 1974), p. 135.

2 Benjamin Mazar, *The Mountain of the Lord* (New York, 1975), pp. 40–49.

3 Shemaryahu Talmon, "The Biblical Concept of Jerusalem," in John M. Oesterreicher and Anne Sinai, eds., *Jerusalem* (New York, 1974).

4 Walter Harrelson, *Interpreting the Old Testament* (New York, 1964), pp. 173–178.

5 See H. Tadmor, "The Period of the First Temple, the Babylonian Exile and the Restoration," in H. H. Ben-Sasson, ed., *A History of the Jewish People* (Cambridge, Mass., 1976), pp. 96–100.

6 Roland de Vaux, *Ancient Israel*, vol. 2, *Religious Institutions* (New York, 1965), pp. 312–330.

7 John Bright, *A History of Israel*, 2nd ed. (Philadelphia, 1972), pp. 284–286.

Chapter 2: Fallen Temples

1 John Bright, *A History of Israel*, 2nd ed. (Philadelphia, 1959), p. 362.

2 *Ibid.*

3 H. Tadmor, "The Babylonian Exile and the Restoration," in H. H. Ben-Sasson, ed., *A History of the Jewish People* (Cambridge, Mass., 1976), pp. 168–174.

4 *Ibid.*, pp. 176–178.

5 W. O. E. Oesterley, *A History of Israel* (Oxford, 1948), pp. 118–127.

6 *Ibid.*, pp. 128–138.

7 Menaham Stern, "The Period of the Second Temple," in Ben-Sasson, ed., *History of the Jewish People*, pp. 185–198.

8 Stern, "The Period of the Second Temple," pp. 189–190.

9 Oesterley, *History of Israel*, pp. 177–186.

10 Stern, "The Period of the Second Temple," pp. 202–205.

11 Oesterley, *History of Israel*, pp. 218–223.

12 Lee I. Levine, "The Age of Hellenism," in Hershel Shanks, ed., *Ancient Israel* (Englewood Cliffs, N.J., 1988), p. 180.

13 Stern, "The Period of the Second Temple," pp. 217–220.

14 *Ibid.*, pp. 233–236.

15 Oesterley, *History of Israel*, pp. 267–287.

16 Emil Schurer, *A History of the Jewish People in the Time of Jesus* (New York, 1961), pp. 74–78.

17 Josephus, *Antiquities*, 13:379–383. Cited in Oesterley, *History of Israel*, p. 293.

18 M. Avi-Yonah, *The Jews Under Roman and Byzantine Rule* (Jerusalem, 1984), pp. 7–11.

19 Stern, "The Period of the Second Temple," pp. 239–245.

20 Oesterley, *History of Israel*, pp. 440–463; Stern, "The Period of the Second Temple," pp. 296–303; Shaye J. D. Cohen, "Roman Domination," in Shanks, ed., *Ancient Israel*, pp. 222–235; Schurer, *History of the Jewish People in the Time of Jesus*, pp. 245–278.

21 Stern, "The Period of the Second Temple," p. 245.

22 Josephus, *The Jewish War*, 2:174. Cited in David M. Rhodes, *Israel in Revolution: 6-74 C.E., A Political History Based on the Writings of Josephus* (Philadelphia, 1976), p. 61.

23 Oesterley, *History of Israel*, p. 396.

24 See Rhodes, *Israel in Revolution*.

25 *Ibid.*, pp. 76–77.

26 Josephus, *Antiquities*, 20:257. See Rhodes, *Israel in Revolution*, pp. 97–98.

27 See the discussion in Rhodes, *Israel in Revolution*, pp. 174–181.

28 Josephus, *The Jewish War*, 4:318. See Rhodes, *Israel in Revolution*, pp. 137–138.

29 Oesterley, *History of Israel*, pp. 453–458.

30 *Ibid.*, pp. 459–465.

31 Yehoshofat Harkabi. *The Bar Kochba Syndrome: Risk and Realism in International Politics* (Chappaqua, N.Y., 1983), pp. 6–23.

32 See Avi-Yonah, *Jews Under Roman and Byzantine Rule*, pp. 13–14.

Chapter 3: Return to Zion

1 M. Avi-Yonah, *The Jews Under Roman and Byzantine Rule* (Jerusalem, 1984), p. 69.

2 *Ibid.*, p. 51.

3 *Ibid.*, pp 64–71.

4 *Ibid.*, pp. 25–31.

5 *Ibid.*, p. 27.

6 Avraham Holtz, ed., *The Holy City: Jews on Jerusalem* (New York, 1971), pp. 59–67.

7 Avi-Yonah, *Jews Under Roman and Byzantine Rule*, p. 27.

8 *Ibid.*, pp. 174–176.

9 *Ibid.*, pp. 208–231.

10 *Ibid.*, p. 222.

11 *Ibid.*, p. 219.

12 Cited in Joan Comay, *The Temple of Jerusalem* (New York, 1975), p. 202.

13 Avi-Yonah, *Jews Under Roman and Byzantine Rule*, p. 271.

14 Holtz, *Holy City*, p. 110.

15 *Ibid.*, p. 113.

16 *Ibid.*, pp. 113–114.

17 *Ibid.*, pp. 122–123.

18 *Ibid.*, p. 127.

19 *Ibid.*, pp. 132–135.

20 Itzhak Ben-Zevi, "Eretz Yisrael Under Ottoman Rule, 1517–1917," in Louis Finkelstein, ed., *The Jews: Their History, Culture and Religion*, 3rd ed. (New York, 1960), pp. 621–629.

21 *Ibid.*, p. 641.

22 *Ibid.*, p. 631.

23 *Ibid.*, p. 650.

24 Yehoshua Ben-Arieh, *Jerusalem in the 19th Century: The Old City* (Jerusalem and New York, 1984), p. 278.

25 *Ibid.*, p. 358.

26 Tudor Parfitt, *The Jews of Palestine, 1800–1882* (Woodbridge, England, 1987), p. 13.

27 Ben-Arieh, *Jerusalem in the 19th Century*, p. 325.

28 *Ibid.*, p. 324.

29 S. Zalman Abramov, *Perpetual Dilemma: Jewish Religion in the Jewish State* (Cranbury, N.J., 1976), p. 32.

30 Ben-Arieh, *Jerusalem in the 19th Century*, p. 287.

31 Parfitt, *Jews of Palestine*, p. 33.

32 *Ibid.*, p. 167.

33 Ben-Arieh, *Jerusalem in the 19th Century*, p. 358.

34 *Ibid.*, pp. 345–347.

Chapter 4: In the Footsteps of Jesus

1 W. D. Davies, "Jerusalem and the Land in the Christian Tradition," in Marc H. Tanenbaum and R. J. Zwi Werblovsky, eds., *The Jerusalem Colloquium on Religion, Peoplehood, Nation, and Land*, Truman Research Institute Publication No. 7 (Jerusalem and New York, 1970), pp. 115–159.

2 *Ibid.*, pp. 126–127.

3 Saint Gregory of Nyssa, *Migne Patrologia Graeca*, LXVI, col. 1010–1015, cited in Walter Zander, *Israel and the Holy Places of Christendom* (New York, 1971), pp. 6–7.

4 For this historical sketch I rely chiefly on Geza Vermes, *Jesus the Jew* (Philadelphia, 1973). Other works consulted were Hans Conzelman, *Jesus* (Philadelphia, 1973); James M. Robinson, *A New Quest of the Historical Jesus* (Naperville, Ill., 1959); William Manson, *Jesus the Messiah* (London, 1956); Rudolph Bultman, *Jesus and the Word* (New York, 1958); Howard Clark Kee and Franklin W. Young, *Understanding the New Testament* (Englewood Cliffs, N.J., 1957); Gunther Bornkamm, *Jesus of Nazareth* (New York, 1960); and Joseph Klausner, *Jesus of Nazareth* (Boston, 1964).

5 For a penetrating study of Jesus as revolutionary zealot, see S. G. F. Brandon, *Jesus and the Zealots* (New York, 1967).

6 *Ibid.*, pp. 129–156.

7 Joachim Jeremias, *Jerusalem in the Time of Jesus* (Philadelphia, 1959), pp. 27–28.

8 *Ibid.*, p. 44.

9 *Ibid.*, pp. 16–17.

10 Kee and Young, *Understanding the New Testament*, pp. 168–175.

11 Vermes, *Jesus the Jew*, p. 35.

12 Jeremias, *Jerusalem in the Time of Jesus*, p. 62.

13 Kee and Young, *Understanding the New Testament*, p. 310.
14 E. D. Hunt, *Holy Land Pilgrimage in the Later Roman Empire, AD 312–460* (Oxford, 1982), p. 197.
15 *Ibid.*, p. 2.
16 Jonathan Sumption, *Pilgrimage: An Image of Mediaeval Religion* (Totowa, N.J., 1975), p. 89.
17 Hunt, *Holy Land Pilgrimage in the Later Roman Empire*, p. 45.
18 *Ibid.*, p. 41.
19 Norman Kotker, *The Earthly Jerusalem* (New York, 1969), p. 134.
20 John Wilkinson, *Jerusalem Pilgrims Before the Crusades* (Jerusalem, 1977), p. 31.
21 Zander, *Israel and the Holy Places of Christendom*, p. 7.
22 Sumption, *Pilgrimage*, p. 91.
23 Zander, *Israel and the Holy Places of Christendom*, p. 8.
24 Speros Vryonis, *Byzantium and Europe* (Norwich, England, 1967), p. 38.
25 Hunt, *Holy Land Pilgrimage in the Later Roman Empire*, pp. 203–220.
26 John Gray, *A History of Jerusalem* (London, 1969), p. 206.
27 *Ibid.*, p. 207.

Chapter 5: God Wills It!

1 W. H. C. Frend, "Christianity in the Middle East: Survey Down to A.D. 1800," in A. J. Arberry, ed., *Religion in the Middle East: Three Religions in Concord and Conflict*, vol. 1, *Judaism and Christianity* (Cambridge, England, 1969), p. 25.
2 Steven Runciman, *A History of the Crusades*, vol. 1, *The First Crusade and the Foundation of the Kingdom of Jerusalem* (New York, 1964), p. 35.
3 *Ibid.*, p. 35.
4 *Ibid.*
5 Frend, "Christianity in the Middle East," p. 43.
6 Runciman, *History of the Crusades*, p. 41.
7 *Ibid.*, p. 41.
8 *Ibid.*, p. 115.
9 Joshua Prawer, *The Latin Kingdom of Jerusalem* (London, 1972), p. 11.
10 *Ibid.*, p. 12.
11 *Ibid.*
12 Runciman, *History of the Crusades*, p. 31.
13 William of Tyre, "A History of Deeds Done Beyond the Sea," trans. E. A. Babcock and A. C. Krey, cited in Meron Benvenisti, *The Crusaders in the Holy Land* (New York, 1970), p. 38.
14 Benvenisti, *Crusaders in the Holy Land*, p. 38.
15 Prawer, *Latin Kingdom of Jerusalem*, p. 208.
16 Benvenisti, *Crusaders in the Holy Land*, p. 40.
17 Prawer, *Latin Kingdom of Jerusalem*, p. 221.
18 *Ibid.*
19 Zoe Oldenbourg, *The Crusades* (New York, 1966), p. 292.
20 C. R. Conder, *The Latin Kingdom of Jerusalem* (London, 1897), p. 178.
21 Oldenbourg, *The Crusades*, p. 289.
22 Prawer, *Latin Kingdom of Jerusalem*, pp. 253–256.

Chapter 6: Who Owns Christ's Tomb?

1 Walter Zander, *Israel and the Holy Places of Christendom* (New York, 1971), p. 16.
2 *Ibid.*
3 *Ibid.*, p. 17.
4 Chaim Wardi, "The Questions of the Holy Places in Ottoman Times," in Moshe Maoz, ed., *Studies on Palestine During the Ottoman Period* (Jerusalem, 1975), p. 387.
5 Bernardin Collin, *Le Probleme Juridique des Lieux Saints*, p. 38, cited in Zander, *Israel and the Holy Places of Christendom*, p. 47.
6 R. Curzon, *Visits to Monasteries of the Levant* (London, 1955 reprint), pp. 162–167.
7 Derek Hopwood, *The Russian Presence in Syria and Palestine, 1843–1914* (Oxford, 1969), p. 38.
8 Derek Hopwood, "The Resurrection of Our Eastern Brethren (Ignatev); Russia and Orthodox Arab Nationalism in Jerusalem," in Maoz, ed., *Studies on Palestine During the Ottoman Period*, p. 395.
9 *Ibid.*, pp. 401–402.
10 John Wilkinson, *Jerusalem Pilgrims Before the Crusades*, (Jerusalem, 1977), p. 40.

Chapter 7: Islam's Triumph in Jerusalem

1 Philip Hitti, *A History of Syria Including Lebanon and Palestine* (New York, 1951), p. 147.
2 Shlomo D. Goitein, "Jerusalem in the Arab Period (638–1099)," in Lee I. Levine, ed.,

The Jerusalem Cathedra, vol. 2 (Detroit, 1982), p. 170.

3 J. Wellhausen, *The Arab Kingdom and Its Fall* (Beirut, 1963), p. 34.

4 Goitein, "Jerusalem in the Arab Period," p. 169.

5 Cited in John Gray, *A History of Jerusalem* (London, 1969), p. 219.

6 Wellhausen, *The Arab Kingdom and Its Fall*, p. 19.

7 According to Alfred Guillaume, "The inference from the Quran, sura 22:25f, is that Abraham initiated pilgrimages there [Ka'ba]." Alfred Guillaume, *Islam* (Baltimore, 1964), p. 70.

8 *Ibid.*, p. 44.

9 Joel Carmichael, *The Shaping of the Arabs: A Study in Ethnic Identity* (New York, 1967), p. 29.

10 Goitein takes the view that Muhammad's decision to change the *qibla* from Jerusalem to Mecca was a natural one, without political motives. He writes: "No 'political' reasons . . . should be assumed for this change ('trying to win the Jews,' 'breaking with the Jews'). One prayed towards Jerusalem because this was the direction of the People of the Book as was known in Medina. It simply was the proper thing to do. When Islam became a separate religion with Mecca as its central sanctuary, the change was natural and religiously cogent." Shlomo D. Goitein, "Al-Kuds," in C. E. Bosworth, et al., eds., *The Encyclopedia of Islam*, new ed., vol. 5, Fascicules 83–84 (Leiden, E. J. Brill, 1980), p. 323.

11 Hitti, *History of Syria*, pp. 481–482.

12 Goitein, "Al-Kuds," p. 324.

13 Hitti, *History of Syria*, p. 524.

14 "The Pilgrimage of Arculfus in the Holy Land," trans. Rev. James Rose Macpherson, *Palestine Pilgrims' Text Society*, vol. 3 (London, 1889), pp. 4–5.

15 Goitein, "Al-Kuds," p. 326.

16 *Ibid.*, p. 324.

17 Al-Mukaddasi, "Description of Syria, Including Palestine," trans. Guy Le Strange, *Palestine Pilgrims' Text Society*, vol. 3 (London, 1892), p. 46.

18 Zev Vilnay, *Legends of Jerusalem* (Philadelphia, 1973), p. 21.

19 *Ibid.*, p. 23.

20 *Ibid.*, p. 24.

21 Aref El Aref, *A Brief Guide to the Dome of the Rock and Al-Haram al-Sharif* (Jerusalem, 1962), p. 20.

22 Goitein, "Jerusalem in the Arab Period," p. 174.

23 Vilnay, *Legends of Jerusalem*, pp. 34–35.

24 Shlomo D. Goitein, "The Historical Background of the Erection of the Dome of the Rock," *Journal of the American Oriental Society*, vol. 70 (1950), pp. 104–108.

25 Oleg Grabar, "The Umayyad Dome of the Rock in Jerusalem," *Ars Orientalis*, vol. 3 (1959), p. 52.

26 *Ibid.*, p. 37.

27 Guy Le Strange, *History of Jerusalem Under the Moslems* (Jerusalem, n.d.), p. 9.

28 Gray, *A History of Jerusalem*, p. 222.

29 Vilnay, *Legends of Jerusalem*, p. 41.

Chapter 8: A Golden Bowl Filled with Scorpions

1 E. A. Belyaev, *Arabs, Islam and the Arab Caliphate in the Early Middle Ages* (Jerusalem, 1969), p. 143.

2 Shlomo D. Goitein, "Al-Kuds," in C. E. Bosworth, et al., eds., *The Encyclopedia of Islam*, new ed., vol. 5, Fascicules 83–84 (Leiden, 1980), p. 323.

3 *Ibid.*

4 *Ibid.*, p. 327.

5 Al-Mukaddasi, "Description of Syria, Including Palestine," trans. Guy Le Strange, *Palestine Pilgrims' Text Society*, vol. 3 (London, 1892), p. 46.

6 Shlomo D. Goitein, *Studies in Islamic History and Its Institutions* (Leiden, 1966), p. 142.

7 Al-Mukaddasi, "Description of Syria," p. 37.

8 Goitein, "Al-Kuds," p. 329.

9 Al-Mukaddasi, "Description of Syria," pp. 38–39.

10 Nasir-i-Khosrau, "A Journey Through Syria and Palestine," trans. Guy Le Strange, *Palestine Pilgrims' Text Society*, vol. 4 (London, 1893), p. 24.

11 Goitein, "Al-Kuds," p. 327.

12 Nasir-i-Khosrau, "A Journey," p. 26.

13 *Ibid.*, p. 57.

14 Philip Hitti, *A History of Syria Including Lebanon and Palestine* (New York, 1951), pp. 487–488, 542–544.

15 Norman Kotker, *The Earthly Jerusalem* (New York, 1969), p. 166.

16 Goitein, "Al-Kuds," p. 330.

17 Emmanuel Sivan, "Le Caractere Sacre De Jerusalem Dans L'Islam Aux XII-XIII Siecles," *Studia Islamica,* 1967, pp. 149–182.

18 Issac Hasson, "Muslim Literature in Praise of Jerusalem, Fada'il Bayt al-Maqdis," in Lee I. Levine, ed., *Jerusalem Cathedra,* vol. 1 (Detroit, 1981), pp. 180, 182.

19 Herbert Busse, "The Sanctity of Jerusalem in Islam," *Judaism,* vol. 17, pp. 456–457.

20 M. J. Kister, "'You Shall Only Set Out for Three Mosques: A Study of an Early Tradition," *Le Museon,* vol. 82, 1–2, (1969), p. 182.

21 Busse, "Sanctity," p. 467.

22 Sivan, "Le Caractere," p. 172.

Chapter 9: Ottoman Indifference

1 Moses Ben Nachman, cited in Avraham Holtz, ed., *The Holy City: Jews on Jerusalem* (New York, 1971), p. 127.

2 Joseph Drory, "Jerusalem During the Mamluk Period (1250–1517)," in Lee I. Levine, ed., *Jerusalem Cathedra,* vol. 1 (Detroit, 1981), p. 179.

3 Oleg Grabar, "Al-Kuds, B, Monuments," in C. E. Bosworth, et al., eds., *The Encyclopedia of Islam,* new ed., vol. 5, Fascicules 83–84 (Leiden, 1980), p. 342.

4 J. Press, *A Hundred Years of Jerusalem: Memoirs of Two Generations* (Jerusalem, 1964), cited in Yehoshua Ben-Arieh, *Jerusalem in the 19th Century: The Old City* (Jerusalem and New York, 1984), p. 168.

5 Drory, "Jerusalem During...," p. 195.

6 Shlomo D. Goitein, "Al-Kuds," in Bosworth, *Encyclopedia of Islam,* p. 323.

7 Drory, "Jerusalem During...," p. 206.

8 Zev Vilnay, *Legends of Jerusalem* (Philadelphia, 1973), p. 208.

9 Ben-Arieh, *Jerusalem in the 19th Century,* p. 109.

10 *Ibid.*

11 *Ibid.*

12 *Ibid.,* p. 111.

13 Moshe Maoz, *Ottoman Reforms in Syria and Palestine, 1840–1881* (Oxford, 1968), p. 18.

14 Ben-Arieh, *Jerusalem in the 19th Century,* p. 110.

15 *Ibid.,* p. 119.

16 C. R. Conder, *Tent Work in Palestine* (London, 1878), cited in Ben-Arieh, *Jerusalem in the 19th Century,* p. 135.

17 Ben-Arieh, *Jerusalem in the 19th Century,* p. 136.

18 See George Antonius, *The Arab Awakening: The Story of the Arab National Movement* (New York, 1946).

19 Cited in John Gray, *A History of Jerusalem* (London, 1969), p. 289.

Chapter 10: Birth and Betrayal

1 Yehoshua Porath, "The Palestinian-Arab Nationalist Movement," in Michael Curtis, et al., eds., *The Palestinians: People, History, Politics* (New Brunswick, N.J., 1975), p. 122.

2 Yehoshua Porath, "The Political Organization of the Palestinian Arabs Under the British Mandate," in Moshe Maoz, ed., *Palestinian Arab Politics* (Jerusalem, 1975), p. 5.

3 Cited in Don Peretz, *The Middle East Today* (New York, 1965), p. 251.

4 Shlomo Avineri, "Political and Social Aspects of Israeli and Arab Nationalism," in Curtis, *Palestinians,* pp. 107–108.

5 John Gray, *A History of Jerusalem* (London, 1969), p. 289.

6 Eugene H. Bovis, *The Jerusalem Question* (Stanford, 1971), p. 5.

7 Chaim Weizmann, *Trial and Error* (London, 1950), p. 161.

8 For statistical information on Jewish immigration and general population, I have relied on several sources: Government of Palestine, Department of Statistics, *General Monthly Bulletin of Current Statistics,* XX (1947), which is cited in Janet L. Abu-Lughod, "The Demographic Transformation of Palestine," in Ibrahim Abu-Lughod, ed., *The Transformation of Palestine* (Evanston, Ill., 1971), pp. 139–163; also statistics from *Municipality of Jerusalem, Office of the Spokesman* (May 1974).

9 Joan Peters's claim that Arab population growth in late nineteenth-century Palestine was caused by in-migration was convincingly refuted by the Israeli historian Yehoshua Porath. See Joan Peters, *From Time Immemorial: The Origins of the Arab-Jewish Conflict over Palestine* (New York, 1985); Yehoshua Porath, "Mrs. Peters's Palestine," *New York Review of Books,* January 16, 1986, pp. 36–38.

10 Daniel Rubenstein, "The Jerusalem Munici-

pality Under the Ottomans, British, and Jordanians," in Joel L. Kraemer, ed., *Jerusalem: Problems and Prospects* (New York, 1980), p. 72.

11 *Ibid.*, p. 74.

12 *Ibid.*, p. 79.

13 Norman Kotker, *The Earthly Jerusalem*, (New York, 1967), p. 147.

14 Cited in Bovis, *The Jerusalem Question*, p. 24.

15 *Ibid.*, p. 27.

16 *Ibid.*, p. 29.

17 Ben Halpern, *The Idea of the Jewish State* (Cambridge, Mass., 1961), p. 358.

18 Gariel Padon, "The Siege of Jerusalem," in John Oesterreicher and Anne Sinai, eds., *Jerusalem* (New York, 1974), p. 101.

19 Meron Benvenisti, *Jerusalem: The Torn City* (Minneapolis, 1961), p. 28.

20 Mohammad Abu Shilbaya, *No Peace Without a Free Palestinian State* (Arabic), cited in Yehoshafat Harkabi, "The Palestinians in the Fifties and their Awakening as Reflected in Their Literature," in Maoz, ed., *Palestinian Arab Politics*, p. 78.

21 Benvenisti, *Jerusalem: The Torn City*, p. 20.

Chapter 11: The Future of Jerusalem

1 For a detailed discussion of "internationalization" affecting Jerusalem, see Yossi Feintuch, *U.S. Policy on Jerusalem* (New York, 1987).

2 Teddy Kollek in *Foreign Affairs*, July 1977, p. 201.

3 Kibbutz Members, eds., *The Seventh Day* (London, 1974), p. 135.

4 Walid Khalidi, "Thinking the Unthinkable: A Sovereign Palestinian State," *Foreign Affairs*, July 1978, p. 705.

5 For an appreciation of Arab attitudes toward Jerusalem as expressed by modern authors, see M. A. Aamiry, *Jerusalem: Arab Origin and Heritage* (London, 1978); K. J. Asali, ed., *Jerusalem in History* (New York, 1990); A. L. Tibawi, *Jerusalem: Its Place in Islam and Arab History* (Beirut, 1969); Islamic Council of Europe, *Jerusalem: The Key to Peace* (London, 1980).

6 The origin of the "boroughs" idea is discussed by Meron Benvenisti, *Jerusalem: The Torn City* (Minneapolis, 1976). See also Saul Cohen, *Jerusalem: Bridging the Four Walls* (New York, 1977), and *Jerusalem Undivided* (New York, 1980).

7 "Vaticanization" is discussed by Terrence Prittie, *Whose Jerusalem?* (London, 1981).

8 These services are discussed by Meron Benvenisti and Terrence Prittie, and by Gideon Weigert in *Israel's Presence in East Jerusalem* (Jerusalem, 1973).

9 Prittie, *Whose Jerusalem?*, pp. 173–174.

10 *Ibid.*, pp. 174–175.

11 *Ibid.*, pp. 197–198.

12 Zeev Schiff and Ehud Yaari, *Israel's Lebanon War* (New York, 1984).

13 Benvenisti, *Jerusalem*, p. 105.

14 *Ibid.*, p. 244

15 *Ibid.*, p. 245

16 Cited in Cohen, *Jerusalem Undivided*, p. 28.

17 Michael Romann, "Jews and Arabs in Jerusalem," *Jerusalem Quarterly*, 19 (Spring 1981), pp. 32–38.

18 *Ibid.*, p. 45.

19 *Ibid.*, p. 40.

20 Benvenisti, *Jerusalem*, p. 246.

21 *Ibid.*, p. 261

22 For a trenchant criticism of Israeli building in Jerusalem, see Arthur Kutcher, *The New Jerusalem: Planning and Politics* (Cambridge, Mass., 1975).

23 Benvenisti, *Jerusalem*, p. 21.

24 Naomi Shepherd, *Teddy Kollek: Mayor of Jerusalem* (New York, 1988), p. 145.

25 *Ibid.*

26 Cited in Prittie, *Whose Jerusalem?*, p. 111.

27 For a more complete account of this incident, see my article, "Greco-Jewish Turmoil in Old Jerusalem," *Christian Century*, January 2–9, 1991. See also the account of Robert I. Friedman, "Making Way for the Messiah," *New York Review of Books*, October 11, 1990, pp. 41–47.

28 See news articles in the *New York Times*, October 9, 10, 11, 1990.

29 Cited in Prittie, *Whose Jerusalem?*, p. 201.

30 Meir Pa'il, "A Palestinian State Alongside Israel," in Alouph Hareven, ed., *Can the Palestinian Problem Be Solved? Israeli Positions* (Jerusalem, 1983), pp. 101–129.

31 The pattern of King Hussein's thinking can be discerned in two books written by his younger brother, Crown Prince Hassan Bin Talal, *A Study on Jerusalem* (Amman, Jordan, and London, 1979), and *Palestinian Self-Determination: A Study of the West Bank and the Gaza Strip* (London, 1981).

A Note on Sources

Seventeen years of research and writing lie behind this book. If I was able clearly to see Jerusalem past and present, it was because I stood on the shoulders of great authors.

My knowledge of the ancient Israelite city of Jerusalem was derived initially from a set of basic introductions to the Old Testament, including John Bright, *A History of Israel* (Philadelphia, 1959); Theodore H. Robinson, *A History of Israel*, vol. 1 (Oxford, 1948); Martin Noth, *The History of Israel* (New York, 1958); Albrecht Alt, "The Formation of the Israelite State in Palestine," in *Essays on Old Testament History and Religion* (New York, 1967); Walter Harrelson, *Interpreting the Old Testament* (New York, 1964); Bernhard Anderson, *Understanding the Old Testament* (New York, 1975); G. E. Mendenhall, "The Monarchy," in *Interpretation*, vol. 29 (1975); J. J. M. Roberts, "The Davidic Origins of the Zion Tradition," in *Journal of Biblical Literature*, vol. 92 (1973).

These works are by scholars who are superbly trained in languages and historical sources to provide lucid and compelling accounts of the place of Jerusalem in ancient Israelite life and thought. If I have a criticism of their scholarship it is their tendency to interpret the monarchy and the Temple from a narrowly religious and moral perspective. This tendency is pronounced in Bright and Noth, who seem to feel that Israel's royal and ritual institutions were sources of corruption when measured by the Covenant law and the moral message of the prophets. A wider view of monarchy and Temple is taken by the Jewish scholar Shemaryahu Talmon, who helped me to see that apart from questions of morality, monarchy and Temple were central to Israel's nationalistic self-conception—indispensable institutions for the confidence, unity, security, and direction of the nation. See Talmon's essay, "The Biblical Concept of Jerusalem," in *Jerusalem*, edited by

John Oesterreicher and Anne Sinai (New York, 1974), to maintain a balanced view of ancient Israel as both a religiously "witnessing" community and a nation in the making through monarchy, army, Temple, and treasury. This balanced interpretation is also strengthened by the superb readings of Israel's history that I found in the contributions of Abraham Malamat and Hayim Tadmor in *A History of the Jewish People*, edited by H. H. Sasson (Cambridge, Mass., 1976).

For specific knowledge of the Jerusalem Temple and ancient Israelite ritual practice I relied on Roland de Vaux, *Ancient Israel*, vol. 2, *Religious Institutions* (New York, 1965), and Benjamin Mazar, *Canaan and Israel: Historical Essays* (Jerusalem, 1974, Hebrew).

Whatever interpetation I encountered, whatever point of view I considered, I checked it against the influential account of ancient Israel rendered by Yehezkel Kaufmann, *The Religion of Israel: From Its Beginnings to the Babylonian Exile* (Chicago, 1960). I also consulted J. Simons, *Jerusalem in the Old Testament* (Leiden, 1952).

The writings of Menahem Stern, W. O. E. Oesterley, Emil Schurer, Lee Levine, Victor Tcherikover, and Michael Avi-Yonah educated me about Jewish life in Jerusalem during the long Hellenistic and later Roman periods. It is a pleasure to acknowledge the wonderful contribution of Avi-Yonah to our knowledge of Jewish life in Palestine after the destruction of the Temple, *The Jews Under Roman and Byzantine Rule* (Jerusalem, 1984). Avi-Yonah's interpretation of this period convinced me that the meaning of Jerusalem in ancient Jewish historical experience was inextricably religious and political. One passage in Avi-Yonah guided me throughout my reading and reflection: "...The Jewish nation as such, and not any metaphysical force, has been the main factor in shaping Jewish history in all periods, from the time of Moses to the present day. National consciousness is like a pulse— sometimes it beats strong and clear, and sometimes it is difficult to catch—but there is no life without it. The national strivings of Israel, the manifestations of which have varied from time to time, existed at all times throughout Jewish history."

The writings of Josephus are indispensable to understanding the Roman-Jewish war of 66–70 C.E. which resulted in the destruction of Jerusalem's Temple; but as every reader of Josephus knows, this Jewish-turned-Roman contemporary chronicler of the disaster was not altogether reliable or accurate in his views. It is with the publication of David Rhodes's *Israel in Revolution: 6–74 C.E., A Political History Based on the Writings of Josephus* (Philadelphia, 1976), that we have available to us the best reconstruction of the events of the war. I also consulted W. R. Farmer, *Maccabees, Zealots, and Josephus* (New York, 1956); Morton Smith, "Palestinian Judaism in the First Century," in *Israel: Its Role in Civilization*, edited by Moshe Davis (New York, 1956); Marcel Simon, *Jewish Sects in the Time of Jesus* (Philadelphia, 1967); S. G. F. Brandon, *Jesus and the Zealots* (Manchester, 1967) and *The Fall of Jerusalem and the Christian Church* (London, 1968); S. Safrai, "The High Priesthood and the Sanhedrin in the Time of the Second Temple," in *The World History of the Jewish People*, first series, vol. 7 (Jerusalem, 1975).

If Avi-Yonah wrote the definitive history of Jewish life in Palestine under the Romans and Byzantines, we are obliged to say that the definitive study of Jews in Palestine under a succession of Muslim regimes, beginning with the initial Arab conquest of the seventh century and ending with the Crusader Kingdom of Jerusalem of the twelfth century, has yet to be written. The reason for this is the lack of historical resources. In this period we simply do not know much about how Jews lived under Muslim governors; what we do know is gleaned from general knowledge of Muslim rule in the region. In this regard I should mention the important essays by Moshe Gil, Avraham Grossman, Shmuel Safrai, and Haggai Ben-Shammai to be found in *The Jerusalem Cathedra: Studies in the History, Archaeology, Geography, and Ethnography of the Land of Israel*, vol. 3 (Detroit, 1983).

With the establishment of the Latin Kingdom of Jerusalem after the Crusader conquest of 1099, we have reliable knowledge of Jewish life in Palestine. Here our premier historian remains Joshua Prawer. See *The Latin Kingdom of Jerusalem: European Colonialism in the Middle Ages* (London, 1972) and *The History of the Jews in the Latin Kingdom of Jerusalem* (Oxford, 1988).

Two authors in particular advanced my knowledge of Palestinian Jewry under Ottoman rule. These are Itzhak Ben-Zevi, "Eretz Yisrael Under Ottoman Rule, 1517–1917," in *The Jews: Their History, Culture, and Religion*, 3rd ed., edited by Louis Finkelstein (New York, 1960), and Tudor Parfitt's excellent study *The Jews of Palestine, 1800–1882* (Woodbridge, England, 1987). The definitive studies of Jerusalem in the nineteenth century were written by Yehoshua Ben-Arieh: *Jerusalem in the 19th Century: The Old City* (Jerusalem, 1984), and *Jerusalem in the 19th Century: Emergence of the New City* (Jerusalem, 1986). It should be noted that Ben-Arieh's studies deal with Christian and Muslim as well as Jewish communal life in Jerusalem.

For a useful anthology of Jewish biblical, Talmudic, historical, and poetic expressions of the significance of Jerusalem to Jews through the centuries, see Avraham Holtz, ed., *The Holy City: Jews on Jerusalem* (New York, 1971). The reading of this work should be supplemented by E. N. Adler, ed., *Jewish Travelers: A Treasury of Travelogues from Nine Centuries* (New York, 1966); Abraham Halkin, ed., *Zion in Jewish Literature* (New York, 1961); Kurt Wilhelm, ed., *Roads to Zion: Four Centuries of Travelers' Reports* (New York, 1948). An important contribution is made by Hayim Hillel Ben-Sasson's essay, "The Image of Eretz-Israel in the View of Jews Arriving There in the Late Middle Ages," in *Studies on Palestine During the Ottoman Period*, edited by Moshe Maoz (Jerusalem, 1975). Altogether these anthologies make it unmistakably clear that the Jewish memory of Jerusalem as national capital and mystical symbol of redemption sustained the ghetto communities of Europe for centuries, right up to the mass immigrations of the 1880s and 1890s.

The origins and development of the Christian esteem for Jerusalem do not lack for scholarly sources—save in one notable respect: Jesus' attitude toward Jerusalem and its Temple. We cannot accept as historically reliable the condemnation of Temple ritual practice put in the mouth of Jesus by the author of Luke's Gospel; certainly not his prediction of the divinely wrought destruction of the Temple: ". . . The days will come when there shall not be left here one stone upon another that will not be thrown down" (21:6). Many scholars have established that these sentiments reflect the attitude of the later church in its concern to separate itself from Judaism.

Is there a "historical Jesus" whose life and thought we can describe? Modern biblical scholarship, influenced by Albert Schweitzer, Martin Kahler, Johannes Weiss, and Rudolph Bultmann, answers negatively. Respecting that scholarship also allows for a historical basis for reconstructing a "historical Jesus" who is not the idealized figure of later church tradition but actually a real Jewish human being, a charismatic preacher of the messianic redemption who lived in the Galilee in the time of Herod Antipas. Our knowledge of this person is advanced in exciting and credible ways by the books of Geza Vermes, *Jesus the Jew* (Philadelphia, 1973) and *Jesus and the World of Judaism* (Philadelphia, 1983). On the basis of these studies it is possible to make educated guesses (no more than that) about what Jesus did in Jerusalem in the last week of his life and what happened to him.

For additional sources of reflection on the figure of Jesus, I relied on Hans Conzelman, *Jesus* (Philadelphia, 1973); Joseph Klausner,

Jesus of Nazareth (London, 1925); David Flusser, *Jesus* (New York, 1969); Paul Winter, *On the Trial of Jesus*, Studia Judaica 1 (Berlin, 1961); Norman Perrin, *The Kingdom of God in the Teaching of Jesus* (Philadelphia, 1963).

The social, religious, and political life of Jerusalem in the time of Jesus is wonderfully described in detail in Joachim Jeremias's *Jerusalem in the Time of Jesus* (Philadelphia, 1969). I also learned from John Wilkinson's little book weaving together archaeology and New Testament themes, *Jerusalem as Jesus Knew It* (London, 1978). Another publication on the same lines is R. M. Mackowski, *Jerusalem, City of Jesus: An Exploration of the Traditions, Writings, and Remains of the Holy City from the Time of Christ* (Grand Rapids, Mich., 1980). I also found Menashe Har-El's *This Is Jerusalem* (Jerusalem, 1985) an excellent archaeological-historical guide to the Christian as well as other periods.

On the important questions of religious claims to territory in early Christian and Jewish Jerusalem, see the monumental study by W. D. Davies, *The Gospel and the Land* (Berkeley, 1974). Also consult his excellent monograph comparing various New Testament attitudes toward Jerusalem and the Temple, "Jerusalem and the Land in the Christian Tradition," in *The Jerusalem Colloquium on Religion, Peoplehood, Nation, and Land*, edited by Marc H. Tanenbaum and R. J. Zwi Werblovsky (Jerusalem, 1970).

In the long period of Byzantine rule in Palestine, Jerusalem through church and monastic architecture was transformed into the "Metropolis of Christendom." My knowledge of this period is drawn from the histories of Edward Gibbon and Jacob Burckhardt. For the creedal controversies affecting Jerusalem I relied on Adolph Harnack's multi-volumed *History of Dogma*.

The hundred years of the Latin Kingdom of Jerusalem represents one the most fascinating periods of the city's history. Here I used Steven Runciman, *A History of the Crusades*, 3 vols. (London, 1952–1954). In my judgment the best interpretive work on the first Crusade remains Joshua Prawer, *The Latin Kingdom of Jerusalem* (London, 1972). Prawer's thesis that the Crusades were at root an expression of European colonial penetration of the Muslim East helps us to understand the arrogance and cruelty of the Franks against both Jews and Muslims.

One should read the contemporary account of the first Crusade by William of Tyre, *A History of Deeds Done in the Holy Land*, 2 vols. (New York, 1943). I also made use of the interesting study of Crusader

Jerusalem written by one of Prawer's most gifted students, Meron Benvenisti, *The Crusaders in the Holy Land* (Jerusalem, 1970).

No one can expect to become acquainted with the literature on Christian pilgrimage to the Holy Land without consulting the memories of the pilgrims themselves. Many of these have been collected and translated in that irreplaceable treasury, the ten volumes of *The Palestine Pilgrims' Text Society* (London, 1894–1899). I also made use of John Wilkinson's splendid studies, *Jerusalem Pilgrims Before the Crusades* (Jerusalem, 1977); and *Egeria's Travels in the Holy Land* (Westminster, England, 1981). Also see the collected travel diaries edited by Thomas Wright, *Early Travels in Palestine* (New York, 1968). The travel account of the fifteenth-century pilgrim Friar Felix should also be consulted. See H. F. M Prescott's *Friar Felix at Large* (New Haven, 1950).

The European "rediscovery" of Palestine and Jerusalem in the early nineteenth century is the subject of a number of interesting books. I highly recommend Naomi Shepherd's *The Zealous Intruders* (New York, 1987) and Barbara Tuchman's *Bible and Sword* (London, 1957); also A. L. Tibawi's *British Interests in Palestine, 1800–1901* (London, 1961). For the fascinating story of the politics and religious idealism that lay behind the major archaeological discoveries in Palestine of the last century see the wonderful account written by Neil Asher Silberman, *Digging for God and Country* (New York, 1982). For an important record of Christian activities in Jerusalem during the mid-nineteenth century consult the diaries of James Finn, *Stirring Times, or Records from Jerusalem Consular Chronicles*, 2 vols. (London, 1878). A colorful account of daily life in Palestine in the 1850s is given in Mary Eliza Rogers's *Domestic Life in Palestine* (London, 1862). Martin Gilbert provides a chronicle of facts about the nineteenth-century city in *Jerusalem: Rebirth of a City* (New York, 1985).

The Church of the Holy Sepulchre in Jerusalem by C. Couasnon (London, 1974) is the best account of that celebrated and much embattled structure. For a moving account of the Holy Fire ritual in the church and the violence that usually attended the performance see R. Curzon's *Visits to the Monasteries of the Levant* (London, 1955). Also see two articles by Ze'ev Rubin, "The Church of the Holy Sepulchre and the Conflict Between the Sees of Jerusalem and Caesarea," in *Jerusalem Cathedra*, edited by Lee I. Levine (Detroit, 1982), and "Christianity in Byzantine Palestine: Missionary Activity and Religious Coercion," also in Levine, vol. 3, 1983.

The important role played by the Greek Orthodox patriarchate of Jerusalem in the politics of Palestine throughout the ninetenth century is covered brilliantly by Derek Hopwood in two studies: "Russia and Orthodox Arab Nationalism in Jerusalem," in *Studies in Palestine During the Ottoman Period*, edited by Moshe Maoz (Jerusalem, 1975) and *The Russian Presence in Syria and Palestine, 1843–1914* (Oxford, 1958). In addition, it is important to consult Maoz, *Ottoman Reform in Syria and Palestine, 1840–1861* (Oxford, 1968). One should also read the devastating report of the British commission which investigated the pitiful conditions of the Orthodox church in later Ottoman times: A. Bertram and H. C. Luke, *Report of the Commission Appointed...to Inquire into the Affairs of the Orthodox Patriarchate of Jerusalem* (London, 1921). See also Daphne Tsimhoni's article, "The Greek Orthodox Patriarchate of Jerusalem During the Formative Years of the British Mandate in Palestine," in *Asian and African Studies*, vol. 12, no. 1, 1978.

The controversies surrounding the Holy Places are discussed by Chaim Wardi in "The Question of the Holy Places in Ottoman Times," in *Studies in Palestine During the Ottoman Period;* also by Walter Zander, *Israel and the Holy Places of Christendom* (New York, 1971).

For a general survey of Palestinian Christianity see Saul P. Colbi's *Christianity in the Holy Land: Past and Present* (Tel Aviv, 1969); also *Tantur Papers on Christianity in the Holy Land*, edited by D. M. A. Jaeger (Jerusalem, 1981).

There are not many sources for understanding the historical development of the Arabic-speaking churches in the Holy Land. A useful summary is provided by Robert Brenton Betts, *Christians in the Arab East* (Atlanta, 1978). One should also consult A. J Arberry's *Religion in the Middle East*, 2 vols. (London, 1969), and Donald Attwater, *The Christian Churches of the East*, 2 vols. (Milwaukee, 1947).

The situation of Arab and European Christians in the Holy Land since 1948 is treated in essays by Gabriel Grossmann, "The Christian Churches in Present-day Israel," in *Jerusalem*, edited by John Oesterreicher and Anne Sinai (New York, 1974); Stavro Danilov, "The Christians of Jerusalem," and Thomas A. Idinopulos, "Diversity and Conflict Amongst the Christian Communities," both in *Jerusalem: City of the Ages*, edited by Alice L. Eckhardt (New York, 1987); Daniel Rossing, "The Christian Communities and the State of Israel," in *Christian-Jewish Relations*, vol. 19, no. 3, 1986; John Oesterreicher, "Christianity Threatened in Israel?" in *Midstream*, January 1983; Chaim Wardi, "Christians in Israel: A Survey," Ministry of Religious Affairs, Government of Israel (Jerusalem, 1950).

Also see the articles by Daphne Tsimhoni: "The Greek Orthodox Community in Jerusalem and the West Bank, 1948–1978: A Profile of a Religious Minority in a National State," in *Orient*, vol. 23, no. 2, 1982; "Demographic Trends of the Christian Population in Jerusalem and the West Bank, 1948–1978," in *Middle East Journal*, vol. 37, no. 1, 1983; "The Armenians and the Syrians: Ethno-religious Communities in Jerusalem," *Middle Eastern Studies*, vol. 20, no. 3, 1984; "The Status of the Arab Christians Under the British Mandate in Palestine," *Middle Eastern Studies*, vol. 20, no. 4, 1984.

We can learn much about the Holy Land by patient perusal of a good guide book. There is none better than E. Hoade's *Guide to the Holy Land* (Jerusalem, 1981).

To understand the place of Jerusalem in Islamic tradition, one should begin with a proper understanding of Islam itself. I began with the reading of some excellent basic introductions: Alfred Guillaume, *Islam* (Baltimore, 1964); Fazlur Rahman, *Islam* (Chicago, 1979); H. A. R. Gibb, *Muhammadanism: A Historical Survey* (New York, 1961); W. Montgomery Watt, *Islamic Philosophy and Theology* (Edinburgh, 1962); Tor Andrae, *Muhammad: The Man and His Faith* (New York, 1960).

For general histories of Arabic cultural influence on Palestine and Jerusalem I relied on E. A. Belyaev, *Islam and the Arab Caliphate in the Early Middle Ages* (Jerusalem, 1969); Philip K. Hitti, *History of Syria Including Lebanon and Palestine* (New York, 1951); J. Wellhausen, *Arab Kingdom and Its Fall* (Beirut, 1963); Joel Carmichael, *The Shaping of the Arabs: A Study in Ethnic Identity* (New York, 1967); Guy Le Strange, *History of Jerusalem Under the Moslems* (Beirut, 1965); C. D. Matthews, *Palestine: Mohammedan Holy Land* (New Haven, 1949).

Two marvelous contemporary accounts of life in Jerusalem under Muslim governors were written by al-Mukaddasi, "Description of Syria, Including Palestine," translated and annotated by Guy Le Strange, *Palestine Pilgrims' Text Society*, vol. 3 (London, 1892), and Nasir-i-Khosrau, "A Journey Through Syria and Palestine," also annotated and translated by Guy Le Strange, *Palestine Pilgrims' Text Society*, vol. 4 (London, 1893).

Our specific knowledge of Muslim Jerusalem is enhanced by the pioneer work done by S. D. Goitein, as in the following: "Jerusalem in the Arab Period (638–1099)," in *The Jerusalem Cathedra*, vol. 2, edited by Lee I. Levine (Detroit, 1982); "The Sanctity of Jerusalem and Palestine in Early Islam," in *Studies in Islamic History and Institutions* (Leiden, 1966); "Al-Kuds," in *The Encyclopedia of Islam*, new edition, (Leiden, 1980); also see his essays in *Studies in Islamic History and Its Institutions* (Leiden, 1966) and "The Historical Background of the Erection of the Dome of the Rock," in *Journal of the American Oriental Society*, vol. 70 (1950).

For more studies on the Dome of the Rock shrine and al-Aksa Mosque, see Oleg Grabar, "The Umayyad Dome of the Rock in Jerusalem," in *Ars Orientalis*, vol. 3 (1959); "Al-Kuds, B, Monuments," *The Encyclopedia of Islam*; Aref El Aref, *A Brief Guide to the Dome of the Rock and Al-Haram al-Sharif* (Jerusalem, 1962); W. Hamilton, *The Structural History of the Aqsa Mosque* (Jerusalem, 1947).

For a splendid anthology of legends and sayings connected with the Dome of the Rock and other Muslim shrines in Palestine, see Zev Vilnay, *Legends of Jerusalem* (Philadelphia, 1973).

A number of important essays in recent years shows the place of Jerusalem in Islamic traditions of sanctity. These are: Emmanuel Sivan, "Le Caractere Sacre De Jerusalem Dans L'Islam Aux XII–XIII Siecles," in *Studia Islamica* (Paris, 1967); Isaac Hasson, "Muslim Literature in Praise of Jerusalem, Fada'il Bayt al-Maqdis," in *Jerusalem Cathedra*, vol. 1, edited by Lee I. Levine (Detroit, 1981); E. Ashtor, "Muslim and Christian Literature in Praise of Jerusalem," in Levine, *Jerusalem Cathedra*, 1981; C. D. Matthews, "A Muslim Iconoclast: Ibn Taymiyya on the 'Merits' of Jerusalem," in *Journal of the American Oriental Society*, vol. 56, 1936; Herbert Busse, "The Sanctity of Jerusalem in Islam," in *Judaism*, vol. 17, Autumn 1968; M. J. Kister, " 'You Shall Only Set Out for Three Mosques': A Study of an Early Tradition," in *Le Museon*, vol. 82, 1969; Hava Lazarus-Yafeh, "The Sanctity of Jerusalem in Islam," in *Jerusalem*, edited by John Oesterreicher and Anne Sinai (New York, 1974). See also the important essay by Joseph Drory, "Jerusalem During the Mamluk Period (1250–1517)," in Levine, *Jerusalem Cathedra*.

I learned a great deal from the essays collected in Moshe Maoz, ed., *Studies on Palestine During the Ottoman Period* (Jerusalem, 1975), as well as the volume edited by B. Braude and B. Lewis, *Christians and Jews in the Ottoman Empire*, 2 vols. I should also mention the careful scholarly work of Amnon Cohen, who in several volumes gives us a penetrating account of life in Palestine under Ottoman rule. See *Palestine in the Eighteenth Century: Patterns of Government and*

Administration (Jerusalem, 1973) and *Ottoman Documents on the Jewish Community of Jerusalem in the Sixteenth Century* (Jerusalem, 1976). A useful summary of Ottoman-governed Jerusalem is provided by H. Z. Hirschberg, et al., "Jerusalem Under Ottoman Rule (1517–1917)," in *Encyclopedia Judaica*.

Additional studies can be found in Amnon Cohen and Gabriel Baer, eds., *Egypt and Palestine: A Millennium of Association, 1868–1948* (New York, 1984); and Richard I. Cohen, ed., *Vision and Conflict in the Holy Land* (New York, 1985).

A number of technical studies published in the Israeli periodical *African and Asian Studies* may prove of interest to the general reader. These are some of the best: Uri M. Kupperschmidt, "The General Muslim Congress of 1931 in Jerusalem," vol. 12, no. 1, March 1978; "The Involvement of Arab States in the Palestine Conflict and British-Arab Relationship Before World War II," vol. 10, no. 1, 1974–1975; and "Islam on the Defensive: The Supreme Muslim Council's Role in Mandatory Palestine," vol. 17, 1983; Aharon Layish, "*Qadis* and *Sharia* in Israel," vol. 7, 1971; Gabriel Baer, "The Dismemberment of *Awqaf* in Early 19th Century Palestine," vol. 13, 1979; Hava Lazarus-Yafeh, "Contemporary Religious Attitudes of Muslim Arabs Toward the Ka'ba and the Hajj," vol. 12, 1978; David Kushner, "Intercommunal Strife in Palestine During the Ottoman Period," vol. 18, 1984, and "A Plan for the Internationalization of Jerusalem, 1840–1841," vol. 12, 1978; Haim Gerber, "The Ottoman Administration of the Sanjaq of Jerusalem, 1890–1908," vol. 12, 1978; Ruth Kark, "The Jerusalem Municipality at the End of Ottoman Rule," vol. 14, 1980. Also see Alexander Scholch, "The Demographic Development of Palestine, 1850–1882," in *Journal of Middle East Studies*, vol. 17, November 1985.

I began my study of modern Jerusalem, 1917 to the present day, by immersing myself in the philosophy of Zionism, the history of British mandate rule in Palestine, and the origins of the Arab Palestinian nationalist movement. The books I found most useful on Zionism and the British mandate are Walter Laqueur, *A History of Zionism* (New York, 1972); B. Halperin, *The Idea of the Jewish State* (Cambridge, Mass., 1961); Arthur Hertzberg, *The Zionist Idea* (New York, 1966); Ahad Ha'am, *Nationalism and the Jewish Ethic* (New York, 1962); David Vital, *The Origins of Zionism* (Oxford, 1975); ESCO Foundation for Palestine, *Palestine: A Study of the Jewish, Arab, and British*

Policies (New Haven, 1947); Bernard Joseph, *British Rule in Palestine* (Washington, D.C., 1948); Gavriel Cohen, *Churchill and Palestine, 1939–1942* (Jerusalem, 1976) and *The British Cabinet and Palestine: April–July, 1943* (Tel Aviv, 1976).

With regard to the Palestinian movement, I found Yehoshua Porath's two-volume work magisterial: *The Emergence of the Palestinian-Arab National Movement, Vol. 1: 1918–1929, Vol 2: 1929–1939* (London, 1974, 1977). I also learned from George Antonius's *The Arab Awakening* (London, 1938); Hazen Zaki Nuseibeh, *The Ideas of Arab Nationalism* (Ithaca, 1956); Ibrahim Abu-Lughod, ed., *The Transformation of Palestine* (Evanston, Ill., 1971); Richard Ward, et al., *The Palestine State* (London, 1977); Joel S. Migdal, *Palestinian Society and Politics* (Princeton, 1980); Michael J. Cohen, *The Origins and Evolution of the Arab-Zionism Conflict* (Berkeley, 1987); Alouph Hareven, *Can the Palestinian Problem Be Solved? Israeli Positions* (Jerusalem, 1983); Gabriel Ben-Dor, ed., *The Palestinians and the Middle East Conflict: Studies in Their History, Sociology, and Politics* (Forest Grove, Ore., 1979); Moshe Maoz, ed., *Palestinian Arab Politics* (Jerusalem, 1975).

Given his delicate position as both crown prince of Jordan and advocate of Palestinian self-determination in the West Bank, I found the books of HRH Prince Hassan Bin Talal's books interesting: *A Study on Jerusalem* (Amman and London, 1979); *Palestinian Self-Determination: A Study of the West Bank and Gaza Strip* (London, 1981); *Search for Peace* (New York, 1984). Fascinating personal accounts of the Arab political struggle are provided by Sir Geoffrey Furlonge, *Palestine Is My Country: The Story of Musa Alami* (New York, 1969),and Nasser Eddin Nashashibi, *Jerusalem's Other Voice: Ragheb Nashashibi and Moderation in Palestinian Politics, 1920–1948* (Exeter, England, 1990).

The intimate connection between Jerusalem and the West Bank in the Arab mind is reinforced by a reading of Shabtai Teveth, *The Cursed Blessing* (New York, 1969), and Rafik Halaby, *The West Bank Story* (New York, 1981).

For specific analysis of the political and social problems facing Arab-Jewish coexistence in Jerusalem, I find no writer more lucid and persuasive than Meron Benvenisti. His most important book is *Jerusalem: The Torn City* (Minneapolis, 1976). See also his personal account in *Conflicts and Contradictions* (New York, 1986), and "Dialogue of Action in Jerusalem," *Jerusalem Quarterly*, no. 19, Spring 1981.

Other works I found useful in understanding the present-day city are Terrence Prittie, *Whose Jerusalem?* (London, 1981); Gerald Caplan, *Arab and Jew in Jerusalem* (Cambridge, Mass., 1980), Saul B. Cohen, *Jerusalem: Bridging the Four Walls* (New York, 1977) and *Jerusalem Undivided* (New York, 1980); Joel L. Kraemer, *Jerusalem: Problems and Prospects* (New York, 1980); Rouhi al-Khatib, *The Judaization of Jerusalem* (Amman, 1979); Michael Romann, *Interrelationship between the Jewish and Arab Sectors in Jerusalem* (Jerusalem, 1984, Hebrew).

One might find it interesting to compare Teddy Kollek's book about his life and administration in Jerusalem, *For Jerusalem* (New York, 1978), with Naomi Shepherd's strong and fair portrait of him in *Teddy Kollek: A Mayor of Jerusalem* (New York, 1988).

Diplomatic and international legal questions affecting Jerusalem in the past fifty years are treated by Evan M. Wilson in *Jerusalem: Key to Peace* (New York, 1970); Eugene Bovis, *The Jerusalem Question, 1917–1968* (Stanford, 1971); Yehuda Zvi Blum, "The Juridical Status of Jerusalem," Leonard David Institute (Jerusalem, 1974); Yossi Feintuch, *U.S. Policy on Jerusalem* (New York, 1987); Ora Ahimeir, ed., "Jerusalem—Aspects of Law," Institute for Jerusalem Studies (Jerusalem, 1980, Hebrew); Richard H. Pfaff, *Jerusalem: Keystone of an Arab-Israeli Settlement* (August 1969); Lord Caradon, "The Future of Jerusalem," National Security Affairs Monograph Series 80-1 (Washington, D.C., 1980); Menahem Kaufman, *America's Jerusalem Policy: 1947-1948* (Jerusalem, 1982).

For specifically Arab and Muslim views of Jerusalem past and present, see M. A. Aamiry, *Jerusalem: Arab Origin and Heritage* (London, 1978); K. J. Asali, ed., *Jerusalem in History* (New York, 1978); A. L. Tibawi, *Jerusalem: Its Place in Islam and Arab History* (Beirut, 1969); *Jerusalem: The Key to Peace*, Islamic Council of Europe (London, 1980).

On architecture and city planning I consulted successive issues, (1967-1985) of *Jerusalem Planning* published by the Jerusalem Committee. I also consulted the published proceedings of the Jerusalem Committee over the years and regularly followed city developments in *Out of Jerusalem*, a publication of the Jerusalem Committee. None of my reading reconciled me to the abysmal record of construction in west Jerusalem and the fringes of east Jerusalem from 1967 to the present—a record accurately described by Arthur Kutcher in *The New Jerusalem: Planning and Politics* (Cambridge, Mass., 1975).

For an understanding of the continuing conflict between ultra-

Orthodoxy and secularism in Jerusalem's Jewish society, I turned to a masterful study: S. Zalman Abramov's *Perpetual Dilemma: Jewish Religion in the Jewish State* (Cranbury, N.J., 1979). A fascinating study comparing traditionalism in Jerusalem's Jewish ultra-Orthodox and Muslim societies was written by Rita James Simon, *Continuity and Change: A Study of Two Ethnic Communities in Israel* (Cambridge, Mass., 1978). Also see Yeshayahu Leibowitz's articles, "State and Religion," and "The Uniqueness of the Jewish People," in *Jerusalem Quarterly*, no. 17, 1980, and no. 19, 1981.

Of general histories of Jerusalem these are worth noting: John Gray, *A History of Jerusalem* (London, 1969); F. M. Abel, *Geographie de la Palestine*, 2 vols. (Paris, 1933–1938). F. E. Peters, *Jerusalem: The Holy City in the Eyes of Chroniclers, Visitors, Pilgrims and Prophets from the Days of Abraham to the Beginnings of Modern Times* (Princeton, 1985) is a very useful source book for original material translated into English. Also see Peters's *Jerusalem and Mecca: The Typology of the Holy City in the Near East* (New York, 1986). Norman Kotker's *The Earthly Jerusalem* (New York, 1969) is a wonderfully well-written popular history of the city. We are in debt to the Ariel Publishing House of Jerusalem for reprinting George Adam Smith's *History of Jerusalem*, a classic work first published in 1907. I should also mention a short but instructive monograph by R. J. Werblowsky comparing Jewish, Christian, and Muslim senses of Jerusalem's sanctity, *Jerusalem: Holy City of Three Religions* (Jerusalem, 1976).

In 1921 G. K. Chesterton published his impressions of Jerusalem which still constitute an accurate and acerbic account of the people of Jerusalem. An updated impression of Jerusalem also written in a biting style can be found in Amos Elon's *Jerusalem: City of Mirrors* (Boston, 1989). *Jerusalem: The Holy City in Literature*, edited by Miron Grindea, with a preface by Graham Greene, is a useful reference work. *Retrievements: A Jerusalem Anthology*, edited by Dennis Silk, is a marvelous account of Jerusalem. Saul Bellow's *To Jerusalem and Back* (New York, 1976) gives us the impressions of a great writer. Lesley Hazelton's *Jerusalem, Jerusalem* (Boston, 1986) represents an intensely personal encounter with the city. And one should take the time to read the memoir of Bertha Spafford Vester, a member of the most influential American family to live in Jerusalem: *Our Jerusalem: An American Family in the Holy City, 1881–1949* (New York, 1950).

Of all the novels and stories which have Jerusalem as their setting, the one that comes closest to evoking the beauty and tragic spirit of the city is Arnold Zweig's *De Vriendt Goes Home*.

My own writings on Jerusalem have appeared in the *Christian Century* and other periodicals and books. The *Christian Century:* "Jerusalem the Blessed: Shrines of Three Faiths," April 12, 1978; "Jerusalem the Blessed: Religion and Politics in the Holy City," May 10, 1978; "The Risks of Pride and Ignorance: Seeking a Balance in the Middle East," March 5, 1980; "Politics, Theology, and Folly in the New Jerusalem Law," October 22, 1980; "A New Patriarch for the Holy City," April 8, 1981; "Holy Fire in Jerusalem," April 7, 1982; "Theopolitics at Jerusalem's Dome of the Rock," November 9, 1983; "Mormon-Jewish Turmoil in Zion," December 4, 1985; "Eastern Orthodox: A New Vision?" November 11, 1987; "Greco-Jewish Turmoil in Old Jerusalem," January 2, 1991. Other publications include "Christians and Jerusalem," in *Encounter,* April 1981; "Religious Colonialism and Ethnic Awakening," in *Worldview,* April 1982; and "Diversity and Conflict Amongst the Christian Communities of Jerusalem, Israel, and the West Bank," in *Jerusalem: City of Ages,* edited by Alice Eckhardt (New York, 1986).

The Revised Standard Version of the Bible was the main source of scriptural citations.

Index

A NOTE
ON THE AUTHOR

Thomas A. Idinopulos grew up in Portland, Oregon, and studied at Reed College, Duke University, the University of Athens, and the University of Chicago, where he received both an M.A. and a Ph.D. He has written widely on the political and religious history of Jewish, Christian, and Muslim communities in the Middle East, including award-winning articles in the *Christian Century* (where his reports appear frequently), the *Middle East Review, Midstream, Encounter, Worldview*, the *Journal of Religion, USA Today*, and other periodicals. He has also written *The Erosion of Faith*. Mr. Idinopulos has been a resident scholar at the Ecumenical Institute for Advanced Theological Studies in Israel; a guest scholar at Mishkenot Sha'ananim, the "Dwellings of Tranquility" of the Jerusalem Foundation; and a fellow to the Patriarchal Institute for Patristic Studies at the Vlatadon Monastery, Thessaloniki, Greece. He is professor of religious studies at Miami University in Oxford, Ohio, and is married with two sons.